SCOTTY

SCOTTY

A HOCKEY LIFE
LIKE NO OTHER

KEN DRYDEN

McCLELLAND & STEWART

McClelland & Stewart and colophon are registered trademarks of
Penguin Random House Canada Limited.

Library and Archives Canada Cataloguing in Publication data is available
upon request

ISBN: 978-0-7710-2750-5
eBook ISBN: 978-0-7710-2751-2

"Fifty Mission Cap" (Johnny Fay, Gordon Downie, Robert Baker, Gordon
Sinclair, Paul Langlois). Copyright © 1992 by Little Smoke Music/
Southern Music Pub. Co. Canada Ltd. Copyright © Renewed.
International Rights Secured. Used by Permission. All Rights Reserved.

Book design by Jennifer Lum
On the cover: Canadian hockey coach Scotty Bowman of the Montreal
Canadiens, dressed in a suit, watches the action from behind the bench,
1970s. © Bruce Bennett Studios/Getty Images

Typeset in Janson MT Pro by M&S, Toronto
Printed and bound in Canada

McClelland & Stewart,
a division of Penguin Random House Canada Limited,
a Penguin Random House Company
www.penguinrandomhouse.ca

1   2   3   4   5   23   22   21   20   19

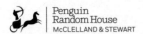

For Sofie (8 months), Dorian, Emmy, Lilliana, Ryan, Graycen, Tyler, Cam, Lindsey, Will, and Ashley (20 years)

AUTHOR'S NOTE

This is the fourth book I have written about hockey. One, I wanted to write. Three of them, including this one, I *needed* to write.

I wanted to write *Home Game* (with Roy MacGregor). I thought that for a reader who knows about hockey, it would tell them a lot about Canada; and for someone who knows about Canada, it would help them to understand hockey. It was the approach Ken Burns used a few years later in his TV series about baseball.

I needed to write *The Game*. It was my first book—and, I felt certain at the time, it would be my only book. I had lived a life fully immersed in hockey, from ball hockey games in our backyard in Etobicoke, Ontario, to the Montreal Forum, to the Luzhniki Ice Palace in Moscow. It was a life that had left me with little time to think or feel. I wanted to stop the rush, to try to make sense of it for myself, and to put it down in words for others. And to do it myself, with no ghostwriter to ease my way and shield me from the test of uncovering my own story.

I needed to write *Game Change: The Life and Death of Steve Montador and the Future of Hockey*. Before I was a player, I was fan—and now I'm still a fan, and a grandfather of kids who play. I thought the mountain of awareness about brain injuries and science was too scattered and too easy to dismiss, and was taking us nowhere. I thought the only way to truly understand the dimensions of the problem was through a person. A life. Steve Montador's life. For us to know the stakes—unmissably, undeniably—in order to generate the will needed to take the decisions that will make hockey just as exciting to play and watch, but less dangerous, for everybody's kids and grandkids. And, most crucially, I thought the only way to inspire this change was to set out how to do it.

I *needed* to write this book for very different reasons. Scotty and I shared a time together—the most important of my hockey life, and one that surely matters to him too. But more than that, Scotty has lived a truly unique life. He has experienced almost *everything* in hockey, up close, for the best part of a century—and his is a life that no one else will live again. It's a life that had to be captured. And it needs to be captured now, because time is moving on. We are both in good health, but we are also at an age when things can intervene. I had thought of writing this book for almost 10 years, and I was sure I would never get to it. I also thought someone would save me the obligation and do it first. But no one did. So on March 26, 2015, at 10:44 a.m., I wrote Scotty an email that said simply, *There is something I'd like to talk to you about.*

Six minutes later, at 10:50 a.m., he replied: *For sure.*

This is the result.

SCOTTY

Robbie Irons was one of more than a thousand players Scotty Bowman coached during his career. He played three minutes and one second of one game for the St. Louis Blues during the 1968–69 NHL season.

I had played with Robbie for the Junior B Etobicoke Indians four years earlier. He was the team's backup goalie. Later, I went to Cornell University, while Robbie played one more year with Etobicoke, then one season with the Kitchener Rangers in the Ontario Hockey Association (later the Ontario Hockey League).

It was a Saturday night in Ithaca, New York, when I sat down to watch the Rangers play the Blues on WPIX. The NHL had expanded from six teams to twelve the year before, and the "Original Six" franchises had made few NHL-calibre players available in the expansion draft. The new teams—St. Louis included—had needed to be creative. Players that were dismissed in earlier years as too old or too small or too soft, or even as "college guys," or Americans, had to be given another look.

Jacques Plante, at age 39, had last played in the NHL three years earlier, having retired after two disastrous seasons with the Rangers. Glenn Hall was 37. The Blues decided that even if Hall and Plante were too old to be the dominant goalies they had once been when playing nearly all of their team's games, they might have enough left as a tandem, each playing about half the time. To save them from any unnecessary wear and tear, St. Louis decided to keep a third goalkeeper on their roster as well—to dress as the backup so Plante or Hall got the night off when the other one played. The Blues rotated three young goalies in this role, and one was Robbie Irons.

Hall was in net that night in New York. The Rangers scored almost right away. Hall, believing that the goal should have been disallowed, argued with the referee and was given a misconduct penalty. Now even angrier, he kept arguing and was thrown out of the game. Immediately, Scotty and Robbie realized the same thing. Robbie was going to need to play.

This much of the story I knew: that Robbie did play, and that a few minutes later he was replaced by Plante. I remember thinking that here was Robbie Irons, my backup with the Etobicoke Indians, playing in a real-life NHL game. But the rest of the story, I didn't know until not long ago.

Robbie, stunned and still disbelieving when Hall was ejected, stayed seated on the players' bench. Scotty, not quite willing to accept his predicament, finally got word to Plante to get down from the press box and dress as fast as he could. Scotty then nodded to Robbie, who skated slowly to the Blues' net. At this moment, Doug Harvey, on the ice, sauntered over to the boards and stood next to Scotty. Harvey was 43 years old and had played only 16 NHL regular-season games in the previous five seasons. The most dominant defenceman of the 1950s, unconquerably hardened and tough, he mumbled to Scotty, "We don't want him to play, do we?"

Scotty said nothing, so Harvey turned and skated even more slowly to the Blues' net, where Robbie was taking some warm-up shots. Harvey said something to him. On the next shot, which was along the ice to his catching-glove side, Robbie did the splits, then threw himself onto his back in agony. He couldn't get up. It was his hamstring, or maybe his groin, or his ankle.

2

Somewhere in the arena, Bill Jennings, president of the Rangers, saw what had happened and raced down towards the Blues' bench. Meanwhile, Plante—who at this stage in his career wanted to play only when he wanted to play—was "taking his sweet time coming down from the press box," as Scotty later related. Robbie, writhing on the ice, was now being attended to by the trainer; his teammates hovering around him in concern.

Minutes passed. Robbie, still on the ice; Plante, still somewhere; the crowd restless; the referee, Vern Buffey, circling near the Blues' bench, growing more impatient. Finally, Buffey said to Scotty, "Somebody's going to have to play." Scotty looked around; still no Plante. Then he looked down the ice at Robbie. Miraculously, Robbie rose to his knees, then to his feet, obviously in pain. The puck was dropped. Three minutes and one second later, the whistle blew. Plante appeared and skated to the Blues' net; Robbie headed to the St. Louis bench; Jennings arrived, too late. "I know what's going on," he roared at Scotty. "I know what you're doing. I'm going to report you to the league. This is a disgrace."

Robbie would go on to play 11 seasons with the Fort Wayne Komets of the International Hockey League, who later retired his number. He never played in the NHL again. His career goals against average: 0.00.

When I watched the game on TV, I didn't know anything about the Doug Harvey moment, or Bill Jennings, or Plante "taking his sweet time." And this was 50 years ago. Scotty remembers everything about everything.

What makes him even more amazing is that, at age 86, he still *sees* everything. He won nine Stanley Cups over three different decades. He won more regular-season games—1,244—than any other coach in NHL history, *by far*. He is the greatest hockey coach ever; he may even be the greatest coach in professional sports history. If anybody has earned the right to live every future moment inside his highly successful past, it is Scotty. But Scotty is not, and never has been, a "been there, done that" person. Every moment of every new game might be different from every moment that has come before. So he keeps his eyes—and his mind—open.

Scotty and his wife, Suella, live from October to May in Siesta Key, Florida, and the rest of the year in East Amherst, New York, a suburb of Buffalo. And except during the holidays when he and Suella visit their kids and grandkids, he drives the hour and a half it takes to get to Amalie Arena in Tampa to attend about 30 of the Lightning's home games—picking up his friend, the former Detroit scout Danny Belisle, along the way. He arrives an hour before puck drop, leaves his car inside the security compound where the players park, walks down a wide back corridor where many of the players—some only just born when he coached his last game in 2002—are stretching or kicking a soccer ball. They look his way, hoping he will look theirs. Then he goes into the media room, picks up a plastic plate and a knife and fork, serves himself at the buffet from the room's stainless-steel containers, and sits down with Jim Devellano—a confidant and long-time Red Wings executive who also now lives in the area—and some media people he knows. They eat, gossip, tell stories, and laugh; then 10 minutes before game time, Scotty gets up and they get up with him. He takes the freight elevator to the press box, gathers a media stats sheet, checks the notice on the wall for the number of his assigned seat, and sits down. A row of TV monitors is above him, the arena's giant screen fills his view in front, and the ice is more than a hundred feet below. He has his iPad and stylus in his hands.

The game begins. As play goes on, he rarely speaks to those on either side of him. Instead, he watches. *Why is this player playing with that one? What is the coach thinking? What is he trying to do?* His eyes are every-where—alert. His eyes are also focused inside himself, searching for something. He taps his iPad, and numbers and letters flicker onto his screen. He thinks. He looks back at the ice.

The next morning in his condo, he watches highlights of games from the previous night on the NHL Network, then watches most of a game he recorded. He gets calls from hockey people who want to know what he thinks. He calls other hockey people to hear what they think. If Chicago played the night before, he goes over the analytics the

Blackhawks had sent him after each period of the game. His son, Stan, is the team's GM, and Scotty is an advisor. Some days, he opens the AHL app and watches the Rockford IceHogs, Chicago's top farm team.

The person who knows hockey if anyone knows, wants to know better. Nobody in hockey has ever lived a life like his. Nobody ever will again.

Scotty was born "down the hill" in Verdun, a working-class neighbourhood of Montreal. He grew up on local, outdoor, snow-covered rinks. Barely of school age, he listened, long past bedtime, to the static and the intermittent voice of the Bruins' radio announcer in faraway Boston. His favourite player was Bill Cowley, number 10. At 11, he breathed the same air as Maurice Richard when the "Rocket" scored an unthinkable 50 goals in 50 games. And all around him were also local heroes with their own legendary stories—some older, some younger—some of whom would one day become heroes on the NHL's big stage: Dollard St. Laurent and Donnie Marshall in Verdun; Gump Worsley in next-door Pointe-Saint-Charles; Fleming Mackell and the Harvey brothers, Doug and Howie, in Notre-Dame-de-Grâce; Dickie Moore in Park Extension; Bernie Geoffrion in the distant east end of the city. And all this time, he played himself—in the streets, back alleys, and parks, and in his imagination.

At 14, he was recruited to play for a team sponsored by the Canadiens. Importantly, he was now old enough to go to the big team's games by himself. With his standing-room pass in hand—the perk of being a member of the Canadiens organization/family—when the doors of the Forum opened at seven o'clock on Saturday nights, ninety minutes before game time, he stampeded with hundreds of others up the back stairs for a spot behind the blues, halfway to the Forum roof. Teenage-quick, he'd always get one of the better ones.

Scotty witnessed the league's first dynasty: the Toronto Maple Leafs, Stanley Cup champions for three straight years from 1947 to 1949. When he was 18, during the 1951–52 season, he was there for all but one of the seven Saturday nights the Detroit Red Wings played in Montreal. The Wings finished with 100 points that year, an astonishing 22 points ahead of the second-place Canadiens. Gordie Howe, Terry Sawchuk, Red Kelly, and Alex Delvecchio were all under the age of 25. They became great before his eyes. And he saw the terrible teams too—Chicago, Boston, New York; half the NHL—at the bottom of the league, year after year, and he saw what made them bad.

In that same season, 1951–52, during his own team's playoffs, he suffered a fractured skull that ended his NHL hopes. A year later, the Canadiens hired him part-time to scout and to coach some minor hockey teams in Montreal. Now he had more time to watch the big team itself—and to watch their GM, Frank Selke Sr., as he put together the team. To a roster that included mid-career stars like Richard and Harvey, he saw them add Geoffrion, then Moore, then later Jean Béliveau and Jacques Plante. Every Tuesday and Friday, he took an early lunch from his job doing general stock-keeping at Sherwin-Williams, the big American paint company, and watched the Canadiens practise. Surrounded by thousands of empty seats, he was the only one there. He saw Dick Irvin Sr. in the last of his 15 seasons as the coach of the team. He saw the players, unguarded and bigger than life—the Rocket, Béliveau. He watched the team inch closer to the Cup.

In 1956, he moved to Ottawa to be Sam Pollock's assistant as coach and GM of the Junior A Ottawa-Hull Canadiens. It was his first full-time hockey job. His players included Ralph Backstrom, Bobby Rousseau, J.C. Tremblay, and Gilles Tremblay, and they played against the best players in the best junior league in Canada—the best junior league in the world—the Ontario Hockey Association (OHA). Scotty was there for two years. In his second season, the team won the Memorial Cup as Canadian champions; in his first they had lost in the final. The next year he moved to Peterborough to become a head coach himself, and the Petes went to the Memorial Cup final again. He was only 25.

Three years later, he was back in Montreal—but really he was out on the road, for seven months a year, night after night, small-town rink after small-town rink, as head scout for the Canadiens in Eastern Canada. He saw all of the top prospects between the ages of 12 and 20, in Ontario and Quebec especially—where nearly two-thirds of the NHL's players were developed. He saw Bobby Orr at 13. He saw Wayne Carleton and Rod Seiling, the other two phenoms of the time. Now more directly associated with the big team, he saw the inner workings of an organization that had won five straight Stanley Cups but was in the midst of *losing* four in a row. He watched the Rocket, Harvey, Plante, Geoffrion, Moore, and Selke all age, retire, or move on. He watched Sam Pollock take over. He watched Jacques Laperrière, Yvan Cournoyer, Serge Savard, and Jacques Lemaire warming up in the wings. He moved off the road to coach junior in Montreal again. All the time, he watched and he remembered what he saw.

In 1966, he moved to the NHL. He was 32. The league was adding six new teams that would begin play a year later. He became assistant to Lynn Patrick, the general manager and head coach of the St. Louis Blues. He was going from Montreal, where he had everything—an established organization, players, fans, tradition, success, expectations, a city with a love of the game—to St. Louis, where he didn't. He had a year to find players who were good enough for the NHL but had never been good enough before. He had seen nearly every player everywhere in Canada—amateur and pro, kid and veteran—since he had suffered his head injury 14 years earlier, and at that time, Canada was where every NHL player came from. But he had seen that special *something* only in very few. In most, he had seen the flaws that couldn't be surmounted to make it to the NHL. Now he had to see past those flaws to what else these players might have in them, *if* they were put in the right circumstances, at this different moment in their lives. So Hall, Plante, Harvey, and Al Arbour, who had been too old, were now no longer too old, and Frank St. Marseille, at 27 and having never played higher than the International Hockey League (IHL), needed to become more than a career minor leaguer.

Sixteen games into the Blues' first season, Scotty took over from Lynn Patrick as head coach. Now he had to both see the possibilities of these players *and* get those possibilities out of them. He was 34, younger than nearly half of his team.

The expanded 12-team NHL had been split into two divisions: East and West. The six new teams formed the West. The Original Six became the East. The Blues emerged from the West and went to the Stanley Cup final in their first three seasons, losing to the much stronger Canadiens (twice) and the Bruins, each time in four straight games. A year later, after a dispute with the Blues' ownership, Scotty became the coach of the Montreal Canadiens. He was 37.

Scotty had grown up in Montreal. He had been immersed in the team. But he was not ready for Montreal, or for the Canadiens. Not at first.

Things had become complicated. The season before, in 1970–71, the Canadiens had come out of nowhere and won the Cup, upsetting the unbeatable Bruins—Bobby Orr, Phil Esposito—who had won a season earlier and would win the following year, and then the power-house Black Hawks—Bobby Hull, Stan Mikita—in the final. After the Cup victory, the Canadiens' long-time captain and leader Jean Béliveau retired. Some players, important to the Canadiens' Cup wins in the late 1960s, were now past their peak; others had not yet reached theirs. The team in 1971–72, Scotty's first season, wasn't ready to win. But the fans and the media weren't ready for it to lose. I was one of the goalies. It was a hard year for the team, and for Scotty. We got knocked out in the first round of the playoffs.

The next year, he was ready—and we were ready. In 1973, Scotty won his first Cup.

Montreal would be eliminated in the first round the next two years, but the Canadiens were piecing together, player by player, something that would become special. Guy Lafleur, then Larry Robinson, then Steve

Shutt, then Bob Gainey—at the same time that Cournoyer, Lapointe, and Savard were getting better, and Lemaire was finding his best game. And so was Scotty.

But how do you coach a great team? Winning once is hard—you've never done it before. Winning the year after is harder, and the year after that. Winning four years in a row is very, very hard, no matter how good you are, no matter how good your team. Scotty had never coached a great team before. No one—except Tommy Ivan and Toe Blake with the Wings and Canadiens in the 1950s—ever had. And a great team in Montreal is a very different story, where even third-line players get a star's level of attention and can get spoiled, complacent, jealous, and think they are stars themselves.

And while the team was becoming great, the Philadelphia Flyers were still in the way. The "Broad Street Bullies"—the Stanley Cup champions two years in a row—were tough. They would hurt you, and in every next moment in every game, they might hurt you more. Every player knew that. There was a phrase that was common at the time—the "Philadelphia Flu," which afflicted a player suddenly (despite him being in the pink of health the day before) when the Flyers were next on the schedule. The Flyers made every opponent focus on *them*, on strategies to survive *them*, not on a team's own strategies to win.

Scotty knew about tough. The original owner of the Flyers, Ed Snider, had once told him that the Broad Street Bullies had been born after Scotty's St. Louis Blues pushed them around in the 1969 playoffs. Snider vowed he would never let that happen again. But push-you-around tough and beat-you-up tough are different, and these Flyers were of a whole new dimension.

The Canadiens needed to stand up to them, to survive Philadephia's game in order to win with their own, because they were the Montreal Canadiens, the "Flying Frenchmen"—in the tradition of the Richards, Béliveau, Geoffrion, and Lafleur. They had to win, but they had to win the right way; and Scotty had to help them believe that they could. Just exhorting them wouldn't be enough. He had to put together the right combination of players that could play this way, and win.

And as all this was happening, he had a new challenge present itself, one that no other NHL coach had ever faced, not in the same way. The Soviets.

Scotty had coached the Ottawa-Hull juniors against touring Soviet teams in the mid-1950s, and lost twice, resoundingly. He had coached the Montreal Junior Canadiens against the Soviets a decade later, before a sold-out Montreal Forum—with Jacques Plante, a year into his first retirement, in goal—and won, 2–1. He had watched with surprise, if not shock, Team Canada's struggles and then final victory in the eight-game Summit Series in 1972. Almost everyone in the NHL, almost anyone who knew anything about hockey, had dismissed the Soviets—they passed too much, they shot too weakly, they weren't tough enough.

Now, after the '72 series, the Soviets were a fact of hockey life. There would be future showdowns, and Canada had to win. The Canadiens represented the best of Canadian hockey. He was the coach. He and the Canadiens had an obligation. He had to find answers to this test too.

On December 31, 1975, all his watching, wondering, and thinking paid off. The Canadiens played an almost perfect game against Moscow's Central Red Army team, tying 3–3 and outshooting CSKA, 36–13. (I was the goalie in the Canadiens' net.) On that Forum ice, he saw right there in front of him the team he wanted. The team he thought we could be. In the Stanley Cup final that spring, the Canadiens crushed the Flyers four straight. It was Scotty's second Cup.

He had learned how to beat the Flyers and at least match the Soviets. He had learned how to win the Cup. He had learned how to coach a great team, and he had done all this in Montreal. There, he would win three more. After his fifth Cup, in 1979, the Canadiens were now the legendary Montreal Canadiens. And he was now the legendary Scotty Bowman.

But there had been some downs along the way, and more were ahead. In February 1979, he coached the NHL All-Stars (all Canadian players, except for three Swedes) against the Soviet national team, in the best-of-three Challenge Cup in New York. After splitting the first two games, the Soviets won the third, 6–0. Two years later, in the 1981 Canada Cup, he coached Team Canada and lost to the Soviets in the final game, 8–1. By this time, he had left Montreal for Buffalo. Sam Pollock, who had always gotten him the players to win, was gone, and Scotty saw no one left in Montreal who could do the same. With the Sabres, as coach *and* general manager, he would at least have himself to trust.

But most of the Sabres' best players were beyond their best years. And in 1979, Buffalo faced a new challenge: with the Canadiens breaking apart—Scotty leaving; Cournoyer, Lemaire, and me retiring—the Islanders were ready to win. And as they were winning, the Oilers— with Wayne Gretzky, Mark Messier, and Jari Kurri—were about to explode onto the scene.

Most seasons, the Sabres were near the top of the league, but they weren't good enough to win. Scotty didn't help himself either. He was 45 when he went to Buffalo. At one level or another, he had been coaching for more than 25 years—and except for a few years as a scout, he had been doing it almost continuously. There is a hierarchy in hockey. To be a coach is good; to be a GM is better. And Scotty had earned *better*. But as a manager, he couldn't get the players he wanted as a coach; and as a coach, he couldn't get the players he had to win. At times, he put others behind the Sabres' bench as coach; at times, he went back behind the bench himself. To the Sabres' fans, media, and ownership, the other coaches were good—but they weren't Scotty. To the fans, media, and ownership, their GM wasn't a Pollock.

In the 1980s, Scotty saw all the game's immense changes up close. He saw how, with Gretzky and the Oilers, the game opened up and the NHL's scoring totals became almost unfathomable. He saw American players and college players enter the league. He saw the rise of the

Europeans—the Swedes first, and a few Finns and Czechoslovakians. He was a part of it. He saw off-ice training come to matter more, and staffs of coaches hired with specialty skills. He was a part of that too. He also saw what it was like to be fired. He knew he couldn't be both coach and general manager any longer—he wanted to manage; the Sabres owners wanted him to coach. There could be no resolution. He saw what it was like to hit mid-life and mid-career and not be as special as he once was; to not have a future that seemed only promising and bright.

Yet none of these changes, of course, could ever impact his legacy. That was already set and determined. He was Scotty Bowman. He'd had a long and incredible run. In a few years, and in every year after that, all that would matter would be his five Stanley Cups in Montreal. His great and glorious teams.

But Scotty never stopped watching. After leaving the Sabres in 1986, he became an analyst for CBC's *Hockey Night in Canada*. Then, in 1990, Lynn Patrick's son Craig—whom he had coached with the Montreal Junior Canadiens and was now Pittsburgh's GM—asked him to become the Penguins' director of player personnel. Scotty and Suella had five kids by this time, all of them school-age, but Patrick told him he could still live in Buffalo and work from there. He took the job. During the playoffs, Patrick had him in Pittsburgh to follow the team, and to be another mind to draw upon for Penguins' coach Bob Johnson if he should need him. Now he was part of another team—Mario Lemieux, Jaromír Jágr, Paul Coffey—that was building, growing, on the verge, and finally, in 1991, winning the Cup.

Then, suddenly, he found himself back in it, when Bob Johnson got sick the following summer. When training camp began, as the Penguins' new interim coach, Scotty was only up to his knees—after all, this was Bob Johnson's team, not his. Johnson would be back soon. Besides, Scotty didn't want to coach anymore. He was too old. And his kids were still young. But then he was up to his waist—Johnson wasn't getting better. Then Johnson died in late November. "Well, it's only until the end of the year," Scotty persuaded himself. Then the Penguins won the Cup again—his sixth. He was fully immersed again. He was almost 59.

He spent one more season in Pittsburgh before moving to Detroit. The great Detroit Red Wings he had watched as a kid at the Forum had not won a Stanley Cup since 1955. In 1997—with Scotty as coach—they won for the first time in 43 years.

He had done it employing no formula, no blueprint from his Cup-winning past. Things had changed in his many decades in the game, and were still changing. The Berlin Wall had come down at the end of the previous decade, and the Russians had well and truly arrived in the NHL. And not just in numbers, though that was important, but in quality. These were stars, or great young talent who were becoming stars— Alex Mogilny, Pavel Bure, Sergei Fedorov.

Non-stars have to find a way to fit into a team. Stars *define* a team. But at the same time a team already *is*, and every NHL team had a history of great Canadian stars who played in the great Canadian way. For Scotty, there were now big questions: How do you coach these new guys, these non-Canadians? How do you make them fit in, and not disrespect the old while adding the new? In Detroit, he had several Russian players, and he put them together in a unit that became known as the "Russian Five"— Fedorov, Igor Larionov, and Vyacheslav Kozlov up front; Slava Fetisov and Vladimir Konstantinov on defence. Together, they played like no other five-player unit in the NHL had ever played. They might have become a novelty act, but Scotty wouldn't let them. He had them play together at times, but not too much—for the team's sake, and for their own. This was about winning the Cup, not putting on a show.

The Wings won again the next year, then lost three times, twice to Colorado in cruel, punishing series. Then they won again in 2001–02. It was Scotty's last Cup—his ninth. He was 68.

He retired from coaching but stayed on as an advisor in Detroit. After his son, Stan, became the assistant GM of Chicago, Scotty became a senior advisor of hockey operations for the Blackhawks, in which role he remains today. Yet this is just part of his still-hockey life—the Lightning games he attends, the gossiping in the media room, the analytics, the phone calls, his iPad, his stats sheets, his NHL and AHL apps. All the watching, all the thinking—his mind as fully engaged as it was as a kid playing shinny at snow-covered Willibrord Park in Verdun. Been there, done that? Never.

When Scotty passes, he will take with him what nobody else has seen, what nobody else knows. After thinking about that for several years, on that March day in 2015, I asked him if he might be interested in doing a book, to try to capture some of this. He had been approached other times, but for one reason or another, not much happened. I thought I knew why. As a rule, away from the ice, most coaches are gregarious. They tell stories. They live in stories, and think in stories. Scotty, though, is not gregarious; he is shy, and he is not a storyteller. He's a coach. He never stops being a coach. He's too practical and focused, and storytelling is too fanciful. When he does interviews or gives speeches and is expected to tell stories, they don't come out the way they do with others, the way his audience expects and wants. He knows he disappoints them.

So ask him to be a coach instead, I thought, not a storyteller. Give him a coach's task. Ask him to pick the greatest teams in NHL history, and more importantly to tell us why. Ask him to talk about the players on those teams, to tell us not just what made them great—because over time, every player comes to be described as great—but also to tell us what they looked like when they *weren't* great. When the Rocket *didn't* score. When Gordie Howe played a lousy game. The same for Orr, Gretzky, and Lemieux—they played lousy games too. What happened then? Why? And how would *he* coach these players, in their great moments and in their bad? How would he coach against them and shut them down? The Canadiens of the late 1950s and the Oilers of the 1980s—how would he coach those teams? How would he beat them?

And of all the great teams, which is the greatest of the great? Why? Why not the others? Scotty has seen them all. He's seen them up close, at their best and worst moments, for more than 75 years. And so I wanted him to tell me. Because nobody else can.

So I asked him to be what he is—the coach—and not what he isn't: the storyteller. And that's how our conversations went, for about a year and a half, mostly when he was in Florida. He'd be in the kitchen of his condo, and Suella would be in the family room. He'd have his binders, his iPad, and stylus on the table in front of him; I'd be in Toronto, at home in my office, with my binders and laptop and my *NHL Official Guide and Record Book* in front of me. For about an hour and a half each time we'd talk, and I would record what we said. We didn't know that it would be for an hour and a half—it just turned out that way. Usually it was on Mondays and Thursdays—we didn't know that either at first, but it turned out that twice a week seemed right. It wasn't every Monday and Thursday; sometimes he had an appointment he couldn't miss or one of his kids and their family would be visiting. But most often it was. And, except for a few times, it was always at 9 a.m. My phone would ring—Scotty always wanted to make the call—and each time I'd look at my digital watch until I knew I didn't need to look at it anymore, because it would always say 9:00—never 8:59, never 9:01. Scotty, in all the years he hasn't coached—and because of all the years he did—is still on "hockey time." And when I answered the phone, it was always the same: "Hi Ken. It's Scotty."

It didn't take long for me to discover something surprising and wonderful: when Scotty is faced with a coach's task—a situation, a player, an opponent, something he's seen, something that he's put together in his mind with other things he's seen and remembers and discovers for

15

himself with some new clarity and meaning—what comes out is a story. Scotty *is* a storyteller. But to him, a story for a story's sake seems too much about him. A story needs a reason. He just needed a reason.

I asked him to pick, in his mind, the top eight teams of all time. I chose eight because we needed to set some sort of limit, and because eight allows for a good, testing three rounds of playoffs—four quarter-final series; two semifinals, and a final. Then I wanted him to pick the best team *ever*. These would be his choices; not mine in any way. I would just question and probe, and try to get out of him what he knew. I told him that he shouldn't worry about selecting teams that ticked all the appropriate boxes—teams from different eras, Canadian *and* American teams, teams from a wide range of cities rather than only from a few franchises. This was about the best—not a representational or political best. My only suggestion was that, where an organization won several Cups in a row, he choose only the one team among them that he considered the best.

I asked him to tell me his eight choices before we began our talks so I could prepare statistical binders on each team—one set for him, one for me, so we both had in front of us resources to jog our memories, uncover some fresh questions, and find new answers.

We discussed the eight teams he chose in chronological order, and talked extensively about each one. I asked him as we began to first set the context—both his own personal context and that of the NHL. For example, if (spoiler alert!) one team was to be the 1951–52 Red Wings, how old was he at the time? Where was he living? What was he doing? What was the league like? Who were the good teams and the bad teams? Which ones were getting better, and which were getting worse? Who were the stars, and the soon-to-be stars? Then, when we had finished discussing all eight teams in that way—and this took many months—I asked him to select the series matchups he wanted, and to think about which opponents might offer the most interesting test for each other. I also suggested that, as he did this, he should have in mind his two finalists and his ultimate winner—but that he shouldn't tell me who they were. In fact, I specifically wanted *not* to know, so I could ask him the same coach-testing questions about each. Of course, I thought I sensed at times who would win each series from what he said, and who his finalists would be—but, as it turned out, I was often wrong.

I had one other thing in mind. I didn't know if he would choose one of *our* Canadiens' Cup-winning teams from 1976 to 1979—when he was the coach and I was one of the goalies—but if he did, I wanted to ask him about it last. I have a stake in that team; a bigger stake now than I thought I would. And I have a stake in what Scotty thinks of me. So I didn't want to ask him about us. I didn't want to ask him about me. I knew I had to, but I would do that last.

So here they are. The top eight teams of all time, in chronological order:

Detroit Red Wings, 1951–52
Montreal Canadiens, 1955–56
Toronto Maple Leafs, 1962–63
Montreal Canadiens, 1976–77
New York Islanders, 1981–82
Edmonton Oilers, 1983–84
Detroit Red Wings, 2001–02
Chicago Blackhawks, 2014–15

Let the games (and stories) begin.

—

A suggestion—many of you may want to skip to the end to find out who wins, but try to resist. How Scotty gets there . . . *that* is the story.

CHAPTER TWO

First, Scotty's own story.

William Scott Bowman was born on September 18, 1933, in Verdun, Quebec—a working-class neighbourhood on the south-central margins of the island of Montreal. His father's name was Jack, his mother was named Jean. His sister, Freda, had been born less than a year earlier; his brother, also named Jack, came three years later, followed by a much younger brother, Martin, in 1946, just after the war ended. For most of Scotty's childhood, the family lived in a rental "flat," as they called it— in a three-storey walk-up at 732 5th Avenue, one of six numbered streets known as "the Avenues" that ran the full width of Verdun; the four blocks between Boulevard LaSalle and the Saint Lawrence River to the east, and Boulevard Champlain and the Aqueduct to the west. The walk-ups connected one to the next uninterrupted, 13 of them on each side of the street, 6 flats in each, 156 flats on their block alone, the staccato repetition of front doors and windows and exterior staircases— same size, same colour—the only evidence of the narrow flats behind.

The row houses of the Avenues were not much different from the terraced houses of Forfar, Scotland, where Jack had grown up. Forfar (pronounced "For-fr") is an old market and mill town which dates back to Roman times. Situated in a wide, shallow valley, in a landscape of farmland, streams, and forests, it lies 80 kilometres north of Scotland's capital, Edinburgh, and 20 kilometres west of the North Sea. Jack's father, Charles—or "Chae"—was a tailor. He and his wife, Jack's mother, Christina—known as "Kirst"—moved often, from Forfar to Dundee to Forfar to Woodside to Coupar Angus and finally back to Forfar, as Chae struggled to find work. Then the children began to arrive: Martin (for whom Scotty's brother was named) in 1894, then Will, then Wilhemina (known as Minnie), then Adam—all two years apart—and finally Jack, in 1902. Chae, it seems, also went to South Africa at some point during these years. The Boer War was on, and soldiers needed uniforms and tailors to make them—or so he hoped. Not many months later, he was back in Forfar.

But in 1903, whether it was because of his recurring struggles in Scotland, the promise of South Africa, or an appetite for adventure that he couldn't satisfy at home, he left again. The South African gold rush had evolved into an immense and sustainable gold industry, and miners had money to buy what he made. Back in Scotland, Jack was less than a year old. He never saw his father again.

Chae never wrote home. Something had happened, the family knew. Jack's oldest brother, Martin, by this time age 9, went to live with their paternal grandparents. The other four children—Will, 7; Minnie, 5; Adam, 3; and Jack himself, 1—remained with Kirst, who raised them by herself in difficult and now further-diminished circumstances. She earned her living working as a sweeper in a jute factory.

It wasn't until 24 years later, in 1927, that the family again heard from Chae. He was still living in South Africa—in Newcastle, a burgeoning city of more than 100,000 midway between gold-rich Johannesburg in the north and Durban on the south coast. He had met an Englishwoman from Middlesborough named Ethel Ingledew, and they opened a store, which they described as a high class ladies' and gent's tailor—which they would continue to run, apparently successfully, until at least the 1940s. Chae had found a place to make his future.

It turned out that, during his years away, Chae had been in contact with his own parents—and it was some bad news from them that had prompted him to make contact with his children: his parents informed him of the death of Kirst, who had succumbed to lung disease after decades of breathing in the jute fibre and dust from the mill. So in 1927, Chae wrote a letter of apology to Will, who was his oldest remaining son. His oldest because Martin, his firstborn—with a new wife and a son less than six months old—had enlisted in the army when the First World War broke out, and had died of his wounds on April 26, 1917, in France. (This news had also been passed on to Chae at the time by his parents.) Martin died never knowing his father's whereabouts. Before he left for the war in France, Martin had named his son Charles, in his father's honour. Chae would continue to live in South Africa—in Newcastle, and later in Durban—until his death in 1966, only a few weeks before his 92nd birthday.

After Chae's departure in 1903, Jack lived with his mother, sister and two brothers, about 20 kilometres outside Forfar. With Martin's death in 1917, Martin's infant son Charles moved in with them; another mouth for Kirst to feed. Jack, by now 14 and too young to join the army, decided to leave school to apprentice as a blacksmith in a small shop owned by Jean's father, in Monikie, about 15 kilometres south of Forfar. A short time later, Jack and Jean met, but Jean, four years younger, was of no interest to him at the time.

Jack worked with the other smiths to forge and shape iron into horseshoes for the myriad horses in the area that ploughed the fields. But with the rise of automobiles and tractors, horses were becoming less important, and Jean's father's business was failing. By this time, Jack *had* noticed Jean— and they began to see each other. When Jack told Jean's father he was leaving to work in another blacksmith's shop, Jean's father told him that if his shop wasn't good enough for him, then neither was his daughter, and to "never come around here again." Jack and Jean were undeterred. Not many years later, Jean would name her first-born son after her father, William Scott.

By the mid-1920s, the local economy had worsened, and Jack had to move from job to job. For two years he rode his bike every Sunday night from Forfar to St. Andrew's, a distance of 40 kilometres, and every Friday night he rode back home again. On weekends, he played for the Forfar Athletic "Loons," a soccer team in the newly created Scottish Second Division. The Loons had won the Scottish junior championship the year before, and Jack—quick, tough, and reliable—was the team's centre-back. They played their games at Station Park, near the train depot and rail lines that brought the raw materials to the mills and took the finished products to Aberdeen or Dundee on the coasts.

But, for Jack, things were no better with Jean's father—nor at work—and the years were passing. Then Kirst died, and there was no longer anything to keep him in Scotland. Jack was 26, and he knew it was now or never for him if he was to make a new life. He just needed something to encourage him to go.

Then he saw an ad—or one of his friends did—placed by the Canadian National Railway, offering free passage by ship to Canada for young men willing to work in the CNR's rail yards in Winnipeg. Jack and three of his friends decided to go. Jean would stay behind; Jack would get settled and then send for her. When Jack left, he knew he had likely seen his family for the final time.

When the four friends arrived in Montreal in October 1929, a CNR representative who met the ship offered them a choice: continue on to Winnipeg, or begin work the following day doing the same job but in the rail yards of Montreal. Two of them went to Winnipeg, but Jack and one of his friends decided Canada was Canada, blacksmithing was black-smithing, and why not get at it. They stayed.

The railyards were in Pointe-Saint-Charles, a grimy industrial area of factories and company row houses inhabited by English, Scots, French Canadians, Poles, and Ukrainians, but mostly by the Irish. It was a place of hard work and simple living; a place for people like Jack to make a start. From his first day on the job, he did what he had always done: he made horseshoes. Trucks were not yet numerous—mostly used for longer and bigger hauls—and so horses were still needed for the routine pulling and towing they had done for millennia. Jack was living with Jim Kydd, another friend from Forfar who had come to Canada four years earlier and had a flat on Ethel Street in next door Verdun. But Jack was also making plans. He found a small flat on 2nd Avenue, also in Verdun, and a few months later Jean, and Jack's sister, Minnie, arrived. On May 20, 1930, Jack and Jean were married. Two years later, Freda was born.

These were the years of the Great Depression. More people were without jobs; more people didn't have the money to buy what businesses made; more businesses shut their doors. The CNR was too big and too important to fail, but they still had to lay off some of their workers. Jack was lucky, and kept his job. Later, he left to go to Mount Royal Metals, which in time was bought by Federated Metals, a U.S. company that made roofing phalanges.

If Jack and Jean had ever heard the name *Verdun* before they arrived in Canada, it would have been Verdun, France. And if they had, they would have assumed their new home in Quebec was named for the French city. But it was actually named for Saverdun, a village near Toulouse in southwestern France that had been the home of Zacharie Dupuis, once the acting governor of Montreal, who in 1671 was granted a fief which he called Verdun.

But the First World War would create a lasting link between Verdun, Quebec, and Verdun, France. In early 1916, the war in Europe had stalemated—the initial excitement and expectation of it was gone. For most monarchs, politicians, generals, and the public alike, victory was now about avoiding defeat. German generals realized that if breakthrough victories weren't possible and this was to be a war of attrition, they needed to develop a war-of-attrition strategy. If they massed their weapons and bombarded the French lines, the British reserves would need to be brought in, French and British casualties would be high, collectively their will would be broken, and then a favourable peace could be negotiated. The biggest and longest battle in this war of attrition would be at Verdun.

By the time the battle at Verdun finally spasmed to its end on December 18—after 303 days—hundreds of thousands had perished, and countless others had their lives permanently altered by their wounds. A few months later, Jack's brother Martin died, also in France. Verdun would become emblematic of the triumph and the futility of the First World War.

The war was 12 years over by the time Jack, Jean, and Minnie settled on the Avenues of Verdun, but it wasn't in the past. Many of their new neighbours had fought in Europe. They had worn Canada's uniform, but they had fought for Britain. Some were English and some Scottish, and they were not many years separated from their ancestral lands. They told stories of home in accents of home. They attended churches of their own denominations—Anglican and Presbyterian. They joined clubs with members of their own ilk.

When the war began in 1914, Verdun's population was 15,000—not much different from that of Forfar. Records show that, in Forfar, 430 local boys died in the conflict—among them ten Smiths, eight Clarks, eight Robertsons, and one Bowman (Jack's brother Martin). In Verdun, Quebec, the exact number of deaths is not known, but it exceeded 150. In 1919, when the Prince of Wales made a royal visit to Canada, he came to Verdun. In a story that was told and retold with pride, long into Scotty's childhood, the Prince of Wales allowed his personal standard to fly from the flagpole at Verdun's city hall, because in the Great War it was Verdun that had the highest per capita enlistment of any city in the British Empire.

Verdun had become a city almost overnight. As Montreal grew, taking in people from farms and distant places to meet its industrial and residential needs, Verdun had stayed isolated and apart, separated by bodies of water—the Lachine Canal and the Aqueduct—when other areas near downtown Montreal were easily accessible. And an even greater obstacle was Verdun's low, marshy land, which was subject to frequent flooding in the spring. From the perspective of developers and buyers, why risk precious money here when they could invest in lots of other places?

But then dykes were built to hold back the water, and while most of the other land nearest to the city had been developed, Montreal still needed more. In 1901, Verdun's population was 1,898. In 1911, it was 11,629. By 1921 it had more than doubled, to over 25,000, and in the next decade it would more than double again, to 60,745. When the Bowmans moved into Verdun in 1930, it was Canada's fastest-growing city, its fourteenth-largest, and the third-biggest city in Quebec.

Verdun was "dry," which meant no alcohol was permitted in its public establishments. Its taverns instead were located on the other side of the tracks, literally, near the CNR rail yard, outsourced to next-door Pointe-Saint-Charles. So too were its factories—Verdun's first factory, Defence Industries Limited, a big munitions plant, wasn't built until near the end of the war, constructed to support the boys at the front. Verdun, instead, was residential, and commercial. Its main thoroughfare, Wellington Street, was busy with cars, trucks, trolleys, and horse-drawn carts, and with people popping in and out of its retail shops. It was the second-most important business artery in all of Montreal, after Sainte-Catherine Street.

Self-contained and isolated for so long, Verdun was developing its own distinct identity by the 1920s. It contained a mix of languages, religions, and cultures that was different from the rest of Montreal, which meant it was different from the rest of Quebec and from the rest of Canada too. It was a mix that didn't vary much over the decades that followed—a few more English-speakers than French-speakers until the early 1930s when Scotty was born; a fifty-fifty split during his growing-up years; then a few more French-speakers than English as he finished high school. Verdun was a place where people moved in and not many moved out.

The words *working-class* and *Verdun* went together, were used together, and everybody who knew of Verdun in Montreal and in other parts of Canada knew that. Verdun was working-class when working-class seemed a good thing to be, when smoke curling out of a smokestack meant progress, when *working* meant being able to care for your own needs and those of your family, in the present and for the future, when *class* meant basic understandings and beliefs that connected and were shared. When working-class seemed like middle-class. When anybody might be your neighbour: a future baron of industry, a hockey player, a member of Parliament—even Canada's official hangman, Arthur B. English, alias Arthur Ellis, who presided over 600 hangings between 1912 and 1935, lived nearby. (The Arthur Ellis Awards for Canada's best crime and mystery writing are named in his honour.)

This was Verdun when Jack, Jean, and Minnie moved onto the Avenues in 1930, when Freda was born in 1932, and Scotty a year later, and young Jack in 1936, even when Martin came along 10 years later. This was the Verdun of Scotty's childhood. Scotty was a Verdun kid, not a Montreal kid.

Verdun was a spirit, and a look. And what defined that look was the Avenues. And what defined the Avenues were the two- and three-storey walk-ups with their outside staircases. And what defined the walk-ups was their size.

732 5th Avenue was part of a six-plex of flats. Two flats occupied the bottom floor, four steps above street level; the Bowmans' was to the right, in the shadow of an exterior staircase fifteen steps high that led to the second floor. Their landlord, Monsieur Leroux, lived in the bottom-floor flat to the left. As it was with most building and shop owners at the time, even in the English-speaking areas of Verdun, he was French-Canadian. He and his wife had two kids, Denis and Maurice. They were about Scotty's age, but, as Scotty recalls, they didn't play hockey.

At the top of the staircase were four identical doors side by side, a foot or two apart from each other. Two of the doors led to second-storey flats; two to interior staircases that connected to flats on the third floor. All the flats were the same—with the ones on the right being the mirror image of the ones on the left. Inside each front door, a narrow hallway ran from the front of the flat to the back. For the flats on the right, like the Bowmans', the rooms extended from the hallway to the right. First was a living room. Then a dining room, separated from the living room by a partial wall. Then a back bedroom behind a full wall. At the end of the hallway was a small kitchen and bathroom. For the Bowmans, the living room also had in it two beds—one for Freda and (until she died from diabetes in 1940) one for Minnie, Jack's sister, as did the dining room, which had one for Scotty and one for young Jack. The back bedroom had one bed, for Jack and Jean; after 1946, there was one for Martin as well. With only two small windows at the front and two at the back, and windowless walls down each side, the apartment was in perpetual dusk.

850 square feet.

When Scotty describes his childhood home, it is this fact that he mentions first and most often. 850 square feet for five people—six after Jack was born, five after Minnie died, and six again after Martin was born. 850 square feet for a family with young kids, three of them close in age, three of them boys. When Scotty and his wife, Suella, went to Montreal a few years ago with their daughter, Alicia, they drove to 732 5th Avenue, knocked on the door, and the woman who now lives there let them in. Alicia took pictures.

The unanswerable question for Alicia—and even for Scotty and Suella—was "How?" How was it possible that so many people lived so close together? And really it wasn't just five, or six. The Bowmans shared a wall with their landlord and his family. They shared a ceiling/floor with the family above them, and the family above them shared a wall with the family beside them and a ceiling/floor with the family on the floor above them, who shared a wall with the family beside *them*. They shared arguments, they shared people coming in late and going out early, they shared crying babies, smells, and sounds that seemed like nothing when they made them themselves, but seemed like a lot when they came out of the blue from somewhere else. Up and down the Avenues it was the same.

Alcide Hébert lived in the flat above the Bowmans. He was a scout for the Verdun Cyclones, where Gump Worsley played, but he had no family and they never talked to him. Above Hébert were the McArdles. Their son, Bobby, played football, until one day his heart stopped and he died on the field. The neighbours all knew about each other even if they didn't know each other. And to make that even more unavoidable, running down the middle of every building from top to bottom like an umbilical cord, connecting every flat, was a ventilation shaft that amplified each sound and smell and drama.

850 square feet. It's what defined life on the Avenues. Or it would have, if Verdunites had allowed it.

Jack left every morning at 6:30, catching a bus at the bottom of the street on Verdun Avenue, his work day beginning at 7. He left work every night at 6 and was home by 6:30. Jean worked three days a week— Saturdays and two other days depending on the week—baking cakes and cookies for the Blue Cake counter at Eaton's, a big, iconic department store in downtown Montreal. She left when the kids departed for school—it took her 45 minutes by bus—and she always arrived home before they did at the end of their school day. Minnie also worked three days a week—Friday, Saturday, and Sunday—staying overnight as a maid for the Brown family in the old-money English neighbourhood of Westmount, where, as she always said, she was treated like one of the family. Minnie had come from Scotland with Jean in 1930, and on days when she wasn't in Westmount with the Browns, she did what Jean needed done around the flat, the cleaning and the laundry, and making lunch for the kids at noon when they came home from school on the weekdays when Jean was at Eaton's. Scotty remembers her as "a beautiful lady."

While Jack, Jean, and Minnie may have had to spend their days at work, and Freda, Scotty, young Jack, and later Martin had to spend their days in school, working and studying also got all of them outside that 850-square-foot space. The CN Yards and Mount Royal Metals were busy workplaces with lots of people, and they were also big spaces. Eaton's was a big space. Woodland Elementary School and Verdun High School were big spaces. So was the Verdun First Presbyterian Church on 5th Avenue. The neighbourhood itself was crowded. The Avenues were the most densely populated section of Verdun, and Verdun was the most densely populated city in Canada. Yet *outside* there was space.

The streets were more than four car widths across—big enough for the large automobiles of the 1930s and 1940s to drive and park in each direction. Yet there were not many cars. The Bowmans never had one, and neither did any of their neighbours. So the streets were wide open for play. The postage-stamp lawns between the sidewalks and the flats had few trees. Not at that time. Trees give shade, but they take up space and take over the sky. Few trees—more space. The 20 metres from the orange-brown brick flats on one side of the street to the orange-brown brick flats on the other meant 20 metres of space to play in. Behind each street were alleys that separated the backyards of the flats. No cars there either—20 more metres. And only a few blocks away was Willibrord Park, with its two outdoor hockey rinks in winter, softball field in summer, and lots of other open space to stimulate childhood imaginations. Verdun's buildings—even those along Wellington Street—were just three storeys high. Only the church steeples extended higher.

And, importantly, at the bottom of the Avenues was the river. At Verdun, the Saint Lawrence River is at one of its widest points around the island of Montreal. Today, the view from Verdun's shore is obstructed by buildings on Nuns' Island. Then—still agricultural and undeveloped—Nuns' Island lay flat, the distant lights of the South Shore visible on the horizon like a string of diamonds. There was also the Boardwalk, one of three big projects constructed in Verdun during the Depression—the Auditorium and the Natatorium, a hockey-rink-sized outdoor swimming pool, being the others—all so-called make-work projects that would become even more important to Verdun as "make-community" projects. A boardwalk might seem insignificant now—a little ambiance for real estate agents to sell—but back then it was really something. The one at Verdun was made of wooden planks many sidewalks wide, and ran along the top of the dyke from the Auditorium all the way to Crawford Park. It was a place of fresh air, river breezes, and wide vistas; where in summer people dressed in their best took life-restoring workday-end walks or romantic weekend strolls under its lampposts, and watched the big ships go by. This was their entertainment. It was also the one place where Verdunites saw people from up the hill in Montreal, who in the rest of their lives had no reason to go down to Verdun. The Boardwalk was as nice as any rich person, even in Montreal, could ever want or imagine.

In his early years in Canada, Jack—with some of his Scottish buddies—had played soccer on a company team, in a league made up of company teams. He brought Scotty along to a few games to watch, but by the time Scotty was old enough to remember, Jack was in his late thirties and soon stopped playing. Besides, he now enjoyed gardening more than he did soccer. He had a tiny piece of land behind their flat by the back alley where he grew flowers, and worked a larger plot as part of a "Victory Garden" that was owned by the city in a vacant lot up the street. Every night from May until October, from dinner until sundown, Scotty remembers, Jack tended his onions, his cabbages, and his cauliflowers. Scotty helped him with the planting—he didn't mind that. It was the weeding he resented—twice a week, which meant twice a week he had less time to play at the park.

Jack was a member of the Verdun Horticultural Society and the lawn bowling club. He was an elder at the church, where with the other elders he helped set the direction of the church and saw that everything that needed to be done for the Sunday services and the church's midweek activities was carried out. The minister of the church, Reverend Coryell, relied on him as a source of quiet good sense, Scotty recalls. They became lifelong friends.

Jack did his gardening, lawn bowling, and his work at the church not just because he enjoyed them—but also because they got him out of the house. When he did need to do something inside the house, he did it on Saturdays when he had the flat to himself—when Jean was at Eaton's, Minnie was in Westmount, and the kids were out playing. He was very handy, as Scotty recalls. It didn't matter if it was carpentry, plumbing, or something electrical, he could fix things. It was an ability that had come from his training as a blacksmith; it was born of an instinct and need that came from his father and grandfather, and from every generation before them. There had never been any money to pay someone else to do something for you, no money to buy anything new. If something was broken, you fixed it yourself. Jack even resoled the family's shoes. Many years later, when they got their first TV, they watched it so often that the black edges of the screen began to creep inward towards the middle, the picture getting smaller and smaller, until Jack went out and bought some tubes and fixed it. Not many people could repair a TV.

Jean, too, wasn't often in the flat. She was there when the kids and Jack were there, preparing meals or baking—she was always baking. During the war, she would send Scotty to the store with ration coupons to buy Crisco. Always Crisco. And always to Steinberg's, a small grocery store around the corner on Verdun Avenue, until one day a giant new Steinberg's opened almost across the street from the old one. It was one of the first supermarkets in Quebec—three storeys high and almost a full city block long. Jean's baking was in part for the family, but mostly it was for the church, because she knew that there was no event, no church bazaar, that couldn't be made better by a cake, or a pie, or cookies. Baking may have kept Jean inside, but baking at Eaton's or for the church also got her out of the house.

As for Scotty, he "lived outdoors," as he puts it. Once breakfast was over, he was gone. To school, then back home to drop off his books, then to the candy store a few blocks away to wait and play marbles with five other kids until the newspapers arrived for them to deliver. Sometimes, on the way there, the guy from the Cheerio Yo-Yo Company would be standing on the corner of 5th and Bannantyne doing his tricks. Around the World, Walk the Dog—he could do them all, and Scotty and some of the others would stop and bring out their own yo-yos, and do their own tricks. If you were good, he might give you a yo-yo string—the strings were always breaking. If you were *really* good, you might get a nice-coloured sleeveless sweater with the company name on it. Scotty did get some yo-yo strings, but he never got a sweater.

At four o'clock, the newspapers were dropped off at the store. He took his 80 copies of the *Montreal Daily Star*, and with a quick twist and tuck he rolled each of them and put them in his wagon. His route was only on 5th Avenue, and only to the English flats—he knew the language demographics of his neighbourhood better than any social science researcher, and most of the English-speaking families were his customers. His routine was simple; all it took was a toss from the sidewalk to a front door, or walking up a few steps on the outside staircase and a few more tosses to the doors that led to the flats on the second and third floors. An hour later, he'd be back home playing on the street.

At 6:30, he'd see his father walk up the sidewalk from the bus stop on Verdun Avenue and join him on his final steps home. Dinner would be ready, and the whole family would sit down to eat. The food was simple—potatoes were a staple, as were shortbread, scones, and lots of mince. There was no particular family dynamic around the dinner table; some talked, and some didn't. There were no usual subjects they discussed—not their days at work or at school, or the happenings of the world. In fact, they didn't talk much. They had things to do, other places to go. Eating was purposeful. So they ate, and then they went.

On Mondays, Scotty had basketball at the YMCA on Gordon Avenue. The program was run by Angus MacFarlane. He was only eight years older than Scotty, but because he was old enough to have fought in the war he seemed much older. Scotty remembers him as a great coach and a great guy. Later, he would become Gus MacFarlane, member of Parliament for the riding of Hamilton Mountain in Ontario, and Chief Government Whip in Pierre Trudeau's government in the late 1970s. He and Scotty remained in contact for the rest of MacFarlane's life.

On Thursdays when Scotty was younger, he had floor hockey at the church, and on other days, Wolf Cubs or Boys Brigade at his school. He was a drummer in Boys Brigade, and 75 years later at his home in Buffalo he still has his Boys Brigade belt, among all his miniature Stanley Cups and other treasures. And, whether he was younger or older, every day and every moment he didn't have something else to do, he played hockey in the winter and softball in the summer. In winter, it was dark by 4:30, but they had "big street lanterns," as Scotty describes them, their games played between one big street lantern at one end, and one at another—the goalies had to see. One night a week, there were games at Willibrord Park, but dinner needn't be rushed because nothing started early and all the kids were local. There was no travel time. There couldn't be. Almost no parents had cars. Scotty got to the park always by the same route—skating up snow-packed 5th Avenue to an alley just before Bannantyne, a right turn, then down the alley, crossing 4th, 3rd, 2nd, and 1st, and he was there. In those days, the alleys weren't paved or ploughed, so once the snow fell, ice formed and stayed put, and the ice on the roads and alleys wasn't much less rutted than the ever-used, Zamboni-less, natural ice of Willibrord Park. Verdunites and Montrealers are good at winter because they have to be.

Verdun wasn't a big area within Montreal, the Avenues weren't a big area within Verdun, and Scotty's world within the Avenues was even smaller. Yet he lived a neighbourhood life. He walked or ran (he was fast) or skated wherever he went. His elementary school, Woodland, was five minutes' walk away; so close he came home for lunch every day. Verdun High School was 10 minutes away. The candy store where he picked up his newspapers, Willibrord Park, and the First Presbyterian Church were even closer. The Boardwalk and the 5th Avenue Theatre, where Jack took the family for Sunday afternoon movies in these pre-TV times, were also only 10 minutes away. To go anywhere else, they needed a bus or a streetcar; there wasn't a subway in Montreal until 1966.

A few times a year they went to church picnics at Otterburn Park on the South Shore. They traded holiday visits with Harry and Esther Smart and their four kids. One year it was Christmas at the Smarts and New Year's Eve at the Bowmans; the next year it was the reverse. The Smarts lived in the far east end of Montreal, at 5682 17th Avenue in Rosemont, more than an hour away by bus. They had come to Canada from Scotland a few years before the Bowmans. Esther was Jean's first cousin, Harry was Jack's best man at their wedding, and they were Jack and Jean's best friends. Harry worked as a painter at the Bank of Montreal.

But except for those excursions and for work, the Bowmans mostly stayed put in Verdun. It wasn't until Scotty was in high school that he was often up the hill and out of the neighbourhood—when his teams played at Lachine Arena or at the Forum, or when he got his standing-room pass to the Canadiens games (the pass itself was free; he just had to pay the tax each time, 50 cents), or when on summer Sunday afternoons he took a bus east to watch Jackie Robinson and the Little World Series champion Montreal Royals play doubleheaders at Delorimier Stadium.

He wasn't often out of Verdun even "virtually." The Bowmans did have a telephone—their number was York 8637, Scotty recalls—but it was a party line they shared with another family, and as his parents always reminded them, a telephone was not a toy, it had a purpose and it was not to be used for gabbing. The kids certainly weren't allowed to call the neighbours. Instead, they had to get up, go outside, and knock on their door. If Scotty had to find out what time a practice was, then maybe ("Why didn't you ask them before?") he might be allowed to use the phone. It was a big moment when the family got their own phone, but that wasn't until just after the Second World War. Until then, they had the radio to take them to other places. And they had newspapers. TV, of course, was still years away.

Of all of the family, only Freda lived an indoor life. She was born with club feet, her legs and feet rotated inward. She had casts put on her legs and feet to reorient them, and by the time she was in school she could move the way most kids did. But a habit had been born in her, and lifelong interests had developed. Freda was a reader; she loved books. She would become the "smart one" in the family—the academic one. Scotty graduated from high school, from Grade ii, which was how the Quebec system worked. Freda took an extra year—said to be the equivalent of the first year of university—and graduated from Grade 12 before attending Macdonald College in Sainte-Anne-de-Bellevue, at the western tip of the island of Montreal, where she got her teacher's certificate in one year and began teaching at 20. Scotty remembers this with pride. "She was an excellent student," he says.

An educated person was prized at the time in a way little else was. Formal education was what Jack and Jean's generation didn't have. But it was what the government was now beginning to provide with everyone in mind; what Jack and Jean's hard work could give to their kids in their new country—in *this* new country—to make a better, heretofore unimaginable future. Scotty and his brother Jack were good athletes. Freda, and later Martin—who got his BA and his master's from McGill University, then earned his PhD from the Université de Montréal and became an English professor at a CEGEP (junior college) in the city—were the special ones.

Scotty did fine academically, but neither he nor anyone else knew how smart he was. He also had his sister's reputation looming over him.

Being less than a year younger than Freda, he hated it when he got a teacher who had taught her—because while Freda got 90s, Scotty got 70s. One year, he had Mrs. Ironside for English. After Scotty scored an undistinguished result on one of his tests, she brought out one of Freda's old report cards as inspiration for him. "Mrs. Ironside," Scotty said to her in return, "you don't know this but my sister doesn't play any sports at all. She studies all the time. She's like a professional student. And I have to play all of these sports, and I don't have as much time as her."

Outdoors is a democratic place. Indoors isn't. Outdoors, for the most part, is the same for everyone, and belongs to everyone, rich or poor. Indoors doesn't. Outdoors, on the Avenues of Verdun, there were English kids, French kids, Italian and Polish kids. There were smart kids and not-so-smart kids. Athletes and non-athletes. Kids with physical disabilities, and kids who "weren't quite right." Kids with very different futures ahead. And adults too, also old people, and women widowed by the war. They weren't all each other's friends, but they ran into each other. They experienced difference, they got used to difference—and, in time, they weren't distracted or frightened by difference. Indoors, you tend to see your own kind.

850 square feet. It's what forced the Bowmans and everyone else on the Avenues outside. And it was these outdoor spaces—not the closed-in world of flats and row houses of Verdun—that defined them.

CHAPTER THREE

Just before the war began, in June 1938, Jean decided to take the kids to Scotland. She hadn't seen her family for eight years. Freda was 5, Scotty was 4, and young Jack just 1, and they had never met their grandparents. They were meant to be there only a few weeks, but then one of the kids got sick, then the other two, then they all got sick with something else— with measles, mumps, and whooping cough, one after another. At times they had to be quarantined.

Months passed. Ships departed. They couldn't get back. They ended up staying in Scotland the entire winter, and then into spring. Jack remained in Canada on his own, working at his job at Mount Royal Metals. Jean's mother fell in love with the baby—young Jack—and tried to convince Jean that he should stay with her, that Jean already had too many kids to care for. After all, 20 years earlier Jack's mother had taken in Charles as an infant after her own son, Martin, had died in France— and that had turned out all right.

Finally, in April 1939, the family—including baby Jack—returned to Montreal on the SS *Athenia*. Five months after that, on September 3— only two days after Germany had invaded Poland and war had been declared—the *Athenia* was torpedoed by a German U-boat and sunk.

Once back home, life for the Bowmans began up again as if

uninterrupted. It would be easy to look back at Scotty's Verdun years and see poverty or at least hardship. If you walked along the streets of fortress-like row houses; if you went inside the door of 732 5th Avenue. But that would be wrong. The Bowmans had the food of their time, the living space and living conditions of their time, the jobs of their time, the schools and parks of their time. They wanted for nothing, or at least nothing that they knew about. They never owned their own place, though some of the French, Italian, and Greek families did—and Scotty always wondered why. But Scots, it seems, were either owners forever or tenants forever. That's how it had been in the old country, after all. And that, primarily, hadn't been about money, it was about class and who you were.

Besides, Scots being Scots, the rent was reasonable—$32 a month—and they were much better off than so many others. After all, through the perilous years of the Depression and the war, Jack kept his job. Many didn't. He also got to stay home. He had been too old to go to war, so Jean and the kids didn't have to go through what many other wives and children went through, even those whose husbands and fathers returned.

Scotty was almost 7 when the Blitz, the bombing of London, began. He was 10 on D-Day; 11 when the war ended. None of the fathers or brothers of his friends died. And so instead of tragedy, he remembers the parades, the photos of the soldiers—local kids—in the newspapers. He remembers Verdun's own George "Buzz" Beurling, who shot down 27 enemy planes over Malta in just 14 days, and the night Scotty and his family and the whole community filled Verdun Auditorium to welcome Beurling home. He remembers all the drives to help "the boys." Verdun's most popular war charity was the "Mayor's Cigarette Fund"—one dollar (postage included) sent a carton of 300 cigarettes to a Verdunite overseas—and a huge number of local organizations, French- and English-speaking alike, organized their own fundraisers in support. Church groups, the air cadets, the lawn bowling club, the Operatic Society, choral and dramatic societies, the Verdun United Church ladies basketball team—even kids with their candy or lemonade stands contributed. In total, 3.7 million cigarettes were sent to the troops, and they were greatly appreciated. As one soldier wrote back in thanks:

When the road is hot and weary
and it's 10 minutes for a smoke
with cigarettes at a premium
and a sapper that is broke
13 more days to pay day
and the post man brings a gift
thanks a million friends
for giving a guy a lift.

For the Bowmans in the 1930s and 1940s, it could have been so much worse. They were lucky to experience only the little challenges and indignities that living in a new country brought. Some things Jack and Jean still didn't understand, even after a decade and more in Canada. (Some things, given their thick, dreichy Scottish accents, others didn't understand about them.) Jean could never stop thinking in shillings and farthings; and so, to avoid feeling embarrassed, she would always pay with bills and get change, rather than fumble around with coins she couldn't comprehend. Jean always had a lot of change.

And then there was Jack, the time that Jean bought that table. She got an employee discount at Eaton's, they needed a table, and one day while on a break at work, she found one. Eaton's would deliver it that day—a Saturday, so Jack was home—and it would be COD. But when the delivery man stood at their door with Jack and the table, waiting to be paid, Jack seemed not to understand. The delivery man pointed to the big box—*COD*, it said, in very big letters on the side. Jack looked at the letters, looked at the box, and finally understood. "What are you trying to pull?" he asked the man angrily. "Do you think I'm some old-country hick because of my mouthful-of-marbles accent? You don't ship cod in a box that size!" That evening, Jean arrived home, looking for her table. Jack had refused the parcel.

But these were little things. The big things, the ones that truly mattered that might have gone wrong, never did—not really. Jack got splashed with molten lead at work and suffered from lead poisoning and burns on his arms and forehead. He was off work for a few months. But he got better. Just as Freda and her club foot got better. Jack and Jean were fine. The kids were fine—they were healthy, and they did either all right or well at school. No disastrous things happened, no awful things that change a life. It's true, no big things went fantastically right either, but they hadn't imagined anything like that for themselves anyway. Jack was never going to run the company and make a million dollars. Freda was smart but she was no certifiable genius; maybe someday she would become what smart women of the time hoped to be—a teacher. Which, of course, she did. And Scotty? He was good at math, he had a good memory, but as he said to Mrs. Ironside, he was too busy playing all his games for him, or her, or anyone to see anything more in him.

As a hockey player, Scotty was good, but he wasn't a prodigy. He was no Buddy O'Connor, who grew up nearby and who later moved onto Foch Street, where Scotty would buy his first house. O'Connor would go on to win two Cups with the Canadiens, the Hart Trophy as the league's most valuable player, and in 1948 be named Canada's athlete of the year. And Scotty was no Dollard St. Laurent, who lived on Osborne Street, only a few blocks away, and would later win Cups with Montreal and Chicago. And he was certainly no Donnie Marshall, who lived even closer in a fourplex at 710 Desmarchais Street, the only street in Verdun that had a median strip—which meant 10 more metres of open space. Marshall was a great athlete; he could do anything. He was the best hockey player in Verdun *and* he played for the Verdun all-star baseball team that travelled all the way to Brooklyn's Ebbets Field, where he batted against Sandy Koufax.

Kids like Donnie Marshall had a future playing hockey. Scotty had a present. And at that time, no kid—Scotty included—ever imagined a future in hockey as a coach. Coaches were former players, so if you didn't make it as a player then you didn't make it as a coach. And besides, as a kid, who ever dreams of being a coach?

There seemed nothing extraordinary about Scotty in his early years. There seemed no extraordinary life ahead of him. But he wasn't disappointed by that. Nor were Jack and Jean. They were living a good life, on the way to a good life.

Unbeknownst to Scotty and his family, however, hockey was getting inside him and he was getting inside it. And it was on the radio where hockey first fully came to life for him. In the 1930s and 1940s, radio was a very big deal. It was also a very democratic experience. Almost everybody could afford a radio, and so almost everybody was able to listen to the same big bands, the same drama and comedy shows, the same news from the war. In winter, they could listen to the same hockey games; in summer, the same baseball games. In the evenings, radio signals would make their way to Montreal from distant places—from New York and (most importantly for Scotty) from Boston.

One night, Scotty heard the voice of Frank Ryan for the first time, on Boston's WHDH—850 on the dial. It was the 1939–40 season, and he had just turned six. The Bruins had won the Stanley Cup the year before; they would go on to finish first that season but get knocked out in the playoffs, then would win again the following year. On the Bruins were first-team all-stars Milt Schmidt and Dit Clapper, and second-team all-stars Frank Brimsek, Bobby Bauer, and Woody Dumart—all of them later elected to the Hall of Fame, as would be three of their teammates: Eddie Shore, Roy Conacher, and Bill Cowley.

Ryan called the home games live from Boston Garden, and recreated road games from accounts he was sent via telegraph; his brother-in-law offering updates between periods in French to New England's French-Canadian audience. The games began at 8:30 p.m. Scotty would listen until 9, the end of the first period. His father listened to the rest, and every morning after a Bruins game, before he left for work, Jack put a piece of paper on the kitchen table for Scotty with the score of the game and the goal scorers' names written on it. Scotty was a Bruins fan, and his favourite player was Bill Cowley, number 10. Even today, when he says Cowley's name, he always says, "Bill Cowley, number 10."

Why the Bruins? Maybe it was the distance of Boston through the crackle of static that fed his imagination. Maybe it was because the Bruins, the first team he listened to, were the Stanley Cup champions. Maybe it was to be different from the other kids. Those Bruins teams of 1938 to 1941 were not much different from the Bruins teams he faced from 1969 to 1972, when he was coaching St. Louis and then the Canadiens. Both teams had the best players in the league. Both teams dominated the NHL for three seasons and were upset by underdogs in the middle year of their run. Both, too, might have gone on to win more Cups and have been considered among the greatest teams of all time. But neither did, and neither is—and each for different reasons. For the Bruins of the early 1970s, the WHA was created in 1972, Bruins ownership decided not to spend the money it would take to keep some of its most important players, and the Canadiens, then the Flyers, then the Canadiens again, also got better. For the earlier Bruins team, their fall happened for a reason Scotty witnessed himself through his radio.

It was February 10, 1942, and with 12 games remaining in the then 48-game regular season, the league-leading Bruins were playing at home against the Canadiens. Scotty was in his bed in the dining room he shared with Jack, taking it all in through Frank Ryan's voice. At the end of the first period, he went to sleep; his father told him the rest the next day.

When the game ended, the Bruins having won, 8–1, the crowd stood and cheered, and the players from *both* teams put Milt Schmidt, Bobby Bauer, and Woody Dumart on their shoulders and carried them off the ice. This was their last NHL game for some time—they were leaving the next day for the war. Scotty was eight years old.

Less than two months earlier, using her employee discount, his mother had bought him a Bruins sweater for Christmas (made of wool and extending up from the shoulders like a turtleneck—at the time these very much were sweaters, not jerseys), and on it she'd sewn the numbers *1* and *0* for Bill Cowley. But this was English-speaking Verdun, not French-speaking Sainte-Justine—the birthplace of Roch Carrier, author and main character of the children's classic *The Hockey Sweater*—so while both Carrier's and Scotty's mothers got their (non-Canadiens) sweaters from Eaton's, when Scotty showed up at Willibrord Park in the black, yellow, and white of the Bruins, the reaction he got was nothing like what Carrier's character faced when he arrived in the blue and white of the Leafs. At Willibrord Park, there were Leafs sweaters too, and at least one Rangers sweater—not just those of the *bleu, blanc, et rouge* of the Canadiens.

Willibrord Park had two outdoor rinks, both natural ice. The ice lasted from never-early-enough, the first week of December, to never-late-enough, the end of February. Winters were colder then, or so it seems now—unaffected by climate change, perhaps overaffected by memory. The kids lost precious days of hockey when the snow fell faster than they could clear it off and when hoping that the ice would still be OK wasn't enough. If the snow got too high, city workers ploughed the streets first, then came to the rink, taking down the end boards and driving their tractor onto the ice. But the kids lost very few days from sudden Montreal thaws. Because there weren't any.

Scotty skated the back alleys to get to the park and he played pick-up with whoever was there—usually the same kids. And, always, he dreamed of "making the team." Organized hockey in Montreal—real teams, teams with their own sweaters—began at bantam, which was under the age of twelve at the time. There was no peewee, or atom, or squirt. Nine-year-olds competed for spots with eleven-year-olds. Anybody younger didn't have a chance. Eleven-year-olds were bigger and stronger, and had five or six years of pickup behind them. Nine- and ten-year-olds had to be extremely good, or extremely fortunate. Maybe somebody moved away, somebody got sick, or somebody didn't grow and they did. If you did make the team, you played two (or three) years of bantam, two years of midget, and two years of juvenile if you weren't good enough to play junior.

The kids who didn't make the hockey team played what was called "park," organized by the YMCA. The Y was important in Verdun. That's where Scotty played basketball and learned how to swim. At his home in Buffalo, with his miniature Stanley Cups and Boys Brigade belt, he still has his YMCA badges and crests—an achievement is an achievement.

If you did make the team, you played Thursdays after dinner. The league was organized by the Verdun Hockey Board; in the less-than-three-month season, you played about nine games in all. If you were French, you played in a different park, on teams organized by the Association sportive de Verdun, the Verdun Sportifs. In the city playoffs, when the English champs went against the French champs, they played on another rink—on neutral ice.

But whether you were French or English, and whether you made "the team" or not, you also played pickup. For Scotty, that meant any time he had on weekdays after he delivered his papers and before his father arrived home for dinner, and sometimes after they ate. On Saturdays he would play from eight or nine in the morning and on Sundays from after church—always until dinner time. If you played on a team you could also get a "permit," and that was important. You had to get it by Wednesday from the man who ran the changing/warming shack at Willibrord Park, and a permit meant guaranteed ice at a guaranteed time on a Saturday or Sunday so you could play with the guys you wanted to play with, and not with the ones you didn't. Most often it would be your teammates, which gave your team a little extra time for practice (at the time, practices weren't much more than scrimmages anyway). If your park team won your division, you would play into March against Montreal's other division winners—and the real prize was getting to play on indoor rinks. The games were sudden death, and every game you won meant one more time on the ice.

43

Lots of things were different year to year for Scotty when he was young, but nothing much changed. As a kid, you moved from grade to grade, but the school was the same, and so were the kids, and your teammates, and the things you did, and your flat, and your church. There was no real chronology to his years. There was place. Whether something happened this year or that, it didn't matter. Childhood was lived in a sweep of years. Life was continuity, not change.

Scotty was an average player in his first year of bantam; he was better in his second year. Then as he faced the jump to midget, again having to compete against lots of good second-year players, he got a break. The league changed the age deadline, and Scotty got another year of bantam. It's this season that he really began to develop, and the following year, when he moved up to midget, he was ready. And they had a great team—Donnie Marshall, who was now a second-year midget, and Bucky Hollingworth, who like Scotty was a first-year, both went on to have NHL careers.

The team was called Norman's Spartons (not *Spartans*)—Norman Bracegirdle, who owned a local appliance store, was the sponsor. They had one goalie, three defencemen who played regularly (and a fourth, Norman's son, who never played), two forward lines, and a spare. Twelve players in all. The team made it to the provincial finals and a sudden-death game at Verdun Auditorium against the Quebec Generals, who were led by Camille Henry—later an outstanding scorer with the New York Rangers who, at the end of his career, played for Scotty in St. Louis. The Spartons won—they were the champions of Quebec. To this day, when Scotty is asked about all the championships he won in his 70-plus-year career, he talks about Norman's Spartons and the Quebec midget championship just as often and just as excitedly as his nine Stanley Cups.

For Scotty, his second season in midget would be a turning point, but not before he got himself into a bit of an awkward situation. It all started when Scotty's mother, Jean, was shopping at Norman's Appliances, which was just down the street and around the corner, on Verdun Avenue near 4th. She wasn't in the store very often—she didn't buy much—but in April, after the team had won the championship, she went in to purchase a toaster. Norman gave it to her free, and he also gave her a player's card, a contract, to take home for Scotty to sign. After all, as a second-year midget, he would be an important player on a defending provincial championship team. Scotty signed the card.

But the Spartons' victory had gotten them noticed, and about a month later, Ken Brown appeared. Sam Pollock—later the general manager of nine Stanley Cup–winning Canadiens teams and Scotty's great mentor—had been given the task of putting together a farm system in Montreal. He had hired Brown, a local Verdunite, to recruit players for a new team they were forming—the Verdun Canadiens. Brown promised Scotty some new hockey gloves and pants if he signed with the team, as well as a standing-room pass to the Forum to watch the Canadiens play any time he wanted. Scotty agreed. But now he had signed two cards.

One evening that July, Brown picked up Scotty and they walked two blocks to the house of Buck Tahamont, the midget league's registrar. Tahamont had a decision to make. He might rule that Scotty had to play for Norman's Spartons, having signed their card first. Or he might suspend him and not allow him to play at all. Instead, he asked him which team he wanted to play for. Scotty told him, "I want to play for the Verdun Canadiens."

Half of the problem was solved. The other half was harder. Scotty's mother was horrified—how was she going to face that nice Mr. Bracegirdle who had given her that toaster? From then on, she avoided going into his store. Gradually, he got over it. It took Jean much longer.

But for Scotty, this was a great and exciting moment. He would now be playing for a team sponsored by the Montreal Canadiens—he would be the *property* of the Montreal Canadiens. *The Montreal Canadiens of the NHL.* Hockey, which had taken up so much of his time and attention, now had a real-life purpose. The Canadiens were now *his* team, not the

Bruins. And now he could get on that 58 bus and go up the Atwater hill to the Forum and watch any game he wanted. Most of the games were on Saturday nights. His own team, the Verdun Canadiens, didn't play that night, he had no homework to do, no school the next day, and church didn't start until 11 a.m.

At the same time, he was playing for Verdun High School, first for the junior team, then the senior. Their games were after school at 4 p.m.— he had given up his paper route by this time. He would bring his equipment in his kit bag to school, and the school would bus them to the rink and back again. They played in indoor arenas with artificial ice—at the Verdun Auditorium, Lachine Arena, and sometimes at the Forum. Their big rival was West Hill High School in Notre-Dame-de-Grâce. NDG was up the hill, richer, had nicer parks, and Verdun could never beat West Hill. But every team Scotty played on meant more time on the ice. It might be only 15 or 20 games in all, high-school team and non-school-team, but this was all that anyone could play—all that even Doug Harvey, Dickie Moore, and Bernie Geoffrion could play. And if your team kept winning you played into March, indoors, on the only ice that remained.

Sports, at the time, were determined by the seasons. You couldn't play baseball in winter, or hockey in summer. So when hockey "season" was over, Scotty played other sports. He had always been a fast runner. He had good range as a shortstop and centre fielder in softball, able to track down ground balls and fly balls, and steal bases. He had been a quarterback in junior football for the Verdun Shamcats. With his strategic mind, he loved to make up trick plays; with his quickness, he ran more often than he passed. In soccer, his speed and ability to "see the game"— its patterns and possibilities—the same skills his father had brought to Forfar Athletic's Loons in Scotland, made him an ideal centre-half.

Scotty played all these sports—to the impatience of Mrs. Ironside— until the demands of junior hockey forced on him a decision, and he chose hockey. By this time he had moved up to the Verdun Canadiens

Junior Bs. A left winger, he had good hands, he didn't need much time or space, and he was a scorer. He wasn't so good defensively, but defence he could learn, he always thought. Then, at 16, he was called up to the big team—to the Montreal Canadiens Junior A team, the best junior team in the whole country. He played only a few games his first year, but by the next season he was a regular.

At Verdun High, Scotty was doing fine in his classes, and would soon be graduating—but there was now the question of what he would do next. A friend of his on the school team, Bobby Fox—who lived on Osborne Street, not far from where Dollard St. Laurent grew up—was being recruited by Rensselaer Polytechnic Institute (RPI), a school in Troy, New York, known primarily for its engineering. RPI's coach had come to Montreal and met with Bobby and his family, and offered him a scholarship. While he was there he talked to Scotty too. He could offer him only a partial scholarship at that time, he said, but he was sure that once Scotty was in school he could find a way to cover the rest. Scotty hadn't thought a lot about what he would do after high school—maybe go to business college for a year or two. He had worked one summer with his father and liked the money he earned, but hated the job. That was something he knew he *didn't* want to do. Another summer, he had delivered milk in Snowdon and NDG. He'd had to be at work early to get his horse ready, to put on its harness and attach it to the wagon. He'd liked that job because he was done with his route by 11 a.m., and he liked the freedom of having the rest of the day to himself. But that was summer stuff. So when RPI's coach talked to him, at first he was interested, but then he wasn't. He didn't think of himself as a student, and certainly not as an engineer. That RPI coach was Ned Harkness, who four years later won the NCAA hockey championship—with Bobby Fox in goal. Fox would go on to graduate from RPI, earn his master's and PhD, and spend 39 years as a professor of mechanical engineering at Purdue University. Ned Harkness would leave RPI in the early 1960s and coach Cornell to an NCAA championship in 1967. I was his goalie.

Verdun was beginning to change. During the Second World War, it had lived up to its reputation as a patriotic city. Its rate of enlistment had remained higher than almost everywhere else in the country, and it was home to Canada's most famous wartime hero, Buzz Beurling. And now the local boys were back home—among them Jim Kydd, whose father, also named Jim Kydd, had come to Verdun from Forfar a few years before Jack, and had put him up before Jean arrived and they had found a place of their own. Canada was booming—and so too was Verdun. Most people, including the veterans, had jobs, and the possibilities of peace were beginning to be imagined and realized.

For the Bowmans in 1950, life was fine. Jack was now a shop foreman at Federated Metals; Freda was teaching; young Jack was playing hockey and football, and was in his early high school years. Jean was busy with Martin, who, born in 1946, was about to enter school.

Scotty's life, however, was about to change dramatically.

It happened in March 1952. It was the fourth game of a five-out-of-nine playoff series against the Trois-Rivières Reds at the Forum. The Junior Canadiens were leading the series three games to nothing, and winning this fourth game decisively. There were 30 seconds left. Scotty, playing on the third line, took a pass and broke into open ice towards the Trois-Rivières net. Chasing him down was Jean-Guy Talbot, the Reds' best player. Talbot had received four penalties already in the game, and knew that his final playoff series in his final season in junior hockey was drawing to a close. He was frustrated. He raced back to catch Scotty, and when Scotty fell off balance into the Trois-Rivières goalie and was lying on the ice, Talbot hit him over the head with his stick. Scotty suffered a fractured skull.

All that summer, he had bad headaches and blurred vision. He had always loved to ride his bike, but now he couldn't. He had loved to play softball, but now he couldn't play. "The odd time when I'd be talking or listening, things would start to race, and it was kind of scary," he remembers. His parents were worried but "they didn't say very much." His father had been scalded by molten lead, and he had seen far worse workplace accidents. "They were hard-working people. They didn't hover over you." When September arrived, Scotty began to feel better, but the Canadiens didn't want him to play anymore. They had other, better prospects; they knew Scotty would never make it, and the risk of him continuing to play was too great. So, instead, he went to the Montreal Junior Royals. But he didn't play the same way as he had before, and he knew it. "I had a decent year because I had experience," he recalls, "but I was no longer a prospect." For Scotty, hockey as a career was over.

As for Talbot, he was given a year's suspension for the incident. In the summer, Talbot got married and wrote Scotty a letter to apologize to him. His wife, Pierrette, wrote to him too. It was "a nice letter," as Scotty recalls. In the fall, the Quebec Amateur Hockey Association held a hearing concerning Talbot and his suspension, which Scotty attended. Scotty was playing again by this time, and the Montreal Canadiens, his team, also owned Talbot's rights, and after all, Talbot was a prospect. Talbot was reinstated in November.

Sixteen years later, Talbot would be nearing the end of his distinguished NHL career. He had won seven Stanley Cups with the Canadiens, had been a first-team all-star, and would end up playing more than 1,000 NHL games by the time he retired. St. Louis needed somebody who could skate well enough and was versatile enough to play a little forward and a little defence. So Scotty brought Talbot to the Blues. At the time, NHL teams could only dress three forward lines and two sets of defencemen, with one spare forward and one spare on defence. If the Blues were behind at the end of the second period, the spares stayed on the bench. If they were ahead, Scotty put together a fourth "shutdown" line—with a defensive centre, Talbot on one side, and the similarly versatile Jimmy Roberts on the other. "We won a lot of games by one goal, by protecting the lead," Scotty recalls. "No question that Talbot was going to help our team." What had happened 16 years earlier didn't matter. Talbot is now 87; Scotty is 86. Each of the last few years, on his birthday, Talbot calls him. They have never talked about the moment in Montreal that ended Scotty's career.

For Scotty, one door slammed shut on that night in March 1952. But another one—as of yet, unimaginable—was about to open.

CHAPTER FOUR
Detroit Red Wings 1951–52

A few weeks after Scotty suffered his fractured skull at the Forum, the Detroit Red Wings played for the seventh and final time of the regular season in Montreal, and tied the Canadiens, 3–3. It was the only home game against the Wings that he missed. After the game, the players on both teams got into their taxis, rushed to Westmount Station, and boarded an overnight train to Detroit, where in the final regular-season game for both sides, the Red Wings demolished the Canadiens, 7–2. It was Montreal's worst loss of the season. It was Detroit's 44th win and 100th point—10 wins and 22 points more than the second-place Canadiens. The Wings would prove even more dominant in the playoffs.

The Detroit Red Wings of 1951–52 are, chronologically, the first of Scotty's eight picks. "They were a powerhouse team," he says.

Detroit had been building up steam for four years. The seasons of makeshift rosters during the war for all of the NHL teams were now past. Players in, players out. Teams could now plan and build. By 1947, the 53-year-old Jack Adams had been coaching Detroit (first named the Cougars, then Falcons, then Red Wings) for 20 years. For two straight seasons, 1945–46 and 1946–47, the Wings had finished in fourth place in the six-team league and been eliminated in the first round of the play-offs. It was time for him to move aside.

Adams became the team's general manager and hired the 36-year-old Tommy Ivan as his coach. After his playing career ended with an injury, Ivan had bumped around as a coach in the senior and minor pro leagues, with years in the military in between—his last two seasons had been with Detroit farm teams in Indianapolis and then Omaha with a 17-year-old Gordie Howe. In his first season as the Wings' coach, 1947–48, Ivan had Sid Abel, 29, as his captain. He had several mid-career, mid-level players, but he also had Ted Lindsay, 22, goalie Harry Lumley, 21, Red Kelly, 20, and Howe, now 19—all of whom, like him, were ready for a lot more. Detroit finished second that season, earning 17 more points than the year before, and went to the Stanley Cup final, losing to the Leafs in four straight games. It was the last time Ivan would finish as low as second in Detroit—the Red Wings won the NHL's regular-season title in his next six years, before he left to become Chicago's general manager in 1954.

The following season, 1948–49—after finishing in first place, nine points ahead of Boston—Detroit again went to the Cup final, and again lost in four straight to Toronto, who had finished fourth, 18 points behind the Wings, with a sub-.500 record. This was the Leafs' third Cup win in a row; their fourth in five seasons. After winning again in 1951, it would be five championships for them in seven years. In sweeping the Wings in 1948 and 1949, the Leafs outscored Detroit 18–7 and 12–5.

The Wings wouldn't make their breakthrough until the following year, 1949–50, winning the regular season by 11 points over the Canadiens and finally overcoming Toronto four games to three in the semifinals— after having lost the opening game to the Leafs in Detroit, 5–0, and winning the seventh game, 1–0, in overtime. Detroit then defeated the Rangers in the final.

Time had been the answer. The Leafs were getting old; the Wings were getting better. Lindsay, Abel, and Howe finished 1–2–3 in league scoring. Lindsay, Kelly, and Howe were still all under 25, and—after having played a few games that season—goalie Terry Sawchuk, 20, was on the horizon.

The next year, 1950–51, Detroit would score 7 more goals than they had the season before, allow 25 fewer against, record 13 more points, and be the first team in NHL history to total more than 100 points in a season. Sawchuk won the Calder Trophy as the league's rookie of the year. Howe led the league in scoring by 20 points over Maurice Richard; Abel and Lindsay were not far behind; and Kelly, in ninth place, became the third defenceman in NHL history to finish in the top 10. But, in a stunning upset, the Wings lost to Montreal in six games in the first round of the playoffs, after finishing 36 points ahead of them during the regular season.

The Wings were embarrassed. But it was the shock they needed to go from being a powerful team to a great one.

In 1951–52, it was as if they were on a mission. They lost only 4 of their first 32 games, and only 4 of their last 25. They finished the regular season 22 points ahead of the second-place Canadiens. They scored 20 more goals than anyone else, and allowed 24 fewer than Toronto, who was second—and the Leafs were a defensive team. The Wings scored 82 goals more than they allowed, 51 better than Montreal, who had the league's second-best goal differential at 31. Howe won the scoring title by 17 points over Lindsay. He scored 47 goals; Bill Mosienko of Chicago was second with 31. Kelly led all defencemen in the league with 47 points. Sawchuk had 12 shutouts—5 more than "Sugar" Jim Henry of the Bruins who was second. As a team, as individual players, this was dominance.

In the playoffs, the Wings were even more overwhelming. They swept the Leafs, their nemesis, in four straight in the semifinals, outscoring them, 13–3. Then they swept the Canadiens four straight in the final, outscoring them, 11–2. Eight straight wins. Zero defeats. For Sawchuk, four shutouts in eight games, a goals against average of 0.62. The Wings of 1951–52 are still the only team in NHL history to go through the Stanley Cup playoffs without losing a single game.

They were just too good.

And Scotty saw it happen. He was 14 when Ivan took over in 1947, playing on his Canadiens-sponsored midget team with his precious standing-room pass. He saw Gordie Howe, big and gangly like a kid, who even at 19 seemed to know where to go and what to do. He saw Ted Lindsay at 22, a tiny aggravating force who zipped anywhere and everywhere he wanted as if he owned the ice, his stick high and in front of him, more a weapon than a tool, always arriving before he did. Scotty saw Red Kelly at 20, beginning to do what no defenceman had ever done, what according to hockey wisdom none should ever do: when Kelly moved up the ice with the puck he kept going and stayed there; he made plays, and set up and scored goals. Scotty watched them *become* Gordie Howe, and Ted Lindsay, and Red Kelly, Saturday-night game after Saturday-night game, *live* at the Forum. And, wonderfully for him, as he watched and learned and wondered, he remembered. Years later, when he was no longer just a kid from Verdun standing miles from the ice at the top of the blues—when he became Scotty Bowman, coach of the Detroit Red Wings—Howe, Lindsay, and Kelly became his great friends and *they* wanted to talk to *him*, and he had so much to say, and they had so much to say to each other.

It is easy to cite statistics, and even easier to dismiss them. It's especially easy if you are Scotty Bowman because *he was there*. He actually saw all those teams and all those players. His memories of them are stuck in his mind's eye like bugs in amber, and they will be there forever. So why do statistics even matter? Twenty-eight goals here, 45 there—times change. Once there was no forward pass and nobody could score. Then the Rocket scored 50; Howe won the scoring title in 1950–51 with 86 points; 35 years later, Wayne Gretzky won it with 215. Does that make Gretzky two and a half times better than Howe? No. Even though he saw all this with his own eyes, Scotty knows that it *does* matter that the second-highest scorer in 1951 didn't finish just a few points back of Howe, but *way* back, and that the second-highest scorer to Gretzky finished *way, way* back. Those numbers *do* say something, just as they do when a team records way more points and leaves every other team drowning in its wake. They say something beyond what even Scotty's own opinion says. Opinions, Scotty knows, are words; and words turn into stories; and in time, the best players and the best teams become those who have the best, most *legendary* stories told about them. Scotty, who saw all this live, and still sees games live, also sees the numbers on his iPad. Numbers are eloquent. Trust performance.

"They had such a strong lineup," Scotty says of that Detroit team, which is still entirely vivid in his head. "They were so deep. You could only dress 16 players at the time: a goalie, three lines, and a spare who hardly ever played—maybe if there was an injury, or to kill a penalty—and two sets of defence and a spare. You had a scoring line, a defensive line, and one that could do a little of both. And if you had a second line that could score more than a little, you made it so tough on your opponent. As a coach," he continues, "if you were Tommy Ivan, you played your scorers against their defensive line, and your defensive line against their scorers. Everybody matched lines, nobody really fought that—the game was slower, there wasn't as much changing on the fly. It was kind of like, 'You can check our guys, and we'll check yours.'

"The teams didn't forecheck in the 1950s, or not much," he says. "The game wasn't wide open. Montreal did play more wide open, until they got against Detroit. But it was still wing on wing. If you're a left winger, your job is to be with your wing [the other team's right winger]. You scored from rush chances, but also from rushing the puck yourself—not passes, or not many of them. The '50s wasn't a 'make plays' time."

Forechecking meant throwing the puck forward into the other team's corner and chasing after it, to win it back closer to the net. It was giving up possession to get it back. But forechecking really only came later, in the late 1960s and 1970s, after the NHL expanded from six teams to twelve—where with half the league, overnight, being made up of minor leaguers, the sizable gap between the skilled players and the rest required a more simplified game. Today, the game is about possession again, but this time it's possession by passing the puck from teammate to teammate, not from rushing it yourself. "In the '50s, it was all man-to-man [defensive] coverage," Scotty says. "Now it's zone. Now the forwards have to be able to skate backwards, they have to have full vision of the puck, to see where everybody is. Then, you just watched your winger, you skated forwards with him, and didn't have to learn anything else."

But whether then or now, you still had to get to the net. "It's why Howe was so good at that time. With man-to-man coverage—first against his winger, then against the defenceman—he was so strong. He was really a big, big guy. He'd challenge them, and he was faster than those guys when he needed to be. He could get an edge. Then he was too much for them. He'd just power his way by." Scotty pauses. "I can see it like it was yesterday," he says. It is something he says often. It's all still there in front of him, almost 70 years later. He can still see Howe, getting the puck from Abel or from rookie Alex Delvecchio, his centres in that 1951–52 season—and coming in off the wing. "He had a terrific shot. Like [Mike] Bossy. Like [Guy] Lafleur. Like [Reggie] Leach. They had those perfect shots in the corner. Now we don't see many angled shots going in. If they do go in, we say, 'Oh [the goalie] should've had it.'" Of course, goalie equipment was smaller then. "It was the same with the Rocket. He was so strong. He'd challenge you. With the Rocket, it was his backhand."

Howe, Lindsay, and Abel were called the "Production Line." But in many ways they were a tandem-plus-one, not a trio. It was Howe and Lindsay together—and Abel (sometimes Delvecchio) helping out as needed. "[Howe and Lindsay] fit perfectly with each other," Scotty says. "They understood each other. They used to have these plays, especially at the [Detroit] Olympia."

The ice surface of the Wings' home rink was more egg-shaped than rectangular, with its sideboards angled gradually towards the net. "One of them would shoot the puck in and it would rebound off the boards in front of the net, and the other would race in after it. They scored a lot of goals that way." But that was only a minor part of what made Howe and Lindsay special together. "They were really tough guys. They were really aggressive. Ultra competitive. And they weren't just guys who put up points; they were so good both ways. They were *feared* by other teams. If they'd had their way, they'd play against anybody. But they didn't have to because [the Wings] developed that Skov line."

This was Detroit's checking line. Glen Skov was only 21 in 1951–52, and it was his first full season. He was tall and rangy, he looked big, and he skated well enough. He was also smart and responsible enough to play against the other teams' best offensive centres—Elmer Lach of the Canadiens, Milt Schmidt of the Bruins, Tod Sloan of the Leafs, Don "Bones" Raleigh of the Rangers, George Gee of the Black Hawks. He had beside him two experienced wingers: Marty Pavelich, 24, already in his fifth season, and Tony Leswick, 28, now in his seventh. "I remember this line," Scotty says. "Pavelich was like the Bob Gainey of his era, and he still scored 17 goals that season. That was a lot then." On Scotty's Cup-winning Canadiens teams of the late 1970s, Gainey was unrivalled as the league's best defensive forward. "And Leswick was a tough guy. A lot like Lindsay—not as good as Lindsay, but the same character. A little guy too. He had his stick up all the time. He was hard to play against."

Then there was the Wings' second line: Metro Prystai, Delvecchio, and Vic Stasiuk. Delvecchio was a talent; Stasiuk a big, awkward skater who several years later became a scorer on Boston's "Uke Line," with Johnny Bucyk and Bronco Horvath. But Prystai is the one that Scotty remembers best, and the one he loves to talk about today. Scotty likes to notice players who make a team better, who players or fans or other coaches might not see. Players who are often now forgotten. In big games, oftentimes the stars balance out each other, and it's the invisible players that make the difference.

In the Wings' Cup-clinching, eighth straight victory in 1952, Prystai had two goals and one assist in a 3–0 game. Two years earlier, he had scored 29 goals and finished ninth in the league in scoring on a last-place

Chicago team. He was then moved to Detroit as part of a nine-player trade—this coming *after* the Wings had won the Cup in 1950. The key player in the trade for Chicago was goalie Harry Lumley—the Wings wanted to open up a path for Sawchuk—and the keys for Detroit were Prystai and defenceman Bob Goldham. "It was a stupid trade," Scotty says now. "Whenever Chicago got a good player, they traded him to Detroit." The Norris family owned both teams. "Chicago was like Detroit's farm team. [Prystai] was only 22 and a really good second centre."

Scotty talks often about the importance of centres on teams of that time. In a rigid-style game, where right wingers played down the right side and left wingers down the left, only centres played all over the ice. They were a team's best skaters because they had to be. Wingers like Howe, Richard, or Lindsay might affect the game because of sheer talent. Only centres influenced the game—engaging all of their teammates and opponents—by virtue of the position they played. They had to be everywhere. And the Wings had the centres they needed: Abel/ Delvecchio, Skov, and Prystai. One offensive, one defensive, and one who could do both.

On defence, Kelly played with Goldham; Marcel Pronovost with Leo Reise; Benny Woit was the spare. Pronovost, 21, was in only his second season. He was a good skater, tough, and with Kelly as his model, he was becoming a more assertive offensive player. Reise was "big and strong," Scotty recalls, "a tough, tough defenceman, a really good player," who had twice been voted onto the NHL's second all-star team. Kelly, always looking to move up the ice from his defensive position, represented for his opponents a troublesome fourth forward when they were accustomed to defending against three. "Kelly scored 16 goals that year [1951–52]. That was unheard of for a defenceman." And Goldham was his perfect partner.

When I was growing up, Goldham mystified all of us as much as Howe and Richard. A puck hurt. A puck shot by an NHL player that seemed to go a thousand miles an hour had to hurt beyond belief. And

here was Goldham—unlike every other defenceman in the league—
who, when his opponent wound up to shoot, would drop to his knees,
purposely, and block the shot with his chest, without even a goalie's
belly pad to protect him. Yet, every time, Goldham seemed just to get
up and get on with the game. As kids we speculated and we argued:
How? *Why?* I can't remember whether it was Goldham himself in an
interview or someone else who explained to us how he did it, but it
seems that in going down onto his knees, the lower part of his shoulder
pads dropped slightly, the upper part of his pants rose slightly, and
together they overlapped slightly and (mostly) covered his chest. We
used to practise being Bob Goldham with tennis balls in street hockey
games, but it never worked. The ball still hurt. "Bob Goldham was like
another goalie," Scotty says. "I talked with Lynn Patrick about him."
This was after Patrick, the Blues' first general manager, hired Scotty
to be his assistant, then to be his coach. "He knew all these players
because he had coached against them with the Rangers, then with
Boston, and he said Goldham . . . for five or six years, if they had a vote
for the best defensive defenceman, he'd win."

Behind Kelly and Goldham, Pronovost and Reise, was Terry
Sawchuk. At 22 years old, it was his second full year in the league. He
was big for a goalie in those days—almost six feet tall and 200 pounds,
occasionally more—but playing in a deep crouch, coiled, he was
remarkably agile. He would play in the NHL for 20 years and for most
of those years he was good to very good, but for his first five seasons in
Detroit he was great. A few other goalies might lay equal claim to the
recognition of being the best ever, but it's almost certain that nobody has
ever had five years better than these. During that time, the Wings won
the regular-season title five times and the Stanley Cup three times.
Sawchuk's goals against averages: 1.97, 1.90, 1.89, 1.93, and 1.96. "I talked to
Ted Lindsay about him," Scotty says. "Ted is a smart guy. He said,
'There's never been a goalie in his prime like Sawchuk. He had all the
mechanics. He had his glove. He just was so focused.'"

Goalies have different personalities than forwards or defencemen—usually quieter, more serious, and more introverted. They also have a different relationship with their teammates than forwards and defencemen do. Some great goalies are loved by their teammates. Other great goalies inspire fear in them. The players know that they cannot, must not, let them down. Or else. On a team of fierce personalities—Lindsay, Howe, Leswick, Kelly, and many more—Sawchuk may have been the most feared among them. He scared them. In the 1952 playoffs, along with his goals against average of 0.62 and his four shutouts in eight games, he didn't let in a single goal in the four games in Detroit. Sometimes *only* numbers tell the story.

But above and beyond Sawchuk, Lindsay, Kelly, and Tommy Ivan, their three strategically balanced lines and two pairs of defence, their power play with Kelly as practically a fourth forward and Pronovost almost a fifth, was Gordie Howe. Even at 23, with more than 25 years of his career ahead of him, he was an overwhelming presence. "Howe was the dominant player," Scotty says. "There's no ifs, ands or buts. There's just no argument over who was the best player in the league at that time. It was Howe, for sure. And that season he really took off. He won the scoring title; he and Lindsay went 1–2, but Howe beat him by 17 points. He scored more than *20 per cent* of the Wings' goals."

In every NHL season before, the league's top scorer would lead the second-place finisher by three points, or five—almost never more than that. With Howe, it had been 20 points in 1950–51, this season was 17, the next would be 24, and the one after that 14. "If you were going to make a model for a player, he was it. He was strong. Very strong. Just a natural. He knew how to play. He had a terrific shot. He didn't need many chances to score. He was a good two-way player, too. And he was mean, he really was. He did things to players . . ." Scotty doesn't finish his sentence. He knows he doesn't need to. High-sticks, elbows—Howe did stuff that didn't just hurt you, it injured you; it put you on the sidelines, and created a memory in you and in anyone else who saw it that never went away. An indelible reminder—you don't mess with Gordie Howe. "He was tough as nails," Scotty says. "And he didn't have many fights. Nobody would dare fight him."

For seven straight seasons, year in, year out, the Wings were the NHL's best team. They won four Stanley Cups; when they lost, it was an upset. And in 1951–52, they were at their absolute peak.

CHAPTER FIVE

Scotty was a good enough player as a kid to make park teams and his high school team, to win the Quebec midget championship, to be recruited to a Canadiens-sponsored team, and to play Junior A. He was good enough to be a hopeful, but he wasn't a real prospect. He knew even as a kid what a prospect looked like: Doug Harvey, Dollard St. Laurent, Fleming Mackell, Donnie Marshall, Dickie Moore, Bernie Geoffrion—but he wasn't like them. And this was before he had suffered his head injury. Afterwards, when he wasn't the same player, he knew for certain he had no hockey-playing future. So what was that future?

Scotty had been a decent student. He'd had no difficulty passing from grade to grade. Ned Harkness had even thought he was capable enough to go to a good engineering school when he'd offered him that partial scholarship to RPI. But Scotty knew he wasn't an engineer. He didn't even think of himself as a real student, not like Bobby Fox or his sister Freda, and he certainly didn't think of himself as a *university* student. University then was only for the richest of the rich and the smartest of the smart, and that wasn't him. He knew that.

Life in Verdun was fine, and it didn't occur to him how much better it could be or what else he might do. His parents had come from Scotland with nothing. No money; no education. His father, once a blacksmith, was now a shop foreman. This could be Scotty's life path too. Not at Federated Metals—after his summer working there, he knew he didn't want to do that—and not in the trades, like his father. But this was post-war Canada. His future could be in some office, not on a factory floor. [...] were lots of jobs around—he'd get one, stay in it, work his [...] his way up, then someday move to some newer, [...] ttle further west in Verdun, and get married and [...], still in high school, living at home, he knew all [...] he didn't need to think much more about any of it. [...] d from high school. Then he fractured his skull. Then [...] ow what?

[...] diens and the other NHL teams had always felt some [...] eir players whose careers were ended by injuries. Hockey is a dangerous game. And while a fractured leg doesn't change a life, a fractured skull or a lost eye does. Governments at the time weren't yet big enough to offer a safety net of much consequence, so it was up to employers to act. If a worker could no longer do one job for a company, that company would find something else they could do. In the case of hockey teams, scouts were always needed. The paycheque wasn't much, but the bragging rights and the standing-room pass were gold.

After Scotty's injury, the Canadiens offered to help pay his way through university—the cost of tuition then was less than $400 a year. But Scotty decided instead to attend Sir George Williams College (now part of Concordia University) while also coaching some Canadiens-sponsored teams in Verdun. Neither path seemed to offer him much of a future, but at this moment Scotty was looking more for continuity than a future. This way he could do what he had always done, what he knew—go to school, and be involved in hockey—in the ways that were still open to him.

But times were changing, and somebody very important was about to enter his life.

In 1952, the NHL had six teams, only two of which were Canadian—the Leafs and the Canadiens. The other Canadian NHL teams had ceased operation years earlier: the original Ottawa Senators, Quebec Bulldogs, Hamilton Tigers, Montreal Maroons, and Montreal Wanderers. Almost every player in the NHL was Canadian, but Montreal and Toronto players were far better known and much more beloved than players on U.S.-based teams. Leafs games were broadcast on the radio all across the country; Canadiens games aired in Quebec.

NHL teams could sign up kids at a young age. The Leafs and Canadiens, already inside the imaginations of Canadian kids and their parents, had the inside track on any player they wanted. Yet from when the league first expanded to the U.S. in the late 1920s until the victory of the dominant Red Wings in 1952, Stanley Cup wins had been split almost equally between American and Canadian teams.

The Leafs, not the Canadiens, had been the first to press their home advantage. Their owner and general manager, Conn Smythe, hired Frank Selke Sr. as his assistant in 1929, and Selke began to put together a web of junior, senior, and kids' teams across the country that would become the Leafs' farm system. In the 1930s, the Leafs won the Cup once; in the 1940s, after Selke's efforts had time to take effect, they would win it five times.

Smythe had fought in France in the First World War, earning the Military Cross. He was later shot down by the Germans and spent the last year of the conflict as a POW. In 1940, Major Conn Smythe insisted on returning to active duty, and put Selke in charge of the Leafs. Four years later, Smythe was badly injured when the Germans bombed an ammunition depot and he was sent back to Canada.

On his return to Toronto, Smythe was ready to resume his job with the Leafs. Selke, however, had outgrown his old one, and in 1946 he resigned. A few months later, he was hired by the Canadiens. Selke set two conditions for taking the job in Montreal: the team needed to expand the Forum from a seating capacity of 9,300 to over 13,000 and it needed to build a farm system. One of the first people he hired to build that system was Sam Pollock. It may have seemed an inconsequential decision at the time, but Pollock would become Scotty's role model and guide—and later his great partner, the two of them winning four Stanley Cups together during the 1970s with Sam as general manager and Scotty as coach. Sam would be the greatest influence on Scotty's hockey life.

Scotty and Sam were sports products of their time. Sam, eight years older, grew up in Snowdon, a neighbourhood in the northeast corner of the middle-class, mostly English-speaking suburb of Notre-Dame-de-Grâce, up the hill and west of Scotty's working-class Verdun. His father had a small clothing store on Wellington Street, not far from the Bowmans' flat on the Avenues. Sam and Scotty both grew up on local rinks and in local parks. At the time, even in minor hockey, there were few teams, few coaches, few officials, few organizers—few adults involved at any level. The kids had to learn to be their own coaches, managers, and referees, even as they scored goals and chased down fly balls. And if they couldn't hit a curve ball or score to save their life, but they were quick enough to get to the shack at the park on Wednesdays to get the precious ice permit for Saturday or Sunday, and reliable enough to call up everybody else and let them know, then they were an indispensable member of any team.

Sam played baseball and hockey, just as Scotty and lots of other kids did. At the time, if you played one sport, you played both—Montreal winters are long, but not long enough for outdoor ice to stay frozen for more than a few months. And what else was a kid going to do with their friends, outside their cramped flat or house, in that healthy fresh air, during all of the other months? And most kids liked both sports equally, even if only a few might make a career in hockey and none in baseball.

Sam and Scotty were a little small; Sam was smaller. Sam was slightly better at baseball than hockey; Scotty was better at hockey. Sam was a good shortstop, but he learned early on that he was an even better organizer. He was like a backroom Duddy Kravitz—without the charm. The protagonist of Mordecai Richler's *The Apprenticeship of Duddy Kravitz* is an irrepressible, inexhaustible spew of schemes and scams. But while Kravitz has a need to perform, with Sam you saw nothing. Things just got done. And when he wasn't doing, he was thinking—he was doing things inside his head. In the rinks and parks of Snowdon, he learned that if you know everything about everything, people listen. And if you're willing to *do* everything, people let you.

At 15, Sam was coaching bantam, midget, and juvenile hockey in NDG. At 18, he put together the Snowdon Stars in the Snowdon Fastball League. Fastball—a variation of softball using a slightly smaller, harder ball—was very popular in Montreal at the time. And if, like Sam, you were putting together a fastball team, you'd want to find the best players. The best players were the best athletes, and the best athletes, of course, were hockey players—and the best hockey players of all were the players of the Montreal Canadiens. The Canadiens' hockey season ended in March, training camp wasn't until September—what else were the players going to do in the other months? In the off-season, it wasn't games that the players missed—it was their teammates. It was the *team.*

Most of the players spent their summers in Montreal. As NHLers, they weren't paid much more than an average wage, so they needed a summer job, and as well-known players for the Canadiens, where better to find one than Montreal? And what better to do in their evenings and on weekends instead of barnstorming the province playing charity games as the Montreal Canadiens but to play as a regular team in the Snowdon Fastball League?

On Sunday afternoons at MacDonald Park, more than 3,000 people watched the league's games. Hall of Fame goalie Bill Durnan, who also happened to be one of Canada's best softball players, was their pitcher.

The Rocket played the outfield, alongside his linemate, Elmer Lach, winner of the Hart Trophy in 1945 as the NHL's MVP. Their third linemate, Toe Blake—the (hockey) team's captain and the 1939 Hart Trophy winner—played second base. Doug Harvey, in years he didn't play minor league baseball, was at third. Ken Reardon, a five-time all-star defenceman and the son-in-law of the Canadiens' owner, Senator Donat Raymond, also played. Sam was the combative shortstop. Even more importantly, he was the manager/do-everything guy. Playing and coaching in NDG had given Sam his hockey training, but it was organizing the Snowdon Stars that got him known by the Canadiens players and their management.

In 1944, the Canadiens began sponsoring his NDG kids' team. A year later, he was put in charge of scouting and recruitment for all Canadiens-sponsored teams in the Montreal area. A year after that, Frank Selke Sr. arrived from Toronto, and in 1947 Selke hired Sam as coach of the Montreal Junior Canadiens. It was Sam's first full-time hockey job. Three years later, in 1950, the Junior Canadiens won the Memorial Cup as Canadian champions. Sam was 24.

Because Sam was *everywhere*, and Scotty was everywhere in Verdun, inevitably they ran into each other. The first time was in 1947, when Sam and his newly appointed Verdun scout, Ken Brown, raised the ante and outbid Norman Bracegirdle and his free toaster to lure Scotty away from Norman's Spartons to play on his first Canadiens-sponsored team. Then in 1950, when Scotty, playing Junior B, was called up to the Junior Canadiens, Sam was the coach. But when Sam was needed for other duties—in brief, anything that needed to be done—veteran Canadiens centre Billy Reay—out with an injury and being groomed as a future coach—filled in. Scotty's first Junior-A game was just down the street from his home, at the Verdun Auditorium. "Billy Reay put me on a line with Dickie Moore," Scotty recalls, "and I scored a goal. I remember like it was yesterday. Dickie had an open net, and he passed it to me." Eighteen years later, Scotty would coax Moore out of a two-year retirement to play with his expansion St. Louis Blues.

Scotty played a few more games for Sam before being sent back to his Junior B team. One of those games was in Quebec, against the Citadelles and Jean Béliveau. Béliveau was a genuine phenom—by far the best junior player in Canada, and maybe the best junior of all time. At 18, Gordie Howe might have been as good, but at 18 he was already in the NHL with Detroit and playing against grown men. In Quebec, Béliveau was playing against teenagers. He was six foot three, but appeared much bigger than that, moved with fluid, graceful power, and shot dangerously hard. He was just so much better than everyone else it was almost embarrassing. Only Mario Lemieux, in more recent times, had close to a similar man-among-boys look about him.

But Dickie Moore, being Dickie Moore, wasn't impressed. He was a Park Extension kid. Tough, Irish, and a scrapper, with an unquenchable willingness to fight and not much skill as a fighter. So he took on Béliveau. Béliveau didn't like to fight, and rarely fought. Moore blackened his eye. But more importantly, in front of his teammates, he brought Béliveau down to slightly more human dimensions. Later, playing together with the Canadiens, they became great admirers of each other, and in their more than 40 years of retirement together were lifelong friends.

The Junior Canadiens beat the Citadelles in the Quebec playoffs that year, then the Halifax St. Marys, then the Guelph Biltmores in the Eastern final, and finally another Canadiens-sponsored team—the Regina Pats—in the Memorial Cup final. Along the way, they'd had to defeat the Montreal Nationals, Bernie Geoffrion's team in the east end of the city. So in 1950, three great juniors had come together—Béliveau, Moore, and Geoffrion. As Scotty described them: "Béliveau was the best, Geoffrion was the goal scorer, Moore was the heart and soul." Three years later, they would come together again, this time on the Canadiens.

Frank Selke's farm system was coming to bear fruit. By 1950, the Canadiens were good. A few years later—led by Béliveau, Geoffrion, and Moore, all of them born in 1931, the "Class of '31," as they came to be called—they were great. They would win five Stanley Cups together.

While Selke ran the show, and Sam was taking on more important roles, Scotty was feeling his way along after his injury. He played his last season with the Royals and began his business course, and the next year, 1953–54, he finished up his studies while coaching bantam and juvenile teams in Verdun. His teams weren't much different from those he had played on a few years earlier. They still played outdoors at Willibrord Park. They still played only eight to ten games a year— on Thursday nights—and whether they played eight games or ten still depended on what days of the week the blizzards hit. And they also still hoped to get in a few more games with a playoff run against the other Montreal "park" winners, to go late enough in the season that there was no option left but to play on the indoor rinks of Verdun and LaSalle, or at the Forum.

Scotty soon discovered that the job of coach wasn't that much different either than it had been in the years he'd been playing. There were still no formal practices. Team "practices" were nothing more than the hours each kid put in playing pickup with friends at the park who also happened to be his teammates. Team "strategy" was still what these kids were able to come up with, looking around at the guys they had and that the other team had. At best on Thursday nights, Scotty might find a way to put into their minds some ideas of how to play that they wouldn't entirely forget the rest of the week. As a coach, "You were more like a cheerleader," as he puts it. "You wouldn't change on the fly or anything like that. You'd change on the whistles. You were mainly trying to encourage them." And in between games, it was his job to encourage them to be there that night. Citing an emergency, he would fight for the family phone to call his players to remind them, even though the games were always on the same night, at the same place. Between Thursdays, he recalls, "You were sort of like a secretary."

Scotty's hockey life was not much changed, but it was very different. This was now his job. He was a coach. His teams were sponsored by the

Montreal Canadiens—they were part of Frank Selke's great farm system. He may have had only eight or ten games a season, plus playoffs, and no formal practices, but he had a responsibility to make his teams better. He didn't have much time to get to know his players, to learn what made them tick, to know how to encourage and prod and manipulate them into something more. And he had too few players to juggle lines or to bench some of them to get their attention. But he was their coach, and he had to find a way to do what needed to be done. He had to do his best, and depending on the game—a good night, a bad night, ahead or behind—he had to come up with a few things he hadn't thought of before. He may have seemed only a cheerleader, even to himself, but in a tone, a gesture, a look in his eye, he needed to get across his message. And do it instantly. "You just played it by the seat of your pants," he says about coaching those games in Verdun. On the rinks of Willibrord Park, he was learning to become a game coach.

1954 was a big year for Scotty. Having finished his business course, he began working at Sherwin-Williams, the biggest paint company in Montreal. Their factory was in a large building on Centre Street, at the foot of the Atwater hill that led from Verdun to Montreal's downtown and to the Forum. He had seen that building and the giant Sherwin-Williams billboard every time he took the 58 bus to the Saturday-night games. Now he was working there. "I was in the general stock-keeping department," he recalls, "because I had a knowledge of French. I was training to be a salesman, to be a representative that would go into the hardware stores in Montreal and take orders." To be a salesman, you needed to know all the products you had to sell—the colours, the code numbers. It was just the right place for someone who remembered everything about everything.

Within a few months, Scotty learned the ropes of his new job. He knew what he had to do, and he realized there was more than one way to do it. He also had some good fortune on his side. "I got a little bit of a break," he says, "because the company built a new warehouse in Ville

LaSalle, and my boss had me go there every day." But Scotty, in fact, made his own break. He knew it would take him half an hour by bus to go from Centre Street to the warehouse to pick up the order sheets he needed, and half an hour to get back. At some point after that, he would need to have lunch. So he took his lunch early, ate the sandwiches on the bus that his mother had prepared for him, and dropped in at the Forum on his way back to the factory because the Canadiens practised between 10 and 11:30, and with his pass he could get in and watch them. He wouldn't make it at the start, but he'd be there by 10:30 and would sit behind the players' bench. Other than the maintenance people, it was just him and 13,000 empty seats. The Canadiens would be away in Boston, New York, Detroit, or Chicago almost every Sunday; they were sometimes away Wednesday when they played in Toronto and sometimes home on Thursday if the Leafs were in Montreal. Saturday was sacrosanct as a home night for both Canadian teams. This meant no practice at the Forum on Mondays—the overnight train from the U.S. cities arrived back in Montreal too late in the afternoon—but there was often a practice on Wednesdays or Thursdays, and always on Fridays. So Scotty adapted his Sherwin-Williams responsibilities to the Canadiens' schedule.

This was 1954–55, and Dick Irvin Sr. was the team's coach. It would be his last season in a 15-year run with the team that had begun in 1940–41 after nine years in Toronto. As a coach, he had won four Stanley Cups— one with the Leafs and three with the Canadiens—and lost an NHL record 11 times in the final. That year he would lose a 12th. "I would always just sit there," Scotty recalls, about watching practice, "[and] I would nod to Dick Irvin, or he would say hello to me. The odd time, I talked to him." An image then pops into his mind. "He used to wear these funny little kid's gloves."

The practices were pretty routine—a lot of up-and-down skating, line rushes, some scrimmages, and a lot of standing around. Scotty would watch the players, and the player he watched most was Maurice

71

Richard. "He practised hard. He didn't joke around. He wanted to score goals. He wanted to score so much, even in practice." And on his face, Scotty remembers, he had this "look"—a look that anyone who ever saw the Rocket remembers. Part desperate need, part bone-deep obligation, in biggest part something that no opponent could stand up to or resist. "He never fooled around."

For the Rocket, life was a never-ending fight. As a kid, it had been a fight against a life of being poor. Then it was a fight to play in the NHL, then to be a great star, then to be a French-speaking star on the only NHL team in a French-speaking province. Then it was a fight to live up to people's expectations and needs, to the duty that had been placed on his shoulders; to be worthy of being so completely depended upon, and not just on the ice but off it—by all those French-speaking Quebeckers who had been under the thumb of the English and the Church, who wanted and needed to feel proud, and who through him felt that pride. His was not an easy life.

Nor was it easy on the ice. He wasn't a puck handler like Gordie Howe. He didn't create distraction and open ice by passing to his team-mates as Wayne Gretzky would do. For the Rocket, there was no open ice. No trickery. No distraction. His teammates got him the puck, and the last 60 feet or so of ice from the blue line to the net was all his. The puck was going nowhere else. Every one of his opponents at every moment knew that. They could focus solely on him. But because he played on the right side but shot left, his body was always between them and the puck, so they had to go *through* him to get it. It was body against body, force against force, will against will. The Rocket going to the net was elemental.

"He was so strong on his skates," Scotty recalls, awe still in his voice. "Guys would just be leaning on him, but he was still driving to the net. He was a tough player. Gordie Howe was bigger, and he was tough too, but the Rocket was really tough. He was so competitive. He was fearless. He was explosive. He got fouled a lot and he had this vicious temper. I would say I've never seen a player so determined." One way or another, he *had* to score.

At these practices, Scotty also watched the other shooters. He had been a shooter himself, a goal scorer. But these players—the Rocket with his backhand (nobody had a backhand like him) and all of the rest of them—they shot so hard. They were men, they were strong, they'd had a lifetime of practice. And when they missed the net, every shot off the boards inside the cavernous Forum just *boomed.* For Scotty, it was magical. "I remember the first guy who could really shoot was Geoffrion. Most players didn't slap the puck then. He started that."

A slap shot was hard to control. A player had no idea where it was going—coaches didn't like that, and the maskless goalies hated it. But players loved it. It was so dangerous and exciting. It also gave Geoffrion his nickname, "Boom Boom." He played right wing, but on power plays "they put him on the right point," Scotty remembers. "He could score from the blue line. He had that good a shot." A few years later, Geoffrion scored 50 goals to tie the Rocket's single-season NHL record; and a year after that, Bobby Hull did the same. Two slap-shooters. The slap shot would soon transform the game.

Scotty didn't sit in those seats at the Forum to be noticed, but he *was* noticed. Dick Irvin said hello to him. He already knew Dickie Moore a little. The older players didn't know him, but they couldn't not see the kid who was always there. Sam didn't see him because he was never at practice, too busy being everywhere else. But Sam and Selke knew Scotty was there. And what Selke and Sam saw in Scotty was somebody not much different than themselves. Neither of them had been players of any note. After they had stopped playing, both had started at the lowest levels, then watched, learned, and did what others—especially those with a player's pedigree—would never be willing to do. Scotty would still need to prove himself, put in lots more time, and demonstrate his dedication. On days off he'd have to seek out a game to watch, any game, somewhere—and, of course, on teams he coached, he had to win. But he wasn't just a rink rat. And they knew, probably before he did, that he might be on the path to somewhere.

In every practice Scotty watched, there was something to see, and it was up to him to see it and then take it back to Verdun for his Thursday-night games at Willibrord Park. Then, after two years coaching the bantam and juvenile teams, he was asked to take over a Junior B team in Park Extension, Dickie Moore's home turf. By junior, age had made a player big enough, or not; genetics and dedication had made him talented enough, or not. And to coaches and scouts, this was now evident. The non-prospects who still wanted to play played juvenile, the possible prospects played Junior B. For them, only Junior A was ahead, then senior, or minor pro, and then the NHL. For Scotty, the stakes were now higher, the job more serious.

His new role was with the Park Extension Flyers—an independent team, not one sponsored by the Canadiens. Montreal's own Junior B team got the best players, and the Flyers and the others in the league had to make do with the rest. Often it was just one flaw that had held these players back—their size, their skating, or that they had just developed too late, making them too old to be prospects. Sometimes there were other complications: a job, or other ambitions. They might be good students and didn't have the time to dedicate their whole lives to hockey. They, or their parents, may have had other things on their minds. So Scotty had to work with what he had. But at least now, in Junior B, he had more games, more practices, and more time to deal with his players.

He did find himself with one challenge he wasn't expecting. The Flyers played their home games in Ville Saint-Laurent on Thursday nights. And as in Verdun, they might have the early game or the late one. The Canadiens also sometimes played on Thursday nights. Scotty's best player was Connie Mandala. "He was quite a player," Scotty recalls. "He never played Junior A because he was more of a student, but his father and uncle owned a parking lot on Atwater across from the Forum, and on game nights they expected him to help them park cars." The Canadiens' games started at 8:30. "If we were playing the early game, I just didn't have him. But if we had the second game, well, there was a chance. I used to worry that his father and uncle wouldn't let him leave until just before the Canadiens' game started. I remember giving him five dollars in taxi fare just to get him there in time."

Scotty was paid $250 that year for coaching the Flyers. "We had a terrific season. We came out of nowhere and made it to the finals. We got beat by the St. Jean Braves, a Canadiens-sponsored team. They had Bobby Rousseau and a lot of good players." The Flyers were a team that wasn't good enough to win, but they nearly did. It had been Scotty's job as coach to help his players find a way to win, and they almost had. More than 60 years later, Scotty still talks of that team with great pride. The same pride he expresses about his midget team that won the Quebec provincial championship, and about his Montreal, Pittsburgh, and Detroit teams that won Stanley Cups.

This was the last year Scotty worked for Sherwin-Williams—he would never use his vaunted memory to sell paint. Sam Pollock had been watching. The unfavoured, unsponsored Park Extension Flyers had made it to the final and brought sweat to the brow of his anointed sponsored team. Sam had a plan. The Montreal Junior Canadiens hadn't won the Memorial Cup since 1950; the Quebec junior league was struggling, and attendance for junior games at the Forum was poor. Sam wanted to try something different. He sold Frank Selke on the idea of moving the junior team to Ottawa, to be both a Quebec *and* an Ontario team that would play in both provinces against teams in more than one league. He asked Scotty to go with him to be his assistant. It would be Scotty's first full-time job in hockey. He was 22.

Scotty would take with him to Ottawa all that he'd learned on the rinks of Verdun, from teams he'd played on and ones he'd coached, from watching Dick Irvin and the Canadiens' practices, and also some lessons that were fresher and more vivid. The year that he coached Park

Extension, he had still taken his lunch break early from Sherwin-Williams, but this time it was to watch the Canadiens' new coach, Toe Blake, and a team that would win the first of five straight Stanley Cups—an NHL record that has never been matched.

CHAPTER SIX

Montreal Canadiens 1955–56

In September 1950, Detroit was easily the NHL's best team and getting better; Toronto was sliding, and Boston, New York, and Chicago were solidly and routinely at the bottom of the six-team league. The Canadiens, second or third most seasons, had on the team a core of future Hall of Famers in Maurice Richard, Doug Harvey, Elmer Lach, and Butch Bouchard, some solid veterans—Floyd Curry, Ken Mosdell, Calum MacKay, and goalie Gerry McNeil, as well as too many ineffectual parts. Because four teams made the playoffs, and the Stanley Cup winner only had to win two rounds, upsets were possible. After all, the Leafs had won a year earlier despite finishing fourth and having a sub-.500 record. But if the Canadiens, in lore and legend, were the "Flying Frenchmen," in reality at this time, and as had been the case throughout most of their history, they were neither "flying" nor were they "Frenchmen." Of all the Canadiens players who dressed for more than 50 games in 1950–51, only three—Richard, Bouchard, and little-used Norm Dussault—were of French-speaking heritage.

For decades, the NHL had been dominated by names like Howe, Bentley, Lindsay, Kennedy, Apps, Conacher, Morenz, Cook, Schmidt, Mosienko, Stewart, Taylor, Malone—British, German, or Eastern European names. Even among the players with French names—Lalonde, Boucher,

Joliat—most were not from Quebec. Newsy Lalonde was from Cornwall, Ontario; Frank Boucher and Aurèle Joliat were from Ottawa. Goalie Georges Vézina, the "Chicoutimi Cucumber," really was from Chicoutimi, Quebec, but scan the history of the NHL's trophy winners, all-star team selections, and scoring leaders, and there are almost no French-speaking players from Quebec. Legend has it right—Maurice Richard really did carry the hockey hopes and dreams of a team, a province, and a people almost single-handedly on his back. In 1950–51, the only French-speaking players of note in the NHL, besides the Rocket and Bouchard, were Léo Gravelle and Marcel Pronovost, who was only 20 and played just half the season with Detroit.

That same year, Bert Olmstead joined Montreal in a trade from Chicago. Defenceman Tom Johnson, 22, became a regular with the team, and Geoffrion, still a junior, came up to the Canadiens and played 18 games. The following season, Geoffrion was there for good and Dickie Moore played half a season, and a year later, in 1952–53, Béliveau—who had stayed on with the Quebec Aces, a senior amateur team, for two long years after his junior career—finally signed with the Canadiens, playing three games and scoring five goals as a teaser of what was to come. Jacques Plante also got into three games.

In 1953, in an upset, the Canadiens won the Cup, and they did it without Béliveau and Plante on their playoff roster. Happily they had found themselves without the need to beat Howe, Lindsay, Sawchuk, and Kelly along the way, as the Wings were upset in the first round by the Bruins, a team that had finished 21 points behind them during the regular season. The next year, 1953–54, the Canadiens continued their climb. Richard finished second in the league in scoring behind Howe; Geoffrion was fourth, Olmstead fifth, and Mosdell tenth. Plante played 17 games. The team that had finished 15 points behind the Wings a year earlier closed the gap to 7. Head-to-head against each other, the two teams scored 27 goals, each team winning six games, losing six, and tying two. When they met in the Stanley Cup final, the Wings went ahead three games to one, and then in an elimination game the Canadiens did what they never did—they won in Detroit. In Game 6 they won again, in Montreal, before losing the seventh in Detroit. The next season, 1954–55, the Canadiens were even better. But still the Wings finished first, and went on to beat them in the final, again in seven games.

Three times in four years—1952, 1954, 1955—the Canadiens just *could not beat them*. Two years in a row they'd lost in the final, each time in seven games, the first one in overtime because of a total fluke, the puck looping through the air, the nonpareil defenceman Doug Harvey batting it away with his glove and instead batting it into his own net. But if that had been crushing, 1955 was even worse. It was meant to be their year. It was *going* to be their year. Plante was now established as the team's goalie. Béliveau, in a single season, had made the leap from phenom to superstar, becoming what he was always destined to be. The team had five of the league's top 10 scorers, Geoffrion, Richard, and Béliveau finishing 1–2–3, Olmstead seventh, and Mosdell ninth. And, crucially, the Canadiens had entered the last week of the season *ahead* of the Wings, who had finished first for six straight years. Head-to-head, the Canadiens had beaten the Wings seven times and lost five, with one week to go. They had outscored them 37–28. They led them in the standings 91 points to 87. The Rocket, age 33, the greatest goal scorer in NHL history, was about to win his first-ever scoring title. Then all hell broke loose.

It was March 13, in Boston. The Bruins were comfortably in fourth place and in the playoffs, going neither up nor down. Only the Canadiens had something to play for. Late in the third period, with Boston ahead, Hal Laycoe hit Richard in the head with his stick. Bleeding heavily, Richard went after Laycoe and slashed him in the face and shoulder. Linesman Cliff Thompson tried to restrain Richard, which infuriated the Rocket even more. He broke loose more than once, the last time by punching Thompson in the head and knocking him out. The Bruins won the game, the Wings beat the Leafs the same night at the Olympia, and the gap between Montreal and Detroit was now only two points.

Three days later, on March 16, before any further games were played, NHL president Clarence Campbell held a hearing at his office in Montreal. The two protagonists, Campbell and Richard, seemed straight out of central casting: Campbell, the proper, patrician-like lawyer and former Rhodes Scholar, who from the French perspective was the perfect stereotype of an Anglo; and Richard, the uneducated, passion-driven player, who to the English was a perfectly stereotypical Franco. The emotions and stakes were high for more than just Richard and Campbell.

Campbell heard from each party. Richard admitted to attacking Laycoe but said that he had been dazed by Laycoe's blow to his head and thought the linesman, Thompson, was a Bruins player. In Campbell's written statement which followed, the NHL president did not accept Richard's explanation. He described how Richard had "persisted in the face of all authority," and how in an incident less than three months earlier, he had acted similarly, the two events demonstrating "a pattern of conduct" that included "flouting the authority of and striking officials."

"The time for probation or leniency is past," Campbell wrote in conclusion. "Whether this type of conduct is the product of temperamental instability or willful defiance of the authority in the games does not matter. It is a type of conduct which cannot be tolerated by any player—star or otherwise. Richard will be suspended from all games both league and playoff for the balance of the current season." That night, Detroit beat Boston, and the Canadiens and Wings were now tied. Montreal had three games to play; Detroit had two.

The following night, March 17, the Canadiens and the Wings played at the Forum. Midway through the first period, Campbell came into the arena and took his usual seat—in the stands and surrounded by fans. A few rows above him, Scotty was in his usual standing-room spot behind the blues. At first, there were boos. Then Campbell was pelted with eggs and other debris. At the end of the period, with the Wings ahead, 4–1, one fan approached him, extended his right hand as if to shake

Campbell's, then instead slapped Campbell in the face and punched him. The NHL president was escorted to safety.

A short time later, a tear gas bomb exploded near to where Campbell had been sitting. Scotty rushed down the back stairs he had run up less than two hours earlier, circled around the end of the rink down a tight corridor, and saw Dick Irvin Jr., son of the Canadiens' coach, who took him into the team's dressing room. The game was suspended, the Forum was cleared, and Campbell and Selke met under the stands where they drafted a note declaring the Wings as the winner of the game.

The Wings were now two points ahead, and the Canadiens had a game in hand.

Two days later, the Canadiens—without Richard—beat the Rangers in Montreal. When Geoffrion collected the point that moved him past Richard in the scoring race, the Forum crowd booed him. The two teams were now tied again. The final and deciding game of the season would be head-to-head—the Wings against the Canadiens—in Detroit. The Wings won, 6–0. They finished first in the league again, which gave them home-ice advantage in the playoffs. Geoffrion won the scoring title, a title Richard would never win. This had been his last best chance. The Wings and Canadiens met in the Stanley Cup final, the series went seven games, the last game in Detroit. The Wings won, 3–1. In 1954–55, the Wings had been as good as they had been in other seasons; but the Canadiens had gotten better and pushed them to their limit, and they had done it without the Rocket.

Sometimes you lose when you are ready to win. Sometimes you think destiny is enough, that the script has already been written with you as the winner—then somebody else writes their own script. Sometimes the window that seemed so wide open, ready for you to jump through, suddenly shuts and the opportunity is gone. Sometimes that window never opens again. Because while you remain good enough to win, you—and everyone around you—become so disappointed that you turn on each other and bring yourselves down. Sometimes adversity makes you weaker, but sometimes it makes you stronger. Which would it be for the Canadiens?

If the Canadiens had been ready to win in 1955, nothing was going to stop them in 1956.

When the 1954–55 season ended, Dick Irvin was fired and Hector "Toe" Blake became the team's new coach. Blake's nickname had originated with his younger sister who, as a baby, in trying to say his name, had the sound come out as "Hec-toe," and her big brother became Toe forever. With hindsight, Blake seems to have been the inevitable choice to become the next Canadiens coach. After all, his teams would come to win eight Stanley Cups during his thirteen years in Montreal. But he wasn't such a clear favourite at the time, in part, because it wasn't evident he wanted the job.

Blake had played twelve full seasons with the Canadiens—eight as the team's captain, during which time Montreal won the Cup twice. He led the team in scoring five times. He played left wing with Elmer Lach at centre and Maurice Richard at right wing on the Punch Line, one of the greatest lines in the Canadiens' history. More than that, he was the team's continuity. He had played with Aurèle Joliat, who had joined the Canadiens back in 1922 in the league's sixth season, when the NHL had only four teams—Montreal, Toronto, Ottawa, and Hamilton. He had played with Howie Morenz—the "Stratford Streak" and the "Mitchell Meteor"—who had lived a legendary career and died a legendary death. Morenz had been the greatest player in NHL history until the Rocket, and died from complications of a broken leg he suffered in a game at the Forum. His funeral was held right there in the arena, his casket at centre ice as more than 10,000 people attended, in the 9,300-seat building, and more than 50,000 later filed past. Blake had played in that game when Morenz sustained his injury. And, some years later, Blake was there when the Rocket arrived—when he wore number 15 before he ever put on his famous number 9. He was Richard's left winger when the Rocket scored 50 goals in 50 games. He was there, too, when Butch Bouchard, Ken Mosdell, Doug Harvey, Floyd Curry, and Tom Johnson joined the Canadiens—pieces of the team that were still there in 1955 and who would be important players for the next coach, whoever that might be. And Bouchard, who had replaced Blake as captain when he retired, would be the captain of this team too.

Blake also spoke French when very few of his English-speaking teammates did. He had grown up near Sudbury, Ontario, with its large francophone community, and now that Selke was creating the farm system the Canadiens needed in order to own the province of Quebec, there would need to be more French-speaking players—and a coach that spoke French. And if all this wasn't enough to ensure Blake the job, it had long been assumed that when Irvin eventually retired or was fired, Blake would succeed him. It was only natural.

But after Blake retired from the Canadiens in 1948, he seemed to have no big ambitions in hockey. He had his tavern on Sainte Catherine Street not far from the Forum. He had his house in a modest neighbourhood in Montreal West. He started coaching a "small market" team in the Quebec Senior Hockey League, the Valleyfield Braves, in a nondescript town an hour's drive southwest of Montreal. Fewer than 2,000 people attended their games—less than half the QSHL's average. Almost none of the Braves' players were on their way up, a few were on their way down, and most were just where they were—in their early twenties, slowly gliding from a hockey life into a regular job and a life back in their hometown. Béliveau had played in this league, for the Quebec Aces. So too Marcel Bonin, Kenny Wharram, and Jean-Guy Talbot. Dickie Moore, Dollard St. Laurent, and Plante had also played briefly for the Montreal Royals, just passing through. But by the mid-1950s, if an NHL team—especially the Canadiens—had any big aspirations for a player, they didn't put him on a team like Valleyfield. So what was Blake doing there? And what was he doing travelling all over the province during the summer as a baseball umpire—Toe Blake, the former captain and star of the Montreal Canadiens? And in 1954–55, the season before, why hadn't he coached hockey at all, anywhere?

So much of the coaching talk instead was about Billy Reay. During his eight-year career with the Canadiens he had been a teammate of Blake's and won two Stanley Cups, in 1946 and 1953. He was the team's second-line centre, very small, and very quick. And unlike Blake, he *had* coached the year before—the Victoria Cougars in the Western Hockey League, then pro hockey's second-highest minor league. "Billy Reay was really well regarded in the Canadiens' organization," Scotty says.

Selke was the team's general manager at the time; Ken Reardon and Sam Pollock were his assistants. Reardon had played with Blake, and in more recent years when Blake had coached in Valleyfield, Reardon had run the team in Shawinigan Falls, so he knew Blake as a coach. Sam and Blake had also been teammates on the Snowdon Stars in the Snowdon Fastball League. "I heard the decision came down to this: that Sam and Ken pushed for Toe, and Frank Selke was kind of leaning towards Billy Reay. I think Toe got the job because Sam and Kenny wanted him." Scotty pauses. "And also Toe's relationship with the Rocket was very good.

"That [Richard] suspension probably cost Dick Irvin his job. Because Montreal was going to finish first until then. You could say it might have cost them the Cup. I think they [Selke, Reardon, and Sam] just said, 'We've got to make a change.' They felt that Dick Irvin had lost control of the Rocket. And that's when Toe came in."

Blake was mature—43 years old—secure, and respected. He knew Montreal, the fans, the media, the organization, and the players. He knew himself. He had in his head a clear sense of how the Canadiens should play, and he believed he had the players to do it.

He also knew Richard was the key. The team had almost won the year before because of the Rocket, and they had lost because of the Rocket. And they would win or lose this season because of him too. Béliveau would get better and better, that was certain, and so would

Geoffrion, and Moore, and Plante. Harvey, Olmstead, Johnson, Curry, and Mosdell weren't going to change; they would still be as good. But the Rocket was getting older. He had been taken down in public by Campbell, told that he had this "temperamental instability," this "willful defiance" of authority, and had conducted himself in a way that "cannot be tolerated." In short, he'd been treated like a child. Blake knew that the Rocket's personality wouldn't change, and couldn't change. He'd known Richard since he was 20. That's who he was, and that's what made him so great. Hockey put the Rocket into a zone where nothing existed except the other team's net. He himself didn't matter, his opponents didn't matter; Cliff Thompson, or any other official, or Clarence Campbell didn't matter. Whether he had been dazed by Laycoe's high stick or not, Richard, almost surely, had thought that Thompson was another Bruins' player. He was that focused.

Irvin, at times, used to push and prod Richard. In some games, the winger seemed to drift, and sometimes the team needed something Rocket-like, for him to go off to "change the temperature" of the game. So Irvin taunted him. He had coached him for 13 years—he was the only NHL coach Richard had known—and Irvin liked to poke the bear. But Blake wouldn't do that. He wanted the Rocket to be the Rocket and no more, because so long as Richard could still score, and still feel proud and important, he knew he would get no less. Richard had almost won the scoring title the year before. He had scored 38 goals, his highest total in four years, tying Geoffrion for the league lead, and this 1955–56 season, he had something to prove. Others might not have thought so because he was the Rocket. But last season hadn't ended right. For somebody who always saw himself as just a hockey player, and who wasn't even comfortable with the attention he got from scoring goals, everything had ended in such a mess. *Nothing* had been about what happened on the ice. *Everything* was about the off-ice stuff—Campbell, politics, French versus English. He hadn't even played when the season mattered most: in those last few games, in the playoffs, in the seventh game of that final. That's when "the boys" needed him, and he hadn't been there. So for Blake, the question was how to give the Rocket his best chance of being the Rocket that was still in him.

The answer, or part of it, presented itself clearly in training camp in September. It was something Blake wasn't expecting, and it had to do with Henri Richard, Maurice's much younger brother. "The Canadiens developed a lot of good juniors," Scotty explains, "but you always finished junior hockey first, whether you were Moore or Geoffrion or anybody." Henri was then 19, and had one year left of his junior eligibility. But in that training camp, Scotty recalls, amazement still in his voice: "He just had the puck the whole time. He came to training camp and just forced his way onto the team." Henri was small, about five foot seven and 160 pounds, but he could skate. He was fast, and he could turn, and turn, and turn again, and in possession of the puck, with his short arms and short stick, he rarely exposed the puck beyond the protective shelter of his body. He was tireless too. At the time, other players changed every two minutes; Henri stayed on the ice for three minutes or more. And because teams matched lines, his opposing centre had to either stay on for three minutes or more with him, and play at Henri's speed, or get off the ice and throw all his team's other lines into disarray. By halfway through a shift, if not earlier, it was "Advantage, Henri."

The Rocket wasn't tall, but he was broad-shouldered and bull-like, while Henri was more like a terrier. Both brothers played the way their bodies allowed them to play. On the ice, they looked completely different, but inside their very different bodies was the same spirit. They were fiery and stubborn. They were proud. They were unconquerable. The Rocket *had* to get to the net. Henri *had* to get the puck and keep it. After training camp that fall, Blake couldn't keep Henri off the team. The two of them would be rookies together, starting out on a hugely successful run. For Henri as a player and Blake as a coach, they would not lose a Stanley Cup until their sixth season.

Maurice was the oldest of his family's eight children; Henri the second-youngest. Maurice was fifteen years older than Henri, and played his first game with the Canadiens when Henri was only six. Almost a generation separated them. Neither of them said much to the other (or to anybody). They didn't seem very close. In fact, they seemed almost purposely to avoid each other. A Richard doesn't need help; a Richard doesn't want help. But Henri was still Maurice's brother, and Maurice didn't have a lot of friends. At training camp that year, Maurice may have been surprised at what he felt when he saw Henri out on the ice for the first time. "I think when his brother joined the team that gave him a lift," Scotty says of the Rocket. "Because he was 34 years old. I think he got a big charge out of his brother coming and playing for the Canadiens."

Every so often, in spite of themselves, a brotherly connection showed itself. There was one occasion, late in the season, when the Canadiens were playing the Leafs in Toronto. Montreal was comfortably in first place and the Leafs would barely make the playoffs, but every Leafs–Canadiens game at the time seemed to be played for now, and before, and forever. The Leafs decided to bring up "Bashin' Bob" Bailey from their farm team in Pittsburgh just for the game. His nickname said it all. A year earlier, he and the Rocket had engaged in a vicious fight. With Maurice's brother in the lineup, Bailey now had one more way to provoke the Rocket.

He targeted Henri. Every time he was on against him, every time he could catch him—or, more accurately, every time his stick could catch him—he whacked him. First period, second period. The Rocket held himself back. Again and again, until he couldn't any longer. Then he went after Bailey. When the officials finally restrained him, there being only a short time left in the period, they sent him to the dressing room. Leafs owner Conn Smythe, seeing the commotion, rushed down towards the ice from his seat midway up in the arena, in the greens. As he arrived, the Rocket was storming up the corridor that led to the dressing room. Several policemen were nearby, as well as a young program seller.

The Rocket headed towards Smythe, and Smythe—who had fought in two world wars and been wounded, who had judged the muted fervour with which French-speaking Quebeckers had fought for king and country as a lack of patriotism, and who was well known for his slurs against French Canadians—held his ground. Everyone knew what would happen next. The cops lunged at Richard and grabbed him. Smythe yelled out, "Take your hands off . . . the greatest player who ever lived!"

So in 1955–56, the Canadiens began the season with a new coach, Toe Blake; an exciting new player, Henri Richard; some stars who were still improving—Béliveau, Geoffrion, and Moore; three new young players—Claude Provost, 22, Jean-Guy Talbot and Donnie Marshall, both 23; and with their greatest star, the Rocket, ready. But there was one more thing that was different about this season.

Gordie Howe was 27, Ted Lindsay 30, and Red Kelly 28—all of them still in their prime. But Terry Sawchuk, 25, was gone. He had been traded to the Bruins. Glenn Hall was the Wings' new goalie. Sawchuk had won the Vezina Trophy three times in the previous five years—including the season before—and the other two times he had finished second. He had three times been the league's first-team all-star goalie, and twice its second. His goals against average in successive years had been: 1.99, 1.90, 1.90, 1.93, 1.94. In those years, as Scotty said about him, "You couldn't put a pea by him." More tellingly, he had beaten the Canadiens three straight times in the playoffs. In 1952, the Canadiens weren't good enough to win, but in the last two years, 1954 and 1955, they may not have been as good as the Wings but they could have won. Sawchuk could be difficult as a teammate—he could be sour and ornery. But he was in the Canadiens players' heads. They couldn't beat him.

Glenn Hall would win the Calder Trophy as the rookie of the year that season, finish second to Jacques Plante in goals against average, and record 12 shutouts in what would be the highest total of his Hall of Fame career. Hall was also a great guy, and the players loved him. But he was new to a veteran team that knew how to win, and knew how they wanted to play. When things went wrong—and things always do—Hall couldn't prey on their minds the way Sawchuk could. He couldn't haunt them and make them so miserable they wouldn't dare to play that way again. Sawchuk had been a brooding conscience on the Wings. He had seemed at times to be more trouble than he was worth—until, as the Wings would find out, he wasn't there. When Blake was named coach of the Canadiens, the players were excited. When Henri made the team, it was the same. But when they heard Sawchuk had been traded, they were thrilled. The Leafs, Rangers, Bruins, and Black Hawks didn't matter that season. This was going to be a two-horse race.

"Toe had his lines, and his defence pairs, he had his power play and his penalty killers, and he didn't change things up much," Scotty explains. "But the top line was Béliveau, Geoffrion, and Olmstead." Boom Boom Geoffrion was coming into the season as the defending NHL scoring champion. When he'd arrived to the Canadiens in 1951, it had been a big deal. Not just because he'd been such a great junior, but because, as Scotty puts it, he was "a French player coming up." He— and soon Béliveau as well—could share the Rocket's load, at least a little. "He wasn't a great skater," Scotty says of Geoffrion, then corrects himself: "He wasn't a speedster as much as a strong skater. He kind of ran on his skates, he had short strides, but he was very strong—and boy, what a shot he had. When he walked in on the right wing he could shoot that puck with the best guys I've ever seen."

Geoffrion had a big shot when a big shot really mattered. Goalies didn't wear masks, and the small equipment they did wear offered little protection. A big shot travelled too fast for them to move the full height and width of the net fast enough to stop it, and it hurt a lot if they did. A big shot could overpower a goalie, and make him a little fearful. Goalies later adapted by moving forward out of their goal crease to "cut the angle," to take away more of the net so they had little distance to move to get to the puck. But until they did, and most times afterwards, Geoffrion hit that bottom left corner again and again.

He was explosive like the Rocket. He scored big goals, and as Scotty says, "He was fearless too. Nobody could intimidate him." But, unlike the Rocket, he was spectacular off the ice as well. "He had a swagger about him. He was a flashy dresser. He was a really flashy guy. Like a *bon vivant*. But a nice guy. A good guy. And popular—he was always talking to the media. He was always into ventures too," as Scotty puts it. "Always opening up a restaurant or something. He had lot of energy. He was up and down, though. He wasn't always up. You had to pump him up."

Things bothered Geoffrion. Hal Laycoe, Bob Bailey, and lots of other players did things that bothered the Rocket, but those had to do with situations, with moments. Anything else, the Rocket was rock, steel, unreachable. You couldn't get to him. You could get to Geoffrion, though. You could hurt him.

The year before, 1954–55, on his way to 38 goals—his then best season—and the team to a first-place finish, in the second-last game of the season against the Rangers—a game they had to win—when he had assisted on a Canadiens goal, and the Forum announcer called out his name, the crowd, realizing he'd passed the Rocket in the scoring race, booed him. *They booed him.* Just because he now had more points than the Rocket didn't mean he thought he was better than the Rocket. But they booed him. The next year, 1955–56, the team would be having its best season ever. Béliveau, Olmstead, Moore, Harvey, Henri, Plante—everybody doing great. Geoffrion ended up with 62 points, 13 fewer than the year before, and scored 9 fewer goals in a season when, at age 24, he should have been even better. But they had *booed* him.

Five years later, in 1960–61, the season after Richard retired, after scoring 19, 27, 22, and 30 goals, Geoffrion got 50 goals to tie the Rocket's record. Doug Harvey had replaced Richard as captain, but when the year was over, Harvey was traded to the Rangers. The Canadiens needed a new captain, and so the team held a vote and the players decided.

Béliveau won. The next year, Geoffrion scored 23 goals, then 23 and 21 in the two years after that. To him, it was as if his teammates had "booed" him in that vote. A body heals; a heart sometimes doesn't.

On March 11, 2006, almost 51 years to the day since they had booed him, Canadiens fans filled the Bell Centre. Geoffrion's family was there: his wife, Marlene, the daughter of Howie Morenz, and their children and grandchildren—two of whom, Danny and Blake, had played in the NHL. Four generations of Morenzes and Geoffrions were on the ice for an almost unwatchably emotional ceremony. Geoffrion's number 5 jersey was being raised to the rafters of Bell Centre. Boom Boom had died that morning.

Back in 1955–56, while Geoffrion still felt wounded and was not quite his same booming presence, he remained important as a slightly secondary player to the Rocket and Béliveau, able to emerge from the shadows and come to the forefront if needed. But it was Béliveau that season who took command. He was tall. He played upright, he took in everything, and he was always aware. He was talented enough to be at the centre of every moment, on the ice or off, but he always put the moment itself at the centre—he made it more important than he was, and made the most of it. As his centreman he saw Geoffrion, he was aware of him, he knew what Geoffrion could do, and he got him the puck. And he showed the same awareness defensively. "He was a superb positional player," Scotty says. "People underestimated that in him. He was always in the right position. In his own end, he'd stand kind of in the middle, and because of his reach, and the length of his stick, he covered so much. Geoffrion didn't play defence much, but he didn't have to."

But while Béliveau had become the team's most talented player, he still wasn't the Rocket, and he knew it. In the Canadiens' dressing room, on a wall above the players' lockers, is a line from John McCrae's poem, "In Flanders Fields." It reads: *To you from failing hands we throw the torch, be yours to hold it high.* On that team, in those years, it was the Rocket who held the torch, and though he was getting older, there was no need for the torch to be thrown to anyone else. Nor did Béliveau or Geoffrion, his obvious successors, ever get ahead of themselves and think it was their turn before it was. And for Béliveau, when or if that moment came, the torch would need to be thrust at him. He wouldn't grab it. But in 1955–56, it didn't matter anyway. This was the Rocket's team, and about that there was absolutely no doubt. It didn't matter if someone else scored more goals or had more points or was the league's MVP; there might be many leaders on the team, but the Rocket was its spirit.

Playing at left wing with Béliveau and Geoffrion that season was Bert Olmstead. "He was a crabby guy," Scotty recalls. "He was always criticizing something. Nothing was good enough. But he was tough, and hockey smart, and he fit in perfectly with the Canadiens." Scotty relates a story that his friend Emile Francis, the former coach and GM (most notably of the New York Rangers), told him. "Olmstead came up in the Chicago organization, and he and Emile were from Saskatchewan," Scotty relates. "They played junior together for the Moose Jaw Canucks. Another guy on that team was Metro Prystai. Anyway, Olmstead played with Prystai and Bep Guidolin in Chicago. They were called the 'Boilermaker Line,' and they were good." At training camp one year, at an exhibition game, Francis was talking to Irvin, who was then still coaching the Canadiens and knew Francis because, as Scotty relates, "they both ran baseball teams in the West." During his playing career, Irvin had settled in Regina, and even after all his years in Toronto and Montreal, he returned there every off-season. "He says to Emile, 'Tell me about Bert Olmstead.' And Emile says, "He's the fiercest competitor I have ever been connected with. I played junior with him. I've never seen a guy so bitter after a loss."" In December, Olmstead was traded to Detroit, and when he refused to go, he was sent to the Canadiens.

In Montreal, "He got hooked up with the Rocket," Scotty recalls. "Then a couple of years later in comes Béliveau. Bert was a very good corner guy. They'd shoot the puck in the corner, he was a big, big man. Tall, long arms, long reach, he'd tangle you up. Béliveau would be in the slot and he'd get the puck to him. The way Bert skated you wondered how he ever got up and down the ice, but he just knew, position-wise. He had exceptional hockey sense. And he was a good defensive player too." In 1955–56, Olmstead finished fourth in the league in scoring, just behind the Rocket. He also had 56 assists, 9 more than anyone else.

The Richard brothers and Dickie Moore—three Hall of Famers— were the Canadiens' second line. Blake had put the Rocket and Henri together the first day of training camp, maybe because the media wanted to see them together—the season was still weeks away, and this could be the one bone he would throw them that year—maybe because he thought one brother would inspire the other, or maybe because he thought they might fit even if in a very unconventional way. Both were highly individual players. Henri was a puck carrier. He wanted the puck *all* the time. The Rocket wasn't a puck carrier. He wanted the puck only at the *right* time. And he wasn't a great defensive player; his focus was on the other team's net, not his own. Henri could be a defensive liability at times because in carrying the puck he might be checked and lose it, but because he generally had the puck so much, the other team *didn't* have it—and if they didn't have it, they couldn't score. Still, someone needed to be a distributor on that line—someone able to get the puck and get it to both of them. The usual distributor on a line is the centre, but on this line it was the left winger, Dickie Moore.

Moore, in his years since junior, with his stick-his-nose-into-anything style of play, had managed not to get himself killed—but only just. He had missed more than half the season in both 1952–53 and 1953–54, but he had managed to play every game except three the following year, so maybe he was learning, if not quite picking his spots. When Scotty thinks of what made Moore special, he pauses, then says, "It was his perseverance. He battled. That's what he did, more than anybody, he battled. He was fiery. He was chippy—oh, he was chippy. When he came to the NHL, they said he's not going to last playing this kind of hockey. And he got into some scraps early. He wasn't really a great fighter, but he would persevere. He was one of those guys, one of the most I've ever seen, who just couldn't stand losing. Who just couldn't stand not doing well."

But, Scotty adds, "He was also pretty good at making plays. If you're going to play with the Rocket, you're going to try to set him up. Dickie liked to be fancy at times. He'd come up with these things, like he'd come in on a guy and be stickhandling like crazy, except his stick wasn't even touching the puck. His stick was passing right over top of it. Just to rattle the guy a bit. He used that a lot in junior. He didn't use it so much in the NHL. But he had a lot of creativity to his game. That's why he won the scoring title in '58 and '59." In 1959, Moore recorded 96 points, more than anyone in NHL history—more than Gordie Howe had ever done. It was a league record that lasted for seven years.

But more than anything about Moore, it was his drive. Scotty had seen it in him in junior when he took on Béliveau, in his early seasons with the Canadiens when he pushed his body to do whatever the team needed—even if his body couldn't do it. He would see it even more unforgettably a decade later in St. Louis, when that body was almost gone. It was February 1968, late in the season, Moore had been retired almost three years, and Scotty signed him. "His knees were awful. He used to ice them for three or four hours before a game. He used to hobble around the rink. It was sad to watch him. I didn't even know if he'd make it to the end of the season, let alone the playoffs." Moore played 27 games and recorded 8 points. In the playoffs, he played all 18 of the Blues' games and had 14 points, 7 of them goals. He led the team in scoring. "He had a terrific playoffs. He scored a huge goal for us. It was in the Western final; Game 7. It was a tremendous goaltending battle: [Glenn] Hall, and [Cesare] Maniago for Minnesota. There was no score for about 55 minutes. I know all these games," Scotty says, all excited. "Walt McKechnie scored a goal with less than five minutes left to put them ahead. And Dickie just threw himself around, and drove around the net, hacking and whacking, and scored the tying goal. We went into overtime, and in the second overtime, we got a breakaway and Ron Schock scored and put us into the Stanley Cup final." He pauses in admiration. "Dickie was some player. He played fearless." And in the 1955–56 season, this was that same Dickie Moore, except 12 years younger, with even more than his spirit to drive him.

Ken Mosdell, Floyd Curry, and Claude Provost were the checking line—two veterans and Provost the rookie. Mosdell and Curry had been linemates for years, knew each other, and knew their jobs. As the team got better around them, to the surprise of many, they got better too. Mosdell, then 33, had had his most productive years the previous two seasons, both times finishing in the top 10 in the league in scoring. Curry, 30, had scored eight goals in the team's twelve playoff games only a few months earlier. Provost fit right in. He was only 22 and had never been a star; he worked hard, didn't complain, and did every job that was given to him. If it was to be a checker and play left wing even though he was a right-handed shot, so be it. And that's what he did.

Donnie Marshall, who had grown up two blocks away from Scotty on Desmarchais, the street with the median, was the extra forward. Marshall had been a scorer with Cincinnati in the IHL and Buffalo in the AHL, finishing near the top of both leagues in goals and points. He was a good skater and able to play as a linemate with the best offensive players or the best checkers if one of the regulars was injured, but not quite good enough on this team to play regularly himself. Bob Turner played the same role among the defencemen, and together they killed penalties and were ready if they were needed for more.

On defence, Doug Harvey partnered with Dollard St. Laurent, Tom Johnson with Jean-Guy Talbot. The two pairings didn't play equally. And Harvey, as well as his regular shift, was on the power play and killed penalties. He seemed to be on the ice all the time. He was 31 years old, but as it turned out he was less than halfway through his professional hockey career. At a time when if someone played one sport they played many, the greatest compliment for any player was to be called an all-round athlete, and Doug Harvey was a great all-round athlete. He played baseball and football as well as hockey, but more remarkably he was a star in all three. He had won the Norris Trophy as the NHL's best defenceman for the first time in 1954–55; he would win six more. In 1956, he was named to the first all-star team for the fifth consecutive year; he would be named to five more in the next six seasons.

Until Bobby Orr, Harvey was considered the greatest NHL defenceman of all time. Period. He wore his salt-and-pepper hair short in a buzz cut. He looked grizzled even after he shaved. It was said he played as if in a rocking chair—unfailingly calm, the world going on around him. No bother. He knew where to be, and when to be there, and what to do when he arrived. He was tough too, as tough as he needed to be. And he was mean, as mean as he needed to be. To his teammates, everything was fine if Doug was fine, and Doug was always fine. As a defenceman, he knew there were lots of things a defenceman might do, but only one thing he *must* do. He had to command—not control—the front of his net. Skaters could skate, puck handlers could make lots of fabulous plays, but ultimately they had to get to the net. They had to come to him; he didn't need to go to them. *See you when you get here.*

Dollard St. Laurent was his ideal defence partner. He was a veteran and yet still only 26—a good skater and very keen, like a golden retriever who can't do enough to please. Harvey played right defence, St. Laurent played left, so when the puck went into the right corner, as the right defenceman naturally Harvey would go after it. Except he didn't. St. Laurent did. Then St. Laurent went after the puck in the left corner, then he went back into the right corner. He went wherever the puck went. And in his rocking chair, Harvey waited until the puck, and the player with it, came to him. St. Laurent did what he did best, and Harvey did the same.

Scotty had known Harvey by reputation and lore in Montreal, but Harvey was nine years older, and, as it was with Moore, he got to know him best in St. Louis when age and injury had taken away most of his skills, and there was little left to see except unvarnished character. Even now—after 80 years of being immersed in hockey and its players—Scotty finds Harvey almost beyond belief. He loves to tell Doug Harvey stories. The Robbie Irons "We don't want him to play, do we?" story. Another from Scotty's first year with St. Louis, when in the West Division the third-place Blues were playing the first-place Flyers in the opening round of the playoffs.

Harvey was then 43. (Scotty was 34.) He had bounced around the minors for four years, and Scotty had signed him to be player-coach of the Blues' farm team in Kansas City. Harvey had spent the whole season there. But, as Scotty relates, "We had lost Game 6 against the Flyers in the second overtime—it was a tough loss, it was at home, we'd been ahead in the series, 3–2, and Doug was playing the deciding game in his own series in Kansas City. But we got a bad injury—Al Arbour had tweaked his groin—and now we had to go into Philly for Game 7. I called Doug at midnight and said, 'I need two forwards and a defenceman,' and he said, 'I've got three guys ready to go,' and he told me the names of the forwards. And then he said, 'The best defenceman is myself.' He came from Kansas City the next morning. I don't think we even practised. Then we took the plane to Philly and he played over 40 minutes and was the first star of the game."

The story doesn't stop there. The next round was against Minnesota. It was the series when Dickie Moore, with his two bad knees, scored the game-tying goal late in the seventh game and the Blues won in the second overtime. But Game 6 had been its own tale. "We'd gone up to Minnesota and got beat, 5–1." Hall had been in goal. "Glenn always lived in fear of not being able to do what he needed to do. I don't know why," Scotty says. "But on the way to the plane he said to me, 'I didn't have it tonight,' which really wasn't true, but he was blaming himself. And he said, 'I'm just not tracking the puck.' I said to him, 'Well, we're not going to play the other goalie.' It was Seth Martin, and he had never played a playoff game in his career.

"I used to consult Doug a lot, and I was telling him what Glenn told me, and Doug said, 'Are we practising tomorrow?' and I said, 'No.' He said, 'Let's have a few guys come out and shoot some pucks at him.' So we did. But before that, because Glenn was complaining he couldn't see the puck, I sent him to our team doctor to test his eyes. He told Glenn, 'Your eyesight is 20/20, and you've got the reflexes of a 20-year-old. There's nothing wrong with you.'

"So we go on the ice, Glenn included, and Doug must've said to the guys, 'Make sure you don't score on him.' So that's what they did, they shot right at him. The next day Glenn's all set to play Game 7. We finish the warm-up, he's coming off the ice and he comes right to see me. 'I'm still having trouble,' he says. 'Keep an eye on me, if I don't have it make sure you make a quick switch.'

"So now I'm pretty uptight, and I'm looking for Doug. It's about seven or eight minutes before we go on the ice, and he's in the washroom having a shave. That's the way he was. He was having a shave. I said to him, '"Ghoulie" came up to me'—that's what everyone called Glenn—and I told Doug the whole story. He said, 'Aw, Scotty, don't even worry about it. I'll keep both my eyes on him. He's going to be fine.' I think he stopped 44 shots."

This was how Doug Harvey was back in 1955–56 too—a great character and a great athlete, and still in his prime.

The team's other defensive unit was a more conventional pairing. Tom Johnson, the veteran, would push the puck up the ice a little more; Jean-Guy Talbot, the rookie, would stay back. Johnson was a second-team all-star that season; three years later he would interrupt Harvey's monopoly and win the Norris Trophy as the league's best defenceman.

Behind the four defencemen was someone decidedly not conventional: Jacques Plante. Goalies have the reputation—put upon them by non-goalies—of being different. And of all the goalies, in all the history of the NHL, Plante was the most different. (Dominik Hašek, another of the very best goalies ever, might be the runner-up.) Plante knitted. Until he was no longer permitted to do so, even after junior, he wore a toque when he played. But mostly he was different because he asked questions when no one ever had, and when he didn't hear answers that made sense to him, he did what he thought he should do instead of what he was told. *Why does a goalie have to stay in his crease all the time? Even when we have the puck and the other team can't score? Even when they shoot it into our zone and rush after it, and will get it, when I could get there first to keep them from getting a scoring chance at all?* But that would mean leaving the net empty, and they could score, the entire hockey world said. Or, in Toe Blake's words, words he used often: "It's hard enough for a goalie to stop a puck when he's in front of the net. It's impossible when he's behind it." *But if I get to the puck first,* Plante argued, *they can't score.* But then the net would be empty, Blake argued back. *But I would have the puck.*

The blind (everyone but Plante, Blake included) refused to see. It didn't matter. Plante went out of his net and controlled the puck for his teammates, while Blake had eight heart attacks behind the bench.

Why can't a goalie wear a mask? Plante also wondered. Because goalies don't wear masks. They've never worn masks. *But if players can now shoot harder, and a goalie might be hit in the face and be injured and not available to play or to play well, or become puck-shy, or lose an eye . . . ?* But wearing a mask would show that you're afraid, and if you're afraid, your coach, your teammates, the fans, and the media don't want you as their goalie. *But, as a goalie, what if, like everyone else, I do get afraid? What if a mask would make me less afraid? What if it made me play even better?* But if you wear a mask you can't see as well. *What if I can see as well?* But you can't.

A few years later, in 1959, Plante put on a mask, and Blake had more heart attacks.

Plante was also different in another way. He was a competitor, as all the great players are, and he wanted to win, but unlike every other goalie before or since—except Hašek—he was also an artist, and goal-tending was his art. And so he needed to play up to, and live up to, his art. If he couldn't—if he felt sick or injured and couldn't be at his best;

if an opponent was too good in some way and would get in the way of him expressing his art—he didn't want to play. Sometimes, especially later in his career, that was a problem. But at this moment in the mid-1950s, he had a more pressing problem.

Oftentimes, someone uses style to hide an absence of substance, and if you're able to get others to focus on that style, maybe they won't notice you aren't any good. Unfortunately for Plante, the reverse was true for most of his goaltending life. His style and his weirdnesses got in the way of others seeing how good he was. A guy who knits, wears a toque, and dons a mask was simply hard to take seriously, It had gotten slightly better for him. His critics had even noticed that the year before—1954–55—his goals against average was 2.12, higher only than those of Sawchuk and the Leafs' goalie, Harry Lumley. Yet after the season, when there were rumours that Sawchuk might be traded and Canadiens GM Frank Selke was asked if he was interested, Selke didn't say, "No, we've got our guy in Plante." He said he *would* be interested. Plante still would need to prove himself. But soon his teammates, the fans, the media, and even Selke and Blake would learn what Plante always knew—that difference is acceptable, if you're good.

The 1955–56 Canadiens had 16 players on their roster: three lines, two sets of defence, two spares, and a goalie. Nine of them—every player on the top two lines, two defencemen, and a goalie—and their coach, are in the Hall of Fame.

When Toe Blake's players talked of him as a coach then and talked of him later, they used the same word. He was *demanding*. It meant that he pushed them—but, well, as they almost admitted, maybe at times they needed to be pushed. It meant they respected him. It meant that he had in his mind what they could be—as a team, and each individual as a player—and if they could be that and do that, then why didn't they? All the time? It meant they liked him but couldn't quite bring themselves to say that, or even think that.

During the 1955–56 season, Scotty was still working at Sherwin-Williams and eating his lunch early so he could watch some of the Canadiens' practices, yet his boss wasn't always asking him to pick up the order forms now, so he couldn't be there as often. But still he had the chance to watch Blake. "He ran a good practice," Scotty says. For a lot of players, practice wasn't much more than time between games, where they had a chance to be with their friends, have some fun, work up a little sweat, and build up a thirst and an appetite for the rest of the day. But for the Canadiens—if the Rocket was always serious, and Blake was the same, even in practice, then what right did anyone else have not to push hard?

"In those days, most guys just stood around at practice," Scotty says. "Toe didn't run practice like a drillmaster, but he got them moving. He never wanted to do just drills. He used to say, 'Drills aren't game situations, so why practise them?' He would do a lot of line rushes like every coach did, three-on-twos [a forward line against a defence pair]. But he used to say, 'When guys are fresh, they can make nice plays. Have them skate up and back once without the puck, tire them out a bit before they make their rushes. That's a real game situation.' So he had them go up and back maybe three or four times."

In today's game, with thirty-five- to forty-second shifts, those line rushes wouldn't make sense. The players stay on the ice *only* when they're fresh. They have to come off before they're tired. Because tired against fresh doesn't work.

"He was also a real stickler about offsides," Scotty recalls. Blake hated it when his players went offside. They'd have possession of the puck, they'd be moving towards their opponent's net, then play would stop with an offside, there'd be a faceoff, then they might lose possession. So, during practice, even when his players were onside but not by much, he'd blow his whistle. It drove his players crazy. "They'd yell, 'Hey, I wasn't offside!' He'd say, 'Why make it close? The blue line's like a cliff. Why fall over it?'" Scotty remembers.

"They used to scrimmage a lot too," he adds. Scrimmages can be just playtime. A coach runs short of ideas and drills, and time's not yet up—so, *let's scrimmage*. But Blake knew the team he had. "They had good players, so they had good, competitive scrimmages." When the puck was dropped, Blake knew it wasn't possible for the Rocket not to go after it, and Henri, and Moore, and Béliveau would do the same, and so on and so on. It didn't matter whether it was 8:30 at night in a game, or 10 in the morning in prac- tice—they would all compete. Line rushes aren't the only game situa- tions. *Competition* is a game situation. So they practised that too.

Years later, after he had retired and Scotty became the coach, Blake would once each season travel with the team on a West Coast swing. During one particular game, Henri Richard had the puck, and Ralph Backstrom, who had joined the Canadiens in the late 1950s as the team's third centre, and who by this time had been traded by the Canadiens to L.A., was chasing him. Richard turned one way, then sharply another, speeding up, slowing down, Backstrom always on his heels. Many sec- onds passed. Seeing what was happening, it was as if suddenly all the other players on the ice, on both teams, decided to stop and watch. Neither Richard nor Backstrom would give up—two great, tireless skaters and unrelenting competitors. When the game was over, Blake talked about that moment. "It was just the way it was in practice every day. Every day," he said, his eyes welling up.

"Toe wasn't a long practice guy," Scotty says. "He would practise maybe 45 minutes to an hour. But [at] a quick tempo." Every Tuesday, almost always either Wednesday or Thursday, and always on Friday. "And always at 10. Even if they played the night before, they never devi- ated from ten o'clock." Among the players, the only exception to their practice tempo was Harvey. To him, it *did* matter if it was 10 in the morning or 8:30 at night, but his teammates knew and Blake knew that at 8:30 p.m. no one competed harder.

On Friday afternoons, Blake would always be in his office upstairs at the Forum. Later, when Scotty was coaching junior in Montreal in the early 1960s, he used to visit him there. "Toe had his ritual. When practise was over, he'd walk down Sainte Catherine Street to his tavern at Guy, have lunch, and then walk back. He was always in his office on Friday afternoons."

Toe Blake's Tavern was part of a ritual for Scotty's championship teams in the 1970s as well. The morning after each Cup win, Montreal mayor Jean Drapeau would issue a press release which always included the same words: "The parade will follow its usual route." With a day to kill before the parade, before the team party that same night, all the players would gather at Toe Blake's Tavern at noon on that first post-Cup day, and sit with him in a back room and drink beer. As every player knew, deep in his bones, you "don't change the luck." (Even if, at this moment, the luck was already safely in the bank for another year.)

When Scotty walked into Blake's office on those Friday afternoons, Toe had sheets of paper spread out on his desk. "It was full, because he had all these game summaries. The league didn't create the stats they do now. But he used to keep these sheets and study them. He was always looking to see who was on the ice for goals. And he was a great matchup guy. He'd have certain guys play against certain guys."

So, on his sheets, if he saw that someone was always on the ice when goals were scored, the other stats didn't matter, and it didn't matter what he had seen from behind the bench; he must have missed something. The sheets said so. "I remember one Friday he said to me, 'Are you coming to the game tomorrow night?' I said, 'Sure.' He said, 'Good, because your friend isn't going to play.'" Scotty had come to know Terry Harper, a new young defenceman on the team. "But the Canadiens were having a hard time against Detroit that year, and Toe decided to take a hard look at things, [asking,] 'Why are we not beating them?'" Right there on his sheets, in the details of so many of the goals the Wings had scored, was Harper's name. "He didn't play that next night."

In practice, Blake also worked on the power play. This was a low-scoring era, and a matchup time in the league. It was hard to score against three good checkers, even for three good offensive players. A power play might be the difference in winning or losing a game, and no team in the league had as many scorers as the Canadiens. Because the shifts were longer back then, one power-play unit might stay out the whole time. It would be Béliveau's line, but with a few adaptations. Béliveau would remain at centre and Olmstead at left wing, but Geoffrion would drop back to the right point; then Harvey would move to left defence, to the left point and the Rocket would take Geoffrion's place on right wing. So it was Béliveau, Richard, and Olmstead up front, Geoffrion and Harvey on the points. It was a very scary power play.

The plan was simple. The puck would go into the left corner for Olmstead. The other team's four defenders would form a box to protect the zone in front of their net. Béliveau would position himself in the middle of that box, close enough to the net and to each defender to bother them, but not close enough for them to leave the box to check him. If Béliveau was open, Olmstead would get him the puck. If not, he would pass it back to Harvey and Harvey would look for Geoffrion. If Geoffrion was moving towards the net—with his shot, another scary sight—he'd get the puck to him. If Geoffrion stayed at the point, Harvey would pass it to him for his big shot, and Béliveau would move to the net to deflect the shot or pick up a rebound. And all the time—circling, hovering, ready to pounce—was the Rocket.

That season, the Canadiens scored 66 times on the power play, almost one-third of all of their goals—that was 17 more than Detroit, who had the second-highest tally. Of his 47 goals, Béliveau scored 19 on the power play, the Rocket had 13 out of his 38, and Geoffrion 12 out of 29. The Canadiens' power play would prove to be too successful for its own good. In the NHL at this time, a penalized player served out his entire penalty no matter whether the other team scored or not. One night that season, with two Bruins players in the box, Béliveau himself scored three goals in 44 seconds. At the end of the season, the rule was changed, and a penalized player returned to the ice after a goal was scored. But that was at the end of the season.

Two lines that could score, an unmatchable power play, the Rocket, Harvey, and Blake—and so the season began. The Canadiens won their first four games, the Wings lost their first three. The two teams met for the first time at the end of October in a home-and-home, with the Canadiens winning in Montreal and the teams tying in Detroit. At the midway point of the schedule, after 35 games, the Canadiens had gone 22–6–7 (for 51 points) and the Wings 11–11–13 (35 points). Then the Wings started to win, but the Canadiens began to win more. The previous two years, the Canadiens had finished second behind the Wings, first by 7 points and then, after Richard's suspension, by 2. This season, with no suspensions and no riots, in their last 27 games the Canadiens lost only 4 times, finishing the year in first place with a record of 45–15–10 and 100 points—24 points ahead of the Wings.

And that was only the regular season.

In the first round of the playoffs, the Canadiens beat the Rangers four games to one, outscoring them 24–9. They would meet the Wings, who had beaten Toronto, in the final. Montreal won the first two games at home and the Wings took the first game in Detroit; then the Canadiens won the second on the road and finished the Wings off at home in Game 5. Four games to one; 18 goals to 9. In the final series alone, Béliveau, Geoffrion, and Olmstead, in five games, combined for 24 points.

The two-horse race proved not to be. The Canadiens accelerated through the finish line; the Wings finished up the track.

CHAPTER SEVEN

"I got the call in July," Scotty recalls. It was from Sam.

"I never expected to go into hockey full time. I wasn't at home waiting for my phone to ring. But he calls and asks if I'd go up and see him at the Forum. I remember like it was yesterday. He said, 'How's your job going?' I said, 'I think I'm doing okay. I'm in my second year, I'm training to be a salesman. It's a two-year program. You've got to learn all these numbers. There are some good benefits, and you get a commission, and you don't have an office so you can be on your own.'

"Then he told me the Junior Canadiens were going to move to Ottawa, and would I be interested in joining him as the assistant coach and manager? He asked me, 'How much money do you make?' and I said, 'I just got a raise from $3,600 and now I'm making $3,900.' And he said, 'That sounds pretty good. This would be a bit of an improvement. The job I'm offering is $4,200.'" Scotty laughs. "Later I kept saying to myself, 'I should've said I was making $4,900.' But I didn't care about the money. Then Sam asked me, 'Do you have a car?' I told him I didn't because my parents never had one. And he said, 'Well, you're going to need a car.'"

It was 1956. Scotty was 22, and for the first time in his life he would be living on his own. He would have a car, and—more amazingly, something he'd never dared even imagine—he'd have a full-time job in hockey. For the Montreal Canadiens. With Sam.

There were so few real jobs in hockey. There were only six NHL teams. Team owners were usually also team presidents, and sometimes they were general managers too. A GM might have an assistant. A coach coached alone. A trainer looked after the team's equipment—sharpened skates and dealt with a player's routine injuries, sometimes with an assistant. With only one goalie on a team's roster, an assistant trainer might also be the emergency backup in the event of a mid-game injury, and might fill the other net in practice. Minor pro teams also had owners, managers, coaches, and trainers, but there weren't many of them; and senior and junior teams had full-time jobs only for the six or seven months of a hockey season. There were always scouting jobs, and as long as you were only looking for a few hundred bucks a year, a standing-room pass, and the chance to drop names and play big shot with your buddies, you were fine. A living wage was a different matter. But for Scotty, this job in Ottawa might really lead to something, and then to something else.

None of this was yet in his mind, of course, when he said yes to Sam. Nor was it when he told his parents, though he might have said a little something about the future when he gave them the news. Hockey was what he loved to do. He was never going to love selling paint. He might be good at it one day. He might memorize all the numbers and make a little game of doing that and amaze all his customers. He might get lots more raises, take some more college courses that the company would require of him to qualify for further promotions. He might build a second-generation Canadian life for himself that was even better than what his first-generation immigrant parents had been able to provide, and create for his own kids the possibility of something better still. But truly, for him, what could be better than this? A chance to work for Frank Selke Sr., who had been lured to Montreal with the promise and for the precise purpose of building what was undeniably the future of any Cup-aspiring NHL team—a farm system—and for Scotty to be able to help him do that. And for Scotty to work directly with the team's resident young genius and Selke's heir apparent, Sam Pollock, who knew him and understood him so well because he saw so much of himself in him. Someone who embodied what Scotty had to hope was real—that you *could* have a job in the NHL at the highest level, not because you were a former player but because you were smarter, more dedicated, and more determined than anyone else. And if that wasn't enough, for Scotty to work for the Montreal Canadiens—the now Stanley Cup champion Montreal Canadiens. The best team in the world, with the game's most compelling and emblematic star, with a roster of players that was only going to get better and with a wave of juniors that would be ready to replace them and keep the team at the top when they were needed.

In Ottawa, with Sam, he would be creating something new. This would be a different kind of junior team, because the Canadiens were facing some different circumstances. At the time, five provinces produced almost all of the NHL's players: Saskatchewan, Manitoba, and to a lesser extent Alberta in the west; Ontario and Quebec in Central Canada, with Ontario developing nearly twice as many players as Quebec—almost half of the entire league. No players came from the territories in the far north, and hardly any from B.C. or Atlantic Canada.

The Canadiens had teams in the top junior leagues in four of those provinces: the Regina Pats in Saskatchewan, the St. Boniface Canadiens in Manitoba, the Peterborough Petes (and Fort William Canadiens) in Ontario, and various teams in Quebec, mostly in Montreal—the Junior Canadiens, Royals, and Nationals. And their approach had been working. Before Sam and Scotty arrived in Ottawa, in the seven years between 1949 and 1956, Canadiens-sponsored junior teams had reached the Memorial Cup final seven times. In 1950, the Junior Canadiens had faced the Pats—an all-Montreal final. Regina and St. Boniface would continue to do well—the Canadiens would see to that—but there were challenges in Ontario and Quebec, each for a different reason.

For Montreal, Ontario would always be a losing battle. This was Leafs country. Toronto had the province's only NHL team, and their games were broadcast everywhere. The logistics of the province also hugely favoured the Leafs. Junior teams travelled by bus on winter roads, so any city much more than a hundred miles from any other was considered too distant to have a team in the same league. NHL regulations also prohibited teams from having a junior affiliate within fifty miles of another NHL team's city. This meant that, for the Ontario Hockey Association (OHA), teams not sponsored by the Leafs were located in a geographic arc around Toronto—Montreal in Peterborough; Boston in Barrie; New York in Guelph; Detroit in Hamilton; Chicago in St. Catharines—while at the hub in Toronto, in by far the province's biggest city with by far the greatest number of players, the Leafs had two powerhouses: the Marlies and St. Mike's. The province's other larger population centres—Ottawa, Kingston, London, and Windsor—had no teams at all.

The Canadiens had to find a way to compete. This was getting harder to do, and would likely get harder still. The Marlies had won the Memorial Cup two straight years, 1955 and 1956, with super-teams which included players that would form the core of the Cup-winning Toronto sides of the early 1960s—Bob Pulford, Carl Brewer, Bob Baun, Bob Nevin, and Billy Harris. And St. Mike's, which for anxious parents offered the unique recruiting advantage of a Catholic school as safe refuge for their small-town, mining-town kids in a big city, had recently won the battle for the north's two most prized prospects—Frank Mahovlich from Schumacher, Ontario, and Dave Keon from Noranda, Quebec, who themselves would become stars on those same 1960s Leafs teams. Even years earlier, Doug Harvey's brother Howie—the most promising goalie of his time—had left NDG to go to St. Mike's. The Canadiens needed to do better in Ontario to keep up, and Peterborough wouldn't be enough.

At the same time, in Quebec, Selke's success in building his farm system had brought growing pains. Quebec's senior and junior leagues were both in trouble. With only six NHL teams and a smattering of minor pro teams across Canada, it meant there were lots of good post-junior players that had no place to play. In a time before TV filled our living rooms, the best hockey team the vast majority of Canadians would ever see was the senior team playing across town at the local rink. And the best players were those who grew up next door, who as kids scored goals playing on your own son's team, who went off to play junior and, for some reason, as the local lore goes—because a coach didn't like him or a knee never healed—came back home to work in the hardware store on Main Street and pick up a few bucks as the hero of the town's senior team. For decades on Friday nights and Sunday afternoons it was standing room only for town-versus-town games across Canada. Then Jean Béliveau came along and presented a problem.

He was of junior age, but he played for the Quebec Aces in the province's senior league. The Aces played in the Colisée, which held more than 10,000 people—and the money from the tickets the fans bought found its way into the pockets of the Aces' owners with very little being passed on to its players. This was senior hockey. Players played for the love of the game, for the town, for the cheers, and for the party after. There was no rule that teams couldn't pay players more than a customary, modest amount, but there had never been a reason. Then Béliveau showed up, and he was just so much better than the rest of the league, and everybody knew that. His teammates and opponents, the thousands of fans now filling the Colisée who had never been there before—everybody could see it with their own eyes. NHL salaries weren't that much more than an everyday average wage; the Aces had the money and the reason to pay him what NHL stars were being paid. So Béliveau stayed in Quebec after his junior years were over, as Frank Selke, Dick Irvin, and the Canadiens fans watched the Detroit Red Wings leave their NHL team in the dust. The Canadiens owned Béliveau's *pro* rights, but because the Quebec league was deemed *amateur* he could avoid the Canadiens and play with the Aces as long as he wanted.

The Canadiens seemed to have no choice: they would have to pay Béliveau much more than any unproven young player had ever been paid—and even more than they were paying the Rocket—and deal with the consequences. But they came up with another solution. They bought the Quebec league—the whole league—and changed its designation so it was no longer an amateur league, but a pro league. And because the Canadiens owned Béliveau's pro rights, he couldn't play for the Aces, he could only play for them. The Canadiens got their man. But in doing so, they created a new problem.

Except for Montreal, the other cities and towns in the QSHL—Chicoutimi, Sherbrooke, Valleyfield, Shawinigan Falls—were much smaller than Quebec City, had much smaller arenas, and couldn't afford to support a minor pro team—especially one in a league now without Béliveau. Teams began to drop out, and junior hockey was in no position to fill the gap. It had never established the same tradition of local passion and support that senior hockey had. Additionally, as Selke developed his junior farm system in the province, Montreal-based teams became much better than those in the rest of Quebec. They got the best players from Montreal *and* they got the stars from these other towns and cities, which further starved local interest in their teams. At the same time, this had an adverse effect on the Junior Canadiens too—with little competition, the players weren't being pushed to improve in these prime development years as much as they needed to be. The team had become *too* dominant in Quebec. And so the Quebec junior league shrank, then disbanded. The Junior Canadiens now needed a league to play in. Ottawa was Sam's answer.

They would be called the Ottawa Junior Canadiens the first season. Every year after that—when they played half their home games across the Ottawa River in a new arena built in Hull, Quebec—they would be the Hull-Ottawa Junior Canadiens. (To confuse matters further, when they later became a minor pro team, they were called the Hull-Ottawa Canadiens.) Located in Ontario *and* in Quebec, but distant from junior and senior teams in both provinces, they played truncated schedules in both the Ontario Hockey Association junior and senior leagues, and in the Eastern Professional Hockey League (EPHL), the successor to the Quebec senior league. Twenty games in the EPHL and OHA senior league, all on the road, and twenty-eight games in the OHA junior league—two at home and two away against each of the other seven teams. Sixty-eight games in total. Then the playoffs. Their junior games would count in the OHA's standings, and also towards what Scotty recalls as a "fictitious" championship, the Laurier Cup, which was more a marketing device than something to aspire to—the winner being the team with the most points in games involving the Junior Canadiens. As the de facto Quebec junior champions, there now being no Quebec junior league, the Junior Canadiens also played the OHA winners in the Memorial Cup playoffs. For the games against senior teams, they would add a few slightly older players. One year they even played five in-season games against NHL teams—something impossible to imagine today—and two against a touring Soviet team, the Moscow Selects.

They were like a barnstorming team. The Junior Canadiens didn't fit anywhere, so they played everywhere. They were allowed their special status because of the influence of the Montreal Canadiens with the other NHL teams, the reputation of Frank Selke among his peers, the working relationships that Sam had been able to develop, and because they were the most exciting junior team in the country. They had their usual strong core of players from Quebec: Bobby Rousseau, Gilles Tremblay, and a short, quick, puck-handling defenceman, Claude Ruel, who—after an eye injury ended his career—would coach the Canadiens to a Stanley Cup in 1969 and be Scotty's assistant coach for five more Cups during the 1970s. They also had Claude Richard—Maurice and Henri's younger brother. But there were players from elsewhere in Canada too: Jerry Wilson, their top prospect, from Winnipeg; Murray Balfour, from Regina; and Ralph Backstrom, from Kirkland Lake, a gold-mining town in northern Ontario.

It's also likely the other NHL teams accommodated the Junior Canadiens because they realized if this experiment failed, the Canadiens would find a new solution that would involve building up the Petes even more, and reconstructing the Quebec junior league with the Canadiens sponsoring even more teams, developing even more players, and making the big team even harder to beat. An outlier team in Ottawa seemed the least of all evils.

Scotty didn't exactly hit the ground running in Ottawa. "It was a completely new team," he recalls, the memory of the challenge still in his voice. It was July, and before there could be a new team on the ice it meant arranging billets—none of the players were from Ottawa—it meant making contact with schools, and it meant selling the team to fans, sponsors, and to the media. And there were only Sam and Scotty to do it.

"We hit the streets, and this was the middle of summer, and we were going out to sell advertising for the program. So the two of us met every morning and went over our possible leads." Scotty laughs. "But little did I know, it took me a month or so to realize it, but all the big accounts, the ones that might buy an ad, Sam kept for himself. I had all the little guys. The guys that sharpened skates that might take a tiny ad. And I mean, I was getting pretty discouraged. The first week or so, I'm just going to these little places and ringing doorbells, and I'm not coming up with much. I'm beginning to wonder if this is for me. I just couldn't stand doing that."

Then he brings himself back a bit. "I didn't like doing it, anyways. We'd meet up at night. We'd always go for dinner and he would review his list, and I would review mine. Sam never got discouraged. But he was a businessman. He was a hockey guy, but he had this business acumen. He was way ahead of his time. I didn't know what I was doing." It turned out that selling paint at Sherwin-Williams probably wouldn't have been his best career.

It also turned out that while the two of them could build a great junior team, they could never make it a *local* team. And they never made it seem like a real team. Sure, they played games, they had referees, they kept score, points were awarded, the Laurier Cup was at stake, but the games had no meaning. The Junior Canadiens, no matter what, *were* going to play the OHA champions in the Memorial Cup playoffs—that had been part of the deal—because now there was no Quebec junior league. They didn't have to earn their way as other teams did. Their "games" were a show, not a contest.

For the Canadiens, the whole purpose of what they were doing was to put their best 17-to-19-year-old players into the deep end of the pool to force them to swim. To see who sped off and left the others in their wake and might have a future, and who drowned. They were creating a competitive test, and a test of character. Great for the Canadiens, not so great for the fans. Attendance was poor, and program ads never got much easier to sell.

Sam was still only 30 years old. "He was moving up the ladder," Scotty recalls. "Besides running the junior team, he was really the Canadiens' director of player personnel. Frank Selke was getting on. Ken Reardon was his assistant, but he never travelled like Sam. Sam was on the road all the time. He never stopped. He never got married until 1961. He just ran all over the place. Watching pro. Watching junior." The Canadiens had a new AHL team in Rochester which they split with the Leafs—each team supplying half the players; each team owning an equal percentage of the franchise. But Sam knew that authority is one thing and power is another, and he also knew that he who shows up rules the day. Ottawa was less than a five-hour drive away from Rochester, and—lake-effect snow or not—Sam always showed up. Sometimes the Leafs didn't, no matter that Toronto was only four hours away. "Sam would leave me with the team in Ottawa," Scotty recalls. "I must have coached two-thirds of our regular-season games and I ran the practices because he was always either going to Rochester, or to Montreal, or to Shawinigan, [as] the Canadiens also had a team there." But when Sam needed to be with the junior team, he seemed always to be there too.

Scotty had known Sam for almost a decade by this time, since Sam had been a part-timer organizing park leagues and chasing prospects for the Canadiens, and Scotty had been one of them. But it was during their two years together in Ottawa that Scotty got to know him as well as Sam ever allowed anyone to know him. "Sam was very private," Scotty recalls. "He was a very, very private person. He was always working. Always planning ahead. Always looking to the future. All the time."

Sam got to be comfortable enough with Scotty that, when the season was over, Scotty inked into his calendar what he knew would soon come. "He'd call me up every summer," Scotty remembers. "We were both single, and we'd go on vacations together. Once, we went to Atlantic City because a friend of his, Irving Liverman, who used to handle all the appliances for the players, was attending a trade convention there. We spent a week with him. Another time we went to a place in Pennsylvania. And if Sam was asking me to go on a trip, I'm not going to say no.

"Another summer we went down to Hampton Beach, New Hampshire, because a friend of mine that Sam knew—a hockey player, Bucky Hollingworth—owned a hotel there." Hollingworth, also from Verdun, had played with Scotty on Norman's Spartons when they won the Quebec midget championship. Scotty pauses. "I don't think Sam had a lot of close friends. He didn't keep up with a lot of people. It was all hockey, but it was more the economic part. I think he recognized early in his career that coaching wasn't consuming enough for him, and he gravitated away from it."

When the Junior Canadiens' first season in Ottawa finally began, the team hit the road. They had to fit into the schedules of three different leagues, and so they had no regular schedule of their own. They had to travel distances as far as from St. Catharines, Ontario, to Chicoutimi, Quebec—more than twelve hours by bus, often on two-lane roads on which snow-clearing equipment was either rudimentary or non-existent. But the players, freed from school—and Scotty, freed from the office—were living their dreams.

On Saturday nights, with no game of their own, Sam and Scotty often drove to Montreal to watch the Canadiens, who were on their way to the second of five straight Cups. On the rare occasion when Scotty wasn't on the road, the first year he camped out in a room he had in a house the team's trainer Les Hynes, and his wife, Ethel, had rented on Clemow Avenue. The next year he moved a few blocks south to a boarding house filled with football players from the Ottawa Rough Riders—Gilles Archambault, Merv Collins, Lou Bruce, and future CFL Hall of Famer Kaye Vaughan. It was at 198 Holmwood Avenue, just across the road and a few houses down from Julia Binks and Ella Wyman, two elderly sisters who lived at 211 Holmwood. Their widowed younger sister Ethel Campbell, who lived in Toronto with her daughter and son-in-law and their three kids, visited them each year for a few weeks—twice with one of her grandsons, during the same years that Scotty lived on the street. That grandson was me.

Having to play in three different leagues meant that the Junior Canadiens played tired from October to March, but still won most of their games. Then, dropping their senior schedule and playing only in the junior playoffs, they could travel less, rest a little, and focus. Led by Jerry Wilson, Ralph Backstrom, Bobby Rousseau, Murray Balfour, and Gilles Tremblay, they dominated the OHA champion Guelph Biltmores in the Eastern Canada playoffs and advanced to the Memorial Cup final against the Flin Flon Bombers. The team boarded a train in Ottawa and two days later arrived in Winnipeg. The first three games of the series were to be played in Flin Flon, except Sam refused to leave Winnipeg, insisting that the games be played there.

The standoff lasted for three days. Finally, Sam was told by the Canadian Amateur Hockey Association, which was responsible for the championship, to go to Flin Flon and play, or go home. The players, Sam, and Scotty piled into taxis, and after more than 10 hours on roads of all sorts and conditions—all of them bad—they arrived in a town that disliked them even more than they had a few days earlier. "We went through The Pas," Scotty recalls. "I mean, they were dirt roads. I don't know why the hell we took taxis. Because that's the way it was, I guess."

In Flin Flon, they settled into the biggest and best accommodations in town—the dormitories at the mine, whose amenities weren't much less comfortable than those the team had stayed in all winter in the small-town Main Street hotels of Ontario and Quebec. But Scotty had learned growing up on the Avenues in Verdun that if your inside space isn't so wonderful, you go outside and make something of it. Flin Flon's Community Arena had been built in the mid-1930s, a few years after the mine opened, and artificial ice was added in 1950. It held 1,141 people, and 200 more seats were added for the series, but more than 2,000 fans jammed inside for the games. One of them, future Hall of Famer Bobby Clarke, was just seven years old. The Bombers won the first game, the Junior Canadiens the next two. Today, in a display case in the front foyer of the Whitney Forum in Flin Flon, built a year after the series ended to replace the old arena, is a program opened to the centre page that shows the rosters of both teams. The player names are impressive, but even more impressive are the two names that appear at the bottom of the list of Junior Canadiens:

Coach: Sammy Pollock

Assistant: Scotty Bowman

Two men who would become the best general manager and the best coach in NHL history.

After a similar 10-hour drive over similar roads into southern Saskatchewan, the series resumed at Regina's Exhibition Stadium. The Bombers won the next two games, during the second of which Sam was thrown out for arguing with the referee, Dutch Van Deelen (who later would become the NHL's supervisor of officials), leaving Scotty in charge of the bench. The Junior Canadiens took Game 6 to tie the series, but Flin Flon won the seventh game, 3–2. Flin Flon, population 10,000—a town that was named after Josiah Flintabbatey Flonatin, the hero of the dime novel *The Sunless City*; a town that existed only because of the copper and zinc deposits nearby, and was almost invisible in the endless expanse of rock, trees, and lakes of the Canadian Shield—was the Memorial Cup champion, the junior champion of Canada.

The next season, 1957–58, Wilson and Balfour were gone, J.C. Tremblay had arrived, and the team—playing out of the new Hull Arena as well as the Ottawa Auditorium—was now known as the Hull-Ottawa Junior Canadiens. The team defeated the OHA champion Toronto Marlies in the Eastern Canada final—decisively, outscoring them 26–9—then played the Regina Pats for the Memorial Cup.

The Pats had on their team future Montreal Canadiens Red Berenson, Bill Hicke, Dave Balon, and Terry Harper, but for the Junior Canadiens, this time the result was different. They were a little better than they had been the year before, and the games were played in Ottawa and Hull, with only a short taxi ride on smooth roads between them. It was Sam's second Memorial Cup championship win, and Scotty's first.

For them, everything seemed to be in place for another year. Then Ted Kennedy resigned as coach of the Peterborough Petes. Kennedy was only eight years Scotty's senior, but he seemed much older. He had begun playing with the Leafs at age 17 during the war years, became a regular at 18, the team's captain at 23, retired at 29, then came back for a half-season at 31 before retiring again in 1957. The next season he coached Peterborough. The Petes were a new team in the OHA, known then as the "TPT Petes" for the Toronto-Peterborough Transport Company, the team's main sponsor. Their first season they had finished where expansion teams always finished—last. When Kennedy took over they more than doubled their number of points, and made the playoffs. But Kennedy found junior travel almost as demanding as travel in the NHL, and now having an additional full-time job as well—with Toronto-Peterborough Transport—it was too much. When the season ended, he stepped aside, and Sam asked Scotty if he was interested in the job. This time he would be the head coach. He would run his own show.

When Scotty arrived in Peterborough he needed a place to stay, and again Ken Brown took care of him. "He had moved from Montreal and he was selling real estate there," Scotty recalls. This was the same Ken Brown who had outbid Norman Bracegirdle's free toaster to sign Scotty for the Verdun Canadiens. One more coincidence that in hockey isn't really a coincidence, but is instead part of the game's web—which begins with street hockey games and neighbourhood parks, extends to local rinks, and spreads to who knows where through stories and memories, especially if, like Scotty, you remember everything. And especially if, like Scotty, you were brought up to understand that no little moment or seemingly small encounter in your past is less important than any seemingly big moment or person in your present. Ken Brown, it turned out, like the character in *Forrest Gump*, would pop up again and again in Scotty's life. "He was still living until just a few years ago," Scotty says of Brown. "He was in his nineties when he died out in Vancouver. He was quite a guy. A real sales guy."

Ted Kennedy also took care of Scotty. "I got to know him very well. He was a very humble man. A very nice man. When I was first named coach, he gave me his phone number and we talked, and he told me not to hesitate to call him, and I took him up on it. He also said to me, 'You'll love this town. It's a great hockey city. The fans are terrific.'" And they were terrific, but for Scotty this also represented something new. Now he would be coaching a team where there *were* fans, where winning and losing and league standings mattered, where his team had to earn its way into the playoffs and on to the Eastern Canada final. In Peterborough he had fans he needed to satisfy, and he had to do it without a team of hand-picked all-stars from across the country. Scotty now had a team that, like every other team, was both strong enough to win and weak enough to lose every game.

He did have one advantage. Even though the Petes had finished fifth out of seven teams the year before and barely made the playoffs, he had taken over a Kennedy-coached team. "They were very well prepared," he remembers. "They knew how to play." Kennedy had won the Stanley Cup five times with the Leafs, twice as the team's captain. "He was some player," Scotty says, admiration in his voice, "and a really good two-way player, along the lines of Bobby Clarke. Scored clutch goals. Terrific on faceoffs. Ultra competitive. It was always about accountability with him; his players had to play both ends of the rink. He told me all about the Petes players he had, the ones I had now, and he'd say, 'You'll like this guy because . . . ,' and he'd give some reason, or 'Watch this guy. He won't help you much in the playoffs because he doesn't know how to play without the puck.'"

Hap Day had been Kennedy's coach with the Leafs. "Day was very tough on fundamentals. The Leafs weren't a high-scoring team. They didn't have the firepower of the Canadiens. They played on the edge. And they were big. They could really run the game, control it, and play it the way they wanted to." The Petes weren't the Leafs—they were only an average team—but they could still play Kennedy's way. It was how they could compete.

"I remember Sam always used to say, 'I really like the guys who light the light.'" These were the guys who could score. Checking and defence were about hard work and commitment, Sam believed. Anybody could do that. But scoring took a special skill. "Maybe it was because hockey was so tight then," Scotty says, thinking back on the NHL of that time. "There wasn't a lot of scoring in the '40s and '50s." As a kid, Scotty himself had been a one-way player, not much interested in anything but going to the net, deflecting shots, snapping in rebounds. "Then, when I went with Sam to coach the Junior Canadiens, we had a powerhouse. We'd score in double figures in maybe 50 per cent of our games." So Scotty's way of seeing the game didn't have to change.

But Peterborough was different. This was no candy-store team. Scotty had only one big goal scorer, Wayne Connelly. Could he try to teach the others to "light the light" when they had never been scorers before, and hope they might learn? Was he going to coach his players to play wide open, again hoping they might learn, and almost certainly lose? As a GM, by all means you seek out the players who can "light the light." But as a coach, you have to know the players you have, and play the best way *they* can play. No fooling yourself. You have a game to win. Fire-wagon hockey only works if you have fire-wagon players.

Sam had been his teacher, and so too had Frank Selke, Dick Irvin, and Toe Blake. In Peterborough, he had a new teacher. From Ted Kennedy he learned even more the importance of a two-way game, of fundamentals. Of faceoffs. And Kennedy was the master of these things. If you win a faceoff, he knew, you win control. If you have control, the other team doesn't. Everything begins there.

"I called Ted one day, and a few days later he came to the Peterborough arena. We used to practice at 4:30. He put on his skates and came onto the ice and said to me, 'You just run your practice,' and he took the centremen down to one end and worked with them on different things about faceoffs. Afterwards, he said to me, 'They're only kids, but they're fine.'"

What Scotty learned in Peterborough was not so much a marriage of two styles—the Canadiens' and the Leafs'—as the creation of a way of thinking. Too basic to be considered a philosophy: *Know what you've got. Get your players to do what they can do. Find a way.* It was essential learning for Scotty and helped him immensely when he took over St. Louis, an expansion team made up of mostly minor-league players. It even served him well with the great Canadiens teams of the 1970s. And it all started in Peterborough, with Ted Kennedy, when Scotty was 25.

At his first training camp with the Petes, other than the players he inherited from Kennedy, one player caught his attention: Jimmy Roberts. "He had been playing Junior B in Peterborough," Scotty recalls. "The guy who ran the B team, Red Creighton, was still upset that a Junior A team had taken over the city, and Jimmy was one of his best players and he didn't want to lose him. Sam came down to see the camp, we were picking and choosing different guys, and, of course, Jimmy stood out. But he was 18 and a lot of the other guys were 16. Still, we wanted to sign him for the A team, but Red Creighton wanted $250 for his release. I remember like it was yesterday. And Sam wasn't interested in buying releases at the time, especially for local players. We said to Jim, 'You just keep practising, we're trying to work something out.' And Jimmy said, 'Mr. Pollock, what's the issue again?' And Sam told him, 'They want $250 for your release and we think it's a little high.' So Jimmy said, 'Mr. Pollock, I really want to play on this team. I'll buy my own release. I'll pay him the money.' And Sam said, "Oh, no, no, we can't do that.' After Jimmy left, Sam said to me, 'I don't want to pay [for the release], but I want this guy on the team. I've never seen a player who wants to play like he does.'"

Roberts would play two years for the Petes, then after the Canadiens' hot prospects—Bobby Rousseau, Gilles Tremblay, J.C. Tremblay— moved on to Montreal's top minor pro team in the newly formed Eastern Professional Hockey League (EPHL), the Hull-Ottawa Canadiens, Roberts was sent to the Canadiens' other minor pro team, the Montreal Royals, that had on it veteran players who were on their way down. After four years in the minors, Roberts was brought up to the Canadiens. Later he joined Scotty in St. Louis, then rejoined him in Montreal. He played over 1,000 NHL games, and won five Stanley Cups.

The Petes continued their climb up the OHA standings that first season with Scotty in charge, finishing second, 21 points behind the St. Catharines Teepees whose roster included future NHLers Pat Stapleton, Vic Hadfield, Chico Maki, Wayne Hillman, Ray Cullen, Denis DeJordy, and Hall of Famer Stan Mikita. But in the playoffs, St. Catharines was upset by St. Mike's, who then advanced to play the Petes. The series went eight games, the final one at Maple Leaf Gardens.

"They made us play it at one in the afternoon during the week, so all the St. Mike's students could go," Scotty recalls, a hint of victim still in his voice. "There were 5,000 or 6,000 of them." The Petes won. For Scotty, this would be his third consecutive year in the Memorial Cup final. Peterborough's opponent was the Winnipeg Braves, with Ted Green, Gary Bergman, and Ernie Wakely. The series was played in Winnipeg and Brandon, Manitoba, and while the Petes won the first game, the Braves won the next four. "It was a tough series," Scotty recalls, and then says simply: "But the best team won."

During that first season with the Petes, Bobby Collins was playing for the Junior B team, but at 15 he was so promising that Scotty brought him up for some games with the Petes. During a pre-game warm-up, skating behind the net, he was hit by a shot and lost the sight in his right eye. A few years later, his younger sister Cathy (one of Bobby's 18 siblings) married Bob Gainey.

The next two years in Peterborough, Scotty was learning all the time, but with no milestone achievements to suggest that he was. After three straight years coaching in the Memorial Cup final, there wouldn't be a fourth in 1959–60. Connelly and Roberts were still there, as well as future NHLers Claude Larose and Barclay Plager, but the team wasn't good enough, and Scotty couldn't make them sufficiently better. The Petes finished fifth in the OHA, with 16 points fewer than the year before, and won one round of the playoffs before losing to St. Catharines, who would go on to win the Memorial Cup. The next year, 1960–61—now minus Connelly and Roberts—the team finished one position lower in sixth, had seven fewer points, and lost in the first round.

In his time in Peterborough, Scotty also learned to live on his own and to live off of the road. In Peterborough, he had a regular schedule. The team practised every day at 4:30, they had occasional games on weeknights, and played and travelled on weekends. But even for the Petes—the furthest east of the OHA teams—none of the other cities were that far or that difficult to get to. Montreal was now too far away to drop in for Saturday-night games with Sam, and there were no games to watch on TV except on Saturdays. So now he had all this other time he had never had before—time to have another life. But now what would that life be? Scotty did get to know some people in Peterborough—both inside and outside hockey. He spent some time with them, he went to movies, he read more often. His life was a work in progress. Then, before it could progress too far, he got another call from Sam.

The Montreal Royals, now of the Eastern Professional Hockey League (EPHL), still were drawing poorly in Montreal, and seeing no improvement ahead, Sam decided to move the team to North Bay. They would be called the Trappers. He'd asked Lou Passador, his top Eastern Canada scout, to be the team's general manager, and so he needed someone to replace Passador. This time, Scotty remembers, "Sam didn't offer me the job. He told me. He said, 'I'm putting you in as the head scout in Eastern Canada. It's going to be a better job.'" Scotty pauses. "And it was. A better-*paying* job." It took him a few months to learn the distinction.

Before he began, "Frank Selke Sr. called me into his office. He said, 'There are a couple of things I want to go over with you.' He was a pretty revered guy. He had been a scout, and had run the Leafs organization for Conn Smythe in Toronto. He said to me, 'When you're a scout, there are lots of temptations. You must be honourable.' I was 28 years old at the time. He said, 'I want to tell you a story . . .'"

Selke told him about a scout he'd once had in Toronto, when both the Leafs and Red Wings were going after future Leafs' captain George Armstrong. Armstrong was a teenager playing in Copper Cliff, in Northern Ontario, and there was a dispute over which team had done what first, and which team should own his rights. To resolve the disagreement, NHL president Clarence Campbell held a meeting in his office. Selke was at that meeting himself, with his scout and the Detroit people—and, as he told Scotty, his scout "lied to the president of the league, and they awarded Armstrong to us." To Toronto. Selke had won; he had gotten his player. Only later did he find out the truth about what his scout had done. "'You cannot do things this way,' [Selke] said to me," Scotty remembers. "Then he said to me again, 'You've got to be honourable.'"

Scotty would be the Canadiens' head scout for Eastern Canada from 1961 to 1963. "For two seasons," he says, "and I didn't like the job at all. I was never home. I lost contact with friends, guys I went to school with, guys I'd hang around with in Verdun. I was on the road all the time. I'd spend the whole month of November in Toronto—the whole month—at the King Edward Hotel. I stayed there and used it as a base, and every night I'd go somewhere to a game, and then drive back. Then I'd spend a month in Northern Quebec and Northern Ontario.

"It was no life. And I was too young. All the other head scouts were in their fifties and sixties. Bob Davidson [Leafs], Jack Humphries [Rangers], Baldy Cotton [Bruins], Bob Wilson [Black Hawks], Jimmy Skinner [Wings]." In the morning on each day he was in Toronto, he had another routine. "I'd go up to Maple Leaf Gardens. The Leafs would be practising. Bob Davidson would be there, Bob Wilson and Jack Humphries—they all lived in Toronto. Jimmy Skinner wouldn't be there much. He worked out of Hamilton. And we'd say to each other, 'Well, where are you going tonight?' And one guy would say, 'I'm going to Oshawa.' We didn't talk much about players. I remember once I think I said, 'I'm going up to Owen Sound to see this guy,' and one of the scouts said, 'You're wasting your time.' But I still went, he was a good player too. But we'd have a coffee and a sandwich in the little canteen there [in the Gardens], and then we'd go off."

Wherever they went, pretty much every team "had a guy" on the ground who was their local eyes and ears. "We called them 'bird dogs,'" Scotty says. "I had Stan Tallon, Dale's father, he ran an arena in Noranda." Dale Tallon later played many years in the NHL, and is now the general manager of the Florida Panthers. "But our main guy there was Ti-Zyme Renaud. He was a biscuit salesman. His territory was northern Quebec—Rouyn, Noranda, Malartic, Val-d'Or, Amos—so he did some scouting too. He got us Jacques Laperrière, Rogie Vachon, Serge [Savard]. And we had the reeve of Kirkland Lake, Len Baird. We gave them all $500 and a trip to training camp. We had a guy in Toronto, Curly Davies, who ran Shopsy's peewees"—a team sponsored by the Leafs, it not being odd at the time to coach a team related to one NHL organization, and be "a guy" for another. (Later, Curly Davies was briefly the coach of the Etobicoke Indians Junior Bs, where Robbie Irons and I were the goalies.) "And Detroit had a guy in Toronto, Jack Harper. He ran a couple of teams. The first time I met Roger Neilson was when he was coaching one of Harper's teams, Bick's Pickles." Later a coach for several NHL teams and a member of the Hall of Fame, Neilson soon became a "guy" for Scotty.

"Roger was a schoolteacher, [and] he was coaching Bick's Pickles and also a Junior B team in Aurora"—a town on the outskirts of Toronto, about an hour's drive north. "In the summer, he coached baseball. I met him at George Bell Arena. It had just opened. I remember like it was yesterday, because he had this decision to make. He had a playoff game at George Bell, and his other team had a big game in Aurora." Scotty laughs. "Roger gave me a tape—an audio tape, not a videotape—and I had to drive it from George Bell Arena in the middle of Toronto to Aurora and give it to the trainer of his team. Roger had taped some instructions for his players. It was about how they should play the game. And I did it." Scotty shakes his head.

"Roger was a unique guy. I'd have to call him, and the only time I could get him was between 7:30 and 7:45 in the morning. I had a 15-minute window. Oh yeah, because before that he had his *Globe and Mail* paper route. The kids on his hockey teams and baseball teams would help him; he had this old Volkswagen bus, and he had more than 700 papers. If I called him a bit early, he'd still be out delivering. If I was a little late, if I called at five to eight, he's gone, he's a teacher, and then I'm done until about 10 or 11 at night because after school he's got some game or practice to go to."

Later, Neilson became the coach and general manager of the Peterborough Petes, then an assistant coach and later head coach of Buffalo when Scotty ran the Sabres. Besides being remembered as a legendary character, Neilson is famous for his many innovations, including the use of video as a teaching and coaching device. His nickname was "Captain Video." But before he was Captain Video—as Scotty, his shuttle driver, can attest to—he was "Captain Audio."

It's also likely that it was Neilson who got me to Montreal. I met him first when I was 12, and through baseball, not hockey. I was playing on one team, Super-Pufft Popcorn, and Roger was coaching another, Parkway

Motors, in a Toronto league, and we could never beat them. To this day, when I drive along Roselawn Avenue on the northern edge of Eglinton Park in Toronto and look at the baseball diamond a few feet away, I cringe. It was the deciding game in a best-of-three playoff series. It was the bottom of the seventh inning, the last inning, and I was the pitcher. We were winning, 1–0, and they had a runner on third with one out. Roger called a squeeze play, his batter laid down the bunt, I fielded it and flipped it to our catcher, Eddie Rose, who applied the tag. The play was close, the runner was out . . . but was called safe. "Rabbit" Sharpe hit a home run in extra innings and won the game for Roger's team. Sixty years later, the kid who scored the tying run is *still* out. Not long after his so-called victory, Roger became Scotty's Toronto-area "guy."

At the time, scouting wasn't about driving around to see junior-age players. "It was about chasing young kids," he says. "I spent most of my time watching bantam players [then age 14]. Once they slipped past bantam, maybe first-year midget, I stopped watching them. You were trying to get them to play for your junior team—Peterborough was for the Ontario kids, Montreal for the Quebec kids." For an NHL team, if you signed one of these young players, he had to play for one of your teams. But this didn't give you his NHL rights; you could only secure those when a player was older and signed a "C" form and received a payment from the NHL team of $100—thus the *C*. But if you did sign a kid at this young age, by the time he was old enough to sign a "C" form his dreams were already so dressed up in the *bleu, blanc, et rouge* of the Canadiens or the blue and white of the Leafs that the game was over. He was already part of the program.

"Peterborough was also a good destination for kids because even though it was further away, we had a pretty good reputation for the kids going to school, as opposed to St. Catharines or Guelph," Scotty relates. "Because it's a big risk for a parent if your kid's leaving home at 15. But St. Mike's was tough to beat if there was a boy from Northern Ontario— especially a Catholic boy. And if you lived in the north you had to go somewhere to get the competition you needed to develop. You'd have a hard time ever convincing his parents to let him go to Toronto to a place other than St. Mike's. The parish priests were pretty persuasive. They had a network that was unbelievable. And Bob Davidson was an excellent scout for the Leafs." Davidson had been the captain of the Leafs in the 1940s. "He was a very personable guy, always well dressed. Worked hard. If he went into a kid's home and talked to his parents, he'd make a good impression. I scouted against him for two years. He was tough to beat."

For Scotty and the others, scouting 14-year-olds meant lots of time in very small towns, on very tough, narrow roads, in very cold arenas, and lots of nights in very cheesy hotels—not the King Edward. Scouting was about seeing in some kids something that no one else could see, but mostly it was about seeing what everybody did see and getting to a kid's house and making a pitch to his parents and to him early enough and better than the other scouts. It was about the chase. And, for Scotty, it was about having to beat back what the other scouts said about the Canadiens.

"'You don't want to go with Montreal,'" Scotty says, imitating what he heard them say again and again. "'They won the Cup five years in a row. You've got no chance playing for them. Really, do you want to play in the NHL or not?'" Or, if they were all chasing an English-speaking kid, "they'd use the French angle against us. 'You don't want to go to Montreal. They're a French team.'" The other scouts didn't even bother to say it in a whisper.

"The players didn't get any real money to sign then. One of the first guys who did was Ron Schock. He was from Terrace Bay"—on the north shore of Lake Superior, near Thunder Bay. The same Ron Schock who less than a decade later scored in the second overtime to send Scotty and the Blues to the Stanley Cup final. "Boston gave him $10,000 to sign. Before that, we were only offering a few hundred dollars. And we tried to get Wayne Carleton too." Carleton was from Beeton, Ontario, a rural community about an hour north of Toronto. He was as big and strong as someone who was five years older, and the hottest prospect of the time. "I had a good relationship with his parents," Scotty says. "He wanted to play for Montreal. Then, all of a sudden, Toronto came in and offered him more." He pauses. "But Rod Seiling was the best example."

Seiling was from a little town near Kitchener called Elmira. "It was between us and Toronto, Bob Davidson and myself. One day, Bob Davidson showed up in Elmira with a set of golf clubs. Soon afterwards I brought along Kenny Reardon and we went to Seiling's house because Sam was busy doing other stuff. We were going to offer him $10,000. I remember what Kenny said to him. He said, 'Well, son, you'll need to make up your mind. Do you want to play for the Montreal Canadiens?' Seiling was only a kid, and he said, 'I'm not sure.' As soon as he said that, and after we left the house, Kenny said to me, 'That's it. I don't want him.' I said, 'What do you mean?' He said, 'I don't want him. Don't go and see him anymore.' And Seiling went with Toronto." A few years earlier, Jimmy Roberts had said something else. Two very different outcomes.

The one player Scotty didn't get was the one he was never going to get—Bobby Orr. Everybody knew about this kid from Parry Sound. He wasn't big like Carleton. At 13, he was only the size of a 13-year-old, but he could skate like no other 13-year-old had ever skated. And he was smart. Meanwhile the Bruins were a horrible team in a great hockey city. "Their crowds were skidding to five, six, seven thousand—not even half full," Scotty recalls. They didn't need to get better step by step, they needed to take a gigantic leap, and Orr was the one who could make that happen. So they went after him, and got him.

For the first few years after the team signed him, he stayed on in junior, and Bruins fans only heard stories about Orr. "Then when he was 16 or 17," Scotty says, "the Bruins set up this tournament in Boston Garden for their two junior teams, Oshawa and Niagara Falls, and also the Junior Canadiens, just so the fans could see him. They drew more people for those games than they did for the Bruins.

"I think what interested Orr most with Boston was that when he was in Grade 7, they told him if he signed he could stay at home, he could stay in Parry Sound and commute [the three hours] to games on weekends.

It was only the second year he moved down to Oshawa." Scotty never did get Orr, but every year he calls him on his birthday.

"The Canadiens always did pretty well in Quebec," Scotty says about the years he was a scout, and the years before. "Rousseau, Gilles Tremblay, J.C. Tremblay, then Jacques Laperrière from Rouyn, [and] later on Cournoyer and Lemaire." Also Vachon and Savard. And from Ontario: "We got Claude Larose from Hearst, and Backstrom from Kirkland Lake, and Mickey Redmond from Peterborough. We had a scout in New Brunswick named Rollie McLenahan. In the early '50s Ken Reardon had put him into Cincinnati in the IHL as their player-coach. Later, when Louis Robichaud became premier of New Brunswick, he made Rollie the director of sports. He started a big hockey program there, and he was also our scout. He sent us a couple of players, and the best one was Danny Grant, from Fredericton." Later, Grant was the NHL's rookie of the year with the Minnesota North Stars. Even a province's director of sports might be a "guy" on the ground.

But during the years he was scouting, Scotty was less often in Montreal and less often with Sam. And big changes were happening with the Canadiens. The Rocket had retired. Harvey and Plante were traded. Selke turned 70, and Sam took over more and more of his duties. The team that had won five straight Stanley Cups had now lost three in a row. "When I was in Ottawa, then in Peterborough," Scotty recalls, "they won the Cup every year—and every year they sent me a watch. They also brought you to the draft. You were in the program." Now he felt disconnected, and even more than he sensed himself cut off from the big team, he felt disconnected from *a team*. From games, from the minute-to-minute, day-to-day ups and downs, highs and lows of a team. From its urgency, its mission and purpose. From the players.

Scotty was no arm-around-the-shoulder guy. He could seem calculating. Emotionless. Cold. But he loved being around players. Around *the team*. But the Canadiens weren't *his* team. They were Toe Blake's. And nor was Peterborough or Hull-Ottawa or Regina his team.

During his years as a scout, Scotty learned two very big things. He learned he didn't want to be a scout. And he learned he wanted to be a coach. "When you're a scout, even though you're following the NHL and pulling for your team, you're not involved. That's the tough part of it. I had coached for five years, and when you're not coaching it's different. There's a void. [So] I told Sam I wanted to coach."

The next season, 1963–64, Scotty was the coach of the Omaha Knights of the Central Professional Hockey League (CPHL). The Knights were a new team in a new league. The NHL teams had wanted a place to put their top young pro prospects and their most promising coaches. All but Toronto were represented in the CPHL's first year, the Leafs joining the following season. Scotty had on his team players he had coached before, coached against, and scouted. He knew them all. He would also be reunited, not for the last time, with Jimmy Roberts, Claude Larose, and Barclay Plager. And behind opposition benches he would face Fred Shero of the St. Paul Rangers and Harry Sinden of the Minneapolis Bruins, two future Stanley Cup–winning coaches, two future Hall of Famers, and great rivals of his in the decade ahead.

At almost the same moment that he was announced as coach of the Knights in 1963, the Leafs were winning their second straight Stanley Cup.

CHAPTER EIGHT
Toronto Maple Leafs 1962–63

Bill Barilko disappeared that summer
He was on a fishing trip
The last goal he ever scored
Won the Leafs the Cup
They didn't win another till nineteen sixty-two
The year he was discovered
    "Fifty Mission Cap," The Tragically Hip

In March 1951, Bill Barilko turned 24 years old. He had won three Stanley Cups with the Leafs, in 1947, 1948, and 1949. That spring, in the Cup final between the Canadiens and the Leafs, each of the first four games went into overtime, the Leafs winning three of them. Game 5, on April 21, was at Maple Leaf Gardens. Tod Sloan of the Leafs tied the game with 32 seconds to go. In overtime, during a scramble in front of the Canadiens' net, a shot by Toronto's Harry Watson was blocked by defenceman Butch Bouchard, the puck deflecting back into the slot. From his defence position, Barilko darted towards it, reaching across his body onto his backhand, throwing himself and the puck into the air and towards the net. His goal won the Cup. Four months later, returning from a fishing trip, his plane disappeared. It's wasn't until 1962, almost seven weeks after the Leafs had won their first Stanley Cup since 1951, that Barilko's plane and his remains were found.

During the first seven of those eleven years between Cups, the Leafs either missed the playoffs or lost in the first round. Boston, New York, and Chicago were never factors, but Detroit and Montreal got better and better as the Leafs got worse. Cup-winning players—and even coaches and owners—get old, are hard to get rid of, and are just as hard to replace. The personality of the Leafs was changing. It was softening. Conn Smythe, now in his sixties, was a little less engaged, and a little less combative. So too were the coaches who had followed Hap Day, the many-time Cup-winning coach of the team in the 1940s: Joe Primeau, who won in 1951, then came King Clancy, Howie Meeker, and Billy Reay. Turk Broda had retired, and the goalies who replaced him—Al Rollins and Harry Lumley—were good, but they weren't quite as hard to live with when they lost.

Yet the biggest impact on the team came when Ted Kennedy retired, then un-retired, then retired again. Kennedy played, as Scotty puts it, with an "edge." He wouldn't let up, he wouldn't give up; in today's terms, he was "hard to play against." And this was how the Leafs played at their best—what made the Leafs different. Even without great stars, finishing a routine third or fourth during the regular season, in the playoffs—at the hardest time of the year to play—the Leafs kept at it until they found a way to win. During the 1950s, as the Wings and Canadiens put together the big pieces that won them Cups and created dynasties, the Leafs were putting together the smaller ones that late in the decade would become the critical mass they needed. First came George Armstrong, Tim Horton, and Ron Stewart in 1952, then even more fruits of their junior farm system began to arrive—Dick Duff and Billy Harris in 1955, Bob Pulford and Bob Baun in 1956, Frank Mahovlich in 1957.

Then three unexpectedly crucial pieces were added within five weeks of each other in 1958. On June 4, in the NHL's Inter-League Draft, the Leafs paid $15,000 to select Johnny Bower from the AHL's

Cleveland Barons. Bower had had a lengthy career already—all but one year of it in the minor leagues. He had been an all-star and was three times the league MVP, but that was in the AHL—and now at age 33, his best years were certainly behind him. Except they weren't. A day later, in the Intra-League Draft, the Leafs took Bert Olmstead from the Canadiens, also for $15,000. Olmstead's skating had gotten worse, and he had been slowed further by injuries and age just as his Canadiens' teammates had gotten faster. Olmstead would bring to the promise of the Leafs' youthful core a crusty reminder of what was still yet to be—if only Olmstead was even barely good enough to play. And then, on July 10, the Leafs signed Punch Imlach as their assistant general manager. By November, he was the team's general manager and its coach. By then, defenceman Allan Stanley had also joined the team in a trade, and Carl Brewer had come up from junior. The next season Red Kelly was added by trade, and a year later Dave Keon and Bob Nevin came from St. Mike's and the Marlies.

Like Smythe, like Day and Kennedy, Imlach brought to the Leafs an attitude and a belligerence. The Leafs' edge was back. That spring, in 1962, the team won the Cup. And the next year, they were even better. For the first time since 1947–48, the team finished in first place during the regular season. But the league had also gotten closer. Chicago, who had been a distant last or second-last for most of the previous two decades, now had the two greatest young stars in hockey, Bobby Hull and Stan Mikita. They had won the Stanley Cup in 1961, ending the Canadiens' five-year dominance. The Bruins and Rangers were still bad, but in the 1962–63 season the top four teams finished in a tight cluster, with only five points separating the first-place Leafs and the fourth-place Wings.

The style of play in the league had begun to change. "Hockey was pretty tough in the early '60s," Scotty recalls. "Chicago was a big, strong team. They were pretty aggressive when they won in 1961. The referees didn't call the game as tight then. The guys could get away with more. As a team, you'd commit, maybe, fifteen fouls and get nailed for four or

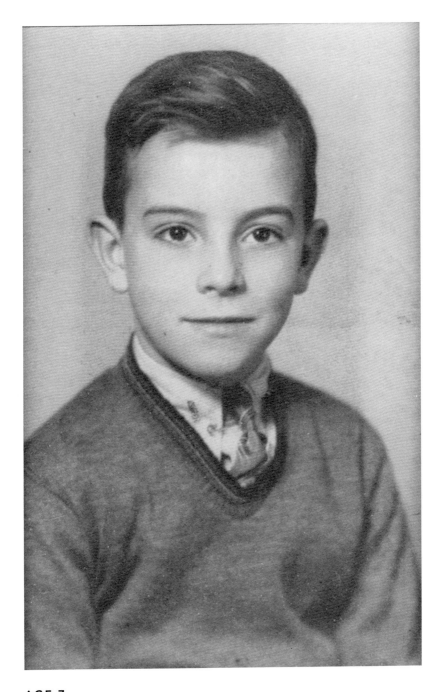

AGE 7

THE AVENUES

Above: 4th Avenue, Verdun, 1938

Right: 732 5th Avenue, 2018

GROWING UP

Top: Monikie, Scotland, 1938. Scotty (with tie), 4, Freda, 5, Jack Scott (cousin), young Jack (in arms), 1, William and Jane Scott, Jean's parents.

Above: Lancaster, Ontario, 1941. Young Jack, Jean, Freda, Jack, Scotty.

Right: 1950

TREASURES

CASUALTY—Scotty Bowman, junior Canadiens' rookie is shown with towel over his head being helped from the Forum ice, on the right, by teammates, last night, after being hit on the head by Three Rivers' star defenseman Jean-Guy Talbot. Talbot received a match penalty. Canadiens won the game, 5-1. Above Michel Labadie (12) the just scored for Quebec Citadels in the second game of the double-bill.

Bowman in Hospital After Stick Attack In Rough Junior Game

By IAN MACDONALD

Rheal Vincent, an obscure lad in local junior hockey circles, earned a thunderous introduction to 6,868 fans at the Forum last night as he paced Nationales to a sensational 4-3 overtime win over Quebec Citadels.

The win evened the best-of-nine series at one game each.

In the opener of the twin bill round, but clinched their second win with Three Rivers as they handily whipped the Reds 5-1, for their fourth straight triumph.

The game was marred by rough house tactics on the part of some Red players.

Jean-Guy Talbot, all star defenseman, played a chippy game, carrying his stick high and slashing heavily and ended up getting a match penalty for what the referee termed "deliberately injuring" Habs' Scotty Bowman, with 30 seconds to go.

Bowman made a rush on the Reds' cage and was brought down from behind by Talbot. The Canadien rookie slid into goalie Gilles Boisvert feet first and the latter toppled on to the ice. Thus pinned to the ice, Bowman was golfed on the head twice by Talbot, who broke his stick on the second crack.

Bowman staggered to his feet, clutched his head, and as he reached mid-ice, collapsed with blood spurting from a five-inch gash across the top of his skull.

Talbot is automatically suspended until his case is brought before the QAHA board.

Bowman was retained in Western hospital for observation, after receiving ten stitches to close the wound.

The match sentence was Talbot's fifth penalty of the game. In the second period he crashed Habs' captain Donnie Marshall and finally threw a few punches back.

Once again with the game on, and held sticks high, with Jean Guy Gendron, Jean Paul Gauthier and Talbot leading the way.

Dave McCready paced the Nats with a pair of goals while Herb English, Billy Sinnett and Sandy Morrison netted singles. Jean Jacques Bernaquier was the only Red able to beat Charlie Hodge

in the Canadien net.

Canadiens can wind up the series by winning in Three Rivers Saturday night but should the Reds stop them they will have another chance Sunday night at the Forum.

The thrilling finish to the second game was fine reward to the fans who had come to see hockey.

For two periods Quebec were far the better team but due to some lackadaisical netminding on their part, Cits were only leading 4-2.

Nats looked pitiful as with Henri Richard out, they lost the services of Charlie Lamblande through a leg injury, early in the middle frame.

The only shining light was the dogged and brilliant display of Nats' "No. 17" who most of the crowd "didn't even know. Rhea! Vincent had been signed by Nats for three months but had been unable to play due to exams at College Ste. Marie.

He seemed a lone star fighting a losing cause for his team first two frames as the rest of his mates were suffering from play-off jitters. Mid-way through the third Vincent set up Phil Goyette and

(Continued on Page 45)

Bowman in Hospital After Stick Attack

(Continued from Page 33)

the slim Lachine product made no mistake. For the first time the crowd began to realise that Nats had a chance to pull the game out of the fire.

Eddie Swartzack, the hurrying sturdy Maritimer with Nats, looked to be seriously hurt when he was crashed head-long into the goal post by Moe Collins in the second frame. Eddie was carried to the hospital. There he found he wouldn't be up for two hours so he was x-rayed for 45 seconds to play. Pete Morin yanked the brilliant Evans and placed the forwards up front and with five seconds to go Swartzack passed to young Vincent and the kid blasted the puck home. Swartzack went back for a neck x-ray after the game.

The crowd went wild acclaiming their new hero and it seemed anti-climactic when Claude Vinet calmly backed away from a player up at the Quebec goal and flipped up the puck over the mob for the winning marker, four minutes after the start of the extra play.

Bert Scullion and Ovilla Gagnon had scored Nats other goals while Gordie Haworth, with two, Jean Pichette and Michel Labadie counted for Quebec.

THREE RIVERS 1, CANADIENS 5

First Period
1—Canadiens, Sinnett (Broden) 10.45
2—Canadiens, Morrison (Bernaquer) 12.52
Penalties — Marshall (5.17), Gendron (7.02).

Second Period
3—Canadiens, McCready (Lilley) 8.19
4—Canadiens, English 15.22
5—Three Rivers, Bernaquier 17.52
Penalties (St. Cyr), Larocque (3.10), Jean (6.21), Chaates (8.51), Dubuc (17.16).

Gendron (13.31), Marshall (16.59), Talbot (16.59).
6—Canadiens, McCready (English)
Penalties — match penalty (30.10)

QUEBEC
1—Nationales, Quebec ...
2—Nationales, (Benoit)
3—Quebec, (15.35)
Penalties (12.42).

1—Quebec, M
2—Nationales, (8.26), Prov major, 10.

1—Nationales, (Vinc
2—Nationales, (Swar
Penalties
misconduct (1.

AU FIL DES SPORTS
par ANDRÉ TRUDELLE

Les pratiques du Canadien vue par l'éclaireur Scotty Bowman

Les gérants d'estrades sont particulièrement nombreux au baseball et au football où les situations se prêtent souvent à de multiples possibilités. Ils le sont moins au hockey. Néanmoins, à l'Auditorium de Verdun, surveillant l'entraînement du Canadien Junior, il n'est pas rare de retrouver, épars dans les estrades, d'anciens joueurs ou instructeurs de hockey et de nombreux amateurs. Tous ont des observations intéressantes, des impressions personnelles à livrer.

Ils savent bien que le dernier mot restera à Toe Blake ou à la direction du Canadien. Leurs remarques n'en demeurent pas moins piquantes, souvent pleines de logique, comme celles de Scotty Bowman, par exemple!

SCOTTY BOWMAN

Qui est Scotty Bowman? Un jeune homme de Verdun qui a été victime d'un accident de hockey chez les juniors. Il jouait pour le Canadien Junior et il a subi une fracture du crâne dans une joute contre les Reds de Trois-Rivières, atteint à la tête par le bâton de Jean-Guy Talbot.

Le geste accidentel avait coûté un an de suspension à Talbot et mis fin à la carrière de joueur de l'athlète de Verdun.

L'année suivante, il devenait, à 20 ans, l'instructeur du Parc Extension dans la Ligue Métropolitaine, puis instructeur du Canadien Junior et enfin, pendant trois ans, instructeur des Petes de Peterborough. Depuis, il est éclaireur en chef du Canadien pour l'Est du Canada, et compte nombre de sous-éclaireurs sous ses ordres, en Ontario, dans le Québec et dans les Maritimes.

Il aime beaucoup le hockey, il peut en parler pendant des heures, raconter nombre d'anecdotes inédites, et malheureusement pas toujours publiables; Scotty se rend rapidement compte des possibilités d'un joueur et ses observations sont toujours justes. Il est bilingue et il se gagne rapidement la sympathie des jeunes. Cela fait partie de son nouveau métier. Il a 28 ans.

"Il y a des adversaires du procédé actuel de participation exclusive à l'entraînement du Canadien, soit sur invitation. Personnellement, je favoriserais une participation massive. Elle ne facilite pas le travail du pilote, Toe Blake en l'occurrence, mais elle profiterait à l'organisation du Canadien", nous dit Scotty. "Tout le monde sait cette année que les vides à combler ne sont pas nombreux. Deux au plus, occasionnés par le départ de Marcel Bonin et d'Al MacNeil. Mais je crois que c'est une expérience merveilleuse pour les jeunes joueurs de côtoyer les Jacques Plante, Jean Béliveau, Bernard Geoffrion, Dickie Moore et autres vétérans du club.

Tenez, par exemple, il y a un joueur qui a

THE END . . .

1952

Junior Playoffs

Vincent, Vinet Upset Cits, Reds' Talbot Faces Suspension

Nationales Top Quebec 5-4 in Overtime; Habs Win 5-1 — Bowman Is Injured

By CHARLIE BOIRE

PETE MORIN isn't the "I told you so" type of coach but he couldn't contain himself last night at the Forum after his Nationales disposed of Quebec Citadels 5-4 in overtime.

Morin was jumping with joy over the outstanding performance of his rookie centre Real Vincent whose driving game carried Nats from the brink of defeat on to victory.

Vincent was labeled a future star by Morin two months ago and he certainly appears headed in the right direction judging from his performance since joining Nats.

His tieing goal with five seconds to go, set the stage for Nats victory and gave them the one-all split in last night's playoff action.

Three Rivers Reds 5-1 to take a strangle hold 4-0 lead in their semi-final series.

This game ended on a sour note when Three Rivers defenceman Jean-Guy Talbot drew a match penalty for "deliberately injuring" Scotty Bowman of Canadiens. Talbot, who usually plays smart hockey, was having a bad game and spoiling for trouble all night. He broke his stick over Bowman's head with 30 seconds to go after the latter slid into the Three Rivers goal trying to score.

Bowman was removed to the Western Hospital where he took stitches to the gaping five-inch cut across his head. Talbot, All Star defenceman, and rated one of the best prospects in the hockey league, jeopardized his hockey career by his foolish action.

Faces Year Suspension

The match penalty automatically suspends him until he appears before the Q.A.H.A. and he may face a year's further suspension for his action. Several Q.A.H.A. officials witnessed the game and saw the incident. Ernie Munday, Referee-in-chief of the Q.S.H.L. termed it the most vicious attack he has ever seen on another player.

Previous to his match penalty Talbot drew four minors and took

several cuts at other players before he cut Bowman who was down on the ice and unable to defend himself. Bowman was detained in the Western Hospital overnight. X-Rays taken today showed no skull fracture or concussion. He was released from hospital at noon today.

Three Rivers apparently gave up all hope of winning after the first period and resorted to chippy hockey that drew them 10 of the 14 penalties called. Three goals were tallied while Three Rivers were shorthanded. Reds were not up to their usual game.

Coach Jacques Toupin who usually fires his team to great heights during the playoffs, didn't seem to care after Canadiens moved ahead 4-0. Dave McCready who played a standout game paced Canadiens with a pair of goals. Herb English, Bill Sinnett and Scotty Morrison got one each with Jean Bernaquez spoiling Charlie Hodge's shutout.

Canadiens can wrap up the series at Three Rivers Saturday night. The Reds have their back to the wall and they have to take five in a row to beat out Habs but they will have to show a lot more hockey sense than last night to even win a game.

Miss Richard

It the second game there was more action packed into the last

See VINCENT, VINET—Page 31

Mr. R. T. Burrows   General Stockkeeping Aug 13, 1956
Mr. S. Bowman   General Stockkeeping
Resignation.

In reference to my conversation with you this morning please consider this letter as confirmation of my resignation from the company.

At this time, I would like to thank you personally for the kind advice you have given me in my stay with the company as it has been a most enjoyable one.

However, there are times in everyone's life that opportunities appear and I feel I have received an offer such as this.

I only hope that I will be able to receive the same friendship and co-operation in my new endeavours as I have had in the past with the employees of Sherwin Williams.

Very truly yours,

Scotty Bowman

AND THE BEGINNING . . .

1956

five at the most. If the other team was committing only half as many [fouls], they'd still get three or four penalties." In the NHL of the early 1960s, it paid to play on the edge.

As the Leafs' general manager, Imlach put together his team to play this way. "[The Leafs] were big, even their forwards," Scotty recalls. "Kelly was a good size. Mahovlich, Armstrong, Pulford, Stewart, Nevin. Big guys. And their defence was very solid. Horton was good. Baun was a good body-checker, not a big offensive player but a tough, tough guy. Stanley wasn't tough but he was pretty hard to play against, always hitting guys with his stick, clutching and grabbing. And Brewer was also a good player in those years. He was very skilful. He was antagonistic, always tripping and hooking, going at you. He kind of hid behind a lot of the tough guys, but he played an aggressive game, and he was hard to play against because he could skate."

The Canadiens had won their Cups in the 1950s by being faster and more talented than any other team in the league. So they built their farm system with this in mind, recruited the best juniors in the country, put them together on the best teams, and made themselves even faster and more talented. Late in the decade and early in the 1960s, they added Ralph Backstrom. They added Bill Hicke. They added Bobby Rousseau and Gilles Tremblay. They added J.C. Tremblay. They became more of what they had been—and Scotty had scouted these players, and coached them, and knew just how good they were. The other teams in the NHL knew they could try to play like the Canadiens—but without the right players, they would lose. Or they could decide to play differently. They, the Leafs included, could choose to get bigger, and play bigger. But that had never worked before. The Canadiens had just skated rings around them. So what was different now? Why were the Black Hawks and Leafs winning, and the Canadiens losing?

"I saw the Leafs play a lot," Scotty says of the 1962–63 season. "They played a tough brand of hockey, but they didn't take a lot of penalties. Keon never took any. Kelly didn't either. Armstrong only a few. Pulford was a pretty aggressive guy but even he didn't get many. It seemed that you could play a strong checking game, a really tight defensive game, you could play on the edge, and not have to kill a ton of penalties. You had only one referee. It was sort of like 'no harm, no foul'—as if a foul, if it occurred but didn't result in a change of possession, wasn't a foul."

It took a while for the Canadiens, and Scotty, to realize what was going on. The Canadiens had lost in 1961—*well, after five straight Cups you're going to lose sometime. Besides, the Rocket just retired.* They lost in 1962—*well, we finished first again, way ahead of everyone else, then we got upset. Upsets happen. The league is just letting too much go; we have to get better and faster still.* Then they lost in 1963—*this is beginning to get serious.* There had been things the Canadiens should have seen, but didn't see. In 1962–63, for the first time in six years, the Canadiens *didn't* finish first. They were third, only three points behind the first-place Leafs, but they won just 28 games, more only than the Rangers and the Bruins, and had 23 ties, far more than anyone else.

When a team ties a lot of games, there's a message. It says they've been in a position to win many times, have got to the end of games needing only a goal, but couldn't score when it mattered. Béliveau, Geoffrion, Moore, Henri Richard, Rousseau, Hicke, Gilles Tremblay, Backstrom—they couldn't score when they needed to score. It also says that late in games—when referees who let things go let them go even more—that the Canadiens' goal scorers, no matter how much faster and more talented they were, couldn't escape the clutching and grabbing of their bigger opponents. It says, too, that in the playoffs, when referees who let things go let them go for the whole game and not just at the end, things would get worse.

The Canadiens also didn't see that on those championships teams in the 1950s, no matter the Rocket's size, he played big. Harvey played big. So did Olmstead. And Béliveau *was* big, even if physically he only played as big as he was. They didn't see that their teams of the 1960s were getting faster and more talented but were also getting smaller. In

1962–63, the big test for them would come in the spring. The Leafs had won the Cup the year before without needing to face the Canadiens. This season, the two teams would meet in the first round. And besides their clutching and grabbing, different from the other teams who did the same, the Leafs were good too.

"On one line they had Kelly and Mahovlich," Scotty recalls, thinking of those teams, "and then they came back with Keon and Armstrong. When you've got two centres like Kelly and Keon, and then Billy Harris as the third . . ." Scotty trails off, then continues. "And they also had Pulford to play centre, or left wing. They had some good right wingers too—Armstrong, Nevin, Stewart—pretty solid players, not just offensive guys. Keon, Kelly, Pulford, Armstrong, Duff, Nevin—they were all two-way players. Duff was like [Ted] Lindsay. Not as good, of course, but tough, chippy, and he could score. Maybe only Mahovlich played a one-way, offensive game. They were a solid team, and they played just the right way in the playoffs.

"I think there's no question that Imlach and Toe Blake were the two top coaches of their era," Scotty adds. "And they had coached a lot against each other, in the Quebec league even before they got to the NHL."

Imlach hadn't been a star player like Blake. He had bounced around, establishing himself quickly as a non-prospect but also becoming a solid Senior A player—first in Cornwall, Ontario, then in Quebec with the Aces. At the same time, and probably before he even knew it himself, he was learning how to coach. Later he would be the Aces' player-coach, then the team's general manager and part-owner as well. "He was in the minors a long time," Scotty recalls. "He served his time. He didn't get to the NHL until he was 40." And when he arrived, it was with two other scrappers, Olmstead and Bower. Olmstead, the product of a life in "the corners"; Bower and Imlach, the products of lives in the minors. "The Leafs were the opposite of a country club," Scotty says. "You know how they talk now about 'changing the culture' of a team? Well, that's what Imlach did in Toronto. He made some good moves. Getting Olmstead.

Getting Kelly. They were important players on the Leafs. Olmstead was a tough cookie, a no-nonsense guy. He was hard on young players." And Imlach knew that, and wanted that.

Kelly was a different story. He had been a big star on the great Wings teams of the early 1950s, and a defenceman like no other in the history of the NHL. From 1950 until 1956, he never scored less than 15 goals a season. Three times he finished in the top 10 in scoring. "No other defenceman in the league was even close," Scotty says. Then the Wings fell off, and so did Kelly. It's one thing to play differently when you're winning, and another when you're losing. When you're winning, what's different seems natural and part of the whole excitement. When you're losing, it becomes a focus itself, and you become a target. For the Wings, the puck that had often ended up in the other guy's net was now more often in their own. And questions were being asked, like: *What's Kelly doing up the ice all the time?*

"On a winning team," Scotty says, "you're not spending a lot of time in your own end, where Kelly was weaker. You're on the attack, where he was at his best. Then the Wings got weaker." But Imlach didn't see in Kelly a defenceman who played the wrong way and whose best days were past. He saw a player who was big, strong, could skate, had offensive instincts, and was smart, adaptable, and could make good passes. He saw him as a centre, as somebody who could get Frank Mahovlich the puck at the right time. "He seemed to fit in perfectly with Mahovlich," Scotty recalls. "They were two good-sized guys, and Kelly was a very strong skater."

Bower was another good fit. He was older, but instead of being embittered by all the years he'd been overlooked in the minors, he seemed grateful for the chance he had been certain would never come his way again. Imlach knew there were lots of players in the minor leagues who weren't just minor leaguers. He had seen them and coached them. Players who were good enough *if* they got the chance—if they got the *right* chance. In the early 1950s, Bower had spent a season with the

Rangers, a poor team with a country-club atmosphere, and he had been sent back to the minors the next year. But on this Leafs team—younger, hungrier, with a growing and developing defensive attitude and conscience—it could be different.

As far as Imlach was concerned, you see what you have, and you develop it into something. You don't focus on what you don't have, and give up. He would do the same with Kent Douglas, another career minor leaguer, a defenceman who couldn't play defence well enough but on the power play could make plays and score, and who in 1963, at 27, would become the NHL's first defenceman and second-oldest player to win the Calder Trophy as rookie of the year. "He was trouble. He was a headache. He was a goofball, really," Scotty says about Douglas during the earlier years of his career in the minors. "Everybody thought [Imlach] was crazy to get a guy like that, but he got a lot of hockey out of him. Douglas was not a kid either. Imlach was adept at resurrecting guys' careers. He liked projects. If other teams didn't think a player had much left, he'd go and pick them up."

Imlach understood players who weren't stars. He had been around them all his life; he had been one himself. He also understood players who were just hanging on, who were vulnerable and knew it. Senior A players in their late twenties who couldn't put off getting a real job much longer; NHL players in their thirties who, with their morning aches and pains, could feel the future closing in.

During Scotty's years with the Petes, the Leafs held their training camps in Peterborough. "I was there in '58, '59, and '60. The Leafs used to come for six weeks and I got to know Imlach a little bit. He was always very respectful, and very nice to me even though I was with another organization. I used to watch them practise and there was no monkeying around," he recalls. "He was really a strict guy. And he really liked older players, but he worked them. His theory was that as they got older they had to work *harder*, not less, to keep their position and to keep up." Imlach pushed all his players, but he pushed the older guys the hardest.

He liked Bower for lots of reasons, but especially because Bower loved to practise—despite being the oldest of them all. "They were a team that was in great shape all the time."

Imlach knew, too, that as vulnerable as these players were, they were also hopeful, and he was giving them a precious gift. A second life. Olmstead was done, Bower was too old, Stanley was going nowhere, Kelly was playing the wrong way, and Douglas was a minor leaguer. Later, Imlach would do the same for Terry Sawchuk, Marcel Pronovost, Pierre Pilote, and Andy Bathgate, after the latter's long and distinguished but frustrating career with the Rangers. And if the old guys practised hard, what right had the young guys not to? Too tough and too proud ever to say so, even to think so, "[Imlach's] veteran players respected the fact that he extended their careers," Scotty says.

Yet in 1962–63, the Leafs weren't as old a team as they seem in memory. Pulford, Duff, and Baun were still only 26, Mahovlich was 25, Brewer 24, Keon 22. It was only Kelly, Horton, and Stanley—and especially Bower, who was 38—who made them seem old. In 1967, improbably, the Leafs won the Cup with many of the same players, and then they *were* old. But in 1963, their young core guys were also experienced and disciplined; they had won championships with the Marlies and St. Mike's. They played old, but they weren't old.

And when a game began, Imlach used his players well. "He was a very good bench coach," Scotty continued. "Sure, he'd use gimmicks. He'd start five defencemen at times, just so other teams didn't have the first matchup. But he matched lines really well. He was really good at getting the right players onto the ice at the right time. And against the Canadiens, he'd always get Kelly out against Béliveau."

Imlach had coached Béliveau in Quebec and knew how good he was. He also knew that while the string of Canadiens Cup wins in the late 1950s may have come to an end, Montreal might start right into another one. They had the best team. For the Leafs to win, therefore, Imlach had to find a way to beat the Canadiens, and not just one year but every year; and to do that he needed an answer for Béliveau. That answer was Red Kelly. An eight-time all-star defenceman for the Wings, Kelly never played a game on defence for the Leafs. He was big, smart, a fluid skater, and bulldog-competitive. Imlach wanted him at centre to get Mahovlich the puck, and to go head-to-head with Béliveau.

When Imlach couldn't get the matchup he wanted, he would put Keon—five foot nine, 165 pounds—against Béliveau, who was six foot three and 205 pounds. "[Keon] was such an exceptional skater," Scotty says. "He was very nimble. He could just fly on his skates. He was always on the puck, always on top of you, never giving you a moment to breathe. He wasn't physical, because he wasn't big, but he was always there, darting in and out, and his hockey IQ was so high. He always knew what to do and when to do it." Imlach knew a small guy in the face of a big guy looks big. He had seen Béliveau brought down to earth before, with the Quebec Citadelles in junior, when a much less talented Dickie Moore went after him and wouldn't let him go, and the Junior Canadiens upset the Citadelles and later won the Memorial Cup.

"[Imlach] loved Keon. He loved Pulford too. He liked those guys who could really check and play good, tight defence. His teams would sit on a goal or two and they were really hard to get through, and if you tried, you paid a price," Scotty says. "I don't think he ever really embraced Mahovlich, because Frank was a big, strong player but he wasn't physical, and he wasn't airtight defensively." Imlach also had a hard time with Brewer. Brewer and Mahovlich, along with Keon, may have been the Leafs' most talented players, but in them Imlach saw more of what he *wasn't* getting. He knew there was no more to get out of Bower, or out of Armstrong or Keon or Horton or Kelly or Pulford or Baun or Stanley. He got out of them all that was there. And he was tough on his players, but Mahovlich and Brewer took his toughness harder and more personally than the rest. It bothered them. Imlach could not just let Frank be Frank, or Carl be Carl. In Quebec, he had let Béliveau be Béliveau, and later in Buffalo he let Gilbert Perreault be Gilbert

Perreault, but they were genuine "franchise players." Béliveau *was* the Quebec Aces. In Buffalo's first years in the league, Perreault *was* the Sabres. During the 1962–63 season, Mahovlich led the Leafs with 36 goals. He was the only Leafs player to finish in the top 10 in the league in scoring; he was fourth. In the playoffs, as the Leafs won the Cup, he played in nine of the team's ten games and collected just two points. In his next few seasons under Imlach, he would become less and less of an offensive force, and become a big scorer again only after he was traded to Detroit, then have his best, most complete and fulfilling years in Montreal with Scotty and Sam in the early 1970s.

More than any of his players, Imlach became the face of the Leafs franchise. "He liked to be in the limelight," Scotty remembers. "He liked to talk to the media. They loved him and weren't critical of him at all because he was such good copy. And he didn't worry about controversy. I was in Peterborough in his early years with the Leafs, and every year at training camp they'd always have a big dispute. There'd always be a contract holdout—Brewer, Baun, Pulford. Imlach seemed to relish that. He never worried about it, he knew eventually it would be solved."

He also knew that showdown moments like these made him look tough. They delivered a message—to the players, the media, the fans— about who was in charge. And they added to the identity that he wanted for the Leafs: to be a team with an "edge," willing to fight on and off the ice for what they believed in. Around the Leafs at this time, "there was never a dull moment. [Imlach] put a lot of life into that franchise."

During the 1962–63 regular season, the Canadiens had a losing record against only one team—the Leafs. Their playoff series proved no contest. The Leafs won four games to one, shutting out the Canadiens in the final game, 5–0, and outscoring them 14–6 in all. "I can't believe how few goals the Canadiens scored in that series," Scotty says, still amazed. Just over one goal a game. For the third consecutive year, the Canadiens had gone out in the first round; the next year, they would make it four in a row. In the '63 series, Béliveau had two goals and one assist; Keon had three goals and three assists. The final was no different. The Leafs beat the Wings decisively in five games to win the Cup.

It's easy to underrate the Leafs of that time. Even though they won three Cups in a row, they were not spectacular. Great teams usually have at least a few very special players—Howe, Sawchuk, Lindsay, Kelly (of the early 1950s), Richard, Béliveau, Harvey, Moore, Geoffrion, Plante. In 1963, the Leafs had no players who today are considered among the greatest of all time. They were a team of their time built for the NHL of the time—when the referees let things go; when, with six teams in the league, there were only two playoff rounds, and so in tough, physical series the older players didn't grind down and wear out.

"In that era," Scotty says, "you only had to win eight games. You only had to go through two series. And the Leafs had experienced guys. Their defence was really solid. They weren't easy to get chances against. They hung in there, and had just enough game-breakers. It really helped them in the playoffs that the referees didn't watch every little thing, and let more go. The Leafs didn't have the individual players some teams have. They won more as a team. And when they got into the playoffs, that's when they made their hay."

CHAPTER NINE

The Omaha Knights of the newly formed CPHL played their first five games on the road, and won them all. Then, returning home to the ancient Ak-Sar-Ben (*Nebraska* spelled backwards) Coliseum, they won their next two. They would go on to far outdistance the other four teams in the league during the regular season, and dominate the playoffs, beating Harry Sinden's Minneapolis Bruins in the semifinals, and Fred Shero's St. Paul Rangers in the final, outscoring the Rangers 28–8 after winning the second game of the series 11–0. But by this time, Scotty was long gone.

The problem began with that first road trip. The teams in the CPHL were in cities many hours apart—St. Louis, Minneapolis, Indianapolis (after its arena was damaged in an explosion later in the season, the team moved to Cincinnati), St. Paul, and Omaha. The Knights' owners— brothers Don and Rod Morrison—were from Saskatoon and had played for Omaha with fellow Saskatonian Gordie Howe back when the Knights were part of the United States Hockey League (USHL) in the 1940s. During the only season the three of them played together, Don finished second on the team in points and Howe was third (he was only 17 years old at the time). After the brothers' own playing careers took them elsewhere, including to Detroit, they returned to Omaha and started a construction company. These were the post–Second World

War years—the U.S. and Omaha economies were growing rapidly, and the Morrisons' company did well. At the same time, the top leagues in baseball, football, and basketball were expanding and moving west, and the NHL would surely soon follow. To the Morrisons—for personal and business reasons—the time seemed right to jump into something else, something they loved and knew.

Maybe for Scotty, the problem was that the brothers thought they knew more than they did, or that Scotty thought they did. They knew Omaha—they had lived in the city for more than a decade—and they were business guys who knew how to run a business. More than that, they had played in the NHL, which Scotty never had, and they had played with Gordie Howe. In both Omaha and Detroit, they'd had Tommy Ivan as their coach, and Tommy Ivan knew a little something about coaching. He was no junior guy from Peterborough; he had won Stanley Cups. And when Ivan was their coach, the teams in the USHL were in cities just as far apart—there had even been one in Houston—at a time when the interstate highway system didn't yet exist. The bus had been good enough for them, and it was still good enough for every minor-league baseball team. So why wouldn't their hockey team travel by bus? But the other CPHL teams travelled by train, Scotty reminded them. Then reminded them again.

Or maybe the problem was because the season had opened with so many games on the road, because this was Scotty's first pro team and he was anxious. Nervous. Maybe it was because he always fixated on things that others nodded politely to at first, then rolled their eyes at: faceoffs, line matchups, on-the-fly line changes. Critical stuff, he thought—no, he *knew*—which in a close game would make *the* difference. Travelling by bus instead of by train, he thought—he *knew*—would be a huge disadvantage for his team; maybe not in the first five games, but certainly over a season.

Or maybe the problem was because, in Omaha, Scotty was truly on his own for the first time. This wasn't Ottawa, it wasn't Peterborough, and Montreal wasn't just around the corner. This wasn't even small-town Ontario or Quebec, which to some might seem the middle of nowhere but really was in the middle of a *hockey*-somewhere. This—Omaha—was in the endless middle of America, and outside the walls of Ak-Sar-Ben Coliseum and every other arena in the league (except in Minnesota), nobody knew anything about hockey. Nobody much cared.

Or maybe the problem was that Sam wasn't around. Because not only was he a thousand miles away, but he was preoccupied with a big team that had lost three years in a row and was about to lose a fourth, and where the central force behind that big team, Frank Selke, was on the verge of retirement and it wasn't certain who would replace him.

Or maybe the problem was that Scotty wasn't mature enough. He knew hockey; his teams won. But maybe he was like a piano prodigy, so absorbed in what he was doing he had no time to do anything else. To learn about people, to pick up cues and clues from what they said and did, to understand them, to trust them, to become comfortable with them and confident in them. In the short term, none of this is a problem for a prodigy because you hit the right notes; for the coach, if you win, a lot is never noticed. A lot is forgiven. But in the long run, it does matter. Most prodigies never play Carnegie Hall. In their lives, so focused on learning the notes, they never create their own music. So maybe Scotty was just a hockey savant. But if he was to have a successful life in hockey, he was going to need to learn some things beyond the *X*s and *O*s of the game, and one of them was that team owners are a fact of that hockey life. The Morrisons were not the Molsons. They didn't leave everything to their managers. They wanted, and needed, to be involved. As to whether the team would travel by bus or by train, Scotty couldn't let it go, and the Morrisons wouldn't let it go.

Maybe the problem was all of these things together. Maybe Scotty had some growing up to do. After the Knights' seventh straight win to start the season, he quit. He had arrived in Omaha at age 30, a wunder-kind. He came back to Montreal not sure what he was.

He had been an assistant coach and manager in Ottawa, and had learned he didn't want to be a manager. He had been a coach in Peterborough, and a scout in Eastern Canada, and had learned he didn't want to be a scout, but that he did want to be a coach. Then he had his first pro coaching job, and quit. All the time, he had been learning, moving up, doing what needed to be done, getting ready for whatever was next, and getting older when getting older seemed an essential part of his development. But now what was left for him? Toe Blake wasn't going anywhere, and if Scotty couldn't handle Omaha there had to be serious doubts he could ever handle the Canadiens. Sam wasn't going anywhere. There also weren't any better jobs with other NHL teams, and after Omaha, teams that had always dreamed of having him on their side had to be wondering now too. Until this point, his downs had always been small ones and his ups had been big ones, but this was failure. And it was November, and teams were well into their seasons; they had their coaches. So Scotty began scouting again, and helping Sam out wherever he needed it.

By 1964, the Junior Canadiens were again located in Montreal and were a full member of the OHA, playing a regular junior schedule with no special privileges. With Yvan Cournoyer, André Boudrias, and the 17-year-old rookies Jacques Lemaire and Serge Savard, the Junior Canadiens were good but not more than that. There was also now a 10-team junior league in Montreal that had a few good teams—the Lachine Maroons, NDG Monarchs, Verdun Maple Leafs, and Rosemont Bombers—with prospects on their roster who a year later might play for the Junior Canadiens, as well as many older players who were never going to be more than hopefuls.

As a scout based out of Montreal, Scotty was now also back watching the Canadiens again and was around Sam more often, but this was not a good moment in his life. He had doubts—and others had doubts about him—perhaps for the first time. Then Alf Harvey, another of Doug's brothers, who coached and managed the NDG Monarchs, decided to give up coaching, and midway through the year Scotty was back. This may only have been the Montreal Metropolitan Junior League, and not even the Junior Canadiens, but it was still coaching. It was a team—his team—something to focus on, to strategize and scheme for, to give every waking hour to and to stay awake numberless other hours for. He also had some good players who might be going somewhere, and not just to the Junior Canadiens but eventually to the big team as well—Rogie Vachon, Carol Vadnais, Larry Pleau, Craig Patrick. A year earlier, Serge Savard had played on the team. Scotty, in fact, even as he was scouting most of the time that season, had had a hand in setting in motion Savard's future in Montreal.

"Serge had come down from Amos, Quebec," Scotty recalls, "and Cliff Fletcher and I put him on a team in Rosemont in the east end of Montreal." Amos was a forestry and mining town of about 8,000 people—50 kilometres northeast of Rouyn and Noranda. Fletcher, who at the time was a part-time scout, would win the Stanley Cup 26 years later as the general manager of the Calgary Flames. "The Canadiens would always bring in 12 young players to Montreal—I don't know why it was 12—not counting the ones with the Junior Canadiens. And the players would be dispersed around the Montreal league. But the owner of Rosemont, Roger Poitras, didn't play Serge," Scotty says. "He was a real tough guy to deal with, and he just wanted to win. He didn't play young guys. At the end of the season, Cliff and I had a meeting with Sam to review the dozen players, and right away Sam scratched off Serge. 'We're not bringing him back,' he said, 'because he didn't play. It wasn't his fault, but that's what happens.'" That was the end of that, except it wasn't.

"So Serge goes back home that summer, and we decide on our 12 guys for the next year, and most of them are new ones. But somehow we didn't inform Serge." Scotty pauses, still embarrassed. "Now it's just past Labour Day and Cliff gets a call from Serge and he'd come down and gone to the same boarding house in Rosemont, and was looking to get his transportation and other expenses straightened away. So Cliff came to me, 'Remember that guy, Serge Savard? Well, he's in Montreal.' I said, 'He can't be.' Cliff said, 'He is. What are we going to do?'"

The two of them had a problem. "And Sam was not always that easy. He could be very demanding, and he was also very busy. So we go to him and I say, 'About Serge Savard, somehow Cliff and I didn't call him.'" It took a moment for this to register with Sam. "And Sam says, 'Well, he's not going to stay here now. We've already got our 12.' It was then Cliff who took the initiative," Scotty remembers. "He said, 'You know, Sam, he never got a chance last year . . .'" Cliff was hoping to change the point enough to change Sam's answer.

"So we made a pact with Sam. If we get him on a team that will play him, we said, can we keep him at least until Christmas? And Sam, he was kind of busy, said, 'Well, okay.' So Cliff got a hold of Doug Harvey to get a hold of his brother Alf who ran the NDG team. NDG never got a lot of good players, but Alf always played young guys." Scotty stops himself again, "And really, it's an amazing story. By Christmas, Serge had developed so much they even moved him to the Junior Canadiens. Serge said to me later that there was a Detroit scout in Amos and if we'd sent him home, he was going to sign with them and go to [the Wings' junior team in] Hamilton."

Savard would play fourteen years with the Canadiens, win eight Stanley Cups, and be awarded the Conn Smythe Trophy in 1969 as MVP of the playoffs; he would be captain and later general manager of the team, be inducted into the Hockey Hall of Fame, and have his number 18 retired by the Canadiens.

There was another remarkable story that same year Scotty took over as coach of NDG. The Monarchs finished with the third-best record in the league during the regular season, and defeated the first-place Rosemont Bombers in the finals. They then beat Victoriaville and Port Alfred to win the Quebec championship, and Summerside (P.E.I.) and Ottawa to advance to the Eastern Canada final against the Toronto Marlies, winners of the OHA title. The Marlies at the time were thought of as the best junior team ever. They had 13 future NHLers, including Ron Ellis, Rod Seiling, Brit Selby, Mike Walton, Jim McKenny, goalie

Gary Smith, and two others who were considered future superstars, Pete Stemkowski and Wayne Carleton. Toronto had dominated the OHA's regular season, and had gone through the playoffs without a single loss, including beating the Junior Canadiens in the OHA final.

"We had 10 days before our first game against them," Scotty recalls. "And I remember I went to Toe Blake and said, 'Toe, we're going to play a team that is at least six or seven goals better than we are,' and we talked about a few things, and he gave me some ideas. One was that we play the way we always did, with two guys forechecking. Another was to have only one forechecking, and to have everybody else lined up in the centre zone. And another was to have nobody forechecking, to have two forwards in the centre zone by their blue line, then the two defencemen, and have our centreman back by the goalie, like three layers of defence, so that if the Marlies couldn't get through the first two and shot the puck in, we'd have a guy right beside the net to get it. I had three different lines, so I decided to have each line play a different system. We practised that for 10 days. And all the players knew they could slaughter us."

The first game was in Montreal, and the Marlies did slaughter them, 7–2. "They were just a powerhouse team," Scotty says. "They were the best junior team I could ever even remember. We played the same way the next game, and they didn't change either, because why would they?"

But this time the result was different. The Monarchs won, 6–4. The Marlies won the next two games in Toronto to take the best-of-five series, then swept the Edmonton Oil Kings in the Memorial Cup final. This great Marlies team, still remembered more than 50 years later as one of the best junior teams ever, lost only one playoff game that season and that was to the lowly NDG Monarchs of the Montreal Metropolitan Junior League.

"That was the proudest moment of my career up to that time," Scotty says. Suddenly uncomfortable with what he has just said, he searches for, and finds a lesson in the experience. "[The Marlies] were just great players that could play by the seat of their pants and beat anybody. And they beat everybody. But they weren't a very disciplined team." He would face other teams just like them in his NHL future—the Bruins of the early 1970s, the Oilers of the 1980s—teams too good to beat until they lost and revealed that they weren't. When later he coached against those teams, he would remember the 1964 Marlies and his NDG Monarchs.

Suddenly he thinks of something else—another lesson, this time a strategic one: "And I liked the fact that we were able to come up with three different systems. I often wonder even now why in the NHL a team plays mostly the same way everyone else does, and every line does. Why wouldn't your third and fourth lines play a different style?"

Interestingly, this juggernaut Marlies team of 1964 that produced so many players important to later Leafs teams, including their last Stanley Cup victory in 1967—Ellis, Stemkowski, Walton among them—produced no great NHL players.

After a tough year, the hardest of Scotty's hockey life, this series and this win mattered to him. It had shown that he could still coach. The next season, he moved back up to the Junior Canadiens.

He was there for two mostly uneventful years. The team, despite having Savard, Lemaire, Vadnais, Pleau, and Patrick on its roster, finished a poor fifth in the OHA in 1964–65 and lost in the first round of the playoffs to the Marlies, being blown out 8–1 in the final game. The next season, the Junior Canadiens moved up to second, only one point behind Peterborough but also only seven points ahead of the sixth-place Marlies in a tightly contested league. They won the first round of the playoffs, then lost in the second. But the highlight of the year came in December 1965, in a game at the Forum against the Soviets.

The Soviet Union's national team had won either the World Championships or the Olympics the previous three seasons (at the time, no World Championships were held in Olympic years), and were only a few months away from a fourth gold, after which they would win five more and one more Olympic gold medal before the 1972 Summit Series. They had become, indisputably, too good for the rest of the amateur hockey world. All of their best players were on this touring team, including some who today are considered Soviet legends: Alexandrov, Firsov, Starshinov, Mayorov, Loktev, Ragulin. Just as it had been with the Monarchs, Scotty and the Junior Canadiens were facing a potentially humiliating night, and in front of a sold-out home crowd.

They added to their roster five players from the Canadiens' minor pro teams, and then one more—Jacques Plante approached Sam and asked if he could play. He had never played against the Soviets, he explained, and he wanted the chance. He hadn't played all that year, having retired after an embarrassing season with the fifth-place Rangers, during which he had even been sent to the minors. He was almost 37 years old and working for Molson. But, Scotty knew, he wouldn't agree to play unless he thought he could, and if he could then Scotty wanted him as his goalie.

For six weeks, Plante trained for this one game. He had seen the Soviets play, had thought about how they played, and developed a plan. Before the game, he got his defencemen together and drew on the chalkboard how he wanted them to play. The Soviets were great passers and poor shooters. When they approached the net on a two-on-one, he wanted the defenceman to protect against any potential pass; he would go head-to-head with the shooter.

The Junior Canadiens tied the game midway through the third period, then scored with 29 seconds left to win, 2–1. Plante was the star of the game. The fans had booed him in his final season in Montreal—difference is acceptable when you win—and now he had come back in triumph. He could still play, something he'd never doubted—and Scotty remembered this a few years later when he was coaching in St. Louis and needed players.

During those years Scotty was coaching the juniors, change finally came to the NHL Canadiens. Off the ice, Frank Selke retired, and Sam took his place. In one role or another, Sam had been with the team almost a full working career, yet he was still only 38 years old. And on the ice, the Canadiens got bigger. In 1963–64, they added John Ferguson, Terry Harper, and Jacques Laperrière to the roster. Harper and Laperrière were tough but not punishing. Ferguson was tough and scary. He had been a career minor leaguer—an awkward, lumbering skater with a scoring touch that surprised you and fists that didn't. Quickly, he became the league's heavyweight champion. From what everyone could see, Ferguson was someone you didn't mess with, but it was his ability to go over the edge and lose it, to do what everyone could only imagine, that made him even more frightening. "And he was competitive," Scotty says. "He was so competitive. He made a big difference to the team." The next season, the Canadiens added another career minor leaguer, 28-year-old defenceman Ted Harris. And after losing four straight years, after being knocked out in the first round of the playoffs four straight times, the Canadiens won the Stanley Cup. They would win three more in the next four years.

The league was facing big changes too. NHL expansion seemed inevitable—the questions were only about where, how many, and how. Or so it seemed.

Professional sports leagues in the U.S. had been formed first in the big cities of the densely concentrated northeast quadrant of the country. This area extended south from Boston to New York, Philadelphia, and Washington, then west to Pittsburgh, Cincinnati, and St. Louis, up to Chicago, and back east to Detroit and Cleveland. Just as bus travel had determined the makeup of junior leagues in Canada, train travel did the same for the pro leagues in the U.S. Any city a day's travel away by rail was fine; any other city was not.

But by the 1960s, airplanes defined our geography. Major League Baseball triggered the change in sports when the Brooklyn Dodgers and New York Giants moved west to California. If the NHL was going to expand, L.A. and San Francisco/Oakland would be obvious destinations as well. So, too, Minnesota, because of its deep history and love of hockey, and also likely Pittsburgh with its size, location and long connection to the sport through its minor-league teams. No other city was certain. Philadelphia had size and location, which had been reason enough for some people in 1930 to move the Pittsburgh Pirates (one of the pre-Original Six NHL teams) there to become the Philadelphia Quakers, but not enough to keep the team there, with the lack of fan interest in hockey in the area proving a reason to go, and a 4–36–4 season not helping. The city's support of its minor-league teams in the decades that followed was also not much better. St. Louis was another story. It had also had a team during the NHL's formative years. A big new rink built in 1929, the St. Louis Arena, had made the city an attractive site five years later when the St. Louis Eagles entered the league. But, like the Quakers, the team lasted only one season, and by the mid-1960s the arena was almost 40 years old, had been poorly maintained for years, and was considered a dump.

So while NHL expansion may now have seemed certain, it wasn't really—at least not then. As well as questions about the new cities, there were other concerns: Why would the existing teams even want new teams anyway? How would they be better off? Sure, they would each receive a franchise fee of $2 million, but that wasn't going to transform the future lives of the Molsons or the Norrises. And big national TV contracts in the U.S.—even in football—weren't yet on the horizon. Besides, the existing team owners already had a good solid business, and one they controlled themselves. The league had little power. It had a head office in Montreal—not even in New York—and almost no employees. These owners, in their own hockey fiefdoms, were lord and master. In their minds, the league existed merely to put together the schedule, hire the referees, and get out of their way. Why did these team owners need six new partners they didn't even know? They didn't even get along with the ones they *did* know.

There would also be the inevitable hassle that came with being a bigger, more complicated league. And if this weren't enough, these new teams would need players—players that would have to come from the existing teams. The Bruins had been a disaster for years, but they had finally put together a farm system, with junior teams in Niagara Falls, Oshawa, Estevan, and Victoriaville, and smaller ones elsewhere. Their pipeline was just starting to produce players. Now, with expansion, they would have to give up some of these players. And, because you couldn't have 12 farm systems in a country with a population as small as Canada's, would they and the others have to give up their sponsored teams entirely? Forever? And have an *open* draft of players where they—one of the Original Six teams—were treated no differently from these new guys? Where the expansion teams would have as much right to—and as good a chance to get—the next Bobby Orr? Boston wasn't thrilled at this. And nor was Chicago. The Hawks had been very bad or worse throughout the 1940s and 1950s, then had finally won a Cup in 1961. Now their superstars were young. They had a chance to win every year. Why mess with that?

But whatever the existing NHL teams' arguments, things were not going to stay the same. There were big cities in the western United States, with big arenas and minor-league teams that almost filled them. L.A., San Francisco, San Diego, Portland, and Seattle weren't going to wait forever. The NFL had put off large-scale expansion, and the AFL, a rival league, had started up to compete against them. The Western Hockey League, which included all these West Coast cities, might decide to go big-time and do the same. So the mood around the NHL shifted, and the teams began to look for reasons *for* expansion instead of against.

Jim Norris, the owner of the Black Hawks and half-brother of Wings' owner Bruce Norris, also owned the St. Louis Arena. At the time the venue was dark most nights—the minor-league team that played there drew poorly, and even St. Louis's NBA team, the Hawks, wanted nothing to do with it, playing in the much smaller Kiel Auditorium. Norris told his fellow owners he would agree to expansion if St. Louis was awarded one of the new teams. Of course, if it was, the team would need to play in the St. Louis Arena.

Jim Norris sold the building to Sidney Salomon Jr. and his son Sid III. In doing so, Norris got out from under a financial burden, got his money from the sale of the arena itself, and received his share of the franchise fee. St. Louis, meanwhile, got its team. And the league got its expansion. To the Original Six, the NHL added St. Louis, L.A., California (Oakland), Minnesota, Pittsburgh, and Philadelphia.

But if the existing teams had to give up players, that didn't mean those players had to be any good. "We [St. Louis] got only three or four real NHL players in the expansion draft," Scotty relates. When Scotty hears the word *expansion*, even 50 years later, he still becomes slightly non-comprehending and angry. "The old teams could protect 11 skaters and a goalie from their NHL roster, and number 13 went to the expansion teams. Then 14 was pulled back, 15 went, 16 was pulled back . . . As an expansion team, you got players 13, 15, and 17, and once an existing team lost three players, that was it. Plus a goalie. They didn't lose any more." And the Blues, and the other expansion teams, didn't get any more. That was it. The rest were minor leaguers—players who couldn't score enough to play on the top two lines of an NHL team, or who couldn't defend reliably enough to play on the third line or on one of the two sets of defence. Players who weren't offensive players *or* defensive players, but who would need to become at least defensive players. None who could "light the light."

Something that went little noticed at the time was that for the following two years the old teams also kept for themselves the best of the next generation of players. There was still the draft of the young players who were not already on an NHL (read "Original Six") team's list, but not a draft fully open to everyone (read "expansion teams" too) until 1969, when the direct sponsorship of junior and younger teams ended. Because of this, the new teams were whatever they would be in their first season, but unlike the existing teams they would stay mostly the same in subsequent years—only get older.

This blueprint for expansion had been put together by NHL president Clarence Campbell and the Original Six team owners, but it was someone else who proved to be the indispensable man. He was only an employee—and just 40 years old—and had been the general manager of one of the Original Six teams for only two years. He had started with his team as a part-timer, but had made himself so essential that a job was created for him, then another, then another. He didn't start out as the most important figure in the expansion process—but he made himself that, because he knew more about the league and how it worked than Campbell or any of the owners. That someone was Sam.

The league office consisted of Campbell, a few senior executives in charge of one thing or another, and some support staff. But Sam knew where all the players were. He knew all the coaches, all the scouts, all the GMs, all the team presidents and owners. He had lived and breathed and thought about hockey every minute of every day for over 20 years. If anybody involved with any team needed to know something about anything, they called Sam. His involvement with expansion was a little awkward, of course. Sam ran an existing team—and not just any team, but the Montreal Canadiens—and Sam was no kindly and benevolent statesman. He was, as Scotty says about only a select few, "ultra competitive." He loved to win. He needed to win. He was *about* winning. He couldn't win on the ice himself, or even behind the bench, but he could get the right players to win. And, as Scotty puts it, "He wanted *every* player. He hoarded players. And once he had them, he didn't want to give them up." In today's way of speaking, players to Sam were "assets." They may not help his team straight away, but they might help someone else now and help his team later—in favours, or in draft picks. But this was a league expansion. He too would lose players in the draft. How was this going to work? And why would the owners of the other teams trust him?

Sam was a few steps ahead of everyone else here too. If expansion was going to happen, its format and approach needed to be right—and to be right, there had to be people involved who knew what they were doing. And no one knew more than Sam. It would mean him spending a lot of time on league matters, but he knew that if there was to be a new system, then to do his Montreal job he had to know everything about it—all its ins and its outs—so that when it was in place, he could use it better than everyone else because he understood it better than everyone else. And an added bonus—something even he likely didn't anticipate—was that by taking on this role he had to deal with owners, who in working with him would see him in action, know him, and come to trust him. The owners of the existing teams knew how much Sam hated to give up players, so they knew the expansion formula, which had to apply to everyone including the Canadiens, would favour them as well. And the owners of the new teams, desperate for additional players because of the expansion formula, knew that only Sam had the players outside the NHL that might help them. Until he left hockey in 1978, Sam would make the new system work for himself and for the Canadiens, not just for others. He was able to deal directly with owners in making trades, while the other GMs could only deal with each other.

When talk of expansion began in the mid-1960s, Scotty had thought about what it might mean for him, of course. How could he not? He tried *not* to think about it, but he could also see what was going on around him, with the other coaches and managers outside the NHL, and with the scouts and the junior and minor-league guys. He could hear the whispers—from the big talkers, from the opportunists, from those stuck in their jobs and going nowhere; they were beginning to rev up their engines. They knew if they waited for the green flag to drop to start the race, for expansion to be officially announced, then the best and fastest would roar past them and win. So they needed to jump off the line before the flag came down, by talking to their buddies rumoured to be on their way to the new teams, and quietly make plans. But Scotty wasn't good at that—at the subtle, behind-the-scenes manoeuvring. When he had tried to do that in the past, he'd seemed pushy. Inappropriate. And how do you leave Montreal? The Canadiens were the Stanley Cup champions again. The torch had been passed from those great teams of the 1950s—it had taken four long years, but now that itself seemed a distant time ago. Toe Blake was Toe Blake. Sam was Sam. Someday Blake would go, he would retire. But Sam would find an answer. To Scotty, you don't give up the best. Where else would he go? What would he do?

But Scotty also knew something else about the Canadiens. Something he had seen many times. It always had had to do with players, but now he could see that it had to do with him as well. Ralph Backstrom had been the best junior player in Canada in the mid-1950s. Scotty had coached him with the Junior Canadiens; he had seen him against all the other good players in the country. Backstrom had come to the Canadiens right out of junior—almost no one did that, and certainly not to a team that had just won three straight Stanley Cups. On the big team he'd played on the third line. He'd gotten third-line minutes of ice time, and was never on the power play. But he scored 18 goals in his first season. In the playoffs, on the way to another Cup win, he had 8 points in 11 games. He was rookie of the year. Béliveau was the number-one centre, of course, and Henri Richard was number two. But Backstrom was only a kid, and he was just incredibly happy to be on the Canadiens, in the NHL, winning Stanley Cups. And the Canadiens kept on winning, and Béliveau and Richard kept on being the best 1–2 centres in the league. And Backstrom continued to be the best number three.

Then Backstrom was no longer a kid. He was still the best third-line centre in the NHL, everybody knew that—and everybody knew he could be a first- or second-line centre anywhere else. But third-line centres get less ice time, play fewer power plays, play with less offensively skilled linemates, get fewer chances, score fewer goals, and don't develop to their fullest. For more than a decade, Backstrom remained that best third-line centre in the league, and by 1966–67, the season before expansion, he had won four Stanley Cups. Béliveau was now 35, Richard 30, and Backstrom 29. Béliveau wouldn't retire for four more years; Richard for seven. For Backstrom, maybe playing behind Béliveau and Richard and being the best third-line centre in the league was enough. Or maybe it wasn't—maybe it was a bargain he was willing to make. If Scotty stayed in Montreal, would he become Ralph Backstrom?

It was Lynn Patrick who gave Scotty his chance. Patrick was the son of Lester Patrick, who had been a great defenceman in hockey's early years, and was later a coach, manager, owner, hockey entrepreneur (he created the Pacific Coast Hockey Association), and innovator (he introduced the forward pass into his league, many years before the NHL adopted it). In 1928, as the Rangers' 44-year-old coach and general manager, Lester Patrick had come out from behind the bench in Game 2 of the Stanley Cup final to replace his team's injured goalie. Lynn Patrick had also lived a full hockey life, as a player and a coach with the Rangers, and as a coach and general manager with the Bruins. His brother, Muzz, had also been a player, coach, and manager with the Rangers. But for Scotty, the most important of his connections to the Patrick family had been with Lynn's son, Craig, who had played for him with the Junior Canadiens. Craig knew what Scotty could do. So in June 1966 when Lynn Patrick was hired as the Blues' first coach and general manager, he signed Scotty as his assistant coach and manager. They began a year before the Blues played their first game—Scotty helping Patrick to put together the team. When their inaugural season began, the team won only four of its first 15 games.

The team's 16th game was in Philadelphia. Scotty was behind the bench with Patrick, changing the defence pairings. The Blues were ahead, 2–1, late in the second period. Scotty suggested to Patrick that to protect the lead going into intermission, he not send out Roger Picard, a high-risk forward, but veteran Gerry Melnyk instead. Patrick left Picard on the bench but replaced him with an equally unreliable forward, Wayne Rivers, and the Flyers tied the game. Philadelphia scored again in the third period and won, 3–2.

"About one o'clock in the morning, I got a call from Lynn," Scotty remembers. "'I know you're upset,' he said. 'The game has passed me by. Starting tomorrow, I want you to be the coach.' [Later that morning] I called Sam. I said to him I wasn't sure I wanted to take the team now. I told him our veterans weren't as good as we thought, and a few other things. He just said, 'I don't know what to say but somebody's going to coach this team.'" Instead of giving him the way out he was looking for, Sam gave Scotty the push he needed.

Patrick stepped down as coach, and Scotty replaced him behind the bench. After all his remarkable ups and surprising downs, at age 34 Scotty was an NHL coach.

The St. Louis Blues were not the Montreal Canadiens, of course. But the Peterborough Petes hadn't been the Junior Canadiens either, and nor had the NDG Monarchs—just as the Park Extension Flyers hadn't been the Canadiens' Junior Bs. You find a way to coach what you've got. If you don't have players who can light the light, you get players who can extinguish the other guy's light. And before you do anything, you extinguish from your mind everything you think you know about a player. Somebody who is too small, too old, too slow, too injured—if you assume they can't, they won't. If you give them a chance, they might.

In that year of preparation before the Blues began play, Lynn Patrick had gotten a letter, Scotty recalls. "It was from a guy who was an opera singer in Los Angeles. He said he had a brother, and his name was Frank St. Marseille, and we should take a look at him. I knew a little about St. Marseille—he'd had a good career with the Port Huron Flags. And I knew the guy who ran the rink there and was the manager of the Flags, Morris Snider. He used to send players to the Canadiens' camp, and [so] I called him." The Flags played in the IHL, a league of players who were neither on their way up nor on their way down, and who were making a pretty nice life for themselves settling into a team and into a community where they would live and work after their hockey careers were done. Just as Robbie Irons did in Fort Wayne.

"I asked him about [St. Marseille], and he said, 'Scotty, I don't know if he's fast enough for the big leagues, but he's one of the best players in our league.' I went to see him one night in Port Huron. Then

I said to Lynn, 'We should sign him. We need some players to play in the minors.' So the next year, [St. Marseille's] playing in Kansas City"—the Blues' minor league affiliate in the CPHL; Doug Harvey was their player-coach—"we get off to a bad start in St. Louis, some of our players weren't as good as we thought they were, some of our veterans, and when I became coach, Lynn said, 'You can bring up anyone you want. We're not good enough.' I used to watch all the Kansas City games, and we brought him up."

St. Marseille was almost 28. He would play 11 years in the NHL, and over 700 games. That season in St. Louis, in 57 games, he scored 16 goals—second-most on the team. In the 18 games of the playoffs he had 13 points—also second on the Blues. "He was a wonderful player to pick up for nothing," Scotty says. Then he adds, "I like those kinds of stories."

Al Arbour was another one. By the time the Blues started play in October 1967, he was almost 35 years old. He had played in the NHL through the 1950s and early 1960s, with Detroit, Chicago, and finally in Toronto—always a fifth defenceman at a time when fifth defencemen didn't play much. He was smart and thoroughly reliable, a "defence first," defence-all-the-time player who would have been invisible except for two reasons. He blocked shots, something he had learned from the master, Bob Goldham, his veteran teammate in Detroit. And he blocked shots wearing glasses. No other player in the league wore glasses.

All this together, for Arbour, had added up to a nice career. A Stanley Cup in Detroit, another in Chicago, two more in Toronto (and later, four more as the coach of the Islanders in the early 1980s). To be so reliable as a player, he had to know himself with no-nonsense clarity, and what he knew by the early 1960s was that his NHL career was behind him. In 1962, the Leafs had sent him down to Rochester, their AHL affiliate. It was a good team, Rochester was a nice place, he was an important player, and he would make a good life there for himself and his family. Also, Imlach knew what he could and couldn't do, so Imlach would bring him up when he needed him, and when the need was over, he'd go back to Rochester, happily. Usually, that meant a few games a season with the Leafs, and the playoffs.

This went on year after year. Except in more recent years, Imlach would bring him up but then not play him. And Arbour didn't like that. So, as Scotty relates, "He put in his last contract with the Leafs that he could not be recalled by Toronto without *his* permission." A minor leaguer who might *not* want to be a major leaguer. "Yeah, isn't that something?" In his five previous seasons, Arbour had played only 14 NHL games. So when the Blues took him in the expansion draft, Arbour told them he didn't want to come. "He didn't come to training camp for two weeks," Scotty recalls. "He was a holdout. Most guys, if they were coming from NHL teams, were getting $20,000 or $25,000 in their new contracts. If they had been in the minors, between $10,000 and $15,000. Al got $81,000 for three years. He was 35. It was the best money the Blues ever spent."

Red Berenson was another story. Just after Scotty took over as coach, the Blues traded Ron Attwell and Ron Stewart to the Rangers for two players who, along with Glenn Hall, Plante, and Arbour, would shape the early years of the team: Barclay Plager and Red Berenson. Scotty knew both of them well. He had coached Plager in Peterborough and, briefly, in Omaha. Plager was an undersized defenceman with an oversized heart who later became the Blues' captain and coach. He was already 26 when the trade was made, and hadn't played a single minute of a single NHL game in his life. Berenson was an enigma. He was fast, physically strong, smart, always in good condition; in junior with the Regina Pats, in college at the University of Michigan, and in minor pro with the Hull-Ottawa Canadiens, he had proved he could "light the light." Prior to that season, he'd had three extended chances with the Canadiens and one with the Rangers, and in 166 NHL games he scored 13 goals. He was a player always about to be something—but now, at 28, it looked like he was never going to be. He had played 19 games with the Rangers that season before the trade and scored just two goals. In the next 55 games with the Blues, he scored 22. The following two seasons, he scored 35 and 33.

This happened again and again with the Blues. Dickie Moore, almost three years retired and 37 years old, on no good knees, led St. Louis in scoring in the team's first playoffs. Doug Harvey, 43 years old, player-coach in Kansas City, dropped into the lineup for the seventh game in Philadelphia after pronouncing himself the best man for the job, played over 40 minutes and was the first star of the game. As Scotty says, "You try everything." Jimmy Roberts, who in Montreal was not quite good enough to be a regular winger and not quite good enough to be a regular defenceman, in St. Louis was good enough to be both. And Scotty also gave him a special additional role. The Blues were a team that could defend but couldn't score, so in order to win they had to get a lead and, in the third period, sit on that lead. They had to shut the other team down. Roberts, a useful first- and second-period player, was put on a checking line with Jean-Guy Talbot and Terry Crisp and became an important third-period player too.

In the team's second season, Jacques Plante was the reclamation project. His story was the same as the others, except Plante being Plante, it was never not filled with drama. He hadn't played in any league since his star turn with the Junior Canadiens against the Soviets three years earlier, but Scotty needed a goalie to take some of the load off Glenn Hall. Why not have two all-time greats in net instead of one?

"So Jacques comes down to St. Louis to sign his contract. It was a Saturday, I can remember like it was yesterday, and we had no secretary around, so Jacques says, 'I can type my own contract,' and he does." Very few players of the time could both knit *and* type. "Then he tells me his plan," Scotty says. Plante had watched the first season of expansion very closely, very carefully. "He said to me that he wanted to start off the year playing only home games. And only against the West." The West Division, of course, was where all the expansion teams had been put; where all the minor-league guys were, who, as Scotty puts it, shot like "pea shooters." Scotty found a way to avoid the worst of Plante's plan, something that would have been particularly galling to Hall, who took pride in *always* playing, insisting that Plante play at least occasionally on the road and against the East. Hall had begun his full-time NHL career with Detroit on October 6, 1955, and didn't miss a game until November 7, 1962. 502 consecutive games. A goalie. Without a mask.

Yet there were still other Plante moments that season. One came late in the year. "Jacques had pulled a muscle in the all-star game, and was out for a month. So we had to play Glenn more. We had two games left, one in Oakland [and] the next night in L.A. The idea was to play Jacques and Glenn half the game in each. Glenn started the one in Oakland, and near the halfway mark of the second period, we got a penalty." Plante was sitting on the bench near to where Scotty was standing. "Jacques grabbed me and said, 'Let him finish the penalty,' which made sense, and I did, but then Jacques went in, and he was rusty, and let in three goals." Scotty pauses, coming to the complicated part. "And going into the game Jacques knows his goals against average was 1.9-something—anyway, under two. He always kept close track of that.

"So now it's the next day, we're in L.A. and Plante comes to me and says he's tweaked a groin or something, and can't play. I was really upset, and I said, 'Jacques, we've got this plan,' because I knew what he was up to. His average was still under two. Then Doug Harvey comes to me and says, 'Scotty, Jacques's not going to play tonight. I know him. Even if you try to make him, he's not going to play.' Then Camille Henry, who'd also played with Jacques with the Rangers, said the same thing.

"Well, now I'm stuck, because Clarence Campbell [the NHL president] has already told us we had to play our best lineup"—because playoff positions for some teams had still not been decided. "So I had to go to Glenn and I told him about Jacques's injury. Well, he really blew up. He said, 'Well, I've got a sore back. I've got a sore leg. Then he said, 'But, goddammit, I'll play.' Christ, he went in there and stood on his head, and we beat the Kings, 3–1.

"But now the players are upset," Scotty says. "They knew Jacques. They knew what had happened. So, after the game, we all had our luggage in the dressing room to go to the airport to fly home, and the players put a white cross on Jacques's bag, and had written on the board: *Number 76, Win it for Jacques.*" The game against the Kings had been the 76th game of the season.

"Well, Jacques got upset. Now we've got a new problem. We're back in St. Louis, and now he's got to show everybody that he really is injured, and the playoffs are about to begin. We're staying at a hotel outside town, and he refuses to come. He says he's got to get treatment. We've got Glenn, but the year before we went to the finals and that's a lot of games, and we're going to need Jacques too. Now it's the day of the first game and Camille Henry comes up to me and says, 'Scotty, I know this guy. He will not play a minute of the playoffs unless we suck up to him. Everybody's going to have to go up and ask him how he's doing.' So they did. Now everything is perfect again. He's back on the team, sort of."

But there was one final twist. When the playoffs began, "We're playing the Flyers, it's in St. Louis, it's the first game, and maybe 15 minutes into the game, Glenn makes a great save and pulls his hamstring. He can't play. And Plante is sitting in the dressing room; he's supposed to be on the bench. The referee was Art Skov, and he comes over to me and says we can't wait any longer, and of course, it takes Jacques at least five or seven minutes to get onto the ice. But he comes in, and we win eight straight games."

That was Jacques. "He was the strangest guy you ever saw," Scotty says. "He was asthmatic. The hotel in Toronto set off his allergies, he said, so he had to stay at another hotel." Scotty shakes his head. "Another time, we're out west and he goes out with the guys to this big restaurant. They order lobster, he orders his little hamburger. He's allergic to lobster, he says. His asthma." Plante, like many other goalies, was known to be cheap. "The next night the owner flew in and had a big spread for us and Jacques is eating lobster, and of course the guys notice, and he explains to them, 'You can't fight it all the time.'" Scotty pauses, then says, "He was his own guy." There's amazement, admiration, and several other things in his voice. "But he was such a goalie."

You coach what you've got.

"When I went to St. Louis," Scotty recalls, "we didn't design the team a certain way. It just happened—it's the players we had, we had good goaltending and we had a very tough defence. We had the two Plager brothers, Barclay and Bob. We had Noel Picard, a big, strong guy who was always all over you. He feared nobody. We had Al Arbour. We didn't set out to play the way we did, it evolved that way. We were tough to play against." In the playoffs that first year, this became even clearer. "We had a very physical series against the Flyers, there were a lot of brawls and we kind of overpowered them. And [Flyers' owner] Ed Snider said at the time, 'My team will never get beat up again,' and he blamed us in St. Louis." That was the start of the Broad Street Bullies.

For three consecutive years, the Blues went to the Stanley Cup final, losing twice to the Canadiens and once to the Bruins. In the expansion draft, the Original Six teams weren't going to give the new teams the players to compete—but they knew they at least needed to create the *illusion* that they could compete. So the expansion teams were put in their own division so they could play against each other most of the time, and in the first two rounds of the playoffs. One of them, therefore, would make it to the Stanley Cup final. One of them, each and every year, would be a Stanley Cup finalist. But every fan not in those expansion cities knew that the real Stanley Cup final was the East Division final between two of the Original Six teams. After that, it was like a four-game lap of celebration for the eastern champions, the race already decided. Time has stripped from memory most of the details of those playoff years, leaving only the fact that the Blues went to the finals. Hindsight flatters them. The NHL's expansion formula, which limited what they could be, has made them seem better than they were. Still, for the Blues, it was a great achievement.

And these were very important years for Scotty personally. The promise that Sam had seen, that others had seen, his three Memorial Cup finals before the age of 25; then the uncertain years; and now making it to the NHL and to three more finals, and not so much fulfilling that promise—that was still ahead—but showing and knowing it was there. It was in St. Louis that Scotty saw perhaps most clearly the importance of getting a chance and giving a chance. Because that was his own story, and the stories of Hall and Plante, Harvey and Moore, Arbour, Roberts, Berenson, Plager, St. Marseille, and the others. It was the story of the Blues, and it is one he is still immensely proud of. But, as always, Scotty prefers to spend most of his time watching, thinking about, and taking in the present—not dwelling on the past. He likes to see what's in front of him.

In those years with the Blues, Scotty also met Suella Chitty, a nurse who grew up on a farm near Marion, Illinois, about two hours southeast of St. Louis. On August 16, 1969, they were married. Scotty's story was about to deepen and grow.

CHAPTER TEN
Montreal Canadiens 1976–77

Great teams aren't born, they are made. They take time. Pieces important to them come at different moments, in different ways. Some unexpectedly.

April 26, 1971. The Canadiens were in the midst of a surprise playoff run. They had just defeated the defending Stanley Cup champion and overwhelming favourite Boston Bruins in the first round, and were tied at two games apiece in a second-round series against Minnesota. Al MacNeil was the Canadiens' coach, having replaced Claude Ruel in midseason. On that day, Scotty resigned, or was fired, by the Blues.

His time in St. Louis should have ended well. The Blues had gone to the Stanley Cup final three straight years—the first three seasons of their existence. They had finished first in the West Division in the last two of those years, by 19 and 22 points. They had ranked ninth out of twelve teams in attendance in their inaugural NHL season, averaging fewer than 9,000 a game. In their second year, after their run to the final, their attendance jumped by nearly 6,000 to sixth in the league, ahead even of Detroit. Then it rose to over 16,000 in the next year, more even than the Stanley Cup champion Bruins. The following season the Blues' numbers soared again, this time to over 18,000—nearly 1,000 more than the Rangers, who were second, and the highest average attendance in

NHL history. In the best baseball city in America, the Blues became "the" team.

For the 1970–71 season, Scotty had decided to make Al Arbour the coach. It often doesn't work when a player moves directly from the ice to behind the bench, because the other players can't quite come to treat him like a coach, and he can't quite not treat them like teammates. This wouldn't be the case here. Arbour was almost 38 years old. He was universally respected by the players as their captain, and had been a coach in the making, it seemed, all of his career. When the season began under Arbour, the Blues did much as they had done in their first three years, except their start *seemed* worse because the league had realigned and Chicago, now one of the best among the Original Six teams, had moved to the West Division. So the Blues were only second in the standings, not first.

Scotty had known all along what the Blues were and what they had only seemed to be in their initial seasons. So had Lynn Patrick. So had the players. And so had the rest of the league. Maybe the only ones who weren't aware that being a very good team in a bad division doesn't make you a very good team were some of the Blues fans, some of the St. Louis media, and the Salomons—the team's owner, Sidney Salomon Jr., and his son, Sid III. The Blues had gone from an anticipated disaster when they were awarded their franchise, to three Cup finals and the top attendance in the NHL. Maybe Sid III, age 34, was a marketing genius. Maybe he was a hockey genius as well.

So when, as an affront to his own personal narrative, the Blues couldn't keep up with the Black Hawks in the standings, Sid III pushed Scotty to replace Arbour and go back behind the bench. About a third of the season still remained, but with Scotty again as coach nothing much changed. The Blues won about the same percentage of games as they had won with Arbour, and finished second in the division—14 points ahead of third-place Philadelphia, but 20 points behind Chicago. Then, in the playoffs, the unthinkable happened. They lost in the first round to Minnesota. No Cup final this year.

When the season ended, things got messy. Sid III pressured Scotty to get rid of Arbour, the team's assistant general manager Cliff Fletcher, trainer Tommy Woodcock, and Glenn Hall, who Salomon now thought was too old, and when Scotty refused, he was either fired or he resigned. In any event, he left. As it had been in Omaha, he had been better at coaching down than managing up.

Meanwhile, in the East Division, the Canadiens went on to win the next two games against Minnesota to advance to the final against Chicago. At that moment, there seemed no path for Scotty to the Canadiens' coaching job. Montreal then beat the Black Hawks in seven games to win the Cup. MacNeil was 35 years old. Cup-winning coaches who are young enough to continue stay on. But along the way, something had happened.

In 1970–71, Henri Richard, also 35 by this time, was playing in the 16th season of his Hall of Fame career. He was still a remarkable and tireless skater, but he didn't score very often, and the team's other two centres— Jean Béliveau, having a resurgent final season, and Pete Mahovlich, emerging in his first full year—were both eating into his ice time. And you don't mess with Henri's ice time; you don't mess with the pride of a Richard. Game 5 was in Chicago, the series was tied, 2–2. In a game that needed to be won, MacNeil benched Henri in the second period. The team lost, 2–0. The next day, tabloid-size headlines screamed across the front page of every French-language newspaper in the province: "MACNEIL EST INCOMPÉTENT." And every French-speaking Quebecker knew what that meant. Not that MacNeil had blown the game/series/season by benching Richard and was a bad coach, but that unilingual English-speaking MacNeil couldn't relate to his French-speaking players.

The Canadiens came back and won Game 6 of the series in Montreal, and then in the seventh game, behind 2–0 in the middle of the second period, they scored three goals—two of them, including the winner, by Richard—to win the Cup. But by this time, win or lose, for MacNeil the writing was indelibly on the wall, in both French and

English. On June 9, he resigned to become the coach and general manager of the Canadiens' top farm team, the Nova Scotia Voyageurs, in his home province, and Scotty was named coach of the Canadiens. He and Suella, and their eight-month-old daughter, Alicia, were on their way to Montreal. He was 37.

For Scotty, while becoming the coach of the Montreal Canadiens was a dream come true, the real dream come true is what you do when you get there, and the Canadiens in 1971–72, his first season, were not a very good team. And, just as problematic for him, the league's other contenders—the Black Hawks, Rangers, and Bruins—were getting better.

The Black Hawks had come from a decade of blown possibilities. When they won the Cup in 1961, Bobby Hull was only 22, Stan Mikita was 20, and the team's other two top scorers, Bill Hay and Murray Balfour, were 25 and 24 respectively. Pierre Pilote had spent years in the minor leagues and—now 29 and in these pre-Bobby Orr times—was about to begin his run as the league's best defenceman. Even Glenn Hall, also 29, had lots of good seasons ahead of him. But just as important for the Black Hawks was the fact that, as they were rising, the Canadiens were retooling, Detroit was sliding, the Leafs seemed good enough to contend but not to win, and New York and Boston, as always, were going nowhere. For Chicago, the path was wide open. Their best players were so good that, in 1963–64, five out of the NHL's six first-team all-stars were from the Black Hawks. They knew that if they needed a big play, Bobby would score or Glenn would make the save. But their strength proved to be their weakness, because in the playoffs details and little plays matter, and they weren't very good at either.

In 1966–67 Chicago ran away with the league, finishing 17 points ahead of the second-place Canadiens. They also had five of the league's top nine scorers; Mikita and Hull finished 1–2. But then they were beaten in the first round by the Leafs.

Fed up with losing year after year, they became fixated on what was wrong with the team, missed what was right and getting better, and overreacted. Phil Esposito had finished seventh in scoring, he was goofy and funny, and had only just turned 25. But in the playoffs he was shut out completely—in six games he got no points—and Chicago decided he didn't have the grit and drive they needed. Ken Hodge had a big shot, but was lazy. He was only 22. Fred Stanfield, also 22, was a slick skater but too soft. The Black Hawks shipped the three of them to Boston. The trade would be the unmaking of Chicago and the making of the Bruins. In Boston, Esposito would be goofy and funny, *and* he would be a force. Orr now had some playmates.

By the early 1970s, Chicago was remaking itself: not with great stars— Hull and Mikita were still there but in their declining years, and Tony Esposito had only just arrived—but with a deep core of solid pros like Pat Stapleton, Bill White, Dennis Hull, Pit Martin, Jim Pappin, Cliff Koroll, and Chico Maki. Yet the Black Hawks' best years were past—they had missed their chance—and other teams had not stood still. The Rangers, whose ambition for decades had seemed only to fill dark nights at the Garden, were now led by a tiny, combative, career minor-league goalie named Emile "The Cat" Francis, who wanted more. By the early '70s, the Rangers were ready to win. But the big team of the time was the Bruins.

Boston had been Scotty's first favourite team. The games he'd listened to on WHDH; Bill Cowley, number 10, his favourite player; the notes his father had left him on the kitchen table the morning after every game, with the score and the goal scorers' names written on it; the night the Bruins *and* Canadiens players carried Schmidt, Bauer, and Dumart off the ice on their shoulders and on to war (carrying off the fortunes of the team with them for almost three decades). For the Bruins, it had been two Stanley Cups in three years, 1939 and 1941, then a drift into the middle of the pack through the rest of the 1940s, falling a little further in the 1950s, then hitting rock bottom in the 1960s. The final years before the league's expansion in 1967, when four of the NHL's six teams made the playoffs, for eight straight seasons the Bruins finished fifth (twice) or sixth (six times). In five of those years, consecutively, they were dead last—23, 26, 32, 23, and 26 points behind the fourth-place team.

In pre-expansion times, Boston was the one NHL city in the United States that had a deep hockey tradition, where the game was *played* and not just watched. In high schools, prep schools, and colleges, by prospects for the U.S. Olympic team—but not the NHL, not yet, because they were Americans and Americans didn't make the NHL. Yet despite these bad Bruins teams, fans still poured into Boston Garden in numbers that averaged thousands more a game than for Bill Russell, Bob Cousy, Red Auerbach, and the incomparable Celtics, who were NBA champions 11 times between 1957 and 1969. Boston was a great hockey city, and it deserved at least a good hockey team.

But during the darkest of those early-1960s seasons—though there was still no evidence of it in Boston—the Bruins were beginning to get things right. They now had a living, breathing farm system extending from Victoriaville, Quebec, to Estevan, Saskatchewan. They had minor-league teams in Oklahoma City and Hershey. Niagara Falls went to the Memorial Cup final three times, losing in 1963 but winning two years later and then winning again in 1968—this time defeating another Boston team, the Estevan Bruins. Players important to later Bruins' Cup-winning teams were being developed—Ed Westfall, Don Awrey, Wayne Cashman, Derek Sanderson, Don Marcotte—as well as others like Gilles Marotte and Jack Norris, who would become important in trades that brought the team much-needed pieces (Marotte and Norris being two of the players, along with Pit Martin, who secured Esposito, Hodge, and Stanfield from Chicago). But it was Orr who brought the dawn.

Even in Orr's first season, 1966–67, when the Bruins finished last again, everyone—the players, fans, media; in Boston, outside Boston—could see something was going on. Orr was different. Unlike everyone who had come before him, he was as special at 18 as he had been at 10 and 14, not undone in any way by time or injury, by a growth spurt that

174

never happened, by the blaze of unforgiving attention he couldn't handle, by expectation or hope or a head that got too big. If anything, when Orr finally arrived in Boston he seemed even *more* special. No longer a figment of hype or doubt, there he was on the ice, surrounded by big, talented NHL opponents, and he really could skate that fast, he really could find space and time in the strait-jacketing confines of Boston Garden to make magic. In his second season—now with Esposito, Hodge, and Stanfield at his side—the Bruins almost doubled their point total, from 44 to 84, and made the playoffs. Things only got better. The following season, 1968–69, the Bruins took the eventual Cup-winning Canadiens to double overtime in the sixth game of the semifinals (the Canadiens went on to overwhelm Scotty's expansion Blues, 4–0, in the final).

But as good as the Bruins were, they were also fun. The Canadiens of the 1950s had been explosive, the Red Wings a force, the Leafs of the early 1960s were dogged and professional, but none of them were *fun* in the way the Bruins were. The Bruins were Boston: fast-talking and street-smart—Derek Sanderson and Gerry Cheevers; South Boston "Southie"-tough—Cashman, Ted Green, Johnny McKenzie; and "across the river"-Cambridge gifted—Orr and Esposito. They were that best mix of Boston: tough enough to be Bruins, and talented enough to be champions. And not perfect. The Celtics were *too* good. They weren't Boston. The Red Sox were *too* bad. The Patriots, at the time, weren't anything. And later, when they became great, they had all this *la-di-da* excellence about them. Like machines. Too much Tom Brady and not enough Rob Gronkowski. A team to be admired and respected; the Bruins were *loved.* (Gronk would've made a perfect Bruin.) And, besides, what's all this *New England* Patriots stuff?

The Bruins won the Cup in 1970, out-swaggered themselves and blew it in 1971, then stormed back and demolished everyone in 1972.

So in Scotty's first year, the Canadiens weren't good enough to compete with these Bruins, nor with the Rangers or Black Hawks. They were a team running out of momentum. It didn't seem so at the time—just as it hadn't in the early 1960s after five straight Cups, when it seemed that every next season the team would do what came naturally and win again because they were the Canadiens. Even when they didn't. But then they had these exciting young players coming up—the best young players in the country. Frank Selke, Sam, and Scotty had seen to that. But they didn't realize at the time how much it meant to lose the Rocket, to lose Harvey, Plante, Geoffrion, and Moore, to retirement, age, or injury. To lose the defining player, the outsized personality, the teammate who was both immensely loved and a little bit feared.

The Canadiens overcame those times, though it took four losing seasons to do so, and between 1965 and 1969 they won four more Cups in five years. But these later teams never did seem like a dynasty, maybe because they lost after they had won only two in a row, then won two more. Maybe because the 1950s teams had cast such a long shadow. And now this next generation of Montreal teams of the late 1960s was also running out of steam. The break point should have happened, the transition should have begun after the 1969–70 season, when, impossibly, the Canadiens *missed* the playoffs—or certainly the next year, after they followed up that failure with a thoroughly mediocre regular season. But then that was capped off with the Cup win, so maybe not.

The young and the promising were also again pouring in—Réjean Houle, Marc Tardif, Guy Lapointe, Pete Mahovlich. I was new too. Yet no one at this time quite realized the effect of Béliveau's retirement. Béliveau had totalled 76 points in his final season, 10th-highest in the league and 27 more than he had recorded the year before, yet he was 39 years old and a diminished player. But his effect went much further than scoring. What had gone almost unnoticed and certainly under-appreciated was that, early in the 1960s when Richard and the others left, Béliveau had not only picked up the torch but had been the steadying presence that saw the team through the bad times to the good ones again. Who would do that now? Not Henri Richard—he was nearing retirement himself. Not the other most senior players on the team—Terry

Harper, Jacques Laperrière, J.C. Tremblay. Not Frank Mahovlich, who had come to Montreal in a mid-season trade from Detroit. Not Yvan Cournoyer. He was the team's best player, and at 27 at an age to take on more, but he was more a bigger-than-life scorer than a bigger-than-life personality. Toe Blake wasn't around either. He had retired after the 1968 championship, having won eight Stanley Cups in his thirteen years as coach—another bigger-than-life figure both loved and slightly feared. In fact, Blake's effect had been so great that the year *after* his retirement, under his successor, Claude Ruel, the players dared not *lose* the Cup for fear it might mean a shift back to a new coach with Blake's heavy-handed ways as opposed to Ruel's passionate, gentle "my boys" approach. So the team did win in 1969. But then came the humiliation of missing the play-offs the year after.

In 1971, two people might have hastened the team's transition, but neither was ready for the task: Scotty and Guy Lafleur. "We arrived the same week," Scotty recalls with a laugh. On Wednesday, June 9, 1971, Scotty had been named coach of the Canadiens; on Thursday, June 10, Lafleur was picked first overall in the NHL draft. And in the hours between, Sam had put Scotty to work. Sam called a meeting. It was about Lafleur and Marcel Dionne.

Lafleur was one of the rare players whose entrance into the NHL was anticipated years before he arrived. Not quite like Béliveau or Orr—they were of a different magnitude still; more like Mario Lemieux, Eric Lindros, Sidney Crosby, and Connor McDavid, who would all come later. But Guy Lafleur was going to be a great NHL player, and anybody who knew anything about hockey knew that. In his second-last year of junior with the Quebec Remparts, he scored 103 goals. In his final season, 130—more than two goals a game. But there was another great junior in the draft that year: Marcel Dionne. His numbers weren't as stratospheric as Lafleur's, but Dionne had played with St. Catharines in the more competitive OHA. In the weeks before the draft, a debate arose about who would be selected first, in part because Dionne was so good, and in part because hockey people love to see what others don't, and to argue.

Here in one draft were two great juniors. And not only that, two great *French-Canadian* juniors. Sam knew this was the moment that could define the next decade of the Montreal Canadiens. Two years earlier, he had lost out on Gilbert Perreault when, after the league's expansion, the draft rules were changed and the Canadiens no longer had the right to preselect two French-Canadian players as their draft picks. Perreault had gone to Buffalo.

To get Lafleur, Sam needed the first overall pick, and so before the 1970–71 season he had to figure out which team in the league would finish last. He decided on the California Golden Seals, and a year before the draft he made the trade, with a player and a first-round draft pick going to each team (Montreal trading its 1970 pick, certain to come much later in the draft, for California's 1971 pick which was certain to be much earlier). The resulting four players turned into three who would have solid pro careers—Ernie Hicke, François Lacombe, and Chris Oddleifson—and Lafleur. With that accomplished, the next season, the year of the draft, Sam began to think about which team might finish second-last.

When he was a kid in Snowdon, when he was hustling players for Selke to build his farm system, Sam had seen how even the Rocket wasn't enough to allow the Canadiens to match up with the Leafs, then the Wings. How it had been the Class of '31—Béliveau, Geoffrion, and Moore—that had put the team over the top, that had made the Canadiens Stanley Cup champions and had made the Canadiens French-Canadian. Lafleur and Dionne might be Béliveau and Geoffrion all over again. They could be the legendary *Draft* Class of '71. As it turned out, Detroit finished second-last and had the second pick in the draft. Ned Harkness was the Wings' general manager—the same Ned Harkness who had tried to recruit Scotty to RPI and who coached me at Cornell.

"We were all at the Queen Elizabeth Hotel [in Montreal]," Scotty recalls. "I remember vividly, there was [head scout] Ronnie Caron, Al

MacNeil, Claude Ruel, a guy named Eric Taylor [also a scout], myself, and Sam. And Sam was really pressing everybody, pressing on the difference between Lafleur and Dionne. Claude had seen Lafleur play a lot. I think [Canadiens owner] Dave Molson had seen him play in Verdun and Lafleur didn't have a terrific game. I don't know if Sam worried about that or not. He told us he was very close to making a trade with Detroit to get their pick. The trade was Phil Myre, a young goalie that had some possibility, and either Terry Harper or J.C. Tremblay, both on the back end of their careers—and also a young player, I could never remember who it was. It could be a done deal, Sam said. [Then] he asked the question, and I'll never forget it. He said, 'If I can make this deal, and I think I can, could this be like getting Béliveau and Geoffrion for the next 10 years?' And somebody said, I think it was Ronnie, 'Not really, because Dionne is not a big guy. He's a small player.' And Sam, when he made a trade, he'd push everybody like hell, but if everybody didn't agree, he wasn't going to do it. And it didn't go through. It didn't go through. Came close."

Still, Lafleur was the prize, and the excitement in Montreal after the draft was about what *did* happen, not what didn't. The storyline was perfect. The great star, Béliveau, and the great star-to-be, Lafleur: both were centres, both had played in Quebec. The great star who for many years and many Stanley Cups had worn number 4 with honour and distinction; the great star-to-be who had worn that same number 4 in honour of his hero. The great star skating off Forum ice one last time with one last Cup in May; the great star-to-be skating onto Forum ice for the first time in October, with many Cups ahead. *To you from failing hands we throw the torch, be yours to hold it high.*

But then October arrived, then November, and Lafleur wasn't Lafleur, and the Canadiens weren't the defending Cup champion Canadiens. Lafleur was doing *fine*, everyone tried to say—and tried to mean it when they did. *He's a kid. He's learning. Be patient. Besides, they have him on right wing. He's a centre. That's what he played in Quebec.* But the

Canadiens had Henri Richard, Pete Mahovlich, and Jacques Lemaire at centre—where was he going to fit in? And they already had Cournoyer at right wing; he'd scored 37 goals the year before and would score 47 this season. All the best scoring slots were taken.

And a few hundred kilometres away, on a lousy Detroit team where he was needed to play anywhere and everywhere, Dionne was piling up points; and in Buffalo, playing on a line with Perreault in the energy-filled atmosphere of a second-year team that was beginning to take shape, Rick Martin, the fifth overall pick of the 1971 draft, who had played with the Junior Canadiens, was scoring goals at a sniper's pace.

Lafleur had a *good* rookie season. He also had a disappointing rookie season. He scored 29 goals. But Dionne scored 28 and had 77 points to Lafleur's 64, and Martin scored 44 goals, a rookie record. In the Calder Trophy voting, five players—including California's Gilles Meloche and Pittsburgh's Dave Burrows—received votes. Lafleur was not one of them.

Many of the team's veteran players were also unhappy that year. Harper, Laperrière, and J.C. Tremblay were all in their early thirties—old enough to feel a little old and banged up, to notice what's *wrong* with everything and not often what's right, and to begin to feel that the best may be past and that Montreal may not be the only place to play. And it had been a sour year for Scotty too. He never seemed comfortable; he never seemed happy. No matter what question he was asked by the media, no matter what he said, everything came out sounding defensive. As if he felt a need to explain how this team really wasn't very good—certainly not as good as the Bruins, Rangers, and Black Hawks—and for three years really hadn't been very good, except for that two-month blip in the spring of 1971. And that, just because he had taken over a Stanley Cup–winning team, and this team, that season, wasn't going to win a Stanley Cup, it didn't mean he was a failure and a lousy coach. In his body language and tone, this seemed to be his message every time he opened his mouth. He was going to need to learn, and to deal with this—and fast—or Montreal and its media were going to eat him up.

But if the season was hard for Scotty, that summer would be even harder.

—

On June 3, 1972, six weeks after the season ended, David Scott Bowman was born. Scotty and Suella now had two children under the age of two; Alicia Jean, named for Scotty's mother, was a year and a half. Scotty had something else to focus him and distract him.

The summer began as it always did. Scotty's parents still had their cottage on the lake in Lancaster, Ontario. Everyone made plans to be there in mid-July: Jack and his family; Freda and hers too. David's eight-week post-natal examination was to come during this time, so Scotty and Suella arranged to have it a week earlier. It was a Friday, and it was the only time Scotty ever remembers going to a doctor's appointment with Suella for any of the kids. David was weighed and tested, and everything was fine. Afterwards, Scotty did recall the doctor saying that David's head measurement was "on the high side of normal," but as the doctor didn't seem to think anything more of it, then neither did Scotty. So he, Suella, Alicia, and David drove on to the cottage. It was a good week, and everybody was having a good time. Scotty's mother even commented on how of all her seven grandchildren, David was "the easiest one to take care of." David, Scotty recalls, was "sleeping all the time."

The following Friday, the family drove back to Montreal. Scotty had agreed to play in a golf tournament. In the midst of his round, someone from the pro shop rushed out to find him. David had had a convulsion.

Scotty raced home and drove Suella and the kids to the Montreal Children's Hospital. David's condition seemed to have stabilized. They saw a neurologist, who told them it could be "a lot of things," and made an appointment for them to see a specialist on Monday. Then they went home.

The weekend was uneventful. They went over to Jack's place—he had two young kids and, as Scotty remembers it, he couldn't stop himself from looking at Jack's kids to see if their heads were also "on the high side of normal." When he and Suella and David returned to the hospital on Monday, a neurosurgeon examined David and right away scheduled surgery for that afternoon. David was hydrocephalic. His spinal fluid was not draining and instead was building up inside his head, putting more and more pressure on his brain. The surgeon put in a shunt to drain the fluid, but as he told them, "Part of his brain has been damaged; we've corrected what we can."

By the end of July, David was home. Scotty and Suella knew what was ahead, but they didn't. David was hard to look after, but any two-month-old baby is hard to look after. And the season was approaching—a season whose training camp begins on a certain day and no other; whose preseason games and opening game are played on certain nights and no others. A season that had to be a lot better. By the time Alicia turned two on October 26, David was almost five months old and getting harder to look after. In August, whatever in their deepest hopes might *not* be ahead for David, for Scotty, Suella, and Alicia, in October *was* ahead. Scotty and Suella decided they would have a family Christmas together at home—all of them would be there. Then, on December 26, Scotty, Suella, and David drove to Notre-Dame-des-Anges ("Our Lady of the Angels"), a residence in the far east end of Montreal, where, as Scotty says, "there were lots of babies like him." Scotty knew, and Suella knew better, that David could not stay at home. Suella had been a nurse; she had seen a lot of things. They also had another child, and at just about this moment, she had found out she was pregnant again. Soon they would have another baby to care for.

"It had been a tough season," Scotty says now, "but nothing was like this. It brought us a perspective. It's like you live two lives—your job and your life. Some things you have to live with, you can't control."

For the Canadiens in 1972–73, it was as if everything just flipped from the season before—though there weren't any big changes of personnel. J.C. Tremblay did sign over the summer with the Quebec Nordiques of the new World Hockey Association (WHA) and Terry Harper had been traded to L.A., but no new significant players had been added. When the games began, Cournoyer, Henri Richard, and Frank and Pete Mahovlich played much as they had the year before, but others—as they were put into and earned new roles—got better, making the team better. Defenceman Guy Lapointe—athletic, strong, a great skater, but who even in junior had been more a talent than a star—began to emerge, then blossom. And Serge Savard, the guy Scotty and Cliff Fletcher forgot to tell to stay home in Amos. He'd won the Conn Smythe Trophy as the MVP of the 1969 playoffs, but he then broke his leg, then broke it again—same leg—and was out for half a year, then another half year, and became the guy who was always around the dressing room but never on the ice, always rehabbing, the team finally having to move on without him. But this season he came back, and got stronger, and stronger, until—with his big plough horse's body and thoroughbred's grace—he became what he had always been, and everyone stopped thinking about his leg. And then there was Jacques Lemaire. A two-way player with a big shot who even in his early twenties scored a reliable 30 goals or so a year. A year earlier he had gone from 56 points to 81. Who could ask for more? Who could imagine more? This season, Lemaire would score 95 points, with 44 goals. Imagine his excitement. Imagine Savard's and Lapointe's. Imagine the team's, the fans', the media's, the city's.

The team didn't lose until its 14th game of the season. In its last 49 games, from December 13 to April 1, it lost only five times. Midway through the season, it got an unexpected boost. The game that night was against Minnesota. Some of the team's defencemen were injured or sick, and when we arrived in the dressing room before the game there was this new person sitting there. I didn't know who he was at first, but it was Larry Robinson. I don't know how I didn't recognize him. We had been at two training camps together, and Robinson, unnaturally tall and raw-boned, is unmissable.

Scotty needed him to play a regular shift that night, and I expected he would do so very cautiously, very defensively, and have a galumphy look about him. Instead, he was composed, comfortable, agile, and in control. I remember thinking, *Where did this guy come from? We've got all these terrific players on this team, and we've got guys like* this *in the minors? This is unbelievable!* I don't remember Lafleur's first game, but I remember Robinson's. It was just more excitement to add to all the rest. In that 1972–73 season, Lapointe emerged, Savard re-emerged, and Robinson appeared. The "Big Three." But for them, and for the Canadiens, the best was yet to come.

Scotty was different that season too. He wasn't just this kid from Verdun any longer, getting older and better and yet—so far as the big team was concerned—somehow always with his nose pressed up against the glass. As he had been with Dick Irvin at the practices he watched when he ate his early lunch working for Sherwin-Williams, as he had been with Toe Blake, and with Sam, as he had been even in St. Louis, and as he had been in his first season in Montreal. But now this was *his* team—not Al MacNeil's or Sam's. He, Scotty Bowman, was the coach of the Montreal Canadiens. And late one night in Chicago—May 10, 1973—he became Scotty Bowman, coach of the Stanley Cup–winning Montreal Canadiens. A month and a half later, he and Suella had their third child. They named him Stanley. Stan Bowman is now the three-time Stanley Cup–winning general manager of the Chicago Blackhawks.

"It was a big, big feeling winning the Cup," Scotty says, "because I grew up in Montreal. I had worked for the team when they won Cups before, but it's not the same. You feel part of it, but it's not even close to when you're with a team all year. It's a very long grind, and when you finally win, then you have so much time. You've got three or four months to really enjoy it before you start up again. It's a big feeling when you know it's finally over."

One time during that Cup-winning season, Scotty and I had a problem. We never had a problem. We never talked for more than a minute or two at a time, and usually for far less, as he didn't really talk with any player. But he understood me, and I understood him, and the team was doing fine, and he and I were doing fine, so there was never a reason to talk more. After the Canadiens' Cup win in 1971 and before Lafleur had truly arrived, I might have been the most important player on the team. Maybe what followed was because I sensed this, or maybe it was because as we got better in 1972–73 I mattered less, but whatever the reason, more often after I let in goals I'd slam my stick to the ice and glare, as if I was angry at myself—it seemed that way to others at first—then as if I was angry at *them*, at all of my teammates, because of the guy *they* had left open, because of the rebound *they* didn't clear. Because, by implication, *they* didn't share the same high standards I did and didn't care as much. Because *they* had let *me* down. In short, I was acting like a diva.

One day after practice while we were still on the ice, Scotty skated over to me. "Do you think you're too good for this team?" he asked in his finesseless way. He mentioned my stick-slamming, my glares, my ungenerous post-game interviews. I was stunned. I was embarrassed. And I was angry. Angry at him. Angry because of what he'd said. Angry because he was probably right and I knew it. I never stopped being angry at him the rest of the season. When we won the Cup, Scotty's first, and he was on the ice hugging all the players, when he got to me, he hugged me and I didn't hug him back.

This new generation of Montreal Canadiens was on its way—like Toe Blake's teams in the 1950s and the 1960s had once been. And to make it easier, as we were getting better, our rivals were getting worse. Bobby Hull had left the Black Hawks for the WHA, and Pat Stapleton followed. The Rangers matched contract offers by WHA teams and kept their best players, but afterwards some of them seemed less driven—as if, after all the team's horrible years, being competitive was good enough. But it was the Bruins that fell the furthest. They had been on their way to becoming one of the greatest teams of all time. They had Orr. They had Esposito. They had an outstanding young coach, Harry Sinden. First, Sinden left after their Cup win in 1970. Then, after the Bruins won again in 1972, Cheevers, McKenzie, and Sanderson went to the WHA. And while Orr continued to pile up his incredible numbers, his knee surgeries were piling up too.

But then the Canadiens stumbled. Houle and Tardif left for the Quebec Nordiques of the WHA. I got into a contract dispute, and, having graduated from law school that spring, left the team to work for a year as an articling student in Toronto. With the door now open, two other teams got their chance and barged through it—the Flyers and Sabres. They didn't bring the Canadiens down; the Canadiens did that themselves. It was a lesson for later.

The Canadiens had played both the Flyers and the Sabres in the 1973 playoffs. They could see how good they were becoming. The Sabres could skate, especially their newly formed "French Connection" line with Perreault, Martin, and René Robert, who, after scoring 13 goals the year before, had scored 40 that season. The Sabres could also defend: Craig Ramsay and Don Luce were becoming two of the top shutdown forwards in the league; Jim Schoenfeld was an exciting young defenceman. And the Sabres GM, Punch Imlach, had added his usual projects and retreads grateful for one final chance—Tim Horton, 43; Larry Hillman, 35; Tracy Pratt, 29. Imlach worked them hard as he had always worked his older players.

As for the Flyers, they were getting tougher and better. A year earlier, Rick MacLeish had scored one goal. In 1972–73, he scored 50. Bill Barber, a rookie, scored 30. Bobby Clarke, still only 23, was becoming the league's most inspirational leader. And the Flyers' storm was gathering—Dave "The Hammer" Schultz, Don "Big Bird" Saleski, Bob "The Hound" Kelly, each of them with more than 200 penalty minutes, the harbingers of the Broad Street Bullies era. The Flyers would be Stanley Cup champions the following two seasons, beating the Bruins in the final the first year and the Sabres in 1975. But as the Flyers were dominating the hockey conversation, things were happening in Montreal almost unnoticed. It was about Sam.

The Canadiens' farm system was beginning to produce again, but it was a very different system from the one Frank Selke had put together in the late 1940s. League expansion had taken away the right of NHL teams to recruit young players and place them on sponsored teams. There was now just a draft, with the teams able to choose one player per round in the reverse order of finish from the previous regular season. All the players were still coming from Canada but there was no longer a home-ice advantage for Canadian teams—everyone was on equal footing. So for Sam, the challenge had been: How do you turn equal opportunity into unequal results? Nobody else understood the value of young players the way he did, or the special player, the guy who could "light the light."

"He was very selfish," Scotty says admiringly. "He hoarded players. We'd have 80 guys at our training camp. [Before expansion] he'd loan out players he couldn't use to the Cleveland Barons, the Seattle Totems, to Buffalo, Cincinnati, and because every one of those teams had the right to have sponsored teams of their own, the deal was that Sam would get a whole sponsored list from them too to add to our others. That meant 18 more players from each of them, and the Canadiens already had 12 sponsored teams. Some [NHL] teams had two, some had four. I think the highest for any other team would have been five. And the players couldn't move."

This was before free agency. Only when Sam felt certain a player would never play for the Canadiens would he trade him to another team, struggling and desperate to make the playoffs with an empty cupboard of players. "Boston was really weak in the early '60s, and Montreal had a surplus of players, guys like Eddie Johnston, Cliff Pennington,

Billy Carter, and Terry Gray, and rather than lose them in a waiver draft, he convinced Boston, 'Look, take these guys. If they make it, give me a draft pick, or a player on a sponsored list. Just give me something.' He was always doing these little deals."

But after expansion in 1967 there was now a real draft, one that involved more than just the dregs from the unsponsored teams. (Scotty refers to that earlier format as "the phony draft.") And so, in return in trades, there was something more certain for Sam than promises or considerations. So he put together a farm system in a different way—the only way available to him. He would have a farm team like everyone else's—the Nova Scotia Voyageurs in the AHL—except this one had a Stanley Cup–winning coach, Al MacNeil, as their coach and general manager. And Sam would also put a smattering of players with the Muskegon Mohawks in the IHL. But, most crucially, he would create a *virtual* farm team of draft picks. Not just a team made up of the single player from each round that every team had a right to select, but lots of others as well. Just as, a few years earlier, the Bruins had needed players *at that instant*, with the six new teams Sam had six new easy marks that were, almost without exception, little supported, underfinanced, uncompetitive, and desperate. In their highly uncertain existence, the expansion teams were looking for a little bit of certainty. Better a devil they knew—a journeyman player who they were sure could play in the NHL and could play right away—than a 20-year-old junior who might never make it, and even if he did, then only someday, certainly not now.

For Sam, this was like shooting fish in a barrel. In 1971, Lafleur's draft year, in a 14-team league, the Canadiens had three first-round picks; the next year they had four, then one, and in 1974 they had *five*. In the seven years from 1971 to 1977, the Rangers had 10 first-round picks, Boston and Toronto eight, Chicago seven, and Philadelphia six. The Canadiens had 20. "That's an amazing number of draft picks when you think of it," Scotty says, still amazed. "In the '74 draft, imagine five draft picks in the first 15 spots: 5, 7, 10, 12, 15. Wow, *five*."

But even Sam, who more than anyone—including NHL president Clarence Campbell—had been the architect of the NHL's expansion process, who knew its rules, regulations, and secrets inside and out, had to find new answers for all its myriad surprises. He was well suited to the task. He was a puzzler. He thought methodically, and never-endingly, about everything.

Sam didn't like to travel by plane, so he went by car to games instead. Most of the time this wasn't a problem, but in the playoffs, when he wanted to be at every game, it was. In 1971, the seven-game series against the Bruins meant three trips back and forth to Boston in little more than ten days, but Boston was only five hours away. After that were two trips from Montreal to Bloomington, Minnesota—without weather or traffic delays, 19 hours each way—and three more trips to Chicago—13 hours there and 13 hours back. Sam had a driver, Rolie Marcil, and he was instructed not to speak. The radio stayed off. It was a time before cell phones. I used to feel sorry for Sam when I thought about his mind-numbingly long stretches on the road. Then I realized this was his time to think.

And so now, after all these miles and hours of thinking, with all these players and draft picks, in this new post-expansion NHL world, what would he come up with?

There were three new complications in the early 1970s: the WHA, free agency, and—because of both—players with agents. A player was no longer tied to his NHL-team master forever (or until the team decided he wasn't of use and discarded him). When his contract was up, the player could leave, and now with the WHA he had another place to go. At first, even Sam struggled with this new order. He decided to hold to *his* "going rate" on contracts he offered, and not to shift to the new, WHA-induced, *competitive* going rate. He lost Houle, Tardif, and J.C. Tremblay to the Nordiques, and me to a Toronto law office for a year. Then he learned. Not every draft pick—not even every first-round pick—was ready to play in the NHL, especially not for a team as good as the Canadiens.

What was crucial was that he sign those players who might be ready. But even signing them wasn't easy. This was the Montreal Canadiens. They were at least Cup contenders every year and had all of these very good players, and high draft picks who had been stars all their lives. Sure, they were also used to winning, they loved to win—and the Canadiens gave them a better shot at that than anyone else—but they also loved to be stars, they loved the ice time and the attention stars got, and they might not even make the Canadiens, and would almost certainly start in the minors. And then they wouldn't get paid as much. So why should they sign with the Canadiens? Why would their agents want them to sign with Montreal? A new league like the WHA may have brought its own uncertainties, but the agents knew the math: 10 per cent of WHA money was a lot more than 10 per cent of minor-league money.

So then Sam figured out something else. Many of his first-round picks had Alan Eagleson or Bob Woolf as their representatives, the two biggest agents of the time. For his best prospects, Sam proposed this deal to them and to their players: sign with the Canadiens and he would guarantee that they stay with the big team all season, get big-team coaching, and be paid big-team money. But big-team ice time and attention they would have to earn themselves. So Steve Shutt and Bob Gainey and a few others signed on, and in the first years of their careers they played little. But they were in Montreal, on the Canadiens, and were available to play when they were *ready* to play.

Yet Sam also knew that players with star potential needed competition and ice time to develop that potential. It made no sense for him to keep them as players but to lose them as future stars. If they weren't going to get much ice time in games, he needed somebody to work with them before and after practice, and to make practices their games. To have someone get them up for practices as if they *were* games. To push them, exhort them, talk with them, bond with them and get them to bond with each other—to create a spirit. And Sam had the just right guy to do this: Claude Ruel.

Ruel had been a promising player until he lost his sight in one eye with the Hull-Ottawa Junior Canadiens. Then he had been a scout. Then he had taken over from Toe Blake when Blake retired, and coached the Canadiens to their 1969 Stanley Cup win. Now he was Scotty's assistant. He coached like a loving parent, like a scout, always looking for possibilities, becoming excited when he saw them, and doing whatever he could to see them realized. Robinson, Shutt, Gainey—and later Doug Jarvis, Doug Risebrough, Mario Tremblay, Rick Chartraw, Bill Nyrop, and anyone else young and new to the team—became "Claude's Boys." When regular practice time ended, it became *their* time. "C'mon, my boys. C'mon," Ruel would yell, and his boys—pretending to be tired from practice—would suddenly leap into action, break into the open for a pass, and race in on goal for a shot. "Six seconds, my Dougie, six seconds." In that moment it was the seventh game of the Stanley Cup final (always the seventh game), the score was tied, there were six seconds to go (always six seconds), and Dougie or Mario or whoever came next had a chance to win it all. (And I or whoever was in goal had a chance to save it all.) Ruel would repeat this again and again, day after day, year after year. Before there was such a title, he was the Canadiens' "development coach."

More than 30 years later, in 2014, much of the team would be back in Montreal for Jean Béliveau's funeral. Before the service began, the players assembled out of public view at the back of the church. It was a real gathering of the clan, one of those deeply felt, funny, and profound moments that comes later in life. And Claude was there too. He hadn't been well for several years; he hadn't been scouting. Nobody ever saw him. He was standing by himself. All of a sudden one of his "boys" spotted him, then another, then five or six more. They started talking, and laughing, and Claude's face, earnest and proud as it always was, lit up. It was fantastic. Less than three months later, he too passed away.

Still, for Sam, it was never easy to keep the players and their agents if not happy, then at least not destructively unhappy. "I remember in 1973 when we were playing the Flyers in the playoffs," Scotty says. "We were in Montreal, Fred Shero was their coach, he was being interviewed and he said, 'Montreal's got four or five players in the press box that would be regulars on our team.' It was in all the papers. And Sam was so upset. He was on a pretty friendly basis with Ed Snider, their owner, and he called him up and said, 'If this guy keeps coming into Montreal and crapping on our doorstep, I'm going to do the same thing in Philadelphia.' Because they were good young players, and they could get unhappy pretty fast and decide they wanted out."

But Sam had another issue—he couldn't sign all his draft picks, and some would continue to go to the WHA. It took him a while to realize—and then even longer to persuade himself—that if they did go, he wasn't losing them, which was a thought completely repugnant to him. He was only losing *access* to them for the length of their contract. Free agency worked both ways. When their WHA contract was up, now the WHA team had to sign them. And if the player was any good, if he had developed and was ready to play for the Canadiens, Sam could sign him then. So he came to think of the WHA like he did the Voyageurs, as another of his farm teams.

And Sam had one more thought. U.S. colleges had never been a place for serious NHL prospects. College teams played too few games and didn't play the "rough and tough" junior style. Colleges required at least some classroom time, and also prepared their players for futures that might not include hockey. Yet all but the highest first-round picks still needed time outside the NHL to develop. So why not in U.S. colleges? "The Canadiens were one of the first teams to draft college players," Scotty recalls. "It was because of [head scout] Ronnie Caron mainly. He got Bill Nyrop [from Notre Dame]. Later he got [Rod] Langway [from New Hampshire] and [Brian] Engblom [from Wisconsin], he got [Chris] Chelios [also from Wisconsin] and [Craig] Ludwig [from North Dakota]. Some pretty good players." Instead of U.S. colleges being a hockey dead end, Sam realized, he could use them as yet another farm team.

So in Sam's hands the 1967 NHL expansion, which had seemed the unmaking of the Canadiens because it was the unmaking of the farm system, became the remaking of the Canadiens because draft picks were now currency, because draft picks, who might be worse than the living, breathing players they would get back in a trade might also be better and be able to help the team. There's no doubt that every NHL team was weakened by players lost to the WHA, but the Canadiens were weakened less, because they had more players to replace them. Selke's farm system had fuelled the dynasties of the 1950s and 1960s; Sam's fuelled the one in the 1970s. It was a one-off, uniquely Canadiens farm system. A Sam system. This is what Scotty had to work with.

Sam took one more step to cement the future. Lafleur's second season with the Canadiens had been even more disappointing than his first. A year older and now on a good team—a team that was about to win the Stanley Cup—it should have been a far better year for him. But he scored one fewer goal, 28, and had 55 points (down from 64). And 900 kilometres away in Detroit, Marcel Dionne scored 40 goals and had 90 points. With the WHA completing its first season, the Quebec Nordiques had finished fifth in the Eastern Division and were out of the playoffs. They needed to do something big, and Lafleur's two-year contract with the Canadiens was expiring.

"I remember Claude Ruel and I were called into Sam's office during the playoffs," Scotty recalls. "The team was staying at a hotel in the Laurentians [a ski area north of Montreal] and we had to drive down early for the meeting, before the team, and this was on a game day." With their season over, the Nordiques were setting the timetable for the negotiations with Lafleur, and Sam needed to make a decision soon. One other piece of information: Lise Barré, Guy's soon-to-be wife, was the daughter of Roger Barré, who owned a car dealership in Quebec City and was a director of the Nordiques.

As the meeting started, Sam gave Scotty and Ruel some background. "He told us that Quebec had offered [Lafleur] a three-year contract for $150,000 a year. He was making something like $35,000 or $40,000 for the Canadiens, so Sam knew he was in quite a fight to keep him in Montreal. He wanted to hit Lafleur's agent with a million-dollar offer—10 years at $100,000 a year. So instead of $450,000 for three years, it would be a million dollars of our money, because [Lafleur and his agent] knew the NHL is here forever. He'd also be able to renegotiate after every three years. It was a risky offer, and Sam was asking us, 'How good is he going to be?'

"I remember Claude talking more than me and saying to Sam, 'Right now he's a third-line player who will definitely be a second-liner.' Sam was pushing us for some names as comparisons. Claude said to him, 'No less a player than Bob Nevin.' Nevin had been a pretty handy player for the Leafs but not a superstar. A guy who would score some goals, and was responsible. Sam was comforted by that. Because he wanted to know first who [Lafleur] would always be able to be. Will he always be at least a regular in the NHL? I remember like it was yesterday because both Claude and I had the same opinion. Because we didn't say he was going to be a superstar."

At this uncertain point in his career, Lafleur needed to know that the Canadiens believed he was a central part of their future. "Sam had to come up with a real novel contract," Scotty says. "It was the 10-year, million-dollar part that did the trick."

Lafleur signed. The team won the Cup.

All the pieces were now in place. The team that had seemed ready for the rest of the decade after its Cup win in 1973, then had taken a step back, was beginning to find another gear by the 1975–76 season. Henri Richard and Jacques Laperrière had retired; Frank Mahovlich had gone to the WHA. Yvan Cournoyer was the new captain—still an explosive goal scorer, if slightly diminished by injuries. After him in seniority came Jimmy Roberts, then Jacques Lemaire, and Serge Savard, who were still finding their best ways to play and still getting better. Then the players acquired in pre-expansion times—undrafted, like Guy Lapointe—and those from the draft of unsponsored-team players, like Pete Mahovlich, Pierre Bouchard, and me. Then Yvon Lambert, who been traded from Detroit. Then those players who had come from the real draft years, beginning with Lafleur, Robinson, and Murray Wilson in 1971, then Shutt, goalie Bunny Larocque, and Nyrop, then Gainey, then Risebrough, Chartraw, and Tremblay. Then Doug Jarvis by trade from Toronto. But more than the strength of this roster, it was a team that needed to win.

For two years they had lost. For two years the Flyers had won. In the second year, the Flyers, Sabres, and Canadiens had all finished the regular season with 113 points. The Sabres beat the Canadiens in the semifinals, the Flyers beat the Sabres in the Stanley Cup final. The Canadiens had been good enough to win, but didn't. After my year in Toronto in the law office, I wasn't as good as I needed to be. The team and I had some unfinished business. From the moment we lost to the Sabres in May, our mission to win began.

Two events in the first half of the 1975–76 season shaped the year. The first was in training camp. "We had to play [the Flyers] home-and-home—Saturday night in Montreal, Sunday in Philadelphia," Scotty recalls. "And they came into Montreal with a pretty aggressive lineup and it was a rough game. I remember Claude saying to me afterwards, 'We were stupid. We played all our hockey players and they came with all these goons.' The next night we brought in Sean Shanahan, we brought in Glenn Goldup, we brought in [Gilles] Lupien. We had Pierre Bouchard, and we had Chartraw. We brought in a pretty hefty lineup into Philadelphia. Players that could fight, and there was a big brawl. And *ohmygawd* it was a wild game. I remember [Gary] Dornhoefer, he was not a big fighter for the Flyers, but he was an instigator, and he ended up at our bench with Shanahan, and he knew me from Peterborough because he played in Niagara Falls, and he was sort of pleading with me to get this guy off of him." Scotty pauses, "After that, when we played them, the games weren't that rough."

The second event came late in December. "I always felt that the team was on its way to winning against Philadelphia after that '75 New Year's Eve showdown against the Russians," Scotty says. "It was the forerunner." In 1972, the Soviet team had come within 35 seconds of a tie against Team Canada in the eighth and final game of the Summit Series, which would have resulted in them winning the series on goal differential. Paul Henderson's goal with 34 seconds to go changed all that. And in the years that followed, the Soviets got better. Tretiak became a dominant goalie, the team's top line of Kharlamov, Mikhailov, and Petrov grew more confident, new young stars were introduced, and in 1974 the Soviets beat the WHA all-stars decisively four games to one, with three games tied. Next was a series of games in late December 1975 and early January 1976 involving two Soviet club teams, the Central Red Army team of Moscow (CSKA) and the Soviet Wings—each of them playing four games against four different NHL teams. The Army team had on it most of the Soviet national team, and on December 28 it demolished the Rangers, 7–3, in New York. Three days later, it faced the Canadiens at the Forum.

"We played such a great game," Scotty says, employing language he rarely uses. "We played a dominating game, and an exciting game, and in an atmosphere that was just electric. That game gave us an awful lot of confidence. The team was building up an awful lot of confidence. To play a game like that against a team as good as the Russians were, that was pretty dominating." The game ended in a 3–3 tie. The Canadiens outshot CSKA, 38–13. (In my memory, it was the best game we ever played. I remember Jacques Lemaire being *everywhere*—offensively, defensively, all over the ice. I remember everyone playing at the top of their game. Except me. It is my biggest regret in hockey.)

Everything that season went right. The team began the year with a 9–0 win against the Kings, and followed that up with a 9–4 victory over the Bruins in Boston. Between November 19 and January 30 the Canadiens lost twice in 31 games; they lost twice in the final 22 games of the regular season; they lost just 11 games in all. In the playoffs, the team beat the Black Hawks four games to nothing, the Islanders in five games, and, in the final, the dreaded Flyers in four straight, including Kate Smith and "God Bless America" live in Game 3 in Philadelphia. Thirteen games. Twelve wins, one loss.

It was Scotty's second Cup.

And Lafleur—finally, fully, and completely—had become Lafleur. In his first two seasons he had scored 29 and 28 goals. Then in 1973–74, after he signed his 10-year, million-dollar contract, after the Canadiens had demonstrated their belief in him, after he had achieved the security he sought—he scored . . . 21 goals. Maybe his really would be a solid, second-line, Bob Nevin career. But then in 1974–75 he scored 53 goals, and in this Cup-winning year, 56. In the four years that followed, he scored 56 again, then 60, 52, and 50.

He was not his hero, Jean Béliveau. He would never be his hero. When Lafleur started with the team, when he was expected to take up the torch, he was 20—half Béliveau's age. He and Béliveau were two very different people, who played two very different ways. One was tall, elegant, commanding; the other, tempered-blade thin, frenetic. *Fast.* One just did, never surprised that he could. The other, Lafleur, always felt a need to prove himself—to fans, to teammates, and most of all to himself. He was never fully sure he could do something until he did it and discovered he could. It wasn't easy being Lafleur in these years, or even in those that followed. Almost certain to be judged a Béliveau-failure. Almost but never quite being able to be judged a Lafleur-success. But at least now he had Lemaire as his centre, and Shutt as his wingman—guys who could score, who could play to his level and make every moment they were on the ice together fun. He was the team's best player. And his breakthrough was the team's final breakthrough. As he soared, the team soared higher. The uncertainty that never left him and kept him from ever finding comfort was hard on him, but it was good for us. It kept us from becoming too comfortable. It made us a better team, and for longer. Meanwhile, first in Detroit and then in L.A., Marcel Dionne piled up his points on teams that didn't matter, and was never talked about in the same breath as Lafleur for the rest of the decade. And if Lafleur was a different Lafleur, my role had now changed too. On a lesser team, earlier in my career, sometimes, not often, I was needed to win games for the team. Now my job was not to lose them.

"We had no goalie coaches then," Scotty said to me as we were working on this book, "[but] what Sam and Claude and I always talked about was how you could concentrate. When the game started, you'd get into a zone. I had another player like that, not a goalie, Steve Yzerman. I used to say, 'He's in a zone tonight and nothing's going to distract him.' That's the way I felt with you. When you started with the team you got a lot of work, then after, maybe a lot at the beginning of a game, and you'd be there to make the big saves, to make the right save at the right time. A lot of people used to say, 'Well, he's extra studious. He's cerebral, he's going to university. He's got a lot of things on his plate.' But I never worried because I thought when the game started there's nothing else that you were trying to do except stop the puck and win the game. You were ultra-competitive, and sort of like Steve, you didn't show it. You were more on the inside than the outside." He pauses. "When you look at it," he says, "in your seven years, you played about 56 or 57 games a year ... 8 losses, 7, 9, 10, 6, 7, and 10, that's 57 losses in 7 years. Forget about the playoffs, that was even better. I mean that and the fact that all the Stanley Cup finals you participated in resulted in victory, that's something you've got to take a long time to digest."

After we won the Cup that year, Team Canada won gold in the Canada Cup in September with Scotty as coach. Three weeks later, "the twins" were born—Nancy Elizabeth and Robert Gordon ("Bob," named for Bobby Orr). Now Scotty and Suella had five kids, all under the age of six. And two days after that, the new year began. It turned out the 1975–76 season was only a warm-up.

Sometimes when a team wins, though it improves on paper the following year, it is not as good. There isn't the same excitement around it, the same sense of mission, the same hunger. But that next season, 1976–77, the Canadiens really were better. They were more self-assured without being complacent; more self-aware without being arrogant. The players and Scotty knew they were good, they knew their team was special; they still felt unmitigated joy in winning, and not yet its burden, nor yet any fear of defeat. Their need to win and beat the Flyers had been replaced by a feeling of satisfaction at how good they could sense themselves becoming. This was a team that was beginning to realize its possibilities—that had the wind fully in its sails. The season was sheer pleasure.

The Canadiens lost the 3rd game of the year in Buffalo, the 7th in Boston, the 13th against the Bruins in Montreal, the 21st in Toronto, then later in New York against the Rangers, in St. Louis (I got pulled at the end of the first period having let in four goals, the last by Bob Plager as the clock was running out, on a loopy, drifty shot "from the parking lot," as a Blues announcer put it), then in Boston again, then in Buffalo again. That's all. Eight losses. Between January 17 and April 3, the end of the regular season—34 games, one loss.

It was, to use Scotty's word for the New Year's Eve game against the Soviets, a "dominating" season. The Canadiens finished first in the league with 132 points; the next highest were the Flyers with 112, then the Bruins and Rangers with 106, the Sabres with 104, then a huge dropoff to L.A., in sixth, with 83—49 points fewer than Montreal. The Canadiens scored 387 goals; the Flyers were second with 323—64 less. The Canadiens allowed 171 goals against; the Islanders were next at 193—22 more. The Canadiens' goal differential was 216. Philadelphia was second at 110. That's a lot of numbers. Sometimes numbers confuse, sometimes they lie, and sometimes they tell a story words can't. On average, the Canadiens outscored their opponent by almost *three* goals a game. "Wow, that's a big discrepancy," Scotty exclaims. "It's amazing. You don't think about it when it happens, but when you look back now—you know, it's hard to fathom. And to lose that few games, and only one game at home. One, all season." If it didn't say so on his iPad screen, he wouldn't believe it himself.

Individually, Lafleur led the league in scoring, Shutt in goals, Robinson in plus-minus with +120. What was more astonishing was that Robinson was on the ice for 218 of the Canadiens' goals. To put that in perspective, 9 of the NHL's 18 teams themselves scored 240 goals or fewer. Yet while the stars were stars, all the attention didn't go on them. Lemaire, Lafleur, and Shutt were the team's top scoring line, but, as everyone knew, and was quick to say, Cournoyer was also a scorer, and so was Pete Mahovlich. *What about them?* And Risebrough, Tremblay, and Lambert were only kids, but they could score too. *What about them?* And Gainey, Jarvis, and Houle hardly scored themselves, but they shut down all the top lines on all the other teams—Esposito's, Clarke's, Bryan Trottier's, Dionne's—and head-to-head still scored more goals than were scored against them. *What about them?* And all the things Robinson did, but what about Savard and Lapointe? And Nyrop? *What about them?* And Dryden may have been the league's top goalie, but Larocque had a better goals against average than he did. *What about him?*

A team doesn't lose only eight games in the regular season—and only two more out of fourteen in the playoffs—unless it is a "what about" team. Even great stars have ordinary nights, and in those games it's the "what about" players that make the difference. Scotty has thought a lot about this. "You know, maybe there are always stars on great teams, but if you get a team of enough good players that keeps everyone sort of on the same level, that's something different." On a team like that, nobody thinks they are too much better than anyone else, because their teammates don't think they are, because the fans and media don't think they are, because nobody can get away with believing and acting like they are. Because they would be shot down so fast, and that would be humiliating. Being a diva doesn't work.

"You know, when Cournoyer started with the Canadiens," Scotty recalls, "he had been a hotshot junior, but he didn't play very much for a few years because Toe didn't trust his defence. He was mostly just on the power play. Then he becomes a big scorer. Six or seven years later Lafleur comes along and he becomes the star. You know, it couldn't have been easy, but Yvan never really complained about Lafleur being the star."

Nor did Scotty try to create a cult around himself and make himself bigger than his players. Those players kept him "sort of on the same level" too. And if things ever did get a little out of whack, as they would slightly the next season, and then even more in 1978–79 when the team struggled to win its fourth straight Cup, there were always the banners hanging from the roof of the Forum and the memories they engendered that were inescapable in the fans' minds to keep things in check. Because as good as Lafleur was, he knew he was no Rocket Richard. And as good as Robinson was, he knew he was no Doug Harvey. And I knew I was no Jacques Plante, and Scotty knew he was no Toe Blake. We knew that— deep in our bones we knew that. And the fans knew that, and the media knew that. Our numbers would never be retired. Our banners would never hang from the rafters of the Forum or wherever the Canadiens played. And, as a team, we might lose only eight games a year and swamp every one of our opponents, but we knew we weren't the 1956–1960 Montreal Canadiens. They were the forever best. In 1976–77, while the league's other teams chased us, we were chasing them. And because we never did catch them, maybe we did.

It was Scotty's third Cup.

CHAPTER ELEVEN

The next season, 1977–78, began pretty much as the previous one had ended. The Canadiens didn't lose until their ninth game of the season, and five of those games were on the road. Then, beginning December 18, the team went 28 straight games without a loss, were defeated by the Rangers at home, won four more, lost in Buffalo, then didn't lose again until the final game of the season. Ten losses in all, then three more in the playoffs—just 13 losses in 95 games. Over three seasons, 1975–76 to 1977–78, the Canadiens lost 29 games in total—11, 8, and 10—and 6 more in the playoffs—1, 2, and 3. In 240 regular-season games and 42 playoff games—282 in total—they lost 35 games. In that 1977–78 season, Lafleur led the league in points, goals, and plus-minus (Robinson was second). I led in goals against average.

The Canadiens made very few changes from the team that had won its second consecutive Cup the year before. Jimmy Roberts, now 37, was gone. Since offering to buy his own release 19 years earlier so he could play Junior A with the Peterborough Petes, except for his four-plus years in St. Louis he had spent his entire career in the Canadiens' system—with the Petes, Montreal Royals, Omaha, Hull-Ottawa, and the Canadiens. Now he was back in St. Louis for one final season, replaced in Montreal by 21-year-old Pierre Mondou, another of Sam's first-round picks. More shocking for the team, early in the season Pete Mahovlich arrived at the Forum one morning a Montreal Canadien, Pierre Larouche a Pittsburgh Penguin. That night, Mahovlich played for the Penguins, and Larouche for the Canadiens. Mahovlich had been one of the top scorers on the team since the early '70s, but now with less ice time, his numbers were dropping and he was looking for a change. Otherwise, the team's lines, defence pairings, roles, and responsibilities stayed mostly the same.

In the rest of the league, the Bruins and Sabres remained close enough in the standings to seem competitive, the Flyers were fading, the Islanders were on the rise. The players who would be at the core of the Islanders' success for the next decade—Denis Potvin, Mike Bossy, and Bryan Trottier—were now all in place. That season, they finished third in the league in points, 18 behind the Canadiens (and two behind the second-place Bruins), and as an indication of things to come, were second to the Canadiens in goals for and goals against differential.

It was Scotty's fourth Cup.

But before the following season, 1978–79, two big events occurred. On the first day of training camp, the team was practising at Saint-Laurent Arena and, as Scotty relates, "Bill Nyrop came into the rink, his van all packed, and said, 'I'm on to different things.'" After three Cups, Nyrop was retiring from hockey and returning to Minnesota. He was 26. After the Big Three of Robinson, Savard, and Lapointe, Nyrop was the fourth. Agile and athletic, a powerful skater, he had gone to Notre Dame on a football scholarship to play quarterback, but more importantly to him, if not to the school, he loved hockey more. With the Canadiens, he had been getting better each year, and one day he might even have turned the Big Three into the "Big Four," if somehow he could also get himself past the minor injuries that seemed too often to sidetrack him.

So now for Scotty, with an important regular gone, he had a problem. But before he could think too much about it, as he relates, "I went back to the Forum and ran into Frank Selke Sr., and he asked me how the team looks. I said, 'Very strong, very good, but we had a big setback today. Bill Nyrop told us he's retiring.' Mr. Selke was surprised too, but he said, 'Let me give you a little advice. When you win it's so hard to make changes, but you have to make them. You've got no choice. You always have to have new players.'" Necessity had presented Scotty with an opportunity, and also an opportunity for three young defencemen— Brian Engblom, Gilles Lupien, and by the end of the year, future Hall of Famer Rod Langway.

But then Sam left. And some changes are harder to overcome.

I first met Sam on Saturday, February 8, 1969, at Lynah Rink in Ithaca, New York. It was in our Cornell dressing room, minutes after we had beaten the University of Toronto, 7–2. Sam had driven to the game with his friend, Sam Maislin. I had no idea he was coming. The University of Toronto, which was routinely the best college team in Canada, wasn't good that night, and I didn't have much to do or need to play very well. Our coach, Ned Harkness, introduced Sam to the whole team, making it clear that he was there to see *us*—not me—play. Sam and I said hello, and he was soon back in his car.

It was about two months later that we spoke again. I had to be in Boston for an event, and the Canadiens would be playing the Bruins in the sixth game of the Stanley Cup semifinals a night earlier. To arrange a ticket, it was suggested I call him in his hotel room in Boston. I think I woke him up. The Canadiens won the game (Béliveau scored in double overtime), and after the team swept St. Louis and won the Cup, and I had graduated, Sam and I spoke a few more times on the phone. He also talked with my agent. I was trying to figure out what to do next. I could sign with the Canadiens and play with the Montreal Voyageurs of the AHL. I could go to Harvard Law School. Or I could join the Canadian national team in Winnipeg, play international hockey in world championships and the Olympics, and also study law.

The next time Sam and I spoke, I was driving with my then girl-friend (now wife) Lynda to Toronto. We were passing through Canoga, New York, a village of about 100 people just south of the New York State Thruway, when it became the time we had arranged for our phone call, and so I stopped at a bar and called him on its payphone. I told him I had decided to play for the national team and thanked him. I think he was surprised. The next time we spoke was nine months later. Canada had withdrawn from international hockey, the national team had folded, and I was looking for a place to play. Sam asked me if I had signed with the Canadian team so I could also go to law school. I said yes. Then he asked if I hadn't signed with the Canadiens because I couldn't. Again, I said yes. Well then, he said, what if you came to Montreal, finished your last two years of law school and played part-time with the Voyageurs? He made the proposal, as Scotty says, because he didn't like to give up players, and he knew that if he had forced a choice on me—*play, or go to law school*—I would have stopped playing. Yet he didn't need me. The Canadiens had won the Stanley Cup the year before, in 1969. The team had Rogie Vachon as their goalie, and Phil Myre in the wings, and I was far from a sure thing. Besides, he was the best general manager in the NHL. He didn't need to do things like this. No other GM in the league would have offered me this option, I am absolutely certain of that. He did so too—and this occurred to me only a short time ago—because if he had been me, I think, he would have wanted to do both things him-self, and he would have resented anybody who stood in his way. Once I was in Montreal, I came to feel he actually wanted me to succeed at both—not just for the team, or for me, but that it would be just kind of nice if I did. Without Sam, my career in hockey and my life in Montreal would never have happened.

Sam also did other things that no general manager is supposed to do. In January 1971, he traded for Frank Mahovlich. The team wasn't very good that season. It had missed the playoffs the year before and was stuck in a nowhere place—both a little too old and a little too young—just when the

Bruins, Rangers, and Black Hawks were at their peaks. Mahovlich, a great talent and great scorer, had been beaten down by Punch Imlach in Toronto and needed support. He had been able to refind himself in Detroit, but to become what he had in him, he needed more. This is where Sam came in. As a manager, just as for a coach, you have to know what you have and make the best of it.

The Canadiens played at home almost every Saturday night, so the team was in Montreal almost every Friday. So on Fridays after practice, Sam would ask Mahovlich to come up to his office and there they'd talk. About anything—the team, the weather, and they both loved art—it didn't matter what. What did matter was that Mahovlich felt that *he* mattered, that he was just different enough from every other player that it was *him* and Sam, and not anyone else, who had these talks. A few months later, Mahovlich was the offensive force the Canadiens needed in the team's upset Cup win, scoring 14 goals and amassing a playoff-leading—and then-NHL record—27 points. Before he left for the WHA three years later, he scored 43, 38, and 31 goals, and twice led the team in scoring. Sam knew he was a rare and special player, so he didn't treat him like everyone else. He helped Mahovlich *be* rare and special.

Two years later, after the team had won in 1973, Sam and I had a problem, and I left the team. The WHA was paying twice what I was making to some goalies who I thought weren't as good. That bothered me, and then it got to me. The fact I still had one more year on my contract bothered Sam, and then it got to him. In the end, we couldn't resolve our differences. I moved to Toronto to do my articling year, and also to watch the WHA up close because I knew I'd be playing again somewhere the following year. But by midway through that season, I knew I didn't want to play in the WHA. I had learned at Cornell the fun and satisfaction—and the need I had—to play where a team matters. The Toronto Toros of the WHA didn't matter to Toronto. Most of the U.S.-based WHA teams didn't matter much to their cities. I knew I would hate playing in the WHA, no matter how much I was paid.

At the same time, the Canadiens were not having a good season. After they were knocked out in the first round, and after I had thought about it for some time, I decided to call Sam. Lee Dillon was Sam's secretary—someone who would now be called an executive assistant. She was in her late fifties, petite, always smartly and properly dressed, and in her efficient and pleasant way she ran the world. We had spoken many times before; and she was always "Miss Dillon." So Miss Dillon answered the phone and I asked to speak to "Mr. Pollock." She said he wasn't in and could I call back later. Then she stopped herself. "No," she said. "You called. *He* should call *you* back." About a week later, Sam and I met—just the two of us. We talked back and forth more than we negotiated. I was going to say yes, he was going to say yes. I was back for five more years.

Years later, Scotty was told a story by journalist Chrys Goyens. Goyens had been interviewing Sam for an article and asked him about my decision to leave the team and go to Toronto. As Goyens related to Scotty, in speaking about me Sam said, "I loved the guy, but it was one of those things that probably had to happen to me sometime in my career. Eventually I was going to come up against somebody like that, where we would fight it out, to be even at the end. But for a year, we both lost." I heard this story only a short time ago. I'd never known what Sam had felt about that time. We shared three more Stanley Cups together. But now, after our win in 1978, he was leaving.

Peter and Edward Bronfman, the Canadiens' owners, had sold the team to Molson Brewery. Now most of the Bronfmans' business interests were in Toronto. They moved to be nearer to these interests, and Sam moved with them. The Rocket had retired in 1960, Selke in 1964, Blake in 1968, Béliveau in 1971, and now Sam in 1978. The five who had defined and shaped the Canadiens. One day, Scotty would be the sixth in this pantheon.

Sam had been with the Canadiens for 33 years, and in those years, from 1946 to 1978, the Canadiens had won 16 Stanley Cups. It was in those years, not the ones before or since, that the Canadiens became the *legendary* Montreal Canadiens. Sam had started as a twenty-year-old gofer who seemed to be everywhere doing everything—especially what nobody else wanted to do. He had played nursemaid to off-season hockey players in a fastball league in Snowdon; he had hung around local parks on nights when blizzards dumped down all kinds of snow (but, this being Montreal, not enough to cancel a game). He had found a way through traffic and distance to see not two, but *three* games a night, at three different arenas, and before every weekend was over was somehow able to get in just one more game in one more town *somewhere*. And all the time in between, he was thinking, puzzling, planning, scheming, and learning—always learning.

He wasn't responsible for creating the Canadiens' farm system. Selke was. But as a scout and a coach he became part of it, implemented it, saw the possibilities of it, shaped it, and made it work better than everyone else's. Then he changed it when times changed and it needed changing, and again made it better than everyone else's. A farm system based on draft picks rather than affiliated teams.

And when doing his job for the Canadiens had meant doing more with the league, he did that too—learning more and knowing more about the league than everyone else. He was the smartest guy in every NHL room *and* he made himself smarter by putting in more time—unglamourous time—than everyone else in that room. An unbeatable combination.

He had his misses, of course. Not every draft pick turned out to be something. Ray Martyniuk, a goalie from Flin Flon and the fifth overall pick of the 1970 draft, never played a minute in the NHL. Robin Sadler, a defenceman from Vancouver drafted ninth overall, showed up to training camp, played one pre-season game, went home, and never came back.

But there was also Larry Robinson, a second-round pick who had played forward, not defence, in his only season in junior. And Steve Shutt, who couldn't do some things but who could really "light the light," and who in his second through fifth seasons with the team scored 15, then 30, then 45, then 60 goals. And Bob Gainey, who couldn't light any light even in junior, but who could skate and skate and check and check and shut down and turn around a game because he could smother the only offensive threats the other team had. But as much of an effect as all of them had, it was the impact of *all* the draft picks together—the 20 first-round picks in seven years *and* the others—because as Selke said, a team always has to have new players, even a team that wins almost every year. And Sam made sure those players were always in the wings.

The 1976–77 Canadiens lost only eight games because of the Big Three, because of Lafleur, Lemaire, and Shutt, and Gainey, but what made the team a nightmare to play against were the *four* lines, the *two* goalies, the Big Three *plus one*; the Lamberts and Houles and Wilsons and Bouchards and Chartraws who, for an opponent, just kept coming at them—in the first period, the third period, in November, May, this year, next year—and never, ever gave them a break. This was Sam's creation. This is what he put into Scotty's hands, and what Scotty put into our hands. When Sam left, this is what went with him.

It would have been a harder decision for Sam five years earlier; it was easier now. Sam had a young family. He had tried for some time to spend fewer hours in the office and on the road, but he had realized, long before he would admit it, that he couldn't do *this* job, in the way *he* needed to do it, in any shortcut way. But really, more than that, at age 52 his job with the Canadiens was too small for him. The "business acumen" that Scotty had noticed in him from their days selling program ads in Ottawa had been put into action to make the Canadiens and the NHL work. It didn't matter the smooth, jargon-smart MBAs that would be increasingly around him in Toronto. The scrappy kid from Snowdon with only a high-school education was a big-time business guy ready for a lot more.

The question the Canadiens faced now was: Who would replace him? The answer seemed easy. Except for his four seasons in St. Louis, Scotty had worked for the Canadiens since 1952—for 26 years. He had scouted and coached kids; he had coached juniors and gone to the Memorial Cup final three straight years, winning once; he had been the team's head scout for Eastern Canada; he had seen every young player in the country for more than a decade—those who made it, those who didn't, and why. He had beaten the bushes of the minor leagues to find every living, breathing prospect possible for the expansion Blues; he had gone to the Stanley Cup final three consecutive years with St. Louis; he had coached Team Canada and won the 1976 Canada Cup. He had won four Stanley Cups, more than any coach in the team's history except Toe Blake. But more than all this—and more than anyone—he had channelled Sam during all these years. He had seen everything. He had done everything. *He* was the answer to the question that wasn't even a question.

Except it *was* a question. After winning the Stanley Cup in 1971, Al MacNeil and the Nova Scotia Voyageurs had won the Calder Cup as the AHL's champion the next year, then again in 1976 and 1977. He had worked with the *non*-sure things that Sam had drafted, the *non*-first-round picks, and helped turn them into NHL players—Robinson, Nyrop, Lambert, Engblom, and others. He and Scotty were greatly respectful of each other, but also slightly wary. They worked together so well because Sam was there. Without him, Sam believed, if either of them was chosen to replace him, the other would leave, and he knew that each of them was the best at his own job. So Sam came up with a plan to keep them both. Neither of them would be named general manager. Instead, Irving Grundman would take his place.

Grundman had been a long-time executive with the Bronfmans. Because he had no background in hockey, he wouldn't attempt to do what he so clearly couldn't do. Instead, Scotty would run the NHL team, having more say in personnel decisions and trades than he had before, and MacNeil would run the AHL team. Grundman would serve as the facilitator. He would be responsible for the administration of the organization, he would conciliate where necessary, but otherwise he would get out of the way and let Scotty and MacNeil do what they did so well.

It almost looked good on paper. In the real world, it gave no consideration to the personalities of those involved—especially Scotty's—or to the circumstances. Whether Scotty was the right person for the job or not, *he believed he was*; and he also believed no one else was. He believed he deserved it. He believed he was ready. So any other logic, no matter how wonderful and tempting, made no sense. Scotty and Sam had formed the perfect partnership—Sam got the players that were needed to win Stanley Cups, and Scotty coached them and won. Scotty needed the right players. He knew that. He couldn't do his job without them. If Sam wasn't around, *who would get him the players?* MacNeil? Grundman? No. If not Sam, the answer had to be him. He had to be the general manager.

Maybe Sam didn't think Scotty would be as good a general manager as the team needed. Maybe he believed Scotty was a great coach, and he didn't want anything to get in the way of him becoming even greater. But if this is what he believed, who in all this *would be Sam?*

"After Sam told me his decision," Scotty remembers, "I just said to him, 'Sam, if you were in my position, would you accept this?'"

Scotty entered the 1978–79 season not in a good frame of mind. He needed for people to know he was unhappy, but he had never been very good at that. He did it with hints, but that came off as whiny and conspiratorial, and challenged the goodwill of his listener. As the season went on, he was able to put his hurt to one side, *mostly*, to obsess on in private moments. He had a job to do, and for the first time he was coaching the Canadiens without Sam. On paper, the Canadiens were better that year. On the ice, they weren't.

There were injuries. Risebrough, Larouche, and Lemaire missed almost half the season. Cournoyer had lost a step, and the steps that remained were less explosive. He'd had back surgery, and his goal production had gone from 47 in 1971–72 to 24 in 1977–78. That season, playing only 15 games, he scored twice. Shutt, who had scored 60 goals in 1976–77, fell off to 37. Lafleur kept scoring at the same rate, but both he and Shutt missed Lemaire. Just as non-players can hit mid-career crises in their late forties, hockey players hit theirs beginning in their late twenties. Cournoyer was now 35, Savard and Lemaire 33, Lapointe 30, and Houle 29. I was 31. Scotty was 45.

After winning three consecutive Stanley Cups, a player wants to win a fourth and he wants not to lose a fourth, but he doesn't *need* to win in the same way. Often, that difference is all it takes. The Canadiens lost 17 games that season. Lafleur didn't lead the league in scoring—Bryan Trottier of the Islanders did—Lafleur was third, behind Dionne. Nor did he lead the league in goals—Mike Bossy did, again followed by Dionne. Neither Lafleur nor Robinson led in plus-minus—that was Trottier, then Potvin and Bossy, and their Islanders teammate Clark Gillies finished fifth. Even more tellingly, the Canadiens went into the final game of the regular season needing only a tie against the third-from-last place Wings to finish first in the league, and lost, 1–0. The Islanders were the NHL's regular-season champions.

The playoffs began predictably. The Canadiens swept the Leafs, the Islanders did the same to the Black Hawks, but then things turned on their ear. The Canadiens, who had won 13 straight playoff series against Boston dating back to 1946, were four minutes away from losing to the Bruins in the seventh game in Montreal. Then Boston got a penalty for too many men on the ice, Lafleur scored, and Lambert won the game in overtime. Meanwhile, in New York, the Rangers—who had finished 25 points behind the Islanders during the regular season—defeated them in six games to go to the final. There, the Rangers won the first game in Montreal, then slowly, decisively, the series turned, and the Canadiens won in five games.

It was Scotty's fifth Cup.

But for him, the unthinkable was now no longer unthinkable. He'd had a year working without Sam, and working with Grundman. He'd had a year to build up in his mind how wrong things were and how they would never be right again. He was a coach; he needed players.

In the summer, the WHA ceased operations after seven seasons and four of its teams were incorporated into the NHL. This was a critical blow to the Canadiens—far more so than it seemed at the time. All those *non*-surefire draft picks who were taken after the first round that the team couldn't sign, but who could develop in the WHA and perhaps be signed later, were gone. The players who might be the team's third or fourth liners, or be traded for draft picks who might *become* the team's next third or fourth liners, or better, were gone. The Canadiens' depth—the thing that had crushed the spirit of all the other teams in those three years they almost never lost, regular season or playoffs—was gone.

"A team always needs new players," as Selke had said, but where were they going to come from now? From the one draft pick per round— per year—they would have, like every other team? The Canadiens weren't *like* every other team. They couldn't *be* like every other team. They hadn't been like every other team since Selke had created their farm system, and certainly not since Sam had perfected it. But going into the 1979 draft, the Canadiens had *no* first-round picks. None. Zero. Even Boston had two. What had Grundman been doing all season?

And even more urgently, the team needed new players for next year. Cournoyer's injured back, which had taken away his speed and joy, wouldn't be getting better, and so he retired. Lemaire decided he wanted to live another life, and went to Switzerland to play and coach a bit. I retired. The team that had won four Cups in a row would need to be very different to win a fifth.

Ahead of their initial season in 1970–71, the Buffalo Sabres had the first overall pick in the NHL draft and chose Gilbert Perreault, a franchise-making player. Punch Imlach was their coach and general manager. The next year, the Sabres drafted a scorer, Rick Martin, then added another, René Robert, as well as two shutdown forwards, Don Luce and Craig Ramsay. In 1972 they got a big defenceman, Jim Schoenfeld, and a hard-driving forward, Rick Dudley; then in 1974 they drafted a two-way player who could score, Danny Gare. That year, their fifth in the league, the Sabres went to the Stanley Cup final, losing to the Flyers. The team was fast and exciting, and the atmosphere inside The Aud was electric.

For the next three seasons the Sabres finished in the top five in the league, but they couldn't get by the Canadiens and Bruins, the Flyers were still strong, and the Islanders were on the rise. And now there were expectations. During the 1978–79 season, after a poor start, Imlach was fired as general manager and Marcel Pronovost was let go as their coach. The Sabres limped to the end of the year, finishing with 17 points fewer than the season before and losing out in a best-of-three preliminary round to Pittsburgh in the playoffs.

Scotty knew how good the Sabres could be. Since their coming-out season in 1974–75, they had played the Canadiens even—which no other team had—with 11 wins, 11 losses, and 2 ties. They had been the last team to win a playoff round against the Canadiens, in 1975. Buffalo's best scorers could score with the Montreal's best; their best defensive forwards could defend with Montreal's best; *and*, most significantly, the Sabres could skate with the Canadiens. They also had two good young goalies, Don Edwards and Bob Sauvé.

The team's owners, brothers Seymour and Northrup Knox, were respected in the Buffalo community. The fans loved their team; in attendance, the Sabres ranked fifth in the league nearly every year, behind the Rangers, Flyers, Canadiens, and Leafs, only because those teams' arenas were bigger. The Aud was sold out for every game. Buffalo was a good hockey city, and it had been a good one even in the minor leagues. The city itself was suffering the fate of other big industrial ports on the Great Lakes—Detroit and Cleveland especially. Its factories were shutting down, its downtown was a disaster, but its parks were beautiful and its suburbs were extensive and pleasant. Buffalo was a nice place to live and raise a family, and Alicia, now 8, David 7, Stan 6, and Bob and Nancy, 2, were entering some life-shaping years.

The Sabres offered Scotty a chance to be both coach and general manager—to get the players he wanted and to coach the players he got. To be his own Scotty, and his own Sam. And the Knoxes were willing to pay him what a general manager and a five-time Stanley Cup-winning coach *should* be paid.

There was one more thing. Before Scotty agreed to sign, he and Suella visited Buffalo and went to see the Father Baker Infant Home in nearby Lackawanna. They left believing that David would be "well looked after."

On June 11, 1979, 21 days after winning the Cup against the Rangers, almost eight years to the day after signing with the Canadiens, Scotty resigned as coach and joined the Sabres. He had left Montreal once before, to go to St. Louis, and then had returned. This time, he would never be back. Four days earlier, Al MacNeil signed as coach of the Atlanta Flames. Sam had wanted to keep both of them, and now both were gone.

Scotty hired Roger Neilson and Jimmy Roberts, two important names from his past, as his assistants. The Sabres bounced back. They finished 22 points higher than the year before—second in the league behind Philadelphia. Their goal differential of 117 was by far the best in the league. Perreault went from 27 goals to 40, and from 85 points to 106, fourth in the NHL. Gare improved from 27 goals to 56, tied for best in the league; Martin from 32 goals to 45. Schoenfeld had the highest plus-minus at +60. Bob Sauvé had the lowest goals against average, and Don Edwards was third. For the fifth straight season, Scotty's goalies had won the Vezina Trophy.

In the best-of-five first round of the playoffs, the Sabres beat Vancouver in four games, then swept Chicago. Back in the semifinals for the first time since 1975, they lost to the Islanders, who would go on to beat the Flyers and win the Cup. The Sabres had had a much better season, but still they couldn't get over that final hump, and the league was becoming more challenging every year. The Canadiens were going back into a pack they hadn't been in for 30 years, but the Flyers were ready for another run, the Islanders were becoming what they had it in them to be, and the Oilers were on the horizon far more quickly, and were far better, than anyone would have guessed. And there was one other thing on that horizon.

"When I went to Buffalo that summer after I had signed, and I started looking around, they had 25 professional players under contract," Scotty recalls. "Twenty-five! And the reason was, and I found out later, the Knoxes were rich people, they had money, but they weren't going to spend it. Punch Imlach, if you look at his history, he let players go to the WHA. He couldn't overpay. His approach was: 'Why do I want to sign a bunch of players for my American League team because if they're any good they're just going to go to the WHA?'"

A team always needs new players. And the Sabres were getting old. The question ahead: Can Scotty be Sam-enough, so that Scotty can be Scotty?

Sometimes teams prepare to win for so long that when it's their time to win, someone else, someone less ready, beats them to it and they never win. *Ready, aim, aim* . . . The Islanders had done almost everything right from the moment they entered the NHL in 1972. They hired as their first employee Bill Torrey, whose prior hockey experience made him unsuited to be the team's general manager, but whose life experience made him perfect. He had grown up in Montreal and knew what great teams—and lousy teams—looked like. He had also worked for the California Golden Seals and had seen how trading draft picks for established mediocre NHL players offers the illusion of somewhere and the reality of nowhere.

With these observations as his touchstones, Torrey put together his team. In their initial season, the Islanders finished a worse-than-lousy—and NHL worst-ever—12–60–6. He then avoided making his first big mistake. The Islanders held the first overall pick in the 1973 draft. Sam wanted Denis Potvin, a smart, tough defenceman who was so talented and physically mature that he had played five full seasons of junior hockey, beginning at age 14. The Islanders had finished the previous year with less than half the number of points of their expansion partner, the Atlanta Flames. Sam offered Torrey a lifeline of players in return for his first pick, to keep him from another season of embarrassment. Torrey drafted Potvin instead.

Then Torrey hired Al Arbour as his coach. The team improved the next season, Potvin was the league's rookie of the year, yet still the Islanders finished last, and far behind the Flames. Torrey then avoided making his second big mistake. The team hadn't fallen short because of Arbour, but because the players weren't good enough. Torrey knew that, and most of the fans and the media knew that too, but he could have made it seem otherwise and offered the critics a fresh jolt of hope by firing Arbour and bringing in someone else. He didn't.

The next year, the Islanders made the playoffs *and* finished ahead of Atlanta. Bit by bit, Torrey was putting together the pieces: some that would make the team more respectable—Ed Westfall (the team's first captain), Terry Crisp; some that would grow with the team—Billy Harris (the team's *first* first-round pick), Gerry Hart, Garry Howatt, Lorne Henning; and a few that would also be cornerstone players on Cup-contending teams in the future—Potvin, Billy Smith, Bob Nystrom. Almost astonishingly, in the Islanders first draft in 1972, Torrey selected three players, none of them first-rounders, who were still with the team when they won the Cup eight years later—Henning (second round), Nystrom (third), and Howatt (tenth). Among their 1973 draft selections, Potvin and Lorimer (ninth) would be on that Cup-winning team as well, as would four more players from the 1974 draft—Dave Langevin (seventh round), Stefan Persson (fourteenth), and two additional cornerstone players, Clark Gillies (first) and Bryan Trottier (second). Two years later, the Islanders selected Ken Morrow in the fourth round, and in 1977 they took John Tonelli in the second and goal-scoring prodigy Mike Bossy in the first. Bossy was the 15th pick overall, after other teams had passed him over for Dale McCourt, Barry Beck, Robert Picard, Jere Gillis, and others, and after the Canadiens had selected Mark Napier with the number 10 pick.

The Islanders were now ready to take on anybody. In the league standings, their point total went from 30 in their inaugural season to 111, and finally to 116 in 1978–79 when they edged out the Canadiens to finish first overall. That year the Islanders could have won the Cup, because the Canadiens were ready to be beaten. But they crashed out against the Rangers in the semifinals and the Canadiens won again.

In the next season, 1979–80, with a score to settle, the Islanders would surely come out of the gate and leave the rest of the league behind. Instead, they didn't reach .500 until their eighth game, won only 6 of their first 21 games, and didn't get to the .500 level again until their 41st game. After that, things didn't get much better. Meanwhile, the Flyers went on an NHL-record run of 35 games without a loss, and Scotty's Sabres almost kept pace with them. The Islanders' window of opportunity, wide and ever-expanding for so long, was shutting fast. They had the right general manager and the right coach; they had Potvin, Trottier, Bossy, Smith, and the rest; they were the best team in the league. But when the best team begins to lose, attention shifts from all the wonderful things that make them the best, to all those suddenly escalating things that have held them back. That's when the right coaches get fired, the wrong players get traded, and teammates turn against teammates.

But, again, Torrey avoided those mistakes, and late in the season he made his big move. He had generated very few trades in his time with the Islanders. He had acquired very few additional draft choices. Instead, the Islanders had picked when it was their turn to pick—in a league thin with players because of WHA signings—then developed and advanced the right ones quickly, and slotted them into the lineup when they were needed. And whether they were entirely ready or not, because the core of the team was so stable and strong, they looked like they were ready. Billy Harris and Dave Lewis had been important players for the Islanders almost since the team's beginning, helping them get to where they were. Now they would be important in helping the Islanders get to where they needed to be next. On March 10, Harris and Lewis were traded to L.A. for Butch Goring, a hard-working, talented two-way centre. With only 12 games remaining in the regular season, the Islanders went unbeaten in all 12. The trade had the effect it did because the Islanders were *that* close and *that* good. In the first two rounds of the playoffs, they defeated the Kings and the Bruins, losing only once in each series, then beat both the Sabres and the Flyers in six games to win the Cup. Bob Nystrom, an original Islander, scored the winning goal, and Trottier was awarded the Conn Smythe Trophy as the playoffs MVP.

Once the Islanders had proven themselves, to others but mostly to themselves, they got better. They went from 91 points in the standings in that first Cup year to 110 in 1980–81, leading the league; then they beat the Leafs, Oilers, Rangers, and North Stars in the playoffs— losing only three games—to win for the second straight year. Yet they wouldn't hit their full stride until the following season, 1981–82, when they finished first overall for the third time in four years before defeating the Penguins, Rangers, Nordiques, and Canucks—sweeping the last two series and winning their final nine games in a row. They seemed to be a team that had been together forever. Maybe it was because most of those at the core—the players, coach, and manager who had created the team and defined it—had remained in place. Torrey was still there, after ten seasons; the team had never had another general manager. Arbour was still there, after nine years. Smith, ten seasons, Nystrom, nine, Potvin, nine, Gillies, eight, Trottier, seven, Bossy, five—they were all still there. And the rest—the younger draft picks and older veterans—just fit in. Even the European players fit in—Stefan Persson, Anders Kallur, Tomas Jonsson. There weren't many Europeans in the NHL at that time. Persson, Kallur, and Jonsson brought different skills, but they played with the same Islanders spirit. Disciplined, focused, tough, and tough-minded; not so much "defence first" as "smart first."

The Islanders played the way Torrey and Arbour saw the game. "Bill Torrey was a hockey guy," Scotty says. It's a term he doesn't often use—it speaks to someone's longevity and dedication to the game, but also to their instincts and singular focus, and finally to their results.

Torrey had passed every threshold and test. "He had been with the California [Golden] Seals," Scotty says. "They were a financially strapped team, and the Islanders were too. Both of them were always under-financed. But he built a good scouting staff, he held on to his picks, and they made some good ones, not just the obvious early ones like Potvin, but some late ones, like Nystrom and Persson. He made some small deals, but basically they were a team that was drafted. And he was a personable guy, always pretty pleasant, happy-go-lucky. The people who worked for him liked him." And nobody more so than Arbour. He and Torrey would be together for 19 years—17 of them as general manager and coach, more than 1,300 regular-season games, and almost 200 playoff games. That's not easy. Even in 17 mostly very good or great years there are lots of bad moments—moments that accumulate in memory, that prompt lots of advice from media and fans, that fuel reasons to make changes. But Torrey and Arbour avoided making the big mistakes about each other. "That's a long, long time," Scotty says, with admiration, about their partnership. He and Sam were together even longer, but only directly and every day as general manager and coach in their two years in Hull-Ottawa and in the 1970s in their seven years with the Canadiens.

"Al was a wonderful guy," Scotty recalls, again using a word he doesn't often employ. "He was our captain [in St. Louis], our captain all the way. He was a stalwart on defence, someone the players looked up to. He had come up the hard way, he had been through so much. He had moved down from Sudbury, he was supposed to go to St. Mike's, but his parents didn't want him to go to Toronto. They thought it was too big a city. But they let him go to Windsor—to Assumption, a Catholic high school there. He was in Detroit with those great teams and won the Cup, but he didn't play much. He was in Chicago when they were really poor, then they won the Cup, but he was always a fifth defenceman. Fifth or sixth, at best. Never a top-four. But he knew how to play. Then he was in Toronto and he won two Cups there. He became a real strong American League player, in Rochester, and they won the Calder Cup twice." In a period of six years, in Chicago in 1961, in Toronto in 1962 and 1964, in Rochester in 1965 and 1966, Arbour won five championships. "But it's tough when you play in the minors the way he did. You're moving around, you can't get established in one place. When we got him [in St. Louis] in '67 he was going to retire unless he got a long-term contract. And then he played four more years.

"With the Islanders, he taught those defencemen," Scotty continues. He had Potvin, and later Persson and Jonsson—talented players with offensive skills and instincts—but mostly his defence was made up of players like Gerry Hart, Bert Marshall, Dave Lewis, Bob Lorimer, Dave Langevin, Gord Lane—defencemen who were not unlike he was. "He had been a defensive defenceman, and he was a stickler on fundamentals. He would be firm, but fair. Not much fooling around with him. And he was a systematic guy. They played a very regimented game in their own end. Not so much Potvin, because he was a great passer, and Persson was a pretty mobile guy. But the others—Langevin, Lane— they were big, strong guys, but they weren't what you'd call puck handlers. The whole team was good-sized, really good defensively and had some pretty tough guys—Gillies, Nystrom, Potvin. Boston had tough teams in those years too, but the Islanders always seemed to be able to handle them.

"They played Trottier and Bossy together most of the time, then interchanged [Bob] Bourne and Gillies on the wing." Bourne—tall, lean, and a fast skater—had the offensive skills to play with Trottier and Bossy. "But he was not an aggressive player, so when they played Boston, they put Gillies in there. He was a very powerful winger who could also fight. And he fought [Terry] O'Reilly a lot." O'Reilly was a crashing, never-back-down, never-stop, highly effective forward for the Bruins. "And O'Reilly was a big, strong guy too." Scotty pauses. "[The Islanders] were a good physical team, they played on the edge, but they didn't play out of control," he says, describing them much as he did Punch Imlach's Leafs teams of the early 1960s. "They had enough scoring, and we had to be careful with them because they could shut you down. Before Bossy, they were a team that was very steady, that played the same all the time."

In the NHL's history, goal scoring had been a put-the-puck-on-the-net, take-ten-shots-one-is-bound-to-go-in exercise. Goalie equipment was small and there were lots of open spaces to shoot for, but sticks were heavy and few shooters could hit them. Until Bossy. He played only 10 seasons, retiring at age 30 with a back injury. In those 10 years, he scored 53, 69, 51, 68, 64, 60, 51, 58, 61, and 38 goals. In 752 career games, he totalled 573 goals, or .762 goals per game. Against that standard, Mario Lemieux is next on the league's all-time list, just behind Bossy at .754. None of the other greatest scorers in NHL history are even close, from Gretzky at .601 to Howe at .453. Before Bossy, the Islanders were a team that with skill and force could pin an opponent in its defensive zone and push and pressure and control and bang, until often enough, given the law of averages, they would score. But very good teams at very important moments in a game establish their own law of averages. They don't get overwhelmed or discouraged, they resist; they counter against their opponent, suddenly caught in the offensive zone, and they score. Bossy was a sniper, the guy who could end all the pressuring and banging with a single shot. He made the Islanders much harder to beat.

For the Canadiens, Bossy was the one who got away. He grew up in Montreal, and everyone in the Canadiens organization knew about him. They had followed him as a kid and as a junior in Laval. They had seen him play hundreds of times. "His father's name was Borden," Scotty recalls. "[Mike] was one of a family of ten, six boys and four girls. I knew Leo Bossy, Borden's brother, who was Mike's uncle," Scotty continues. "We played against each other when I was at Verdun High School. He was at Catholic High. And there was this guy who used to come around the Forum when I was playing Junior A in the early '50s. His name was

Roger Bolduc, he owned a restaurant up in the Laurentians and had some money. Later he owned part of the team in Laval, and he told me about this guy they had, Mike Bossy."

On a rare night off in 1977, Scotty went to see him play. Some days later, he got a call from Claude Ruel. "Claude didn't call me very much. Very, very seldom. But he had gone to Laval to see Bossy, and he was very excited. 'I just saw this guy play,' he said, 'and it's the first time I've been out of my seat in a junior game since I saw Lafleur.'"

A few weeks later, "We had this meeting with Sam. I remember it very, very clearly. Ronnie Caron [the Canadiens' head scout] was there. Claude was there. And Claude said to Sam, 'There's this kid playing in Laval that you might want to watch.' And Ronnie got mad. He didn't like people telling him what to do in the draft, and he said, 'Just worry about your team, I'll worry about mine,' something like that. Then Ronnie said to Sam, 'Why don't you go see him next Friday. He's play-ing in Sherbrooke'"—about an hour east of Montreal, not far from Sam's summer home in North Hatley. "So Sam went, but Sherbrooke had a goon team, and Laval wasn't that great, and they got beat up that night and they never had the puck. And Bossy didn't either."

When draft day came more than a month later, the Canadiens took Mark Napier with the 10th overall pick. "He was really a pro," Scotty says of Napier. "He was playing in the World Hockey Association." Napier would go on to have a solid 10-year NHL career, winning Cups in Montreal and Edmonton.

But it wasn't only the Canadiens who missed Bossy—11 other teams did too. And the Rangers and Leafs, each with two selections prior to the Islanders' pick, missed him twice. "Jimmy Devellano told me the whole story of what happened," Scotty relates, "and he was with the Islanders at the time." Devellano later worked for the Wings when Scotty was there, and now lives in Florida where he often meets up with Scotty in the media room prior to Tampa Bay games. "Anyway, the Islanders had a Quebec scout, Henry Saraceno, and he brought up

Bossy's name at their draft meeting and the Islanders weren't sure of their pick. It was between Bossy and Dwight Foster, and somebody asked Al Arbour, 'Do you want a guy that's a good checking forward, or this guy who can't check but can score?' And Al said, 'We need some scoring. We can teach him to check. Let's go for the guy who can score.' Bossy was the game changer for them. Before him, they didn't have anybody that scored easy goals."

It was Bryan Trottier who often got Bossy the puck. Trottier didn't look like an offensive star. He was a little short and thickly built. There was no flash about him, and he played almost without expression. Yet even as a rookie, having barely turned 19, he nearly always did the right thing—on offence and on defence. If Arbour had been a forward, and had had the talent, he would have been Trottier. Torrey and Arbour offered the Islanders continuity and direction, Potvin was their cornerstone, but Trottier was the one who turned the team from a likeable underdog into a contender. He was that mixture of talent and force that defined the team.

When the Islanders played against the Flyers, Arbour would have Trottier go head-to-head with Bobby Clarke. Clarke, with Reggie Leach and Bill Barber, played against every opponent's best line, or often their shut-down line. He was once asked who he found the hardest player to play against. He loved playing against Esposito, he said. You could just be on him. You could disrupt him. Upset him. Clarke said he didn't find Lemaire that difficult. You could push him. He found Jarvis and Risebrough hard, but the toughest guy he ever played against, he said, was Trottier. "He was strong, he was tough, he was mean," he said. "He kind of played like me but he had more force about him."

Trottier changed the Islanders. He allowed Bossy to be Bossy, and he brought out the best in Potvin. Potvin was the best of all the Islanders, except when he wasn't. But with Trottier around, Potvin no longer had to carry so much of the load, and with the team winning more often, he could begin to see himself as part of something bigger.

"What I remember about the Islanders more than anything was Potvin," Scotty says now. "He was their key. He was an exceptional defenceman, a really strong, physical guy. And he could play a lot. He was as close as anyone I ever saw to Doug Harvey. They were similar in size. Their passing was right on the mark. And he was mean like Harvey. If you tried to hit either of them, you were going to pay a price. Potvin was maybe a little more fiery. Doug was fiery too, but he didn't show it as much. And for a guy who could play both ways, Potvin was a real offensive threat. He had a good shot. He was a hell of a point man. He probably didn't get as much attention as he should have, because when he started Orr was still in his prime."

Orr and Potvin played together in the 1976 Canada Cup when Scotty was the coach. Scotty remembers that series for lots of reasons, but among the most vivid was the defence he had. Orr, Potvin, his own Big Three of Robinson, Lapointe, and Savard, along with the Flyers' Jimmy Watson. Five of the top defencemen of all time, all on one team, and at the very top were Orr and Potvin. "It was sort of Bobby's last hurrah," Scotty says. "He hadn't played in '72 [the Summit Series], this was his first international series, and he was really injured. He would go to the rink early in the afternoon and ice down his knees just so he could play that night. They gave him the MVP [of the series] and he was very good. But Potvin was too. And [Potvin] was really upset when they gave the MVP to Bobby."

Potvin had been so good as a junior that people would compare him to Orr, but he wasn't Orr and he couldn't be Orr, and everyone would say that too. Then, finally, in the Canada Cup when he might have been as good as Orr, people didn't see it—or they wouldn't let themselves see it. Instead of this being *his*—Potvin's—moment of triumph, when he turned whiny, and complained of being overlooked, what everyone *did* see was his petulance. His lack of generosity. This was Orr's last big moment, after all, and everyone knew it. Let him have his time. Potvin had earned more recognition in the series than he got, but by insisting on it, people gave him less.

But as the Islanders continued to get better, Potvin seemed more willing to give up a fight he couldn't win and win the one he could—the fight to be Denis Potvin, captain of the ever-improving, top-contending, soon-to-be Stanley Cup champion New York Islanders. That didn't stop him from having run-ins with Arbour, however. Potvin could get himself a little "heavy" at times, a little overweight, and Arbour loved to notice. In fact, to Potvin it seemed like Arbour loved to notice *every* imperfection about him. But what Arbour mostly noticed was the little bit of diva in Potvin, which Potvin was learning to temper, but which was never not there and which Arbour could always see. "He used to lock horns with Al, I know that for sure," Scotty says. "One time he was late for their bus to Philadelphia and Al wouldn't let him on. He said, 'We're going without him.' And they did."

Another source of tension—which, as they won more often, became more a source of amusement—was Potvin's brother Jean, four years older and his teammate on the Islanders. Jean was a modestly talented player. He skated and passed well for a defenceman, and had a good shot. But to Arbour's eyes he wasn't quite talented enough to play as a skill player, and wasn't quite disciplined and consistent enough to play the Islanders' defence-smart style. He drove Arbour crazy.

Arbour had learned from his very first breath: know yourself, know what you are, know what you aren't. That's how he'd made it to the NHL; that's how he played in the league for more than 10 years; that's how he won four Stanley Cups. That's why he was the coach of the New York Islanders. And, in a hundred different ways and a thousand different times, that's what he would say to Jean. *Look around: Hart, Marshall, Lewis, Langevin, Lane, Lorimer, everyone else. You're* not *Bobby Orr. Just get the puck out of our zone!* But sometimes Jean would forget.

"Al didn't exactly embrace Denis," Scotty explains, "because Denis could be a little bit of a prima donna, but Al knew how good he was. But he'd also give him a hard time. But then he gets Jean on the team, and he doesn't like Jean as a player at all. So Jean is practising and practising, but not playing, so that's all right, but then they get some injuries and they start to call up guys from their farm team and Jean's still practising and not playing. So Denis goes in to see Al and says, 'My brother's been practising, why isn't he playing?' Finally, Al agrees to play him, and Denis convinces him to play the two of them together. At least that way, Al figures, he'll get the best out of Denis too because he's going to push like hell for his brother."

A few nights later, the Islanders were playing the Canadiens on Long Island—there were about five minutes to go and the score was tied. The puck was in the Montreal end, and Denis saw the loose puck and pinched in after it—something he was very good at—but this time he got caught, and now his brother had to defend Lafleur and Shutt alone. Lafleur had the puck, he faked a pass, Jean went for the fake, and Lafleur put it through his legs and scored the winning goal. Five minutes to go. Arbour was livid—livid because of what Jean had done, and most livid because he had Jean on the ice with five minutes left in the game.

So, after the game, Jean went into the shower. It happened that there was another way out of the shower, so Jean could get dressed and out of the room quickly before anyone could see him, but Arbour knew this too. So Arbour was waiting when Jean came out. And Arbour said, "Well, what've you got to say?" Jean tried to be contrite, and said, "Al, it was all my fault. Denis got caught, but I know, I know what you always tell me. I shouldn't have been looking at the puck, I should've been looking at [Lafleur's] waist, and I made a bad mistake and it won't happen again." This is a story Jean loves to tell on himself at sports dinners, especially the way it ends. Arbour then said to him: "No, Jean, you didn't make a mistake. Your mother made a mistake."

"What really saved their team," Scotty says, "was when they got Goring. That was the trade." And 600 kilometres away, in Buffalo, Scotty felt it. "Boy, now they were strong down the middle. Trottier, then Goring, and Brent Sutter was a very useful player for them, and Wayne

Merrick. They had four pretty good centres. They had such depth. They were tough too—Gillies, Nystrom; they had Howatt, [and] Tonelli was a good pickup for them from the WHA. And Duane Sutter. When they got up against a tougher team, they had enough muscle. They had a big, strong defence too." Near the end of the 1979–80 season they added Ken Morrow, and he gave them another boost. He had just won a gold medal in Lake Placid as part of the U.S. "Miracle on Ice" team, and he was big, smart, and steady, and gave them a little bit more offence. Morrow, it turned out—like the Canadiens' Doug Jarvis—wouldn't *lose* a Stanley Cup until his fifth season. (Henri Richard didn't lose one until his sixth.)

The Islanders' goaltending had also grown up with the team. Billy Smith and Glenn "Chico" Resch were far from sure things in the early years when the team's future was still uncertain. They were promising, then good when the team became promising, then good. When the team was an underdog and needed infectious enthusiasm, they had Resch. When the team needed a killer to put them over the top, Smith emerged. "Smith was a good playoff goalie," Scotty says. "He probably cut his goals-against by half a goal a game then. They were a pretty stingy team when they had to be. They had enough guys to play that way. Though they didn't seem to have a lot of skill, they did. They were a very well-rounded team."

After the Islanders won in 1980, their challenge changed. "Obviously, when you win, your confidence level is very high, but now there's pressure from the other teams that are trying to knock you off. So you look back and think, 'How did we do it before? Let's not change anything.' But you have to be ready for anything that might happen. The best thing, after you've won one, and then two, is that when you go into that third year"—as the Islanders did—"you've had some adversity and you've overcome it, and you know you can again. You know how. It's the experience. It's the confidence you have now. You don't notice it at the time, but it's such a big advantage.

"That's what probably saw them through. Maybe you add a piece or two that you didn't have before. Somebody comes in and really fits in perfectly. That's what you're trying to do. Confidence can become complacency, and you can depend on that confidence a little too much, especially during the regular season. But it's less of a problem in the playoffs, because you know the grind. You know what you have to do. There's a bit of a formula, which you don't go back to, but it's there, sort of ingrained in your thought process. You have highs and lows. If you lose a big game you should've won, you've got to come back and win the next one, no matter what the circumstances. Pretty simple, but it's true. I think what you've learned before helps you because a lot of things are different, but a lot of things are similar. And you get the hunger. You know that what you've accomplished all season doesn't really matter. You're in the playoffs, you've got a new opponent. You know it's a grind. It's not a surprise for you."

After the Islanders won two straight Cups, they had one more thing going for them the next season, 1981–82. The Oilers were coming. They'd been young and good, then they were on the horizon, then suddenly they were right there. The year before, they had totalled 74 points. That season they had 111—an increase of 37—and finished second overall to the Islanders. They scored 417 goals, the first team in NHL history to score more than 400. Wayne Gretzky won the scoring title, his second straight, with 212 points, Bossy was next with 147. Even more ominously, Mark Messier scored 50 goals, Glenn Anderson 38, and Jari Kurri 32—and all of them were 21 years old.

So much of the media and fan focus that season was on the Oilers. *They* were the ones to watch, not the two-time defending Stanley Cup champion Islanders. The Islanders had seemed always to be overshadowed—first by the magical flair and dominance of the Canadiens, and now by the jaw-dropping possibilities of the Oilers. It was as if *they*, the Islanders, were the ones who had to prove themselves. It was as if they weren't the champions at all. But, unlike in 1980 when they'd also had to prove themselves, this time they knew how. Once they got into the rhythm of the playoffs, it was no contest—they won their last nine games and had two straight sweeps—and they were the champions again for the third straight year. They would win again the following season to make it four in a row, this time facing the awesome and thrilling Oilers in the final. Edmonton had four scorers in the league's top 10 and had again scored over 400 goals—424—but the Islanders blew them away in four straight.

"They were a very complete team," Scotty says now, thinking back. And maybe more than anybody, more than Torrey and Potvin and Trottier and Bossy, it was Arbour who set the tone. "He won one Cup with Detroit, one with Chicago, and two with Toronto," Scotty says, "then four as a coach with the Islanders. He's got eight Cups." Scotty is shy, and often awkward, and rarely expresses himself this way. But he says this about Arbour because he knows it's true, because it's proper recognition, and because he's proud of him.

The Islanders in 1980 won four playoff series to capture the Cup. In 1981, they won four more, and then again in 1982 and in 1983. In 1984, they won three playoff series before losing to the Oilers in the final. Maybe the team's biggest accomplishment was a real Islanders-like achievement. "I read this when Al passed away [in 2015]," Scotty says. "They won *19* consecutive playoff series."

CHAPTER THIRTEEN
Edmonton Oilers 1983–84

"I saw some interviews [Gretzky] did on TV," Scotty says. "He said right after they'd lost four straight in '83 that he and some teammates were walking by the Islanders' dressing room and looked in and saw the players with all their cuts and bruises. And they realized for the first time what it took to win."

It was at that moment that the Oilers began to win the Cup.

The Oilers had always had it easy, though it didn't seem that way to them. When they and their WHA cohorts, the Winnipeg Jets, Hartford Whalers, and Quebec Nordiques, entered the NHL in 1979, they were a team literally out of their league. Now, suddenly, they were up against the Canadiens, Islanders, Bruins, Flyers, and Sabres, but without the strength, depth, or experience to compete. Night after night. That first season in the new 21-team NHL, the ex-WHA teams finished 20th (Winnipeg), 19th (Quebec), 16th (Edmonton), and 13th (Hartford). The next year wasn't much better; the Jets, with a 9–57–14 record, finished 24 points behind the league's next-worst team. But when you are young and talented, it *is* easy—today is no burden because tomorrow is so close at hand. And the Oilers were young and they were breathtakingly talented.

They had so many players who had been outstanding as kids, who were highly drafted, yet who turned out to be even better than anyone had imagined. Even Gretzky, who had been astonishing since he was scarcely old enough to walk. Early videos show him on the backyard rink his father built, looking like Tiger Woods did hitting golf balls as a two-year-old on *The Mike Douglas Show*. Gretzky's incredible future was all there to see. As he got older, he was too good for his age group, then too good for his hometown of Brantford, Ontario. He had to play against older kids, and then had to move to a bigger city, and everyone in hockey knew of his exploits. During the 1978 World Junior Hockey Championships in Montreal, after a Canadiens' workout one day, Scotty and many of the players—me included—stood by the boards and watched Team Canada practise. "Which one is Gretzky?" we wanted to know. He was 16, and we were winners of two straight Stanley Cups and on our way to a third and a fourth.

Yet until this time, Gretzky had been only "kids' hockey" dominant, like scores of phenoms before him who had been bigger, stronger, and smarter, with some kind of biological head start—hitting puberty sooner—until others caught up and closed the gap—which would surely happen to him too. And yes, Gretzky was a great junior in the only season he played, finishing second in the OHL in scoring behind future NHL first overall pick and Calder Trophy winner Bobby Smith, who was three years older. And yes, at 17, unwilling to wait around to be old enough for the NHL draft, he then signed with the Indianapolis Racers, and in his only WHA season, against opponents who were sometimes 10 years older and stronger, finished third in the league in scoring. And yes, the next year, at 18 and as an NHL rookie, he was second in scoring behind Marcel Dionne (he had the same number of points, 137, but scored two fewer goals). Yet in these junior, WHA, and NHL seasons, he had been only remarkably good for his age. He wasn't league-dominant. Not like he had been as a kid.

Then things got ridiculous.

In 1980–81, his second NHL season, he won the scoring title by 29 points. He was 19. But that was nothing, because the following season he totalled 212 points, demolishing his own league record by 48 points and finishing 65 points higher than the league's second-highest scorer, Mike Bossy. He also scored 92 goals, 16 more than Phil Esposito's league record that had stood for 11 years. Then, in his next five seasons, his point totals were 196, 205, 208, 215, and 183, while those of the league's *second*-highest scorer in those same years were 72, 79, 73, 74, and 75 points behind him.

This was the "live puck era," as Scotty describes it. Average shooters were suddenly putting up superstar numbers. Superstar goalies were suddenly like Swiss cheese. But it was the live puck era for everyone, not just Gretzky. So while Gretzky's absolute numbers can be misleading, his comparative numbers still tell the tale. This was the NHL, these were the best hockey players in the world, and for six straight years Gretzky totalled, on average, more than one and a half times the number of points per season than the *second*-best of the best. These second-best scorers were named Lemieux, Bossy, and Kurri, among others. Howe, even at his most overwhelming in the early 1950s, never came close to this degree of supremacy. Gretzky dominated the NHL like he had once dominated kids' hockey. And this wasn't Brantford anymore.

More than the live puck era, this was the "Gretzky era."

But he wasn't the only Oiler who proved far better than anyone had dared imagine. When Mark Messier was 17, he too decided not to put off his money-earning career and signed with Indianapolis. He was eight days older than Gretzky. He had always been a strong and powerful kid, and could skate with a force and tireless drive that was stunning. His minor hockey opponents also quickly realized what his NHL opponents would later learn: you don't mess with Mess. Because Messier could be mean. Scary-mean. But unlike Gretzky, Messier at 17 wasn't yet ready for the WHA. In his only season, he played 52 games and scored only one goal. When the year ended and the NHL and WHA merged, the Oilers were allowed to designate Gretzky as one of their two protected players. Messier went into the draft. Forty-seven players were chosen ahead of him. He would go on to play 1,756 NHL games, more than anyone in league history except Gordie Howe. Back in 1979, the Oilers could have had no idea what they were getting.

They had no idea about Glenn Anderson either. He was chosen 21 picks behind Messier in the same draft—the 69th selection. In his first six years in the league, Anderson scored 30 goals (as a 20-year-old rookie), then 38, 48, 54, 42, and 54.

Nor could the Oilers have known about Jari Kurri, who was drafted a year later—also in the fourth round, also with the 69th pick overall. Swedes had been making their mark in the NHL for almost a decade. Finns had not. They were the country cousins of their more worldly, sophisticated neighbours. Swedes expected success, in business, in the arts, in sports—think Alfred Nobel, IKEA, Greta Garbo, Björn Borg, ABBA, Ingmar Bergman—and they got it. The Finns did not. Kurri averaged over 47 goals a year in his 10 seasons with the Oilers, and was the team's best two-way forward.

Imagine the feeling around the Oilers in these years as they began to realize what they had. Imagine how the fans felt, and the media, the coaches, and the players, discovering how good they were, how good they made each other, how much better they were than just a few months, a few weeks, a few days ago. And how much better they might be. And could be. And would be.

And the way they played was so exciting. There was such joy. For every other team, even for the Stanley Cup champion Islanders, getting up the ice was such a slog. They moved like infantry grunts. The Oilers were the *flyboys*. In their first NHL season, they finished with 69 points. In their second, 74. In their third, 1981–82, 111. The Stanley Cup–winning Islanders might still have been the best team, but the Oilers were inevitable. They might even win that season. If not, the next. Life was great.

Yet in the first round of the 1982 playoffs, the Oilers lost to L.A. The Kings had finished 48 points behind them during the regular season. It was stunning. But when you're young and talented, everything seems like a lesson, nobody's a disappointment, and nothing is disappointing for long. They had just gotten ahead of themselves that season—that was the problem, people said. They would be even stronger the next year, and everyone knew it.

And after a slow start, they were. In the last 18 games of the 1982–83 season, they lost only twice, and only once in the first three rounds of the playoffs, sweeping both Winnipeg and Chicago. They averaged more than six goals a game, and now they had seven days to get themselves rested and ready for the final.

The Islanders had defeated the Bruins in a hard, grinding, six-game semifinal series. They would have three days and a flight to Edmonton before the first game. The Oilers were ready to win. They knew it, the fans and the media knew it. The torch would be passed.

For the Oilers, in most ways, the opening game couldn't have gone better. They were a team that could always score; their challenge was to avoid the indiscipline that led to too many easy goals against. And in that first game, they allowed only two goals. But Islanders goalie Billy Smith shut them out, 2–0. In Edmonton. Two nights later, the Islanders won again, 6–3. In New York, the Islanders completed the sweep, 5–1 and 4–2. In four games, the unstoppable Oilers had scored just six goals. It was after that Cup-losing final game that Gretzky and his teammates took their walk down the back corridor and learned what they needed to learn.

"The Oilers had never played against a team as tough as that," Scotty says of the Islanders. "They weren't used to it. They weren't battle-ready." Edmonton played in the Smythe Division of the Western Conference (then known as the Campbell Conference). Every NHL team played eight games against each of their division opponents—in the Oilers' case, Calgary, Vancouver, Winnipeg, and L.A.—and three times against each of the other sixteen teams in the league's near-barnstorming format. In those years, Calgary finished about 10th during each regular season, Vancouver and Winnipeg a few spots lower, and L.A. near the bottom. Theirs was not a strong division, and it was known for its wide-open style of play.

For the Oilers, it meant that 32 of their games, 40 per cent of the schedule, were a feast. (In 1983–84, they would win the Smythe Division for the third consecutive year with a 27–3–2 divisional record, outscoring their opponents 201–126.) The Islanders, on the other hand, played their regular season in the tougher, more competitive, more defensively focused Patrick Division. Learning from their playoff defeat the year before, the Oilers came to play every game that 1983–84 season as if it were against two opponents—the other team on the ice that night *and* the Islanders—and as if it were taking place at two times—the date of the game itself *and* late in May during the Stanley Cup final. However great the Oilers might be on any given night against any given opponent during the regular season didn't matter; it was how they would stack up against the Islanders in a showdown final that counted.

The Oilers won the first seven games of the 1983–84 season, then not many nights later started on an eight-game winning streak. In a 20-game stretch between December 14 and January 27, they lost only once. But in early February, in a testing trip east, they lost to the Capitals, 9–2, the Islanders, 5–3, the Flyers, 4–3, the Bruins, 4–1, and the Whalers, 11–0. Learning their lesson was one thing; applying it was another.

"Their game was all attack," Scotty explains. And it wasn't just Gretzky, Messier, Kurri, and Anderson. It was having two of them—two centres, Gretzky and Messier—go back-to-back. More than that, it was having Gretzky *and* Kurri, then Messier *and* Anderson, back-to-back. Teams might be able to match up against one great star, maybe two, but against two great tandems? Maybe they could for a few shifts, or a period or two, but not the whole game. The concentration and effort that took, let alone the skill, were too much. Then there was Paul Coffey on defence, who was really a third member of both tandems and a fourth forward on every line, flying at you every time he was on the ice. Coffey didn't just join the attack, he was a full-fledged member of it. He had the hands to play with the great offensive players, and the shot, but it was his skating that set him apart. Lots of baseball players have a good swing—and then there's Ken Griffey Jr. Lots of goalies are graceful and athletic—and then there's Carey Price. "Of all the defencemen I've seen," Scotty says, "nobody else except Coffey could skate stride for stride with Orr. He had a beautiful glide. He skated effortlessly, and I don't think he ever got tired. And for him, it was all offence. He didn't pay much attention to defence. He didn't sense danger." Instead, he sensed opportunity, just as his teammates did. The Oilers just kept coming at you.

But it was Gretzky who had set the Oilers in motion, and it was Gretzky who kept them there. Even Scotty has a hard time explaining him, making sense of him. When he tries, he begins in one direction, then when his words don't sound right to him, he tries another, and another, as if hoping somehow that everything he says will somehow add up to something. Gretzky was skinny. He was a slightly awkward skater. He wasn't strong. And nobody should've been that good.

"He did so many things differently," Scotty starts. "He was unpredictable. He was a scoring machine." Not satisfied, he tries again. "He had such vision on the ice. He had so much hockey sense. That's such an underrated quality. He was brainy, and his quickness was underestimated. Maybe he didn't skate all over the ice and everywhere, but I don't remember him hanging around. He was always a busy guy." And when you do play "up high" in the defensive zone, near the blue line, like Gretzky did, you don't get caught in the mire and scrum of the action; you can see what's around you, you can anticipate, you can set yourself in motion and give yourself a head start and get to where you want to go before anyone else can. You have open ice, as much open ice as there is in a hockey game. And you don't have a lot of guys to beat— some of them are trapped in their offensive zone—so you don't have to wrestle for space with players who are bigger, stronger, and tougher. You can play *your* game, not theirs.

"He could pass the puck as well as anybody who's ever passed it," Scotty says. "Backhand, forehand, over the stick, through guys." And then, if you're Gretzky, because you have time, you can be patient and make even more plays. You can go behind an opponent's net and, using the net as your protection, stay there, and wait, and wait, and see the other team's players run around and see their minds twist into knots. "He'd get the goalie and the other five guys looking at him, then at his teammates, then at him," Scotty recalls. He put their heads on such a swivel they couldn't focus on anybody just when, with the action near the net, they needed to focus on everybody. "In that position, you have to commit and go after him, but you can't fully commit." You can't fully do *anything*. "Then he can make a forehand pass, or if you chase him— and teams would always say, 'Chase him onto his backhand'—well, he can make a backhand pass too." Pick your poison.

If you're Gretzky, with time, touch, and a mind able to use both, you can make magic.

"I don't know why we didn't play more guys 'up high' like Gretzky did," Scotty wonders now. "But you have to have a special player. Buffalo did that with [Alexander] Mogilny. And Vancouver with [Pavel] Bure. I remember in Montreal, talking with [Anatoly] Tarasov before the New Year's Eve game with the Russians [in 1975]." Tarasov, the former coach of the Soviet national team and CSKA, more than anyone had been responsible for creating the Soviet style of hockey. He and Scotty spoke through an interpreter.

"He had watched us practise, and he mentioned Lafleur, and also Savard, Robinson, and Lapointe, and he said, 'You have players who are calm, who don't get flustered and can really pass the puck. Why don't you have Lafleur break out of your zone [without the puck] past the point man? Now you'd have both defencemen looking at each other, each having to make sure that one of them covers Lafleur. Now you've got a four-on-four in your own end, and if Lafleur is like a lot of our offensive players in his own zone, he's not a defensive player. So he's not going to make good defensive decisions anyway.'"

Tarasov had employed this strategy with waterbug-quick Valeri Kharlamov—who, in the 1972 Summit Series, drove the Team Canada defence crazy. "Cournoyer used to do that a little for us," Scotty adds, but not as often as Kharlamov. Cournoyer and Lafleur, after all, were Canadian, and this was the NHL, and the NHL was the best league in the world, and Canadian players were its best players, so whatever they did was the best. Anything else was Soviet stuff—until a few years later, when Gretzky did the same and made it his own.

"Nobody will ever score goals again like this guy," Scotty says of Gretzky. "Over a six-year period: 92, 71, 87, 73, 52, 62—437 goals. Nobody's ever going to come close to that. I don't think anybody could think the game, and think *ahead* of the game, the way he could. Players would try to cover him, but then he'd be gone." His father, Walter, might have taught him to "skate to where the puck is going, not where it has been," but it was Gretzky who taught himself to "skate to where the big guys aren't." To open ice, where he could have that ice to himself.

He had no space in his own defensive zone; he was no good there. He was no good in the offensive zone either, unless he could create space. He knew if he couldn't, he couldn't play in the NHL, and he had known that from almost the first moment he played. "From the time he was 12 or 13 he played against players who were much older," Scotty explains. Against them, he knew he couldn't do everything himself. He wasn't the pituitary freak who had matured early to be as big as they were. He'd have to find a way to play *with* them, and he could do that only if he could make size not matter. If he could make something else matter more.

So while the young phenoms who *were* big learned to take the puck from end to end and score because they could, their teammates standing around doing the *doo-wahs*, Gretzky learned to *see* his teammates, to pass to them, to make them matter, to make *himself* matter. He played a game that others would learn—*if* they learned it—only much later. For Gretzky, *this* was Brantford, and its life lessons that stayed with him wherever he went. And in this Brantford, he learned something else, at an even younger age. "He played a tremendous amount of shinny on his backyard rink as a young kid," Scotty says. "When you're playing shinny, you're not thinking defence."

Scotty has an easier time explaining Messier, and he speaks about him with deep admiration. He can't believe how strong he was. He can't get over the sheer force of him: his personality, his total *being*. But he understands him, just like he understands Gordie Howe, Ted Lindsay, and the Rocket.

Scotty has a memory of Messier that has stayed with him. "I remember the Oilers coming into Buffalo one year, it was a Sunday night. Messier had done something in an earlier game, and [NHL vice president] Brian O'Neill had held a hearing to decide if there'd be any further penalty, and I knew Messier was going to get suspended. But [O'Neill] wouldn't make his ruling until Monday morning. So Messier played that night, and I'm telling you he ran the whole game. I remember like it was yesterday. We would've won if he wasn't there." That night, Messier scored the tying and winning goals in an Oilers 5–4 victory, and the *something* he had done was crack the cheekbone of Calgary defenceman Jamie Macoun with a sucker punch two weeks before. He got suspended the day after the game in Buffalo. For Scotty, justice delayed was justice denied.

Messier was suspended for ten games for that incident. The year before, in 1983–84, he was suspended for six games for hitting Vancouver's Thomas Gradin over the head with his stick, and for an additional game later in the year after receiving his third game misconduct that season. In 1988, Messier was suspended for six games for hitting the Canucks' Rich Sutter in the mouth with his stick, breaking four of his teeth. A few years after that, he got one game for his stick-swinging duel with Ulf Samuelsson, two games for hitting Mike Hough from behind, and two more games for spearing Martin Štrbák. In between, there were all the slashes and high-sticks that served their purpose and brought no suspension at all.

"He had a big mean streak in him," Scotty says. "He played on the edge. No other player I can recall had as many suspensions as he did." Howe had been tough and mean, but he was calculatedly mean. If somebody did something to him, nonchalantly and *with* premeditation he would destroy him. No muss, no fuss. Maurice Richard was out-of-control mean. If somebody did something to him, he'd lose it. And Messier was the same. Their eyes turned from fierce to spooky in a flash. Some players go stupid and weak when they lose it. Messier became superhuman. "He and the Rocket were very similar. When the Rocket was out of control, nothing could stop him."

All of this was on top of Messier being an immensely talented player. "He was an exceptional skater, and in super condition in an era when not many were. He had defensive instincts—you had to if you played with Glenn Anderson. Anderson was a little like Cournoyer. He could fly, he didn't handle the puck that well, but if you could get him the puck in flight he could really cause you problems, and Messier was really good at finding him. Anderson had a knack around the net and he didn't need much of an opening. A lot of guys just don't finish, but what I remember about Anderson [is] he could finish. He'd come from that off wing and put his leg out, and with his speed and strength, you couldn't stop him. He was a hell of a player. He and Messier played so well together. They were tough guys and they played tough. And they were both mean."

On another team, Messier could have been "the man." Later, after Gretzky was traded to L.A., and with Messier as captain the Oilers won the Cup, and later still, after he went to New York, and with him as captain the Rangers won the Cup—he *was* "the man." But that wasn't how it was in Edmonton then, nor could it be. Messier could have insisted on a larger role. He and Gretzky could have been rivals. The team could have divided itself into a Gretzky camp and a Messier camp, but that didn't happen. It wouldn't have occurred to either Gretzky or Messier, or to any of their teammates, or to the media, or to the fans. And even if it had, Gretzky wouldn't have allowed that division to happen. He admired Messier as much as everyone else did, because Messier was like his hero, Gordie Howe; and if Messier had ever needed more—whether attention or credit—Gretzky would have made sure he got it. But Messier never imagined or expected or needed more. To him, Gretzky was *the one* and he had always been *the one.* They had played together since they were both 18, eight days apart in age, and it was Gretzky who had piled up all those points, won all those awards, and was the making of the Oilers. It didn't matter how much better Messier got, or what everybody began to say about him—Gretzky was Gretzky, he was beyond any*one* and any*thing.* It had been the same with the Bruins in the early 1970s. Phil Esposito was fabulous, but he wasn't Bobby Orr and he never could be, so any fantasy anyone might have about anything else could be buried 10 feet under, where it belonged.

Instead, Gretzky and Messier were a great partnership—two centres, back-to-back. Survive Gretzky, good luck with Messier; make it through Messier, good luck with Gretzky; survive the first period, good luck with the second and the third. Different bodies, different skills, same attitude, same *need.* Gretzky was the inspiration—for his teammates, he was what they could never be. Messier was the model—he was who they might be; he played the way they played, only amped up and better. The two of them needed each other, needed for the Oilers to win the Cup, and then to win more. They needed to be as great as they had it in them to be.

By 1981–82, when Edmonton jumped from 74 points to 111, Gretzky and Messier knew the Oilers weren't just a bunch of young guys having fun. They had something special, and with that recognition came a feeling that took them over and grew. *They could be, so they had no right not to be*—so they, Gretzky and Messier, had to remain that partnership. "In the history of hockey," Scotty says, thinking, "maybe a little bit Béliveau and Henri Richard, but I don't remember a team having two centres like that. If you were to rate the greatest centres of all time, it would be hard to say that Gretzky and Messier wouldn't both be in the top 10. [And they were] on one team."

Everybody else took their places around them. Anderson with Messier, Kurri with Gretzky. "Kurri, for all those 600 goals he scored, was such a dependable two-way player. He killed penalties. He knew where to be. He was always in position. He was such an outstanding defensive player, and so important for Gretzky. He played down low [near the net in his defensive zone] so Gretzky could play up high. He had a terrific shot. He could put the puck where he wanted to, and he didn't need many chances. Gretzky, a left shot, liked to come up the right side, his wrong side, and Kurri, a right shot on the left side, would move into the scoring areas. He was a very good skater—not big, but a good size and very strong. And durable. I don't think he missed many games. And yet he was overshadowed completely by other star players. By Canadian players. I don't know, was it because he was European? Because when people talk about top players they never talk about Kurri, but this guy's record is fantastic." In Kurri's 10 years in Edmonton, the team won five Stanley Cups, and Kurri scored 32, 32, 45, 52, 71, 68, 54, 43, 44, and 33 goals—474 goals. In the playoffs, when scorers are more tightly defended, he scored even more often.

"It is pretty unusual for a team to have two right wingers [Kurri and Anderson] who scored as many goals as they did. Gretzky and Kurri, and Messier and Anderson, they had all kinds of guys on left wing, just like Bossy and Trottier did. They had Dave Hunter, and Willy Lindström. They had [Dave] Semenko. They had [Jaroslav] Pouzar. And, on that 1983–84 team, they had seven players who had over 100 penalty minutes: Messier had 165, [Kevin] McClelland 127, [Lee] Fogolin 125, [Don] Jackson 120, [Ken] Linseman 119, Semenko 118, Coffey 104. And Hunter had 90. Nobody was going to out-tough this team. I don't think there's ever been a team that had seven guys with over a hundred minutes in penalties. They didn't take any guff at all. And they had guys who played a lot but didn't get penalties: Kurri 14, Gretzky 39, even some defencemen—Kevin Lowe, who played a ton, had only 59 minutes, and Charlie Huddy 43."

Yet even when killing penalties, the Oilers thought offence. "They scored 36 shorthanded goals that year!" Scotty exclaims. On a team that generated countless outsized numbers, this one jumps out at him. The Islanders and Minnesota were next, they had 18; Gretzky himself had 12—only six entire *teams* (including his own) scored more shorthanded goals than he did. Again, this was Gretzky and the Oilers, always in motion—even killing penalties.

"They had a good-size defence," Scotty recalls. "Lowe played with Lee Fogolin. Lowe didn't have a lot of natural ability, but he had a lot of desire. He had toughness. He could block shots. He was a valuable defenceman because the Oilers didn't have a lot of guys like that. And, of course, Coffey was a terrific offensive player. In some games he was so good. But he was high-risk, there's no other way to say it, and he was never going to shut things down defensively. But he played with Charlie Huddy, who was solid. Randy Gregg played with Don Jackson. Huddy, Gregg, Jackson, and Fogolin weren't really top-notch guys, but they got a lot of hockey out of them, and with that team, with all their scoring, they fit in perfectly."

"In goal, [Grant] Fuhr and [Andy] Moog were a good combination. They were like Billy Smith and Chico Resch with the Islanders. They shared the job during the regular season, then in the playoffs, *boom*, they'd stick with one goalie. With Fuhr. The Oilers were such a wide-open team, he had to make a lot of tough saves. He got breakaways, but he seemed to have the right temperament for that team. He looked like he was never concerned about anything." Fuhr allowed a lot of goals because this was the live puck era and because the Oilers played with offensive—and defensive—abandon. In his 10 years in Edmonton, Fuhr's goals against average was 3.69 a game, only slightly less than the league average of the time, and more than a goal a game higher than other Hall of Fame goalies of recent years—Martin Brodeur, Dominik Hašek,

Patrick Roy—whose careers managed to miss much or all of the 1980s. But to goalies, the *whys* and *hows* don't matter. They don't like letting in goals. Goals embarrass them, and fans and media notice goals.

Because of the maturity the position requires, goalies take longer to reach the NHL, but the Oilers couldn't wait, and so Fuhr was barely 19 when the team made him a regular. He had to learn fast what any goalie for the Oilers had to learn: don't allow the goals you're going to let in to get you down. Your team can score, better than anyone else in the league, and they *will* score. Just keep the game close, and if a shot beats you, make sure you stop the next one, even if it's harder to stop than the one before. Because if you do, Gretzky, Messier, Kurri, Anderson, or someone else will get the rebound and take the puck up the ice and score, and they'll make what you did not only a tough save, but a *big* save. A save that matters, and makes you—the goalie for that Oilers offensive machine—matter too. Fuhr was important to the Oilers. So was his co-goalie, Andy Moog. Their teammates trusted them. In turn, they gave their teammates the freedom they needed to do what they did best.

The Oilers also had the right coach. They were a "swashbuckling team," as Scotty puts it, and Glen Sather was a swashbuckling coach. Street-smart, funny, irascible, charming, with a tongue as sharp and quick as his mind. He was a star. He looked like his players, who were 20 years younger, with his mop of longish blond hair. He dressed like his players, but *impeccably*. He had two great stars, Gretzky and Messier, and lots of outstanding players. He had a team owner, Peter Pocklington, who liked to conduct his business in the deep shade and his personal life in the noonday sun. Sather had to bring out the best in his players, and avoid the worst in his owner. He had to coach down, and manage up. But for Sather, that was a piece of cake.

He had always been a manipulator. If he'd had the talent he might have been a star as a player too, but he didn't. He was a little undersized, and without the speed to compensate. He was scrappy, always on the puck, or even more happily always on a more talented opponent in the vicinity of the puck, jabbing at him with his stick, hooking him, holding him, trash-talking him, distracting him, making him ordinary. Making himself matter, and getting a star's attention from the fans: at home from those who loved him; on the road, from those who loved to hate him. He was a pest. A disturber. He played three years in the minor leagues, ten years in the NHL, and a final season in the WHA, and he never once scored 20 goals. Near the end of his career, he played in Montreal. Scotty was his coach, and I was one of his teammates. "Sam took him as a role player," Scotty recalls. "He knew he was a rah-rah type of guy and wouldn't disturb anybody if he didn't play. And he didn't. He was a good guy and a good teammate. He knew who he was." This was 1974–75, the year before the Canadiens began their run of four straight Stanley Cups. At this stage in his career, and on this Montreal team, Sather knew he couldn't offer more. So that's what he offered.

After a couple of wind-down seasons—one in Minnesota, and another with Edmonton while they were still in the WHA—Sather started into coaching with the Oilers. As a coach, he might have taken one of two approaches, one far more likely than the other. He had been a journeyman player. He had experienced the game through a journeyman's eyes. He knew the importance of dogged, never-say-die players, of good guys and good teammates who are almost always overlooked and underappreciated. He might have put together a team in his image, coached them to be what he was, made them a team that was gritty and tough and aggravatingly hard to play against that would be fun to watch, almost always made the playoffs, and some years got into the second round. Then there was the less likely approach, which is what he actually did, because of what he had also experienced as a journeyman. He had played on some good teams—notably the Rangers in the early 1970s—and he knew the importance of star players. He knew you can scuffle and try, but that you can't go far just with players like him. What he did as a player mattered only if he was surrounded by stars. If he wasn't, it was all show. All pretend. Sather respected great players. He needed them to be great—not just great, but also a little more gritty and hard-nosed like him until they weren't great anymore. *Great.*

"He was good with players like Gretzky and Messier," Scotty recalls. "He let them play their style, be creative, then he reined them in at the right time. He didn't try to force his own personality on them. He didn't try to make them what they weren't. He trusted people. He was the manager-coach. John Muckler [his assistant coach] was the strategist, the *X*s and *O*s guy. Muckler ran their workouts, and later was their head coach. Sather trusted Barry Fraser too, his head scout. He made some great picks. They were a team built on a lot of great selections.

"[Glen] didn't do any scouting himself. He didn't put in his own hands things he couldn't do. He was the number-one guy, and he made the final decisions, but he delegated a lot of authority. He had a good feel—for a team, for players. He wasn't afraid to take a chance on a guy who had been a problem child with another team. He would take on guys as projects, because he knew that the core of the Oilers was very solid. Gretzky, Messier, and the others had a real feeling among themselves, and they were going to run things the way they wanted to. Glen knew that, and he just kept them on the straight and narrow. They needed that a bit, and he wasn't afraid."

Sather wasn't afraid of trying to make the Oilers great, or of them *being* great. He wasn't afraid of being a star himself, as a coach—of standing centre stage, the spotlight on him. He wasn't afraid of taking on his star players if he had to, and because he wasn't, and his stars knew that, they were a little afraid of him. He was intimidating. He had as big a personality as they did. On the ice, they were in command, but off the ice, they were no match for him. He had funnier one-liners and more soul-punishing barbs than they did, and the media loved him. He wouldn't have been easy to take on. But he was too smart to take his stars on. They were great players, and it was his job to make them greater, not to bring them down. They had the right instincts, they had the right talent; his job was to use a little manipulation here, some finesse there, and that's all it took.

"Even a team that wins Cups," as Scotty says often, "needs to change. But when all of a sudden changes are made, what happens to the relationship between the coach and manager, and the players? If [the coach and manager] have looked after the core, the players don't question every move that's made. They'll embrace the new guy coming in. They have full confidence in the coach. They roll along. Glen could do what he wanted to do in Edmonton."

In that 1983–84 season, after the Oilers had lost five in a row against eastern teams in February, they returned home and won eight straight, 18 of their last 22, and finished first overall, 15 points ahead of the second-place Islanders. Gretzky led the league in scoring by a margin of 79 points over Coffey, and in goals by 31 over Michel Goulet of the Nordiques. But this was only the preamble. This season was about the Cup.

In the first round, the Oilers swept Winnipeg. Next up was Calgary. During the regular season, Edmonton's record against the Flames was 7–0–1, the Oilers outscoring them, 53–28. Their opening playoff game followed the same pattern: a solid 5–2 victory for the Oilers in Edmonton. But then the series took a turn. Calgary won the next game, also in Edmonton, in overtime, and now the Flames were returning home. Again the Oilers found a balanced playoff style and won the next two games, 3–2 and 5–3, and now they were heading home to finish off the Flames. But Calgary won the fifth game, and the sixth at the Saddledome in overtime, and the series returned to Edmonton for Game 7. The Oilers won, 7–4. In the next round against Minnesota they hit their stride, sweeping them in four games and averaging 5.5 goals a game for—and, more importantly, only 2.5 against.

Now, finally, the Islanders.

The series opened in New York. For the Islanders, it was their 97th game; for the Oilers, their 95th. But nothing about that regular season or the earlier playoff rounds now mattered. The Islanders had won the Stanley Cup four straight times; the previous two years, the Oilers had lost when they seemed ready to win. Worse, the last time they had been swept by the Islanders. Worse, in the opening game of the 1983 series, in Edmonton—in a statement game—the Oilers had shown the Islanders that they could defend and not just score, allowing only two goals; but it was the Islanders who had delivered the real statement, showing the Oilers they could shut down their scorers, winning 2–0.

Now this was another statement game, this time on Long Island. Were the Oilers ready to be champions? Were the Islanders still the Islanders? Which would it be? When the game ended, the statement was clear—not only could the Oilers beat the Islanders in the playoffs, and win on the road, but they could beat the Islanders on the road *and* in a low-scoring game. The team that couldn't defend had shut out the Islanders, 1–0. New York won the next game, but that didn't matter. This Oilers team was different. And when they reinforced this message in Game 3 in Edmonton, the series was as good as over, and became more decisively over with every minute that passed. The scores of the last three games: 7–2, 7–2, 5–2.

The Islanders had won 19 straight playoff series. During that time, from 1979–80 to 1982–83, they played 78 playoff games; the Oilers 33. For the Islanders, four years, four Stanley Cups—that's a lot of wear and tear. They had finally discovered they couldn't outscore the Oilers, they couldn't out-defend them, or out-steady them, or out-tough them. They couldn't discourage them. They couldn't beat them or get them to beat themselves. They had no answers. "The playoffs take an awful lot out of you," Scotty says. "Eventually, the Islanders finally hit a wall, and the wall was a bunch of young guys who had learned from their previous loss."

The Oilers in the early 1980s had gone through so many ups and a few downs that it's hard to remember they were so young. Yet when that 1983–84 season began, Gretzky, Messier, and Coffey were all 22, Anderson and Kurri 23, and Fuhr just 21.

They won the next year, were upset the next, and then won twice more. Then in August 1988, Peter Pocklington sold Gretzky to L.A. "I wonder how Glen [Sather] felt when Gretzky left," Scotty says now. "I mean, you're standing there on the podium and your franchise player is taken away."

The Oilers won again in 1990, but this time *that* was the upset, then they drifted out of sight. Sather stayed 10 more years, then joined the Rangers in 2000. "He got fed up," Scotty says. "He knew that this thing wasn't going to work"—that the Oilers couldn't win again with Pocklington as the team's owner. "It's like when I decided to leave Montreal. I didn't think things were going to work, and I'd be the victim."

CHAPTER FOURTEEN

The 1970s was a great decade for Scotty. The 1980s wasn't.

In his first season in Buffalo, 1979–80, the Sabres had earned 110 points and finished second in the league behind the Flyers, then won two rounds of the playoffs before losing in the semifinals to the eventual Cup champion Islanders. During the rest of his eight-year tenure with the team, the Sabres recorded 99, 93, 89, 103, 90, 80, and 64 points, finishing fourth overall, then sixth, ninth, fourth, eighth, thirteenth, and twenty-first (and last), and won one, zero, one, zero, and zero playoff rounds, until in Scotty's last two seasons they didn't make the playoffs at all.

That initial season in Buffalo still haunts him. "We had a very good first year," he says with pride. "We squeezed every last ounce out of all the players, and finished second overall." The team surged into the playoffs on a 14-game unbeaten streak, then beat Vancouver, and swept Chicago in four straight games. But this is where the story begins to change. "And then we had a eight-day layoff before we played the Islanders." The layoff should have given the team the fresh boost of energy they needed to take on the big, strong, desperate Islanders. Instead, in dialing back their emotion to wait out the days, the Sabres never quite got it back. The first two games were in Buffalo, where, during the regular season, the Sabres had beaten and tied the Islanders.

In the opening game, the Sabres lost, 4–1, and they lost again in the second, 2–1 in double overtime. The Islanders won the series in six games. This was the season that should have set the team and Scotty on their way. But as the Sabres' non-Cup-winning years piled up during the 1980s, it became the season that might have been.

The best player for the Sabres in those playoffs, as it had been in the years before and would be in the years after, was Perreault. He had been with Buffalo since the team's beginning—their first-ever first-round pick; the prize first overall selection of the 1970 draft. Almost instantly, he became the league's second-most exciting player, after Orr. Not the second best. He was a mix of the fluid grace of Béliveau and the quickness of Lafleur, and through much of the 1970s he made the Sabres—after the Bruins, then after the Canadiens—the second-most exciting team in the league. Not the second best. He and his teammates generated loud sold-out crowds in the bandbox-tight Aud—never more so than when the Sabres made it to the Stanley Cup final against the Flyers in only their fifth season. In their first decade in the league, the team was good and exciting, and promising.

"He was the best player on the team by quite a bit," Scotty says of Perreault. "I don't know if he realized that, or if he was of the type of temperament to notice. There aren't a lot of players who can make plays and also score goals, but he could pretty well do anything. You were always hoping, 'Is he going to realize tonight that he can take over the game?' And you always had the feeling he could. He was easy to coach too. He practised pretty well, he was never involved in any controversies, he wasn't a rebel at all. He had none of that in him. Yet he was ultra-competitive in his own way. He played with Martin and Robert, but when we traded Robert that didn't bother him either." The trade happened six days before the opening game of Scotty's first season, breaking up the French Connection, which had been the identity of the team during its first decade.

"You could play him with whomever you wanted. You could ask

him to do certain things, and he'd try. Not many superstars were like that. As a teammate, you couldn't find anyone better. He never had a negative part in him. But he had no leadership at all. None. He didn't want that responsibility. He didn't want to be 'the guy.' I don't think that came from him having to carry the team in his first years there; I think it was just his makeup. He didn't want the attention. I always thought that if he had gone to Montreal with all the great players there, it might have made a difference to his career. But I think going to a market like Buffalo fit his style. He was a simple guy. He was the most popular player ever to play there, and maybe still is."

Scotty had coached Perreault before, in the 1976 Canada Cup. Orr and Potvin may have been Team Canada's best players in that series, but on a team that included such great scorers as Bobby Hull, Phil Esposito, Bobby Clarke, Guy Lafleur, and Marcel Dionne, Perreault and Hull led the team in goals, and Perreault may have been Canada's best two-way forward. He didn't seek out the spotlight, but on hockey's biggest stages he still shone. And in Scotty's first season in Buffalo—a critical transition year for both the team and the franchise, where the best needed to be "squeezed" out of everybody—Perreault finished fourth in the NHL in scoring, and registered 21 points in only 14 playoff games. Yet in the next few years as Perreault remained the constant, some of the team's other stars fell back, and others were traded—Gare and Schoenfeld among them—mostly for players whose best years were also past them, but also for Mike Foligno and draft picks. Big defenceman Jerry Korab and sniper Rick Martin brought a pair of first-round selections, a sixth and a fifth overall, which Scotty turned into Phil Housley, who was second in the Calder Trophy voting the next season, and goalie Tom Barrasso, who won the award the following year.

The Sabres had three first-round picks in each of those 1982 and 1983 drafts. As Sam had done, Scotty the manager was getting Scotty the coach the players he needed to see the team into the future. But it wasn't enough. As the Sabres had become too old to win, now they were too young to win.

What Scotty needed was to add to these young stars a few veterans who were excited about the team's future and their own fresh possibilities; to fill roles and add depth for games against the Islanders and the Oilers and other big contenders, for the four grinding series of the playoffs. But Buffalo was a "small market" team. They had the money to pay the stars, but not to pay the players who were able to keep the game close until the stars got back onto the ice to win it. The Sabres' new players slowed down the team's decline, but they didn't stop it.

Scotty's time with the Sabres never did feel comfortable. After that initial season, everything seemed off. He could never get the coach-manager balance right. He was a coach. He'd learned that when Sam had made him head scout for Eastern Canada and he hated the job. Always on the road, but mostly it was because he was not with a team. The intensity of a team—even the everyday-ness of it. Guys in slumps, sick or hurt; a hot team coming in, everything urgent, the need to find an answer; the buzz, the *now*. The full immersion of a team. He loved that. Not many people understood that about him. He often seemed awkward around others, and so everyone thought he didn't like being around people, but that wasn't it at all. He was a hockey genius, but he was no pointy-headed academic focused only inside his own head, his eyes open wide but blind to everything around him. He looked outward, always searching for something new. He didn't want to be shut away in any office. His instincts were those of a player. He wanted to put everything of himself into a few hours of a day, then have the rest of the day to himself. He wanted to put all of himself into a season, then escape into the summer.

As a manager, he found all those hours and months get stolen away. He had seen it happen with Sam. "The toughest part when you're doing both jobs is that when you're not coaching you're doing the phone calls, you're doing the paperwork, and you'd rather be doing something else. When you've been a coach and you become a manager, you still have that coaching in you. Once you've coached and you're not doing it anymore, the part of the game that is the most enjoyable is gone."

Still, somebody had to get the team the players to coach, so he tried to coach less and manage more. Others could do a lot of the coaching, he thought; they could run practices and take care of the moment-to-moment things that came up, and he could be behind the bench for the games. He hired good people—Roger Neilson as the teacher, Jimmy Roberts as the motivator, and later Red Berenson—but when the team's record didn't get better (and later got worse), the question for the team's owners, fans, and the media, was obvious and loud: Why isn't the world's best hockey coach coaching? And when he was coaching but seemed to be giving a lot of authority to his assistants: why isn't he coaching *more*?

Then Neilson left and took the head coaching job with the Canucks. Berenson became coach at the University of Michigan. Scotty then brought in Schoenfeld as head coach, but a half a season later he was gone. Scotty's even bigger problem, however, was that too many other teams got better. The Islanders became too good, then the Oilers, but also the Flyers, then at various times Calgary, Quebec, and Washington. For the Sabres' first decade, they had been good and exciting *and* promising. Then they stopped being good and exciting. Then they stopped being promising and became boringly mediocre. Scotty, as always, was better at coaching down than managing up; inept at soothing and finessing ownership to buy himself more time. And by the mid-1980s, it was becoming clear that more time wasn't going to matter anyway.

For perhaps the first time in his career, he seemed out of answers. He had always had answers. As a kid at Willibrord Park, in his Thursday-night games, in pickup games on Saturdays and Sundays, then with Norman's Spartons and the Junior Canadiens. But there always are answers when you're a kid. You win, or you think you can win, and you know you can win the next time, and that kick to the belly of disappointment is gone in an instant. Then with Sam in Hull-Ottawa, then in Peterborough by himself, and with the NDG Monarchs against the

Toronto Marlies, then playing the World and Olympic champion Soviets with a bunch of junior kids, and one old guy who couldn't play anymore but who thought he could. There had always been answers.

Even in St. Louis. They were an expansion team. The Original Six teams gave them practically nothing. He'd had to go anywhere and everywhere to track down bodies—ones that weren't even remotely warm; that were one step from the cold, cold ground. He'd followed up a lead from an opera singer in L.A.; he'd signed guys who were years too old and who had knees too injured. He'd had to, if not believe, then at least make himself too focused to *dis*believe—and suspend every bit of evidence to the contrary. The world had known, and he had known, that he couldn't win. The Canadiens, the Bruins, the Leafs, the Black Hawks, even the Rangers and Red Wings were far too good. But he didn't have to beat *those* teams. He just needed to be better than the other five new teams, to win often enough to slowly fill half-empty arenas, to survive long enough to get better, to win often enough. To be a Stanley Cup finalist. To be good *enough*. And then, gradually, to believe they could win the Cup.

In St. Louis he found those answers, because he was Scotty Bowman, and in Montreal with Sam he had those answers in spades. And he'd had them when he arrived in Buffalo. But now, eight years later, he was Scotty Bowman, and he had no answers.

After beginning the 1986–87 season 3–7–2, he was fired.

For the Bowman family itself, these had been good years. The 1970s had been lived in such a rush. Scotty and Suella had been married in St. Louis in August 1969, the summer after the Blues' second run to the Stanley Cup final. Fourteen months later, Alicia had been born. Less than a year after that, Scotty, Suella, and Alicia were on their way to Montreal, Suella with the additional challenge of having to meet a family's needs in a new city and a new country, and in a new language. Then came that disappointing first season with the Canadiens. Then, less than two months after it ended, David was born; and a few weeks after that, a far, far bigger challenge: the slow, then sudden discovery of David's condition, and the slow, then sudden and deep realization of what that meant, for David and for them. Then the incredible turmoil of emotions the following year: David, and also the new baby on the way; and then the Canadiens—and Scotty—finding themselves and running away with the league. Then, in May and June, the Cup run, David's first birthday, and the birth of another son, Stanley, named after you-know-what. Scotty now had his first Cup win; Scotty and Suella now had three children under the age of three, one with a life-transforming disability.

And then those two Cup-losing seasons that followed in Montreal, then another Cup win, and five months after that, in October 1976, three weeks after Scotty had coached Team Canada to victory in the Canada Cup and two days before the Canadiens opened the season with a 10–1 win over the Penguins, Suella gave birth to twins, Nancy and Bob. Suella and Scotty now had five children under the age of six. Then, just over a month after that, on November 15, 1976, the Parti Québécois—dedicated to the separation of Quebec from Canada, and the creation of Quebec as its own independent country—won the provincial election and became the government of Quebec. Before a referendum vote could be held, the PQ government passed laws to reinforce the primacy of the French language—in offices, on street signs, and in schools. Suddenly English-speaking parents, including Scotty and Suella, were confronted with thoughts about their children's future that don't usually occur until later. Alicia was already in school; the other kids would soon follow. Would they be able to attend English schools, or only French ones? Whatever the answer—what about their future lives, and where they could best live them? These weren't yet questions that preoccupied Scotty and Suella—they didn't have the time, and the team was winning. Then Sam left. And some place other than Montreal was not so unthinkable.

In Buffalo, they could finally settle into a life. The city was both big enough and small enough. It had a beaten-up downtown core but it also had an expanse of lazy green suburbs that visitors rarely see. In time they bought a house on an out-of-the-way, tree-lined street that backed onto an established golf course. As they got older, the kids got involved in their schools, they joined clubs and teams, they formed friendships. Scotty and Suella also found a more permanent place nearby for David, and doctors who in time could come to know him and understand him—David is unable to speak. They became friends with many of the parents of their kids' friends. Buffalo had become their home.

But now what?

Scotty was 53 years old, and his coaching career was almost certainly over. In time, some team going nowhere might want to bring him in to calm the most turbulent waters and set them on an even keel. But he was Scotty Bowman, he didn't coach teams like that—he coached to win Stanley Cups with owners and general managers who shared his ambitions and had the wherewithal to get him the players he needed. Otherwise what was the point? Besides, even if he never coached another game, his legacy was more than assured. He had already won more games (739) than any other coach in NHL history. He had won more Stanley Cups (five) than anyone else except Toe Blake (eight); and, at worst, after Blake he was considered the second-best coach of all time. He had been coaching a very long time, in ever longer seasons, with ever longer playoffs, and with ever greater media and public attention, and pressure. It might be time to go.

His mind was telling him all this. And down deeper, where he doesn't often dwell, he was feeling old for the first time. He had always been "the kid"—as Sam's assistant in Hull-Ottawa, as the head coach in Peterborough, as the head scout for the Canadiens in Eastern Canada, as the coach in St. Louis. Not when he was hired as the coach of the Canadiens—he was 37 by then—yet by the time he left with his fifth Stanley Cup at age 45, for someone who had done something so legendary, he was a kid then too. Getting fired at 28 or 35 isn't easy. But getting fired at 53 sucks. It makes you think something is over. That you are over. Done.

But that feeling wouldn't last long. And it didn't last because the most fundamental part of his life hadn't changed. He had been a player, a coach, a scout, and a manager, but throughout it all he had also been a hockey watcher. That's what he had been first as a kid, and what he had been all those years in St. Louis, Montreal, and Buffalo, and that's what he still was and always would be. He now had no team to be involved with, but he still had the *game*, and for the next few months at least, until the season was over, that was enough. It turned out he didn't even have to wait that long. *Hockey Night in Canada* asked him to watch hockey, publicly, as a commentator, and share what he saw with a national audience.

"The most appealing part of [the offer]," Scotty told journalist Chrys Goyens, "was that they were looking for someone to come to Montreal, and my parents were still there. They were in their eighties. I would come on Friday night and do the game Saturday and then fly back to Buffalo." He did a few games in 1987, then more in 1988 and 1989. "I did the Calgary team quite a bit in the 1989 season, which is when they won the Cup. They had a hell of a team." He also did games in Toronto and Edmonton. "The biggest advantage for me was that while I was doing it I was able to keep a book in my own mind on the players in the league. I didn't really know if I was going to get back in." But he would be ready just in case.

On *HNIC*, "I tried to be like a coach," he recalls. "Always analyzing. 'This is what they should do, or should have done.'" It wasn't easy for him. Anything he had to say had to wait until a whistle and for his play-by-play partner to stop talking, and then he had to be done by the time the puck was dropped. "[The directors] wanted you to go in and out, quickly," he explains. But Scotty's mind doesn't work that way. He'd see something, he'd say something, and in the middle of saying it, something else, new and more interesting, would come to mind and he'd begin to say it—then run out of time. TV analysts had to say what they already knew. Or be a personality. That was all they *could* do in the few seconds allotted. There was no time to puzzle or wonder.

"After doing the broadcasts for about a year, you start to get into a bit of a rut. It was nice coming to Montreal and watching [the Canadiens] play, but by the next year it all felt kind of empty because you're not cheering for any particular team. You don't care who wins or loses. The non-competitive part was hard. It wasn't me. I didn't like it." And there was another thing he didn't like. As the playoffs went on there were fewer games, and *HNIC* needed fewer analysts. "I'd do about one round then get bounced by the senior crew. I remember saying to myself, 'If I continue to do this, I'm never going to get past the first round.'" That wasn't him either.

"Then, all of a sudden, I got the chance to go to Pittsburgh."

It was the summer of 1990 when Craig Patrick called. Scotty had coached him with the Junior Canadiens in the mid-1960s, and it was Patrick, Scotty thinks, who recommended him to his father, Lynn, when he was putting together the expansion Blues. Now, more than 20 years later—and after being Herb Brooks's assistant coach on the U.S. team that won gold in Lake Placid in 1980—Craig Patrick was the Penguins' general manager. He explained to Scotty "that the Penguins were in final negotiations with Bob Johnson to become their coach, that he knew I knew Bob, and would I want to come in as their director of player personnel?" Johnson had been a legendary coach at the University of Wisconsin—so much so that even after several years in the NHL, he was still known as "Badger Bob."

After speaking with Patrick, Scotty had all his arguments ready—for himself and for Suella. If he took this job, he wouldn't need to coach. They wouldn't have to move. A lot of the games he'd watch could be in Buffalo, and he could drive the hundred and fifty kilometres to Toronto for others. He wouldn't have to go to the East Coast much—to New York, Boston, or Philadelphia—and never had to go west, and Pittsburgh was only three and a half hours down the road. (He became so familiar with that road that 30 years later he remembered there were always cops lying in wait for speeders near the Meadville exit, and not long ago, when I told him I was about to drive to Pittsburgh myself, he warned me about them. The cops were still there.) For someone in his mid-fifties like Scotty, who wanted to stay in hockey, *Hockey Night in Canada* was as good as it gets—away from a team. But the Pittsburgh job was as good as it gets *with* a team—though away from coaching.

When that first regular season was over, Scotty joined Johnson and Patrick as another set of eyes and another mind in the playoffs, travelling with the team and getting that much closer to it. So close that he could feel again how distant he really was from it all. How being in a press box was not the same as being behind a bench. It was this "non-competitive part" of it that he found so unfulfilling. That season the Penguins won the Cup, but this was Bob Johnson's team, not his.

At almost the same time, Scotty got a phone call telling him that he had been elected to the Hockey Hall of Fame. Scotty thinks a lot about a lot of things. He likes his quiet time, and he is able to turn the noise around him into silence by retreating into himself in order to think ahead and to work through almost every possibility before it happens, so he knows what to do and say and feel if it does. But he didn't see this coming. He'd thought—hoped—that someday it might happen, but he was still working in hockey, and he knew that for players and coaches Hall of Fame selection waits until after they have retired.

The ceremony was in Ottawa, and that too had special meaning for him. His first full-time job in hockey had been in Ottawa, with Sam— those program ads he hated to sell; a team that played in three leagues and had no home except the road. Now, 35 years later, he would be recognized for something that had started right there. His mother and father were still alive, his dad was 89, his mother 85, and they were at the ceremony—his sister, Freda, had driven them from Montreal for the night. His brother Jack was there. His youngest brother, Martin, was away on a trip and couldn't make it.

Each inductee is asked to select his own presenter. It might be anybody, and in Scotty's case it could have been any one of the biggest and greatest names in the sport. Scotty chose Jack. "We were only three years apart in age," he says. "We shared the same bedroom, we both loved hockey, we grew up together." The family—all of them—were put up at the Château Laurier, the castle-like hotel right beside the Parliament Buildings. Not exactly the 850 square feet of their flat in Verdun. Suella and the kids were there too, along with some friends from Montreal. More than anything, what brought the moment home for his parents was seeing the other inductees—former NHL linesman Neil Armstrong, and former players Mike Bossy, Denis Potvin, Bob Pulford, and Clint Smith. His mother and father knew that all of them were big deals. And if they were, then their son must be too.

The induction was in September, and some weeks earlier Bob Johnson had gotten sick. When training camp began and he wasn't better, Patrick asked Scotty to take over as coach on an interim basis, just until Johnson came back. Again, Scotty had all his arguments ready, for himself and for Suella. He would coach the Penguins as if they were Bob Johnson's team. Because they were, and because Johnson would soon be back. "Never in my mind did I think I would coach the whole season," he says.

But with Scotty coaching as if he were the substitute teacher, the Penguins played as if he were the substitute teacher. "I didn't have my sleeves rolled up the way you do when you're the real coach." The players wanted "flow practices," to use Scotty's phrase. To be always on the move—skating, passing, sweating, everything but defending. "They were never a big practice team."

Lemieux could rarely practise because of his chronic bad back, and had to go easy when he did. But this set the tone for players who did need to practise. "The Penguins always wanted to play offence," Scotty recalls. "They didn't want to play defence." Then Johnson died. It was late November, and Scotty had no arguments left. He had to become the coach again, and be what he was and needed to be.

If Scotty had never coached another game, he would have retired as the great Hall of Fame coach Scotty Bowman. But he got a chance at an an unexpected encore—one that would last more than a decade.

Now that the Pens were Scotty's team, he had to coach them as if they were his team. But still, the Penguins were "meandering around in the standings," as he puts it—not in danger of missing the playoffs, but not going anywhere. Late in the season, they traded Paul Coffey to L.A. and Mark Recchi to Philadelphia, in a three-way exchange that, by the end of the trading day, saw Pittsburgh with Rick Tocchet and Kjell Samuelsson. Tocchet "was a very tough winger who had good hands," Scotty says. "There was no monkeying around with him." Samuelsson was one more piece to add to the Penguins' patchwork of defencemen, replacing Coffey—who had become less of an offensive force and no less of a defensive liability. The Penguins also had a solid core of veteran forwards—Ron Francis, Joe Mullen, Bryan Trottier—who could defend if that's what the team needed.

Trottier had come from the Islanders the previous season. After New York's Cup-winning years, as they went down, Trottier went down with them. He became less important to the team, and ended up as the Islanders' third-line centre after Pat LaFontaine and Brent Sutter—which he didn't like, and didn't deal with well. "He had outlived his usefulness with the Islanders," Scotty says. "He was unhappy with his role as a third liner and was getting to be a nuisance. He and Al Arbour were at odds. We took him in Pittsburgh and he found his niche as a third-line centre playing 10, 12 minutes a game. He was a valuable faceoff guy. I had a good rapport with him."

Unwilling or unable to be a role player on a team on which he had been a star, on the Penguins Trottier didn't expect to be the star. That was Lemieux; and Jágr was the star of the future. "Jágr was just 19 and had only one year under his belt, and he was very moody. He was always worried about his ice time. Trottier was the guy he looked up to, and who quieted him down and got him focused."

Pittsburgh was undoubtedly Lemieux's team. He had made it respectable in his first few years in the league, when he had bad players around him. He made it a contender and a champion when Patrick got him some players to play with, and hired Johnson and then Scotty to coach them.

"Mario had health issues most of his career," Scotty says. "Before I got there he'd had back surgery, then that got infected, and his back problems never went away. He was on medication all the time. I remember a couple of nights he could hardly lace up his skates because of his back. He rarely practised, and he was always in pain. He was very calm and mild-mannered. He never got emotional. He wasn't interested in the limelight, and he wasn't a guy who was always knocking on your door as the coach and wanting you to do this, or do that. He just wanted to do whatever you wanted him to. But you had to fit players in to play with him. He needed a lot of ice time. Some nights he played over 30 minutes, and for a forward that's a lot."

He played "up high" near the blue line in his own defensive zone the way Gretzky did, and as Gretzky had Kurri to help him defend, Lemieux had Joe Mullen, who "was smart, he'd stay back and make passes. He wanted Mario to play up." The team also had to adapt to Lemieux's injuries. Scotty and the players knew he would play if there was any possibility he could—and sometimes even when there seemed to be none. If he was in the lineup, the Penguins would play one way; and if he wasn't, they'd play another. "It was tough on the team," Scotty says, especially in the playoffs. But as he had learned decades earlier, you coach the players you have, and you adapt to your great players far more than they adapt to you. Sometimes that might not seem right, but this wasn't about him being right, or about his convenience, or his philosophy of play or his system or his own remarkable genius. This was about the team, and finding a way for that team to win.

Lemieux was just so good. He was about six foot four, but he looked and played far taller. The first time Scotty ever saw him he had been almost the same size, but he was only 12 years old. It was on a Saturday morning at the Montreal Forum during the 1977–78 season. At that time the Canadiens helped sponsor a youth hockey exchange involving a Montreal-area team and another—usually small-town—team from elsewhere in Quebec, or sometimes from Ontario. The Canadiens had just finished their short day-of-game practice, and as Scotty would do with Gretzky a year later, he went out by the boards and watched.

With Gretzky—among all the junior-age players around him, some of whom were much older—you had to watch closely to see his specialness. With Lemieux, a glance was all you needed. He was just so big, and so good. And as he got older, even when he reached the NHL, a glance was still all it took. "I always thought two things made him so different," Scotty says. "His reach—he had this wingspan, he was pretty much impossible for one guy to stop. And also around the net. At the side of the net, or in behind, he was so unpredictable as to what he might do. He'd bank pucks off the goalie's pads. Do wraparounds. Players didn't do that then."

Then, thinking about Lemieux's injuries and health problems, he adds, "I don't think he could ever put everything into the game he wanted to." In his 17-year playing career, Lemieux missed on average about one-third of the Penguins games a season, and he played injured in many of the others. Yet he averaged almost two points a game during the regular season and not much less in the playoffs. Very few players in the NHL then or now—even counting Gretzky and Howe—have been so noticeably better than the other best players on the ice that they just jumped out at you so dramatically. Maybe only Orr is comparable. Lemieux could embarrass good defenders and good goalies and make them look completely inept. Orr's unsurpassed superiority came from his speed; Lemieux's from his size and reach and the ridiculous ease with which he seemed to overwhelm his opponents.

In spite of Lemieux's placid demeanour, "He also had an inner fire about him." One moment sticks in Scotty's mind. "The year I took over from Bob Johnson we played Washington in the first round of the playoffs and they had a good team. They had some terrific defencemen, and we got down three games to one, but we came back and won Games 5 and 6. The seventh game was in Washington and Mario controlled the entire game. We shut them down completely, a team that could really score, and we just played a completely different style, because Mario wanted to win so badly. I'd never seen him play defensive hockey before—play *without* the puck. But guys like that have so much talent, they can apply themselves and play defensive hockey if they need to. And he did.

"Then we went on and fell behind the Rangers two games to one, but then we won three in a row. Then we swept Boston. In the finals, we went down in the second period in Game 1 at home, 4–1, we scored twice, and then Jágr stepped out of the corner and beat two or three guys and then [Chicago goalie] Eddie Belfour on a backhander to tie the game. Then Mario won it with 15 seconds to go. He got 34 points that year in the playoffs, in 15 games," Scotty says, still amazed. "The year before he got 44, in 23 games. Back-to-back years, they couldn't stop him. Don't forget, he had health issues that never went away. You were always just waiting for him to make a big play, to score big goals."

After Lemieux's late-game goal against Chicago, the Penguins won the next three games. It was Scotty's sixth Cup.

The next year, 1992–93, Pittsburgh finished the regular season first overall, 10 points ahead of second-place Boston. Lemieux won the scoring title by 12 points over Buffalo's LaFontaine, despite playing only 60 games to LaFontaine's 84. He missed so many games because of the radiation treatments he received—and the recovery time he needed—after he was diagnosed with Hodgkin's lymphoma. The Penguins lost the first game after his return, and the next, then won 17 straight, before tying the last game of the regular season. But on their way to what seemed certain to be a third straight Cup, the Penguins were upset by the Islanders in the seventh game of the second round, in overtime.

Then the trouble began. When Bob Johnson had gotten sick and Scotty became head coach, he had asked Craig Patrick for the same deal that Johnson was given. Later, Scotty discovered that Johnson's pay package included a signing bonus that Scotty didn't receive. He wasn't happy.

Word got out that Scotty wasn't going back to Pittsburgh. A few days later, he got a call at home from his friend Jim Devellano, then with the Red Wings. "We're making a coaching change in Detroit," Devellano said. "[Wings owner] Mike Ilitch wants to talk to you."

CHAPTER FIFTEEN
Detroit Red Wings 2001–02

"I was only going to go for a couple of years, and I stayed nine," Scotty says. It was his longest stretch as an NHL coach. "The move to Detroit was superb because it gave me financial stability, and gave me the opportunity to get paid for what I had done in my past. I just about tripled what I was earning in Pittsburgh. I was going to an organization that was very financially stable. Mike Ilitch wanted to build a good team, and he had the financial wherewithal to help me—to help all of us—do it. I didn't feel any pressure. I mean, you have pressure to win in the playoffs, but they were patient, and it turned out to be the best move I could have made. When your kids get older and are in university, your life changes because it can change." At the time, Alicia was 22, David 21, Stan 20, and the twins, Nancy and Bob, were 16.

Scotty was turning 60. His own great hero, Toe Blake, had retired at 55 after the Canadiens' Cup victory in 1968. But Scotty was off to a new adventure, and this time, not like in Pittsburgh, he wasn't the reluctant, accidental coach. He knew what he was getting into, and he knew he wanted to get into it. And beyond tripling his salary, Ilitch promised him something else, which to Ilitch may have seemed like a throw-in but which mattered to Scotty. "He said whenever I wanted to stop coaching, I could stay on."

When Scotty was 15, playing midget hockey for a Canadiens-sponsored team and taking the 58 bus up the Atwater hill to the Forum to watch the big team from his standing-room perch, the Wings were becoming great. For seven straight years they finished first, and in those seven years they won four Stanley Cups, the last being in 1955. For the next few seasons, as the Canadiens began their Cup streak, the Wings seemed like contenders—they had Gordie Howe, after all—but then they fell off, then bounced back a little, until in the mid-1960s they made it to the Stanley Cup final on three occasions, the last time in 1966, as Scotty was about to leave for St. Louis. But from that point on, over the next 17 years, the Wings made the playoffs only twice; and for a period of 20 years, between 1967 and 1987, they did not win a single playoff series.

At the end of 1979, the team moved into Joe Louis Arena in Detroit's increasingly derelict downtown core, and things continued to get worse. The NHL's newest and biggest rink was now filled with the NHL's highest number of empty seats. Two years later, Ilitch bought the team. He was born in Detroit and had graduated from high school in Detroit, and after four years in the Marines and four summers kicking around baseball's minor leagues dreaming of playing for the Tigers, he was back in Detroit full time. He and his wife, Marian, decided to open a small pizza shop in Garden City, west of downtown, and called it Little Caesars. This was 1959, and Ilitch was 29. By the time he died in 2017, Little Caesars had over 5,000 locations and was the third-largest pizza chain in the U.S. after Domino's and Pizza Hut.

Ilitch had been a baseball player, but he was also a sports fan, a fan of Detroit sports teams, and a fan of the city. His kids played hockey, and by the late 1960s Little Caesars began sponsoring youth teams. Then more and more of them. Massachusetts and Minnesota had always been the heartland of hockey in the U.S. Detroit—just across the river from Windsor, Ontario, with an NHL team, a hockey climate, and in range of *Hockey Night in Canada* broadcasts—produced lots of fans but not many players. But as Little Caesar's became more involved in youth hockey, so did Compuware, owned by Peter Karmanos Jr., who would one day also own the Hartford Whalers and Carolina Hurricanes. Ilitch, a Macedonian-American, and Karmanos, a Greek-American, were rivals. Today, Michigan has more kids playing hockey than any other state except Minnesota, and more than any Canadian province except Ontario, Quebec, and Alberta. Little Caesars graduates include Mike Modano, John Vanbiesbrouck, Derian and Kevin Hatcher, Ryan Kesler, and Zach Werenski. By the time Ilitch bought the Wings in 1982, his hockey legacy was on the way to being established. A year later, Detroit selected Steve Yzerman in the first round.

But progress for the Wings was slow, and Ilitch wasn't accustomed to slow progress. As a Detroiter, he was excited that the Pistons were contenders every season (they would win the NBA championship in 1989 and 1990). He would also have been absolutely thrilled that his beloved Tigers won the World Series in 1984—had they not been bought a year earlier (a year *after* he had bought the Wings) by his bitter rival, Tom Monaghan, who also had gotten into the pizza business a year after he did and turned Domino's into the *biggest* pizza chain in the country. So, then, why not the Wings? After improving slightly in his first season as owner, the team made the playoffs the next two years, losing in the first round each time. But then, just as they seemed on their way, in 1985–86 they hit rock bottom, winning only 17 games, scoring the fewest number of goals in the league, allowing the most *by far*, and finishing dead last. The team improved again after hiring Jacques Demers as their coach, then missed the playoffs, then improved again with Bryan Murray—even finishing third overall in the league in 1992, and fifth the following season. But both times, they were knocked out of the playoffs quickly.

For Ilitch, enough was enough. He had just bought the Tigers from Tom Monaghan of Domino's. A few years before that, he had taken over the once-great Fox Theatre, built in the 1920s, which had been a 24-hour-a-day movie refuge for shift workers during the Second World War and, with its capacity of over 5,000, where Elvis, the Motown greats, and countless others had rocked the city. But, like much of downtown, it had been abandoned by its audience, who had gone to the suburbs. Ilitch, like most Detroiters with a choice, could also have thrown in his chips with the city. Instead, he doubled down. He doubled down with the Fox Theatre, with the Tigers, and later with the Tigers' new home, Comerica Park, right across from the theatre. And he would double down with the Red Wings as well. Good coaches hadn't been enough. He went after Scotty.

Once he had him, he let Scotty be Scotty. Initially, Bryan Murray, who had been the team's coach and general manager the previous season, stayed on as manager. But that was never going to work—one chef too many—and when the team did no better in Scotty's first year, finishing fourth overall but losing in the first round of the playoffs, Murray was fired. Now Scotty was in control. But in control *how?* It had never been entirely clear just what letting "Scotty be Scotty" meant, maybe most of all to Scotty himself. He knew he was a coach, and he knew he wasn't a general manager, but he also knew he didn't want to be *just* a coach, and he knew he didn't *not* want to be a general manager. Not entirely.

He knew he didn't want to do everything, and he knew he *couldn't* do everything, but he wanted the right people to do what he couldn't do, and the right people weren't necessarily the best people. Glen Sather, for example, wouldn't have been a good match for Scotty. Sather needed to run his own show, and he was too visible. What Scotty needed was what every coach needs—someone to get him the players. Like Sam had. A coach is the one who is out there exposed, even more so than the players—after all, there are 20 of them—and not the guy behind the desk. A coach is in a manager's hands, and a coach has to trust those hands so he can coach.

Yet Scotty didn't really need a Sam. He had won six Stanley Cups. He had become more than a coach, and he knew the team he wanted—the team he and Ilitch needed. He would be the architect, the team would be created with his design. Someone else would build it, but to *his* specifications. And Ilitch would be his banker. That is what "letting Scotty be Scotty" now meant. Scotty would be a coach-plus.

Devellano would be the trusted figure. Scotty had known him in St. Louis, and later when Devellano had been with the Islanders. He had begun as a volunteer scout for start-up NHL teams who needed all the underpaid help they could get. He was the guy who was everywhere and always around, making himself useful until he made himself indispensable—a confidant, insider, and right-hand person to all the right people. Most importantly to Scotty, he was "a hockey guy," a rink rat, just as Scotty and Sam had been. A rink-rat in a tailored suit, as all of them were, but someone who was still watching, thinking, scheming, and breathing the game. And Devellano knew Scotty. He knew how great a coach he was, and he knew that nothing could be allowed to get in the way of him being that great coach.

Devellano would hold the title of general manager. "Jimmy did the contracts and looked after the scouts," Scotty recalls. "Kenny Holland was his assistant." Holland, a former minor-league goalie, had begun as a scout in the Detroit organization. He would be responsible for the Wings' system outside the NHL—their minor-league team and scouting. Scotty would be the director of player personnel. "I did the trades, but I had to consult with the owner if I wanted to do something." In the event that Scotty, Devellano, and Holland couldn't agree, neither Devellano nor Holland had the authority or presence to take Scotty on, and both of them knew that—and Scotty knew that. And crucially for all of them, and for Ilitch, they knew that this was the right way to go. More than in Montreal, more than in Buffalo or Pittsburgh, this would be Scotty's team.

And now, finally, Detroit had something to coach. In the NHL drafts in the 1980s, as Devellano once said to Scotty, "After Yzerman [in 1983], we just got players who could play. We didn't get players you could build a team on." That changed in 1989. With the Wings' first two selections, they made conventional picks—Mike Sillinger in the first round with the 11th pick; Bob Boughner in the second round with the 32nd pick—and got solid, conventional results. But in the third round, with the 53rd selection in the draft, the Wings chose Nicklas Lidström; in the fourth round, the 74th pick, Sergei Fedorov; and in the 11th round, with the 221st pick, Vladimir Konstantinov. Two future Hall of Famers, and a player who might have been one if not for a car crash that ended his career. Two Russians, one Swede—three Europeans.

By the time Scotty came to Detroit in 1993, Lidström and Konstantinov were on their way to becoming stars, and Fedorov had been a star from the first day he arrived. Also there in his first full season were Vyacheslav Kozlov and some other recent draft picks—Martin Lapointe, Darren McCarty—not cornerstone pieces, but "players who could play"; role players who would take on even more important roles as the team got better. There was also Keith Primeau, a third overall pick who would have his best seasons on other teams but who, in a trade a few years later, brought to Detroit one more player on which to build the team—Brendan Shanahan.

After the Wings lost in the first round of playoffs in 1994, Scotty sat down with Steve Yzerman, his captain. "I said to him, 'You've got to play a lot differently if this team is going to win.'" For Scotty, everything had become clear. "The team was good offensively, but really weak defensively, and when it got into the playoffs it didn't perform. Yzerman had been there since '83. He had been the captain for a long time. One year he had scored 65 goals, another he had 62. The year before I got there he had 58. But they still couldn't do anything in the playoffs. He wasn't playing a two-way game at all."

His meeting with Yzerman was a big risk, but as always, so absorbed in the team that personal feelings often didn't occur to him, Scotty may not even have realized it. He knew that, deep down, deeper even than stardom and money, a player wants to win. He knew that because he knew that about himself, and he knew that even the pain of being "called out" and embarrassed is nothing like the pain of losing. He knew that Yzerman wanted to win. He knew that Yzerman couldn't win playing this way, or with the team playing this way. Still, not every player can see past a kick in the gut to the prize on the other side.

Yzerman was a star. He had been the one source of excitement for Wings fans during the team's dark years. He was young. He was promising. He offered hope. With him on the ice and in that jersey, tomorrow really might be a better day. And he was such a good person. Respectful. He didn't do stupid things. He was such a competitor. He didn't miss games with routine injuries. He either played a near-full season of games, or he played 51 or 64 or 58. He missed games in long stretches because he had *real* injuries—usually to his knees.

Hearing Scotty's words, Yzerman might have sulked, or he might have turned against Scotty and fought back, and though Devellano and Holland had no chance in taking Scotty on, Yzerman did. He was the guy who had saved the franchise. It wasn't Ilitch giving away cars at games that had started to fill the acres of empty seats at "The Joe." It was Yzerman, and Ilitch knew that. If Yzerman wanted to, he could play the media too. Scotty was never any good at that. Yzerman could turn the fans passionately and angrily against Scotty. It wouldn't have been hard.

Scotty had had a similar talk with Jacques Lemaire 30 years earlier, and that hadn't turned out well. At first. "I coached Jacques in junior," Scotty recalls, "and he would come down the wing and score goals just on his shot alone. But he never played a checking game at all. I couldn't play him against any top offensive guy. He was just interested in scoring. I called him in one day and said, 'Jacques, if you don't start to play a different kind of game, you're never going to play for the Montreal Canadiens.' And of course, his dream all through growing up was to play for the Canadiens." Now Scotty's tone changes. "I didn't know this at the time, but Jacques's father had died a couple of years before when Jacques was very young, and he was raised by his mother and older brother. I remember getting a phone call from his mother. She wanted to tell me that Jacques was devastated by what I had said. I think she came down to the Forum to see me, and she said he's broken-hearted that you told him he would never play for the Montreal Canadiens. I said to her, 'No, no, no, he didn't understand. I meant that if he kept playing like *this* he would never play for the Canadiens.'" Scotty pauses. "And then Jacques became one of the best defensive centres in the league, a real two-way player."

But in this case, Yzerman's mother wouldn't be around to call Scotty if things went off the rails with her son. Yet whatever the risk—and there was a risk of Yzerman not understanding what Scotty was saying, because he was often more blunt than clear—not having the talk was far worse. Yzerman was the core player on the team. Scotty was the coach, this was his team, but the Wings were going to play mostly in the style and spirit of their most important player. That's how it is on any team.

Likely, Yzerman was ready for a conversation like this. He could see that while the Wings were improving, other teams were improving more. He was a responsible person, he had been the captain of the Wings since he was 21, and he was proud of that. (As it turned out, he would remain the captain for 20 years and more than 1,300 games—longer than any captain in North American professional sports history—and someday he would be very proud of that too.) He also knew that even great one-way teams like the Oilers, or the Penguins, had to find a two-way game in the playoffs. And he knew the Wings were *not* the Oilers or the Penguins.

Yzerman had carried so much of the team's load for nearly a decade that maybe this talk with Scotty was a lifeline. Maybe it allowed him a chance to finally be what he truly was, just as that conversation with Scotty had done for Lemaire. During all those dreary seasons in the 1980s, the team and the fans had needed spectacular Steve. Now they needed solid, all-round, winner Steve. Different times, different needs, and the true team player does what his team needs when his team needs it. Also, he was almost 29 years old. He had already played over 800 NHL games, and his knees were not getting better. Maybe he didn't think he could keep up his high-flying game much longer. Maybe he looked at all the amazing things Fedorov could do, and thought: *I can't be the go-to offensive guy much longer, but I don't need to be. If I want to be as important to this team as I need to be, and as the team needs me to be, it's going to have to be a different way.*

However Yzerman worked through his conversation with Scotty in his head, by training camp the next season he was ready. In the five years previous, he had finished in the top ten in the NHL scoring five straight times. In the remaining eleven years of his career, he would finish in the top ten only *once.* In the first eight of those eleven seasons, until 2001–02 when Scotty retired, the Wings finished first overall in the league four times, and won the Stanley Cup three times.

By the start of the 1994–95 season, most of the core players were in place and young enough to get better. But the Wings had some big obstacles in their way: other teams. That season, which was shortened to 48 games because of the lockout, Detroit finished first overall; Yzerman, playing in all but one of the team's games, was sixth on the *team* in scoring; the Wings rolled over Dallas, San Jose, and Chicago in the playoffs, winning twelve games and losing only two, but were swept in the final by New Jersey. The Devils would remain the best team in the Eastern Conference for most of the decade.

The next season, the Wings blew away everybody, not only finishing first overall but doing so by 27 points over Colorado, which had just moved from Quebec, and by setting an NHL record with 62 wins. But in December of that year, in a trade with Montreal, Colorado had gotten what it lacked—a big-time goalie who lived for centre stage, Patrick Roy. After beating Winnipeg and St. Louis in the playoffs, the Wings lost to Colorado in the semifinals. A historic, almost perfect season for the Wings ended in defeat, just as it had for 41 consecutive years before. Great teams win. The Wings needed to get better.

The team in Detroit was very different from any Scotty had coached before. In 1973, in his first Cup win, the Canadiens were made up of 20

Canadians—twelve Francophones and eight Anglophones. There were no Americans, and no Europeans. Every one of the players had grown up and developed in the Canadian hockey system, where play was tougher and rougher; where the puck was dumped ahead and then chased, not moved forward by passing; where practices mattered less and games a lot more; where off-season and off-ice training mattered almost not at all. It was this game, this team, and these players that Scotty had to coach, and to win with. Even in 1979, for his last Cup win in Montreal, the team had on its roster 22 Canadians—eleven Francophones and eleven Anglophones—and one American. No Europeans. Thirteen years later in Pittsburgh, when he won his sixth Cup, he had eleven Canadians (only one of whom, Lemieux, was Francophone), seven Americans, and four Europeans—two Swedes and two Czechoslovakians. Only half the team was Canadian. Gretzky's Oilers had introduced European-style passing and open-ice play by this time, and had brought in the live puck era. Bob Johnson had brought with him from the University of Wisconsin a fitness trainer to make off-ice, off-season training matter more. Yet the mainstream game had still been old-time Canadian. This was now the game, the team, and the players that Scotty had to coach, and win with.

Just five years after that, things were very different again. The 1996–97 Wings had on their roster twelve Canadians, one American, and seven Europeans—two Swedes and five Russians. The Europeans were now not just specialty players who added a little extra skill in moments when a little extra skill was needed. Nor were they just prodigies like Alex Mogilny or Pavel Bure, so skilled they were almost solo acts, on the ice to do their thing until they went off and the rest of the game resumed. In the 1970s, there had been a few Swedes in the NHL; for most of the 1980s there were more Swedes, a few Finns and Czechoslovakians, and no Russians. By 1990 there were many more Europeans and even some Russians—defectors, or dissenters like Fetisov and Larionov—and then, after the Wall came down, a new

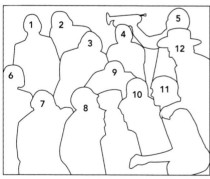

THE FIRST CUP

1972–73

1. Guy Lapointe
2. Me
3. Guy Lafleur
4. Johnny Davis (assistant trainer)
5. Bob Williams (trainer)
6. Jacques Laperrière
7. Edward Bronfman (team owner)
8. Serge Savard
9. Eddy Palchak (trainer)
10. Scotty
11. Michel Plasse
12. Henri Richard

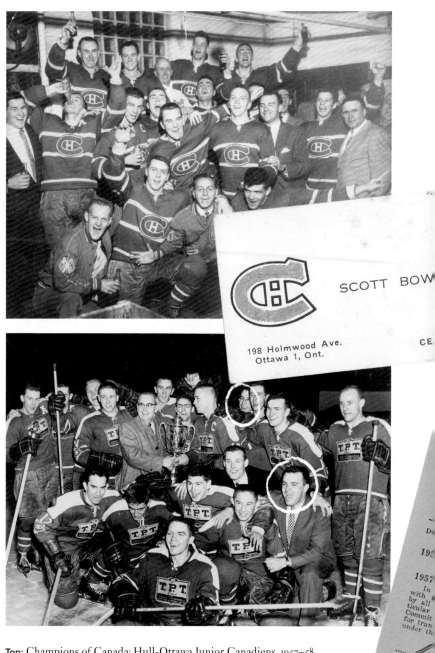

198 Holmwood Ave.
Ottawa 1, Ont.

SCOTT BOW

CE

Top: Champions of Canada: Hull-Ottawa Junior Canadiens, 1957–58, including Bobby Rousseau, Ralph Backstrom (captain), J.C. Tremblay, Gilles Tremblay, Claude Richard, Sam Pollock, and Scotty.

Bottom: Jimmy Roberts and Scotty, Peterborough Petes, 1958–59.

Centre: $250 + this signature = 1,006 NHL games + 5 Stanley Cups

Top: Student and Teacher, Scotty and Toe Blake, 1963

Bottom: Scotty and Suella, 1969

29- Dryden

Teams	Shots	Saves	Gls	W	L	T	average	1st Pd	2nd Pd	3rd Pd	EMP NET
Feb 10 Det	28	1	52	53		1		2.16	0	0	1	
Feb 7 Pitts	27	3	55			1		2.18	1	2	0	
Mar 1 Buff	32	1	56			1		2.15	0	1	0	
Mar Van	37	0	56			1		2.11	0	0	0	
Mar 2 Phila	26	0	53			1		2.07	0	0	0	
Mar 8 Pitts	38		40	7		1		2.11	3	0	1	
Mar 9 St Louis	46		58			1		2.07	0	1	0	
Mar 11 Chi	30	1	57			1	1	2.06	0	1	0	
Mar 12 Phila	29	1	58			1		2.05	0	0	0	
Mar 15 Tor	43			260		1		2.05	0	2	0	
Mar 18	35	3	61			1		2.06	1	0	2	
Mar 19 Minn	36			7		1	1	2.14	2	2	3	
Mar 22	36		64			1		2.16	0	1	2	
Mar R 25	40		67			1		2.17	2	1	0	
Mar 26	39			572		1			2	3	0	
	11			375								

Sun. Jan. 2 London at

23 12-9-4=28   1

M°Cauley

Rose - Bruno
Valdamir - friemont
Staunton - hamilton
Pleau - Grenier - Cullerton
Staunton Fergeson Cote

First Period
1—Montreal, Lapalme (Grenier, Lemaire)
2—Montreal, Ferguson (Stewart)
3—London, Kyle
4—Montreal, Stewart (Ferguson, Cote)
Penalties — Bazey 6:25, 19:11, Grenier 7:20, Clairmont, Vadnais (double minor) 18:45.

Second Period
5—Montreal, Lemaire (Lapalme) 11:36
Penalties — Bazey 13:02, Descoteaux 15:40, Lapalme 5:44, Murray, Vadnais 17:07, Burns 18:41

Third Period
6—Montreal, Grenier (Lemaire) 2:50
7—Montreal, Vadnais (Pleau, Lapalme) 14:16
8—Montreal, Lemaire (Grenier) 14:16
Penalties — Dorey 4:27, 7:17, (double minor) 16:59, Clark, Lapalme (double minors and double majors 6:09, Bazey 6:28, 9:50, Ferguson (double major) 9:50, Clairmont 15:08, Murray (minor and misconduct) 16:25, Grenier 16:59
Shots on goal by:

| Montreal | 10 | 13 | 8—25 |
| | 13 | 13 | 23—51 |

Goals Against   Goals F
5-20-6-12 (Even)   ① 15-20 — ⑪
(3 Pen. 0 Gls)   ② 15-20 — 17-
100 Pen - 23 Gls 5 Fo ③ 4-18 — ⑰
                      ④ 15-20 — 11-②
                      ⑤ 4-12 — 11-21
                      ⑥ 12-⑮ 6-11
                      ⑦ 11-㉑ 10-6-19
Game (6 P. Ply - 1
Season (120 P. Ply - 24
#3 Out - K
#8 " - K

ONTARIO JUNIOR "A"

	G	P	W	L	T	F	A	Pts
Oshawa		28	16	9	3			37
Peterborough		28	16	11	1			35
Niagara Falls		28	15	9	5	135	103	35
Montreal		25	13	12	0	118		
Hamilton		27	12	14	1			
Toronto			12	14	2			
St. Catharines			11	17				
London			6					

μ A-B-C 1960-1

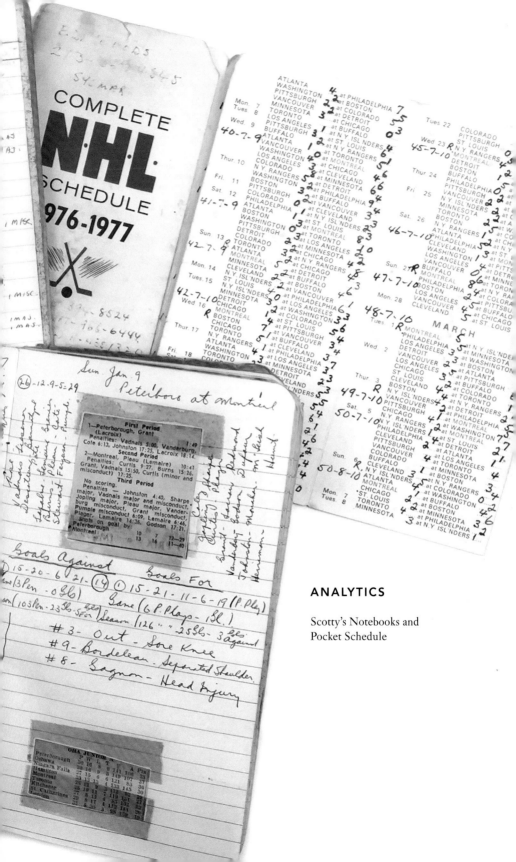

ANALYTICS

Scotty's Notebooks and
Pocket Schedule

60-8-12

Montreal Canadiens, 1976–77

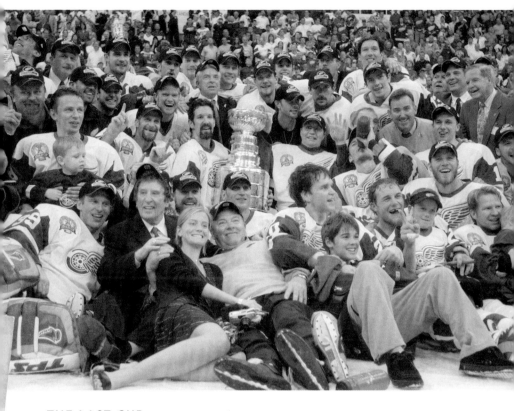

THE LAST CUP

Detroit Red Wings, 2001–02. With daughter Nancy.

HOME TEAM

New Buffalo,
Michigan, 2017

young wave who were in their prime or with their prime still ahead of them. The kind of players that can not only change a game in an inspired moment, but change a team.

That's what Scotty had in Detroit. Yzerman and Shanahan were outstanding players, but what drove the Wings and made them special in 1996–97 were Fedorov, Lidström, Konstantinov, Kozlov, Larionov, and Fetisov. Players who had grown up and developed within a very different hockey tradition; who were less rough, though no less tough; who passed the puck and kept possession of it and knew how to use open ice; who trained in-season and out-of-season, off-ice and on-ice.

It was a new world for everybody. Almost all of the league's coaches were Canadian. Almost all of its general managers and scouts, and almost all of the media that counted were Canadian. To them, European players were at least *different*. In the early years, you didn't want them as your players, then you didn't want many of them, then you didn't want them as your leaders or go-to stars because they weren't dependable enough or committed enough. They were still seen as a little "soft," and would disappear in the tough and rough going. They didn't play like never-say-die Canadians, who pushed and drove themselves to the very last second of the very last minute of the very last game. They didn't grow up like *our* guys did; they didn't believe as *we* do. They were cynical Europeans. Realists. They knew—really, truly—that lots of times the game *is* over before the fat lady sings. It just is. So why pretend otherwise?

And really, truly, they just did not *get* the Stanley Cup. Anyone who knew anything knew that. They understood the Olympics and the World Championships, where they would play a few games against opponents who would never beat them, then a few sudden-death games against the very few teams who could beat them for a gold medal. But they didn't understand the cruel slog of four rounds of best-of-seven playoffs, ten weeks of game after game—every one you have to win. What team had ever won the Cup with a European captain, or with a

European as its best player? Since 1980, when the Europeans really began to arrive, the captains of Cup-winning teams were named Potvin, Gretzky, McDonald, Messier, Lemieux, Carbonneau, Stevens, Sakic. Not one European; not one American. And on these Cup-winning teams, the other best players were named Trottier, Bossy, Roy, Brodeur, Niedermayer—all of them Canadian. Even Jari Kurri, a Finn, and Joe Mullen, an American, were mostly just really good support players. Colorado's Peter Forsberg might have been the sole exception, but he played like a Canadian.

So what would Scotty do with the Wings—*his* team—when the best players were not only not Canadian, they were Russian?

He did as he always did—he saw past conventional wisdom to what was actually there. To what was real. Theory is theory, but results are results. Peter Šťastný had been the second-highest scorer in the NHL during the 1980s—higher even than Lemieux, higher than Messier and Kurri; behind only Gretzky. Šťastný was from Czechoslovakia. Alex Mogilny (Russia) scored 76 goals in 1992–93, as did Teemu Selänne (Finland). Nobody else scored more. That year, Selänne and Chris Chelios (U.S.) were on the first all-star team. Tom Barrasso, Al Iafrate, Kevin Stevens, and Pat LaFontaine—four Americans—and Mogilny were on the second team. A year later, half the first all-star team was non-Canadian—Fedorov, Bure, and Hašek; Brian Leetch and John Vanbiesbrouck (both U.S.) were on the second team. The next season, Hašek, Jágr, Chelios, and John LeClair (U.S.) were on the first team; Alex Zhamnov (Russia) and Keith Tkachuk (U.S.) were on the second.

In 1979–80, in his first NHL season, Gretzky finished second in the league in scoring, after which he won the scoring title for seven straight years, and in the seven years after that he won three more times and Lemieux won four. Two Canadians. In the entire 77 years of NHL history, every scoring champion had been Canadian—no Europeans, no Americans. Then, in 1994–95, Jaromír Jágr won the scoring title. He was from Czechoslovakia.

Not theory. Not conventional wisdom. Results.

It would have been far more natural for Scotty to do something else. He had won six Stanley Cups. He was the best, so whatever he had done before and however he had done it had to be the best way. It only followed. And he was Scotty Bowman. If anybody had the right to believe, and say "Been there, done that," it was him. What else was there in hockey for him to see? What else was there to know? You do what you've always done and you keep doing it. You dance with the one that brung ya. Except if he had shut his eyes and shut off his mind after his Cup wins in Montreal, he never would have won with Pittsburgh.

Scotty's players had to adapt to him, but he also had to adapt to them. They had to learn, but he had to learn too. And he and they would have to continue to adapt and learn, because Colorado was really good, and Joe Sakic and Forsberg—two centres going back-to-back like Gretzky and Messier, Béliveau and Henri Richard—had lots of years ahead of them. And New Jersey was really good. Dallas was becoming really good. And some other team was also bound to emerge because some other team always does. Detroit was now not many years from getting old, and Yzerman's knees were always in doubt. To win, Scotty had to see things expressly as *not* "been there, done that," but as something new. What he has. What had *brung* him weren't Canadians or Americans or even some Europeans. What had brung him were his always-open eyes and always-open mind.

Five of Scotty's seven European players were not only Russian, but three of them played forward and two played defence. Perfect. They could all play together. And because they could—of course they must. So they became the "Russian Five": Fedorov, Larionov, and Kozlov up front; Fetisov and Konstantinov in back. Fedorov and Konstantinov had arrived in Detroit before Scotty, then came Kozlov, then Fetisov who wasn't playing much in New Jersey, then Larionov who, his buddy Fetisov knew, wasn't happy in San Jose. On October 27, 1995, the Russian Five played together as a unit for the first time.

"I remember that night. They were just completely different from everyone else," Scotty says. "They would never shoot the puck in. They'd circle around in the neutral zone, they'd have guys chasing them. It was the way the Harlem Globetrotters used to do it—run around and around then one guy would peel off and get a lay-up—and with them it was Konstantinov who ended up with the breakaways. It was amazing. I've seen footage of it recently. I don't remember those guys *not* having the puck a lot.

"But I always sort of held them back. I played them in some games, but I didn't play them exclusively, and not in others. I didn't want anybody to target them, to find a way of playing against them. They played such a unique style. I wanted them to change the game when we needed that push. We used them together in the playoffs more than during the regular season. I also didn't want the other players thinking this was just a Russian sort of team."

For Scotty, this was the problem within the opportunity. They were the Detroit Red Wings, not the Harlem Globetrotters. The Russian Five were not—and must not be—a side show. Once they had become important, it was critical that they didn't become *too* important. "We wanted to make sure they weren't the most important part of the team," Scotty explains. "We had some high-end guys. Guys who were proud of what they had done." Putting the Russian players together in the first place had to do with the team. It wasn't about getting attention. It was about winning the Cup.

Four days after the 1996–97 season began, the Wings made a trade. If this was Scotty's team, it would be a team that won Stanley Cups, not just one that had record-breaking seasons. Keith Primeau and Paul Coffey were sent to Hartford for Brendan Shanahan and Brian Glynn. After the trade, the Wings had an indifferent regular season, finishing only fifth overall, but in the playoffs they beat St. Louis and Anaheim, losing only twice, and in doing so—crucially—they allowed only 20 goals in 10 games. But ahead of them in the semifinals was Colorado, who had finished first overall, and Patrick Roy. Roy loved to turn every series he played into a mano-a-mano—a goalie-against-goalie contest. Two years earlier, the Wings had traded for goalie Mike Vernon, who had won a Cup with the Flames in 1989, beating the Canadiens and Roy in the final. Vernon wasn't as good as Roy, but he was just as combative, and was willing to go eyeball to eyeball with him.

The Wings beat Colorado in six games, allowing only twelve goals, then swept Philadelphia in the final, allowing only six. The Wings were Stanley Cup champions for the first time in 42 years—since 1954–55; since Howe, Lindsay, Sawchuk, and Kelly. Doubling down on Detroit, Ilitch got what he needed. The city did too. And Scotty had been the architect, the designer and shaper, the coach. Coach-*plus*. More than in Montreal or Pittsburgh, this was Scotty's team.

It was his seventh Cup.

But before Scotty and the Wings had even begun to think about the challenge of the next season, just six days after they had won and were still celebrating, everything turned upside down. Konstantinov, Fetisov, and the Wings' masseur, Sergei Mnatsakanov, were leaving a team party at a golf course and going to a restaurant—the team had thought ahead and hired limos for the players. The driver crossed several lanes of traffic and slammed into a tree. Fetisov received major injuries, but he healed and was able to return the next year. Mnatsakanov was paralyzed from the neck down. Konstantinov suffered a major brain injury, never played again, and has never healed.

"Konstantinov was a hard-nosed tough guy," Scotty recalls. "He wasn't big, but he was solid, rock solid, and he hit hard, and he played hurt. You couldn't get him out of the game. He was 30 years old then, and was just coming into his own. He made some mistakes, maybe more than most players, but he was good offensively and really really solid on the back end. He liked to have contact with guys, and if there was a good player on the other team, he had to keep his head up. He was a different kind of player, but boy, what a player he was. If he hadn't had his accident, he might have challenged Lidström for the best defenceman in the league."

A champion usually ends one season and begins the next as the Cup favourite, but now Konstantinov was gone, and the Wings would still have to beat Colorado and Dallas in the west and New Jersey in the east. Then things got even harder. Fedorov, looking for a contract befitting a league MVP who had twice been its top defensive forward, was a hold-out, and the 1997–98 season began without him. October extended into November, then December, then into the new year. Finally, late in January, Carolina extended Fedorov an offer sheet, which he accepted. This would pay him, beyond his annual salary, a $14 million signing bonus and an additional $12 million in bonuses over the six-year life of the contract, which had to be paid immediately, *in full*, if the team made it to the 1998 conference finals. In return, the Wings would receive five first-round picks from Carolina. Behind the offer was Carolina owner Peter Karmanos, Ilitch's great Macedonian-American-versus-Greek-American, Little Caesars-versus-Compuware foe.

The NHL contested the validity of the offer sheet, but a month later, after the Olympic break, an arbitrator ruled that the contract was valid. The Wings had a decision to make: let Fedorov go and receive the first-round picks, or match the offer, knowing that with him in their lineup they had a good chance of getting to the conference finals and therefore being on the hook to pay him, over the period of only a few months, the two bonuses plus his salary—about $28 million in all. It was Ilitch's call. He had a Stanley Cup winner, *finally*, and then his unfriendly rival had presented this poison-pill offer sheet.

Ilitch decided to match. The Wings now had back in their lineup an outstanding, yet not entirely happy player for the last quarter of the season and the playoffs. And, just as important, the players had received from Ilitch a message that was very clear: the Detroit Red Wings mat-tered to him enough to match the offer, and this year's team—these players—mattered enough to him to risk him paying out $28 million.

The playoffs were not easy. The Coyotes took Detroit to six games in the first round, then St. Louis and Dallas did the same. The final was easier, and the Wings swept Washington. Beyond every other motivation to win, Fedorov had had one more—his $12 million bonus. "He was terrific in the playoffs that year. He had 10 goals and 10 assists, nearly a point a game, and he was a terrific defensive player to boot."

It was Scotty's eighth Cup.

He thought about retiring. He would turn 65 before the next season began. He had reached an age where people do retire, and when others can't stop themselves from asking them about it—especially after a Cup win when it seemed to them, at least, that he had no other mountains to climb. He *was* the mountain. He had won the past *and* he had won the future—surely nobody was ever going to win more games than he had. He had also just tied Toe Blake's record for the most Cup wins by an NHL coach, and nobody else was ever going to coach that many great teams for that many years—teams that could win year after year. Besides, a career has to end sometime, and maybe this was the perfect moment. He'd had his knee replaced a year earlier, and his brother Jack, three years younger, had died. That was a shock. He could no longer *not* think about his health or his age.

But more than that, he had the right and proper script in front of him. Ilitch, the players, the public, the media, Suella and the kids— everyone would understand. No backward glances. No regrets. He had lived a coach's life all of his life, where when the puck drops everything is out of your control, but now he had control over whether he went or stayed. And whichever he chose, it would be on his own terms. That's a level of control a coach or player almost never has. A script he could even sell to himself.

No one was telling him he had to stop. Ilitch wasn't, Holland wasn't, Suella wasn't. The Wings' fans and the media certainly weren't. There was, however, one big risk to staying on, and he knew that because he had been a sports fan all his life. He had seen it happen with players. He had seen it with coaches. Vince Lombardi ended his career not as the Super Bowl–winning coach of the Green Bay Packers, but as the non-Super

Bowl–winning coach of the Washington Redskins. Casey Stengel had gone from the Yankees' penthouse to the expansion Mets' outhouse. Even the great Red Auerbach, whose coaching career had ended with another Celtics championship, then kicked himself upstairs to be the general manager, then president, then chairman of many non-title winning teams.

But Scotty wasn't telling himself to stop. Retiring now was someone else's perfect script, not his own. Not yet. Not then. He, Devellano, and Holland worked well together. Scotty had been responsible for the Larionov, Fetisov, and Shanahan trades, but he believed now—and Ilitch and Devellano did too—that Holland was ready to be the team's general manager and could get him the players he needed, just as Sam had done. He and Holland saw the team in a similar enough way that they would have no reason in the future to come to an irreconcilable divide.

So after the Wings won the Cup, Scotty didn't say anything, and each week that he didn't announce his retirement brought him one week closer to the next season, to a point where it began to seem a little unfair to the Wings if he left, then a little more unfair, then too unfair—and then training camp began. Until, with the 1998–99 season underway, suddenly his next right opportunity to retire wouldn't be at the end of the following season but would come only after the next Cup win—because you can't go out with a loss, and because the team would be still close to winning again, and because Ilitch had been so good to him. As Scotty puts it, "You win two in a row and then start losing, and lose a couple of times, and then you want to win again." And that's what happened. The Wings finished sixth overall, swept Anaheim in the first round, then lost in six games to Colorado, who lost to Dallas, who beat Buffalo to win the Cup. The following year, the Wings were second overall, swept the Kings in the first round, then lost in five games to Colorado, who lost to Dallas, who lost to New Jersey in the final. In 2000–01 the Wings again finished second overall, but this time they lost in the first round in six games to L.A.

Suddenly, it was three years later. Instead of having won two in a row, the Wings had lost three in a row. Instead of having done it all, now

Scotty had something to prove. That he wasn't too old, that time hadn't passed him by, that he was still the best.

But if they were to win again, something was going to need to change. In those three lost years, the same names kept recurring: Colorado, Dallas, and New Jersey. And backstopping those three were three other names: Roy, Belfour, and Brodeur. In the six years since Patrick Roy had arrived in Colorado, the Wings had played the Avalanche four times in the playoffs, and lost three of them. The first of those series, in 1996, was screamingly thrilling and punishingly cruel. Both teams were talented—Sakic and Forsberg; Yzerman and Fedorov. Both teams were tough. The sixth game had been in Colorado, with the Avalanche ahead in the series, three games to two. The puck was near the boards, and Kris Draper, a hard-working defensive forward for the Wings, had just lost possession. With his back to the play, he was turning to his left to see Sakic skating towards him. To his right, coming at him unseen, was Claude Lemieux, a bull-like, highly competitive, and much-disliked winger for the Avs. He hit Draper from behind, driving his head downwards onto the top front edge of the boards. Draper suffered a broken orbital bone, broken cheekbone, broken nose, and broken jaw. The whole right side of his face was caved in. "It was just a total destruction of his face," says Scotty, someone not known for overstatement. "It was just such a vicious hit to an unsuspecting player with the boards right there." The Avs won the series, and went on to win the Cup. It was the start of a heated rivalry, in which the two teams hated each other, and also respected each other.

The next year, the Wings won the matchup—and the Cup—with Mike Vernon in goal. But then Vernon was traded to San Jose, and the Wings went into the 1997–98 season with Chris Osgood as their number one goalie. Osgood was only 24, but he had already played more than 150 NHL games with Detroit, and in his first big playoff year, the Wings won again. But in doing so, they hadn't had to meet Colorado along the way—the Avs had been upset by Edmonton in the first round.

Over the next three seasons, Osgood improved and matured, but no matter how much he developed, he would never be Roy or Belfour. Twice the Wings lost to Colorado, and once to L.A. A feeling grew: the Wings were not going to beat the Avs or the Stars with Osgood in goal, and they couldn't win the Cup if they didn't. They—Scotty and Holland—had to do something.

During Scotty's eight years in Detroit, they had moved many players in and out. "We were able to add free agents. We added guys every year. When you look at the core we had, Lidström and Konstantinov, Yzerman and Fedorov, then we traded for Shanahan and Chelios; when you've got a core, you can fit in people. We got Datsyuk in right away in 2001–02. He was a rookie, we didn't know much about him, but at training camp he just took off. He was an extra-special player. He wasn't on those first two Cup teams, but we kept adding."

The Wings could keep on adding because this was a pre-salary cap time, and Ilitch was always willing to find extra money to make the team better. "Ilitch really wanted to win. The Fedorov thing was unbelievable," Scotty says. One year early on, Scotty had needed a defenceman, and Bob Rouse was available as a free agent but the team had already reached its budget limit. "I was dealing with [Mike's wife] Marian Ilitch. She was looking after the money. She said, 'No, we can't go over the budget.' But Mr. Ilitch had told me that if there was a discrepancy between us, to call him. So I did. And we signed him." Rouse gave them four solid seasons.

Larry Murphy came in a late-season trade in 1997 and helped them win two Cups. Vernon, who came from the Flames in 1994, won one. A few of the players they added then stayed—Larionov, Shanahan, and Chris Chelios among them. Chelios was already 37 years old when he came to Detroit late in 1998–99, and he had played more than 15 hard, body-punishing seasons—over 1,000 games. It was thought he would be a good, quickly fading player for a year or two and then be gone. Instead, he played nine full seasons with Detroit, finally retiring at age 47, having played the sixth-highest number of games in NHL history (1,651).

The 2000–01 team hadn't been good enough. It had lost in the first round. By this time Ilitch was 72, Scotty was 68, Yzerman was 36 playing on 70-year-old knees. The window was closing. So, for the 2001–02 season, the Wings decided to go all in. During the off-season, Detroit signed Brett Hull, Luc Robitaille, and Fredrik Olausson as free agents, and, crucially, traded Vyacheslav Kozlov and a first-round pick to Buffalo for Dominik Hašek.

Hull was 37, Robitaille 35, Olausson 35, Hašek 36. They were joining a team that included Chelios 39, Shanahan 32, Larionov 40, Lidström 31, Fedorov 31, and defenceman Steve Duchesne 36. Even the "kids" on the team's shutdown line were now veterans—Draper was 30, McCarty, 29, and Maltby, 28. Of the other regulars, the only ones under the age of 30 were Tomas Holmström 28, Mathieu Dandenault 25, Pavel Datsyuk 23, Boyd Devereaux 23, and Jiří Fischer 21. The team's average age was a staggering 31.7 years. Of their top eight scorers, none were under 31.

It was like no other team in NHL history. On its roster were *nine* players who are now in the Hall of Fame—Yzerman, Lidström, Hašek, Hull, Chelios, Fedorov, Shanahan, Larionov, and Robitaille— and one, Datsyuk, who likely will be someday. And a Hall of Fame coach. Yet in 2001–02, none of these nine players, except Lidström, were in their prime years. Almost all of them had been the best players on their teams, many had been captains, and all had been those who were sent onto the ice entrusted with the most crucial moments in the most crucial games. All were proud and all were intensely competitive—not only with their opponents, but also with each other and with themselves. All but Lidström had moved from their glory years, to the difficult middle years, to now, and the realization they weren't perfect and weren't just a few slump-breaking games away from being perfect again. They were getting old and feeling old. They knew they had no great individual achievements left in them. In this season—in any season ahead—they would never put up more goals, more points, or more shutouts than they had in their earlier years. Robitaille and

Hašek had never won a Stanley Cup. The others might never win another. More than anything, they just wanted to feel good, they wanted to feel young, they wanted to be excited again. Their only success would be the team's success. The team's success would be their success.

From the time these players were six or seven—from the first team they played on—the world had revolved around them. Now it didn't. And now, probably for the first time, they were feeling *grateful*. To be around these other players; to be on a team like this with a coach like this; to have a chance to win the Cup. A second chance. A last chance.

"When you get to this stage in your career, you know what you can do, and you know what you can't do," Scotty says. "These guys came here for one purpose. They didn't have a lot left, and they weren't going to rock the boat. I felt we had a team that could play any style. We had enough toughness when we needed toughness. We were a pretty good-sized team; we weren't small. And once you get close to the top and there's only one or two teams that can beat you, you're in pretty good company."

This was the team, these were the players, that Scotty had to coach and to win with.

"The toughest part was trying to get ice time for all these players." They were used to having so much more, but they could live with less if the others next to them, who were also stars, were getting less too. "We had Yzerman, Fedorov, and Shanahan—that was our number-one line. Then we had Hull, Devereaux, and Datsyuk. Larionov, Holmström, and Robitaille—that was a two-way line. Then McCarty, Draper, and Maltby was our checking line. We had four really good lines. We also used Hull and Holmström on the power play, so we had two power-play units. We were tough to play against, even when we were on the road and couldn't match up as much. When we couldn't get Draper's line on against their best, we could get them against their second-best and get Yzerman out there. He had become such a good two-way player. He could kill penalties. He blocked shots, because you can't kill penalties if you don't block shots. He could take faceoffs. He became a complete player. So when you have a couple of guys that can play two ways, you're not desperate."

Yzerman was the key, just as he had been in so many different ways since he came to the team 18 years before. If *he* was willing to score less and defend more, if *he* could deal with less ice time, if *he* could accept less than a superstar's attention, then so could they all. "He wanted so much perfection. Some guys show their emotion, but he didn't wear his on his sleeve. But if something didn't happen the right way, he'd blow his stack."

Yzerman had an awkward, slightly arm's-length relationship with Fedorov. They had been teammates on the Wings for 11 years—longer than with anyone else on the team. They had played on promising, then disappointing, then thrilling, then disappointing, then promising Wings teams together. They had won two Cups together. They needed each other and they knew it, but they were rivals too.

"There was a competition there. In my mind [as a coach], I had to keep a balance between them. You wouldn't give one something without giving something else to the other, but never forgetting that Yzerman was the captain, of course. Keeping him number one, but making sure Fedorov wasn't pushed aside. I deferred to Yzerman a little more."

Ice time was a big thing, especially to Fedorov. For any player, it was the true indicator of his place on the team, and in his coach's mind. Yzerman and Fedorov both killed penalties, they both played the power play, they both took faceoffs, they both played their regular shift. "One thing I remember most about Sergei is that as soon as the game was over he couldn't wait to look at the stats sheet to see how much ice time he got. I was always concerned about keeping a balance between him and Yzerman on ice time."

In personality, and within the dynamic of the team, Yzerman was like the big brother and Fedorov the little brother. Yzerman the serious, responsible, driven one; Fedorov the precocious one. Because Yzerman was as he was, under his protective veil Fedorov could use his incredible talents and do whatever he wanted to do whenever he wanted to do it. And Fedorov could do everything.

"He was a powerfully built guy. Bigger than people thought—he played bent over a bit. And like most Russians, his core, his leg strength was tremendous. He was such a skater. He could skate backwards and forwards with equal dexterity. He had speed. He had balance. You couldn't knock him off his feet. His skating was off the charts. And, unusual for a Russian player, he was airtight defensively. I don't know how he became such a good defensive player because, for the Russians, defence is holding on to the puck and not giving it away. But he just knew how to play. On offence he was able to accelerate, slow down, cut in—again, it all came down to his skating. He was a left shot, but he'd go up the right side and put the puck through the left defenceman's legs, and jump around him and pick it up again on the other side. And his shot was terrific. He was completely offence and defence together."

In his own way, Yzerman almost delighted in the antics of his "little brother," but at the same time he was always a little disapproving. That's how he kept the slight upper hand he needed. "Sergei would compete in games, but sometimes he should [have] compete[d] a little more," Scotty recalls. "Maybe he'd do that the odd time when you're playing a weaker team, but never in a crunch time. Yzerman never took a night off. I think what bothered Yzerman more than anything was that he thought Fedorov could have pushed the envelope more like he did." Yzerman played hurt—and the more hurt he was, the more determined he was to play. "Fedorov didn't get hurt. He hardly missed any games at all, but one year in the playoffs, he hurt his shoulder. With Yzerman, you didn't worry, you know he's going to play, but we didn't know about Sergei. He didn't play with pain. We had to go to Chicago to play two games. Mark Howe was on the team then, and he had a suggestion. His dad was around the team a bit, and Mark got Gordie to come down to the rink before we left. Sergei was going to try out his shoulder. And they went on the ice together, and Gordie was talking to him about how you don't always get an opportunity to be in the playoffs and you never know when the next time will be. Blah blah blah. And how sometimes you play with pain—to stroke him on the one hand, and get his message across on the other. And Sergei played.

"I think Sergei looked up to Yzerman. He didn't want to steal his thunder, and I think that's why when he went somewhere else later in his career [Anaheim, Columbus, Washington], he just dropped off completely. It wasn't because he was too old, but maybe that competition with Yzerman was good for him."

Meanwhile Igor Larionov had had a full and storied career before he ever arrived in the NHL. He had played with Sergei Makarov and Vladimir Krutov on the famed Soviet "KLM Line"—perhaps the greatest line in the history of international hockey—and had won Olympic gold medals and World Championships. By 2001–02, he had already played 11 seasons in the NHL, but he wasn't a perfect fit for every team or every coach. He had played with the Wings, then wasn't re-signed and he went to Florida, and there "he got into a big hassle with [Panthers' coach] Bryan Murray," says Scotty. "He didn't want to ever shoot the puck in, and they were a young team on the rise and he didn't fit into their system. And he rebelled, so we got him back. He could be a bit of a clubhouse lawyer if you didn't treat him the right way, but I found he was always very supportive. I think he liked the way I treated him."

Larionov had been part of the Russian Five during his first stint in Detroit, but now his role was different. On this team and at his age, "He gave us depth. He killed penalties, he was on the power play a bit. He played with Robitaille and Holmström—they were a fourth line but we used them more like a number three. Draper's line was a real fourth line, but it was our go-to line for work ethic and penalty-killing, so they were almost our second. The most underrated part of Larionov's game was how terrific a player he was in the last minute or two of the game. It was because of his hockey sense. He knew where the puck was going to go, and he'd be there to get it. We used to move another player to the wing, or move him to the wing, just to get him out there."

During the rest of the game, "He was a feeder more than anything. He was one of those guys who knew how to play with a scorer. Whoever he played with would get a lot of opportunities. He detested anybody who shot the puck in. He wanted to have it. People would say the Russians aren't good defensively, but their defence was having the puck. They didn't put themselves in defensive positions very often."

To these determined personalities, with their long-established roles and ways, Scotty had to somehow fit in his two new forwards, Robitaille and Hull. "Robitaille was superb. He was a very top player in L.A., but then he kind of moped around in Pittsburgh, then New York, but he was a good person on this team. He was pretty happy-go-lucky. His nickname was 'Lucky.' He'd score on tip-ins and rebounds. His touch around the net was unbelievable. He had never been a great skater, but he wasn't any slower than he was before, and he just knew his position on the team. He was big on our power play. He didn't act like a big star. He just fit in. He knew his role, which is the most important thing for a guy who isn't in a primary role. And the thing is, he accepted it. He was there because he wanted to win a Cup. This was his first. He never won another."

And then there was Hull, who had come to the Wings from Dallas. "[He] was a fun-loving guy. He talked a lot, but he was such a skilful player. He would be friendly with everybody. Everything was always okay. He never let things bother him. I never saw him other than happy and smiling. And he had such a great shot. Earlier in his career, he didn't play in his own zone much, he seemed always to be up at centre. He'd get passes, and come in on breakaways—and, of course, he could pick the corners like nobody else could. I mean, he's the fourth all-time goal scorer in league history." And Hull scored in the playoffs too, not only in the regular season.

"I think people thought of him as just a one-way player, but we got him into killing penalties. It was like what we did with Frank Mahovlich in Montreal. If a guy is a goal scorer, he has that special talent of knowing the areas to go [to], so he knows where to go defensively too. It's about applying yourself, and Hull was willing to do that. I remember in the playoffs, and this was the closest we came to losing that [2001–02] year, but the Canucks beat us in the first two games at home and then we had to go out there. We won three in a row, but then in the sixth game back in Vancouver, the game was tight and Hull was killing a penalty. He just got himself in the right spot at the right time, and they were a little careless, and the next thing you know he scores a shorthanded goal." His linemates were Datsyuk and Devereaux, two young guys. "Hull definitely wasn't playing a top-line role, so his line wasn't up against the other team's best, and that's a big advantage. He could kind of go unnoticed. Then he'd also be on the power play, so he was always playing at moments where he had an advantage."

In the playoffs, Datsyuk and Devereaux each averaged about 11 minutes a game; Hull almost 18. He led the Wings with 10 goals in 23 games. "He was at the end of his career but he didn't concern himself with not being a top guy. I think he kind of relished it."

Remembering that 2001–02 team, Scotty says, "We had a very stacked deck up front. And we got a lot of hockey out of our defence because we didn't play in our own end a lot." Lidström was paired with Olausson; Chelios with Fischer; Duchesne with Dandenault. In the playoffs that year, Lidström played 31 minutes a game, and Chelios 26. Lidstrom was 31 years old, Chelios 40. They were on power plays (Chelios only sometimes), they killed penalties, and they had their regular shifts as well. Olausson and Fischer played less than 20 minutes a game; Dandenault and Duschene less than 14.

"Lidström was the cornerstone. Whoever was the best line on the other teams, he played against them. We never tried to spot him. And sometimes his defence partners were not that good. He would make them. You'd never see him getting trapped up the ice. His mindset was 'I'm going to defend.' But being such a good passer, and having such a good shot, and having such smarts, and knowing where to put the puck at the net, he got a lot of points. If you gave him time and space, you were done. He played a lot too, but he never tired because he didn't skate unnecessarily. And when he had a chance to rest, he rested. He played almost every game."

In his then 10 seasons with the Wings—not counting the lockout year—he had played 80 games or more every year but one. "And some of those games he missed were near the end of the year, where we'd just take him out and rest him. He played nearly 20 seasons without a major injury. And he wasn't a big man. There wasn't much meat on him. But even big, physical guys didn't bother him. He was fearless. You always worried that someone would take advantage of him, and you just hoped he'd push back a bit. But nobody did. Knowing him, if they had, he'd step up. He never disappointed us.

"He wasn't spectacular. He wasn't flashy. He wasn't a guy the media clamoured to get to. He roomed on the road with Fedorov. His best friend on the team was Holmström. Usually the guys that are the core of the team have a lot to say, but he was quiet. As a coach, he wasn't the kind of guy you went to and asked, 'You think maybe we shouldn't practise tomorrow?' or, 'You think we should take a later flight?' Because he would just say, 'Whatever you want to do is fine.'" In many ways, Scotty says, Lidström was like every other Swedish player he coached. "They go about their business. They don't complain. They never get rattled. They compete. They're much more competitive than some people give them credit for. They're good team guys. They're very appreciative of what they have. They don't take anything for granted. They love Canada, they like the U.S., but when the season's over they zip back to Sweden, and then they come back and do their job again. There's no maintenance to them at all.

"I'm always just amazed when I look at his stats," Scotty says of Lidström. "I never think of him as an offensive player. I always appreciated what he did defensively. Then, at the end of a season, there he is, he's got more than 50 points, and he's playing against good players all the time. If you were a forward during those years in Detroit, you could count on one hand the number of times he didn't put the puck right on your stick—on the rush, or coming out of your own end. It was amazing."

Chelios was a different story. Or he seemed to be. "He was the exact opposite type of player [to Lidström]. He got a lot of penalties, but he used to get away with a lot too. He'd be hooking, holding, jabbing; he'd be all over you all the time. He used to really bother the good players. He was always looking for that little bit of an edge, and he didn't worry about the consequences. And in those days there was only one referee."

Lidström knew exactly what he could do and what he couldn't do, and did it. Chelios did whatever he wanted to do, and it was up to the referee to tell him he couldn't. "He was a fantastically conditioned guy. A real horse. I remember we had to take the door off the sauna because he insisted on bringing a stationary bike into it. It was the craziest thing I ever saw. And when practice was over he'd go to the gym and hang around there until the middle of the afternoon, because he just loved to train. He was all hockey. All he lived for was to play. And he was 40 years old."

Because he was in the shape of a 25-year-old, Chelios thought he could do what 25-year-olds do—even if he hadn't been able to do some of that himself when he was 25. But sometimes a lack of self-awareness makes you better. "He wanted to be on the power play. He really wanted to be on the power play. We put him there, sometimes, but we had Lidström, and Olausson was a pretty good offensive guy. And we could put Fedorov back there. And Yzerman." As much as Lidström was no-maintenance, Chelios was not. "But he was a hang of a player. He liked to play, and he fit in perfectly with our team."

Then, the final piece. Dominik Hašek had gotten a late start in the NHL. He had been drafted by Chicago in the 10th round in 1983, the 199th player selected, but it wasn't until seven years later, in 1990–91, that he got into even a few games with the Blackhawks (in 1986, the team name had changed to one word instead of two), then two more years before he was a regular in Buffalo. He was 27 by this time. It took him so long because Ed Belfour was ahead of him in Chicago, but mostly because Hašek played like no other goalie had ever played. Certainly no other goalie that was any good. He was all over the place in his net—up, down, on his back, flipping and flopping around. Goalies were supposed to be in control, in position, composed, predictable—so everyone else on the team could feel secure, solid, confident. Mostly it was Hašek's dives that were so off-putting. Every other goalie set themselves in butterfly position, knees on the ice, feet splayed out to each corner, body upright, and then slide a few inches one way, glide a few inches the other, ready for any shot, in position for any rebound. Hašek dove like a soccer goalie, horizontally on the ice on his side, arms and legs extended, the upper part of his net fully exposed, leaving himself totally out of position, beached, for any rebound. And because he dove like a soccer goalie, and soccer goalies don't use sticks, Hašek was always throwing off his stick, or otherwise losing it. Outside the crease, he was hopeless. He couldn't handle the puck—and worse, he didn't know it. And because he was all over the place so much, it was hard to notice that he stopped pucks. Just about every one of them. He broke every rule of goaltending but that one.

By the end of the 2001 playoffs, having been a regular for less than 10 years, he had won the Vezina Trophy as the NHL's best goalie six times, been the league's MVP twice, won an Olympic gold medal for the Czech Republic, and had gone to the Cup final with the Sabres, but he had never won a Stanley Cup. At 36, time was running out for him as well. He wanted out of Buffalo, and the Wings made the trade. The price was high—Kozlov and a first-round pick—but Scotty knew the price of *not* making the trade was higher. It was Holland who made the deal. If the Wings didn't have a Stanley Cup–winning goalie—no matter all these Hall of Fame players and this Hall of Fame coach—they weren't going to win a Stanley Cup.

"Hašek was good during the year," Scotty recalls. "He wasn't spectacular. But he *was* spectacular in the 2–0 win in Colorado."

The Wings had a good regular season. They finished first overall—15 points ahead of second-place Boston. Scotty spread the ice time around, and all four lines played. "We didn't have to overplay a lot of guys," Scotty says. "Except maybe for Lidström." Older players get hurt more often, and when they're hurt, they take longer to heal. But because Scotty didn't have to overplay them, "We had almost no injuries, and no serious ones."

The team had all this great offensive talent—Yzerman had finished in the top ten in the league in scoring six times, Hull and Robitaille three times, and Fedorov and Shanahan twice—yet that season not one Wings player finished in the top ten. This team and this coach weren't here for another first-place finish and a nice, injury-free, stats-filled season. This was about the Cup.

The Wings started the playoffs slowly, losing their first two games at home against the Canucks, but then came Hull's shorthanded goal in Game 6 in Vancouver, and they went on to win. Then they defeated St. Louis in five games. But now the preliminaries were over, and Colorado was next. The Avalanche had won two tough seven-game series, against L.A. and San Jose, and were playoff-ready. The teams split the opening two games in Detroit, and the next two in Colorado, but in the crucial fifth game at Joe Louis Arena, the Avalanche won in overtime, 2–1. Now ahead three games to two, the Avs returned to Denver, where they could close out the series on home ice. It was for a game like this that the Wings had signed Hull, Robitaille, and Hašek. It was for a game like this that Hull, Robitaille, and Hašek had signed with Detroit.

Hašek was like Jacques Plante. He was a competitor, but also an artist—more than competing against his opponent, he competed against his art and himself. He had faced Patrick Roy once before in a showdown game—in the semifinals of the 1998 Olympics in Nagano, Japan. The game had ended in a 1–1 tie. Then came overtime, and with no goals scored, the ultimate showdown: a shootout. Of the five shots taken by each team, Roy allowed one goal—Hašek none.

It was hard to play mano-a-mano games with Hašek. He was unaware of what Roy was trying to do, or he didn't care, or maybe he thought it didn't matter; he had his art and himself to live up to. "That sixth game was 1–0 until the middle of the second period, then we got another." And, as Scotty says, Hašek was "spectacular."

Now it was Detroit that was returning home. Now it was the Wings that could close out the series on home ice. They blew the Avs away. It was 4–0 by the 13-minute mark of the first period, and 6–0 by seven minutes into the second period, at which point Roy was gone. The final score was 7–0. For Hašek, it was two straight shutouts.

In the final, the Wings beat Carolina in five games.

It was Scotty's ninth Cup.

CHAPTER SIXTEEN

Moments earlier.

"Once that empty-net goal went in with 45 seconds to go, I started thinking, 'When can I leave?' I couldn't go then because there was still enough time if they scored a quick goal, but there was another faceoff with five or six seconds to go, and I left the bench. My skates were ready. I'd told the trainer before the game to get them sharp. I knew it was going to be the last time I'd have a chance to be with the Cup."

He had begun to think about retiring in February. "We were on a family holiday in Orlando"—him, Suella, and some of the kids and their families. The NHL had shut down for three weeks for the 2002 Winter Olympics in Salt Lake City, and as Scotty relates, "I said to myself, 'Gee, I'd like to do this all the time.'" His mind, which had always been tentative and conflicted about retirement, was suddenly clear—and he hadn't seen that coming. "Before, I always worried about the big question: How do you really know when your time is up, or when you want to decide it's up? My decision that February was not like before. It was automatic. I knew it was time. I made up my mind that, win or lose, I was not going to coach again."

Now the Wings had to win. Four more months to go.

"I began to think about how it would be nice if I could win that last game as a coach. I felt if I could go out a winner, it wasn't that it was going to make the decision itself any easier, but it would make the post-decision a lot better. If we could win, I wouldn't be able to second-guess myself."

He didn't tell anyone what he'd decided—not in Orlando, and not in the weeks that followed. He didn't even say anything to Suella—not in so many words—but she knew, though she also knew him well enough to understand that she didn't quite know, because he didn't either. With him, there always had to be some wiggle room. Just as in a game you have a plan, and it's the right plan, but things will happen and you have to be ready to adapt. But what he did know absolutely was that he didn't want a farewell tour. "I was concerned about being a distraction," he says. He had seen that happen before. A farewell tour is nice but winning a Stanley Cup is a lot nicer, and if you're thinking about what you shouldn't be thinking about, it's a whole lot harder to win. Besides, a farewell tour makes it harder to change your mind if that's what you decide to do. And then you're stuck.

Now that he had put retirement into his head, he couldn't not think about it, but he had a lot of coaching left to do. He had to keep managing the egos of his veteran stars, which meant managing their ice time. He had to keep managing their aging bodies, which meant keeping the team at the top of the standings to ensure home-ice advantage in the playoffs—while not wearing the players out to achieve that. This was a special team. It was so strong in so many ways, but it was also vulnerable. "If we didn't have a good regular season that year," Scotty says, thinking back, "I don't know if we would have won. This team wouldn't have been able to go right down to the last game, playing everyone in all 82 games, then winning the Cup. We wouldn't have had the stamina."

As for himself, "I was feeling a sense of relief. And I was going to make sure I enjoyed everything, knowing it was not going to happen again." It was a Scotty kind of relief—one that comes without ease; a Scotty kind of enjoyment that came with fresh, intensified focus. For him, a *real* farewell tour wasn't the endless spotlight of interviews, applause, and backward glances, but a chance to pace that space behind the players' bench one last time in games that had new meaning.

He loved coaching games. He had always loved that, even with his park teams in Verdun where the players just showed up and played and he wasn't much more than a cheerleader. "When you stop coaching, if there's anything you miss, it's [coaching games]," he says. It's the ultimate test. "When they drop the puck to start the game, and you're behind the bench and you make decisions that affect the team or an individual player, that's the best part. That's the most fun. When you're coaching and there are two minutes to go and it seems like you've got an insurmountable lead, 98 times out of 100 you do, but there's the two times you don't, and that's what I was always concerned about. You never really feel totally in control of a game until it's over. Until the final whistle goes, you're still in the same mode. You're still trying to win that game."

He continues: "You must always be ready. You have to have your next five players ready. Ninety-five per cent of my thinking when I was on the bench was who I was going to put out next. Maybe some coaches don't think that way, but I was always trying to figure out the situation of the game, the situation with the opposition, what could you do to combat what they're trying to do. You're sort of thinking two benches at the same time, but you're only in control of one. You've got to know the score, and you've got to know your players. One of the things I used to think about a lot is that every player is different. Some, if they don't get out there early in the game, if they don't have a good start to their game, they never recover. Sometimes it means double-shifting [them]. As a coach you have to cater to their style.

"This also has an effect on the other team because they have plans on how to stop these guys from playing their game. I used to work on this a lot, not allowing the other team to really know what my next move was. Most times it's pretty difficult to camouflage, but the odd time you can do it. You go 1–2–3 [with your lines], then all of a sudden you go 1–2–3–4 and see how they react." Other coaches did the same with him. "Some would put out a bunch of heavyweights against you, hoping you'd bite. But I never wanted to match my heavyweights against theirs. We didn't always have them, but what I did sometimes was put out players I knew *wouldn't* get involved with those guys— good skilled players who can control their emotions. Because when there's a guy on the other team looking for a brawl and he can't get one, that exasperates him. He's also eating up the ice time of his team's good players."

More than anything, Scotty needed to sense the mood of his bench—if the players were fearful, if they were nervous or excited or complacent or bored or distracted—and give back to his players the emotion they were missing. When a team is ahead by three or four goals, he says, sometimes "players get a false sense of security, and if you don't take steps to prevent that, you're in trouble." So at moments like that, he would get yappy and frenetic just to shake them up. "In a tight game, there was never a problem, because the players knew what was on the line." Then he would go quiet—solid like a rock.

He wasn't always this way. "When I first started coaching, I was always excited behind the bench. I always thought you had to have a lot of energy." One time in junior, the Petes were playing the Marlies on a Sunday afternoon in Toronto. "They had a couple of really tough guys, and one of them, Roger Côté, went after one of our players. I got so upset, I grabbed . . . it must have been about eight or nine sticks, and I threw them on the ice at the referee. They gave me a three-game suspension." He learned then, and would learn again: "If you're not calm on the bench, the team can become restless; a high-energy level is important, but not all of the time."

June 13, 2002. Game 5. The Wings were leading the Carolina Hurricanes three games to one in the Stanley Cup final. The situation was clear.

Scotty's players knew it, and he knew it. One more win. One more time he had to give his players—and now himself—the emotion that was missing.

"I was pretty nervous that day," he says, "I was thinking—your mind races ahead—'If we win tonight, it's all over. It's the icing on the cake.'" All the thoughts he knew he shouldn't have, and couldn't have; that would keep him from being ready and getting the team ready; that could backfire and keep him and them from winning, from that icing on the cake. "You play games in your mind," he says: "'If we lose this game tonight, and then go [to Carolina] and lose Game 6, and now we're in Game 7, which to me, for a home team, isn't as much of an advantage as Game 5.' So you're saying to yourself, 'Game 5 is our advantage game. We can use it to wrap up the whole season.'" But his mind was also telling him that playing a Cup-clinching advantage game at home could be a disadvantage too, because "everybody at the rink, and everybody you meet on the street, that's all they're talking about . . . 'Isn't it great, we're going to win the Cup tonight.'" And, he knew—better than anyone—that a Cup isn't won until it's won.

"You've got to be careful not to get carried away," he kept telling himself that day. But even he found it hard to focus. "I remember being very nervous, and hoping it would go our way, but knowing that hoping didn't matter—that this wasn't going to happen unless we did it ourselves." So to distract himself, he focused on the little things in front of him that he needed to do—on what he *could* control, not on what he couldn't. "I remember going to the game at five [o'clock]. You have a game routine, and you keep to it." You do *this* and you check *that*, and in every way but one this is like a thousand other games. It takes two hours to do what you need to do, so you give yourself two hours to do it.

Then the puck was dropped, then the Wings went ahead, then the empty-net goal, then the faceoff with five or six seconds to go. Then he was on the ice in his freshly sharpened skates, the crowd screaming, the players hugging. It was *all* over. What had begun 63 years earlier with those Bruins' broadcasts in that six-plex on the Avenues. But, in that instant, his hockey life didn't flash before him; he didn't think of glorious Cup wins past. He thought, instead, of what he had to do next—"[I] pretty much just focused on the moment. It's mid-celebration, you're conscious of what's happening—now they'll present the Conn Smythe Trophy; now they'll give us the Cup." The Cup would go first to the captain—Yzerman—and it did. Then something happened Scotty wasn't expecting; something the players had cooked up.

"Steve got the Cup from the commissioner, and he gave it to me." Quickly, he had to refocus. "When you're skating around with the Cup, and it weighs 35 pounds, and all the confetti they'd thrown on the ice—I was worried I was going to fall and drop it." But he didn't. For Scotty, this was a moment of triumph—and relief.

Then, just as the players had also arranged, the Cup went to Hašek, Robitaille, Duchesne, Olausson—their teammates who had had long, honourable careers and who had never won before.

Next the team picture—the whole team, the more the merrier. Players, coaches, trainers, Ilitch, others of all sorts, some sprawled on the ice, some sitting, some kneeling, some standing, pressing up tight against whomever was next to them. Scotty lay on the ice in front in the middle, half leaning on Ilitch to his right, half propped up against Hull and Draper behind him, and Robitaille on his left. Hašek was beside Ilitch, an un-Hašek-like grin and glow covering his face. Suella, Stan, Bob, and Nancy were there too, standing near the boards, out of view of the cameras. Then, as more photos were being taken, all of a sudden Nancy, as Scotty puts it, "just decided to get in the picture," and there she is, propped up on the ice, Scotty's arm around her.

As the celebrations moved from the ice to the dressing room, Scotty told those who needed to know what they already knew—that this was his final game. "The first person I told was Ken Holland," he said, "I also mentioned it to a couple of the players, Yzerman and Shanahan. Then I told Mike Ilitch at the bench. He said, 'I understand.'" But what Ilitch didn't understand at that moment was the importance of the promise he had made to Scotty nine years earlier, something that Scotty remembered like it was yesterday: "Whenever I wanted to stop coaching," he said, "I could stay on."

Scotty was retiring as coach. He wasn't retiring from hockey.

Players and coaches think they retire when a season ends and they announce they are leaving. They don't. They retire when the next training camp begins and they're not there. Scotty *was* there at that next camp in Traverse City, Michigan, the following September, but he wasn't on the ice, he wasn't behind the bench, and when camp ended, he and Suella were back in Buffalo.

Then the season began. And when it did, he was like a swallow in Capistrano—he did what he had always done. He watched games, because it was his job as special consultant for the Wings, and because that's what he had done every fall, winter, and spring of his life, and mostly because that's what he wanted to do, what still absorbed him, what he loved to do. "I went and watched some junior games for the team, and a little bit of college hockey," he says. "I watched the farm team a few times, but I didn't have to spend much time in Detroit, not until the playoffs, and even then I didn't watch the Wings as much as I did other teams—the teams they might meet."

When he could see a break of games in his schedule, he would fly to Florida for a few days, and then fly back for a game he thought he needed to see. "I didn't really move to Florida full time in the winter until about 2005. Then I decided I wanted to travel a little less. And that's when I started to watch the Lightning; I'd go to their games. I'd watch hockey on TV at night. There were so many games on all the time."

But he was no longer a coach. The decisions he made about the team or any of the players had no urgency about them. He had no skin in the game, and this was now the way it was and always would be. But just because he wasn't behind the bench anymore didn't mean he had to stop watching as a coach, or stop thinking, scheming, looking for an edge, for something new, imagining a way to get himself one step ahead of the other guy. Why would he? In fact, why couldn't he watch, and look for, and see even more—and think and scheme even better?

So he started arriving early at the Lightning games, and on his way to the media room, or when he was in line to eat, he stopped to talk to anyone who stopped to talk with him—because who knows what he might pick up, and because hockey guys love to talk. He didn't hold court. He didn't pronounce. He was a rink rat, just like them, only with nine Stanley Cup rings.

In many ways, they wish he *would* pronounce. They want to be able to tell others that they've just talked to Scotty Bowman, and to say what Scotty Bowman told them—from God's lips to their own ears. But Scotty doesn't pronounce. Pronouncing would mean knowing something now and forever, and he doesn't know anything forever, and doesn't want to. He knows there are no timeless strategies. A truly great player is truly great, but that doesn't mean what he did then or does now is what everyone should do. Because otherwise what would be the point of watching? Playing? Coaching?

Even some things he talks about with what sounds like absolute certainty come with their own little caveats. Faceoffs, for example. He always somehow brings up faceoffs. Yzerman scored all these goals *and* "he was a good faceoff guy." Fedorov, *and* he was a good faceoff guy. And Béliveau, and Trottier, and Ted Kennedy. Faceoffs *are* important, but there aren't as many of them now, with fewer clean saves by the goalies, fewer icings, and—with Toe Blake smiling in his grave—fewer offsides. Faceoffs matter because possession matters, and now the focus is on other ways to get possession—and keep it. So, faceoffs, he'll have to think about that more.

And while coaching is still about getting the right players on the ice, the shifts are so short you can't match lines, so—for a few seconds, at least—maybe *everybody* has to be the right player. Maybe that's how you need to coach now. He'll have to think about that too.

And the most important player on the ice now, maybe it's not the centre. It was always the centre because only the centre went everywhere on the ice. Now it's the defenceman who does, and he's on the ice a lot more minutes of the game. So he'll think about that too, and find a way to bring it up with his buddies when they call him in the morning or when he sees them at the Lightning game at night.

And analytics. He knows there is something to it. It's information, it's watching, it's seeing something, it's thinking about it, it's figuring out what it might mean. It's what he's been doing all his life. What Toe Blake did on those Friday afternoons in his office when he spread out those stats sheets—and there weren't many of them—on his desk. Looking for something, looking for what is there, looking for what he's missing. Neither he nor Scotty had the electronic tools and staffs of analysts that coaches have today. And the information he gets now after every period of every Blackhawks game matters. He just wonders why all those people who all of those years in the past knew nothing because they had never played the game at the highest level—those stats guys—now know everything precisely because they didn't, because their minds haven't been misdirected and poisoned by what they saw and what they learned. He'll have to think about that some more.

Scotty doesn't need the comfort most experts do of knowing once and forever, of always being right and never being wrong. Much more interesting to him is seeing something new—what he doesn't know— then trying to figure out what that means and what to do. It requires of him an ability to make himself an expert again, and again, and again. Even when sometimes the result of all this thinking is some idea that actually isn't very interesting—or even doesn't make much sense—and that does happen. *What do you think about putting in a ringette line, at the top of the faceoff circles, so you can't pass all the way from your end boards to the far blue line? So you have to work your way up the ice a bit, and also create a forecheck?* Well, maybe.

But more important than any of his ideas is that, at age 86, he still has them.

"I like to watch the warm-up," he says. "You see who's playing, and in the drills you see who's playing with who. I write the lines down, [and] you see the teams start the game that way and if they change, you notice the difference and you wonder why. It used to be that everybody was trying to match up their lines, but now they don't do it as much because of the speed of the game and players can't stay on as long. Now they only match on whistles, and at home when they have the last change." As a result, offensive players, freed from their defensive shadows, should get more chances. They should score more goals. But until recently, that hasn't happened.

"I'd like to see the stats now compared to before they did all these rule changes, taking out the centre line and making the end zones bigger. That long stretch pass to the far blue line, they brought that in as an offensive move because if you can get the puck to the guy moving up the middle he might get a breakaway. But then the defencemen in the offensive zone have to have in the back of their minds that somebody might get behind them. Then one of them for sure, maybe both, has to bail out and leave the offensive zone. So for the team trying to make the long pass, their guy isn't open, so they don't gain any offence, and for the team in the offensive end, with their defencemen now back in the neutral zone, it has no pack of players going after the puck, so they don't have any effective forecheck." The result: no offence either way.

"When I first started to coach, and later too, you would cram your opponent into their own end. They couldn't get out, and there would be a turnover. Philadelphia was the best example. They'd come up the ice and throw the puck into the corner and that wing would come tearing in, and with their defence pinching, when they were on their game with a heavy forecheck, you might not recover. It was the same in Boston and Chicago [with their small ice surfaces]. I really think the bigger end zone now has curtailed the ability of a team to forecheck. The thinking of the league was to create extra room for the attack, but they didn't take into consideration that the defensive team now also has more room to manoeuvre around, to spread out."

A few years ago, he was at a Lightning game and saw his former great Red Wings defenceman, Nicklas Lidström, and he tried his thinking out on him. "Nick was saying how it's not very difficult to play defensively now. The end zone is so big that teams don't forecheck you. Your defensive partner spreads out to the side, and you pass to him. If you can't get the puck to him, you look up the middle and try that pass all the way to the far blue line. If there's any risk, you just fire it up the side, and you've got the time to do it. I go to a lot of games now where there's not a lot of offence until there's a power play."

Scotty doesn't say this as if it's wrong. He's a coach; there's no such thing as "right" or "wrong." It's the results—whether something works or not. If it doesn't work, you do something else. His answer, more often now, relates to the defence. Just as Sam loved the guy who "lights the light," Scotty loves defencemen. They play the wild-card position on every team. They defend, but they also set the offence in motion. They are the extra guy, the *three* of a three-on-two, the *four* of a four-on-three, that an opponent doesn't always expect and can't cover. They are the game changers. And because they can pick their spots and jump into the play one moment and not the next, they don't get tired as fast as forwards do and can play up to 26 minutes a game—not just 18. So, as an opposing coach, if defencemen are the game changers, Scotty thinks, you get on them so they can't change the game. So, when he watches, he wonders: *Why don't these coaches do that?* And why does the league make it so easy for even an average defenceman, with all this space and time, to do what only special ones like Lidström and his own Big Three should be able to do? But while these are questions that should be puzzled over, and considered and reconsidered, he's not laying blame on anyone. He's not interested in wallowing in the wonderfulness of his own time, and finding unwatchable what seems incomprehensible to him. Instead, Scotty watches, trying to comprehend what's there and trying to find an answer better and faster than anyone else—just as he always did. Just as they should do.

There's something else that he really thinks about—forwards blocking shots. When he was growing up, even when he was in his twenties, Bob Goldham blocked shots. So did Al Arbour. Scotty can't even imagine the Rocket blocking shots, or Howe, or Esposito, or Lafleur, or Gretzky, or Lemieux. It's not that forwards are braver now; it's because when the NHL lockout ended in 2005, and new penalties for obstruction were introduced and a bigger end zone was created, it became easier "for good puck handlers to beat their checkers one-on-one." And, as Scotty says, "You can't have skilled guys walking out of the corners, so coaches pulled their forwards back from near the blue line to the scoring area, which, with the goaltending equipment being so big, has shrunk and now is only right in front of the net." If league officials were going to expand the zone, coaches would shrink it themselves. The result: a defending team's forwards aren't close enough to their opponent's point men to intercept the passes intended for them, or to reach out their sticks to deflect their shots, so they have to throw their bodies in front of these shots, which means more injuries and which eliminates the quick breakout attack.

What if the blue line were moved in a few feet? Scotty wonders. Would the point shot itself be more dangerous—and not just for the screens, deflections, and rebounds it creates? Would the defending forwards have to play out higher? Would more quick breaks be more possible? Or what if the goal line was moved further from the boards?

"I talked to a guy at a Lightning game"—something that Scotty says a lot—"and he does analytics for three or four teams. He's quite a sharp guy and he's always asking me questions. He's trying to figure out the relative strength of teams. He wants to eliminate the lucky goal from his analytics, the one that the goalie doesn't see, or deflects off somebody, or misses the net but hits a defenceman's skate and goes in. He wants to take the luck part out of his equation for scoring chances and goals. He wants to get it down to how many legit scoring chances there are in a game." The ones that come, as Scotty puts it, "from what they call the 'home-plate area'"—the triangle-shaped space that runs between the top of the faceoff circles and diagonally to the net. "He told me, I forget the exact number, but the percentage of goals scored in that area is so high. It's where all the goals are scored from."

But if what this analytics guy says is true, doesn't this mean that the actual "legit" chances *are* the lucky ones, and therefore the ones you *shouldn't* factor out but instead should plan for? For Scotty as a coach to coach for? And he also knows that if one coach decides to do things this way, by eight o'clock the next night, 15 more will be doing the same, and then a few hours after that 15 more, depending on time zones, because they'll have seen something on the NHL Network, or one of their assistants will, and they'll have to answer questions from their GMs and the media later the following day if they don't.

Scotty has had to learn, and then un-learn, and then learn again many times in his career. And while learning isn't easy, un-learning is far harder. But he knows that nothing is new for long. There is no final edge. You have to keep coming up with your own next edge, and you can't do that if you think you know something forever, and you can't do that with information that already exists. You've got to create new information yourself. That's the scary part for most, but for him that's the fun part, because that comes from watching and thinking, and listening to the analytics guy at the Lightning game. His feet are no longer behind the bench, but his mind has never left.

Between all these games, life has gone on. The kids have gotten older, finished college, and are off on their own, with their own lives to live and their own families. Scotty and Suella have grandkids. David is well settled into his group home in Buffalo. He has people he sees, and who see him, every day. He has a very special doctor, Dr. Jeff Steinig, who when something isn't right—and with David's condition, even something small can become life-and-death very quickly—has always been there. He knows David, and while David cannot speak, Dr. Steinig understands him, so "when he goes into surgery," which he often does, "we don't have much concern," says Scotty. "He treats David like his own son." David is now 47.

Buffalo has remained home for Scotty and Suella; it was even home when Scotty was in Detroit or on the road for nine months a year. In a life that has felt always in motion, having one place that doesn't move and has never changed has been important for all of them. It is still their home, even though they now spend seven months a year in Florida. And right outside their back door, where their lawn ends, the golf course begins. Scotty has shot three holes-in-one there—"in '87, '88, and '89," he laughs, "the three years I wasn't coaching"— and he plays as often as he can. But as much as he likes to play, he likes to watch too. He has gone to many of the big tournaments on the pro tour. "It's a great way to walk," he says, "but the crowds are so big." So some years ago he decided to take up a friend's offer. "He's the head scorekeeper for some of the USGA events and he invited me to be a 'walking scorekeeper,' that's what they call it, for the final round of the 2000 U.S. Open at Pebble Beach. You get assigned to a golfer, and you walk around with him. You're within ten yards, maybe even three or four sometimes, and you've got to keep moving. When the last putt goes in on each hole, you have to write the player's score on a piece of paper and then tear it off and give it to a person there at the green—it's different now with the technology—but then you have to hustle to the next tee because the marshals close off access pretty fast." The golfer he was assigned to was Tiger Woods.

Woods began the round with a 10-shot lead and ended it with a 15-shot victory, the biggest margin in grand-slam golf history. "I walked the whole 18 holes with him," he says. Scotty, 66, an eight-time Stanley Cup winner; Woods, 24, about to win his third major title. They had met once before, briefly—a year earlier at *Sports Illustrated*'s 20th Century Sports Awards at Madison Square Garden.

When the round was over that day, Scotty remembers, "You go into this little scoring trailer. Tiger was sitting in front of me. He signed his scorecard, then turned around to get up, and he saw me. He said, 'Scotty, what are you doing here?' He didn't know I was his scorekeeper. I had been scoring for, like, four and a half hours."

Today, Woods's 15-shot win is considered the greatest performance in golf history (his Masters win in 2019, the greatest comeback). But what struck Scotty most about it? His power, the amazing precision of his iron shots to the green, his steely-nerved putting? "He was so focused," Scotty says. "He doesn't look at the crowd, the only person he ever looked at was his caddy. I've never seen anybody so focused."

Scotty continued to be a walking scorekeeper for some years after. "I went over to St. Andrews [in Scotland] when Jack Nicklaus played his last game." It was the 2005 British Open. "It was the second day; he didn't make the cut. I scored his last game." Nicklaus birdied his final hole. He was 65; Scotty was 71. He also went to Dayton, Ohio, later that same year. "Arnold Palmer was playing his final U.S. Senior Open and I scored his last game too. I got to see golf at its best." It was a chance for him to watch up close, just as he had done on his lunch breaks at the Forum, watching Dick Irvin Sr., Toe Blake, the Rocket, and Béliveau; just as he has done all his life.

When Scotty stopped coaching in 2002, it seemed as if everything would change, but not much did. Then, in 2008, Stan—by this time the Blackhawks' assistant general manager—suffered a recurrence of Hodgkin's lymphoma. After thinking about it a lot, and talking to Suella, Scotty decided to see Mike Ilitch and ask him if it was all right if he left the Red Wings and joined Chicago. Scotty was almost 75 years old; he had been with the Wings for 15 years. Ilitch said to him: "This is no decision at all. It's a no-brainer. You have to go to help him."

At that moment, Scotty's job title changed from *Special Consultant* to *Senior Advisor, Hockey Operations*, but his life didn't.

CHAPTER SEVENTEEN
Chicago Blackhawks 2014–15

Jonathan Toews and Patrick Kane, both first-round picks, joined the Blackhawks in 2007. Kane, the first pick overall, would win the Calder Trophy as the league's rookie of the year. Toews, the third overall selection the year before, finished third in the voting. Just before the start of that season, in September, the Blackhawks' long-time owner, Bill Wirtz, died and was succeeded by his son Rocky. Over many decades, Bill Wirtz had managed to alienate, then anger, Chicago fans and media with his determination to re-fight every lost cause—the local TV blackout of the team's home games, the WHA, higher player salaries—to demonstrate his own rightness, no matter what anyone thought. In doing so, he had only weakened the franchise. The team hadn't won the Stanley Cup since 1961, and had made the playoffs only once in the previous nine seasons.

Toews and Kane offered hope. Rocky Wirtz, at least until he showed otherwise, offered a respite from despair. The Blackhawks missed the playoffs in Toews and Kane's rookie year but had a winning record for only the second time in 11 seasons. Then, in October 2008, four games into the following year, former Blackhawks star Denis Savard was fired and replaced as coach by Joel Quenneville. With Toews, Kane, Rocky Wirtz, and Quenneville, the four core pieces that would result in three Cups for the Blackhawks in the next seven years were in place.

Also in the team's favour—the league was in transition. The best of the Wings' teams had passed, and so too had those of Colorado, New Jersey, and Dallas; and the best of the Penguins and Kings was yet to come. The 2004–05 lockout had produced a salary cap, and the big-spending teams were still trying to sort out its implications. There was now also a shootout, and every game that was tied at the end of regulation time had a two-point winner and a one-point loser. What this meant for coaches and GMs for their in-game strategy and roster decisions wasn't yet clear.

Amidst these uncertain times, the Blackhawks had a solid coach, a solid owner, a goal scorer, an on-ice leader mature far beyond his years, and a city of passionate fans ready to explode at any excuse. And Scotty, the Blackhawks' new "Senior Advisor, Hockey Operations," was there to see this happen.

In this remaking of the Blackhawks, if the team had one indispensable player, "It would be Toews," Scotty says. "He was solid all the way through. He was consistent. He was ultra-competitive. He's got that work ethic. He's very conscientious. He plays as hard without the puck as he does with it. He'll chase guys down. He'll forecheck. He's very good at faceoffs. He's physically strong. Others might be better in certain areas, but not overall, not when you look at everything. And he judges his game by *every* standard, not just his points. He's not the biggest offensive threat, but in crunch time he can make the big individual play. And if you're his teammate, it's hard to slack off when you have a guy who does everything at such a high level. He prides himself in who he is, in the reputation he has, and he lives up to that reputation."

In many ways, Toews is like Steve Yzerman, Scotty's captain in Detroit, but Yzerman—a more dynamic player—was needed by the Wings in the first decade of his career to play a bigger offensive role. It took Scotty's arrival, Yzerman's bad knees, and their heart-to-heart talk to reorient him towards his most impactful role. Toews had taken on that role with the Blackhawks almost from the day he arrived. He was named the team's captain at age 20. He was the captain of the Stanley

Cup champion Chicago Blackhawks at 22. "Captain Serious." Some nicknames are perfect.

Toews's father is an electrician from Winnipeg; his mother, the manager of a credit union, is from Sainte-Marie, a small town in the Beauce region south of Quebec City. In Scotty's first season in Montreal, the Canadiens played an intrasquad game in Saint-Georges, only 50 kilometres away. Toews's mother might even have been there. "His mother is really a French Canadian," Scotty relates. "Even when she's on the Blackhawks' parent-son trips, she always wants to speak French. [Jonathan] grew up speaking French to her. He's fully bilingual. It's really something."

Kane is different. He grew up a rink-smart kid in Buffalo. Always the most talented, the quickest, the best; always able to find a way out of every situation. A kid that was going to be great, if something didn't happen along the way. Unlike Toews, a kid you worried about and worried for.

The two of them arrived on the Blackhawks together, and that was important. Neither had a head start, neither had an upper hand, both could see how good the other guy was with their own eyes. And both could imagine, right from the beginning, where all this might go: a team that was getting better and better, and fans that were getting more and more excited. The year before Toews and Kane arrived, the Blackhawks averaged 12,727 fans in the 19,717-seat United Center—second-lowest in the league, ahead of only St. Louis. In their first season, attendance rose to 16,814, 19th in the 30-team NHL; and the next year to 22,247, tops in the league. An arena two-thirds full sounds empty; an arena jammed to capacity and beyond sounds like 50,000. And Toews and Kane were still only 19.

They came to the team completely as advertised—something that almost never happens. Toews, a bona fide third overall pick, not just special for year one, but for year two and three and every imaginable year after that—and, in his case, for every game and every shift as well. And Kane, a true first overall pick, with such brilliant, game-breaking skills. With the two of them together, Mr. Reliable and Mr. Excitement, the Blackhawks had no regrets—there was no looking back, only looking forward. The two of them competed against each other, of course they did, but they had so many other more important things to compete *for*—that were right there in front of them, that were excitingly, thrillingly in their grasp. They seemed right from the beginning to know that they needed each other, and that there was room for both of them. Toews could be the Toews he wanted to be; Kane could be Kane. Neither would get in the other's way.

And Toews—unmistakeably, indisputably—was the captain because he was born a captain. And Kane—unmistakably, indisputably—wasn't, and didn't want to be. "[Toews] took his captain's job pretty seriously," Scotty says, much in the way he describes Yzerman. "He doesn't shy away from it. The other players lean on him, and as a coach, you run a lot of stuff through him." Coaches know that every player, even a captain, looks for his own edge—something a little more and a little better for themselves. Something they can take advantage of. Even if they don't initially, even if it seems unthinkably contrary to their character, circumstances can change, the player can change. Everyone has their weakening point. So coaches are wary. But with Toews, Scotty relates, "He was so committed to the team and making it better that they didn't worry."

Teams were different in the post-lockout era. The salary cap, part of the 2005 NHL–NHLPA settlement, meant that a big-money team could only spend so much and a small-money team could only spend so little—and the gap between the two of them wasn't that great. Any additional money a team wanted to expend to gain a competitive advantage had to go towards coaches, scouts, trainers, training facilities; the cheap-money stuff that wasn't subject to the cap. The legendary diamond-in-the-rough player hidden away in Nunavut, Norway, or North Carolina, that only your own bird dog/local biscuit salesman guy saw—and whose name was announced out of the blue as your sixth-round pick on draft day—doesn't exist anymore. Everybody has seen everybody. Nor does that one great super-scout exist who sees what no one else sees, or that GM, rendered dumb as a rock by desperate circumstances, that is ready to be fleeced. Even Sam would have a harder time in this NHL.

The competitive edges that remain are small; the competitive differences on the ice are almost non-existent. Not only can any team beat any other on any given night, but in any given week or month and nearly any year as well. More than half of the NHL's teams—16—make the playoffs. Every season begins with a third of them seemingly certain to make the playoffs, another third certain not to, and a final third that might go either way. And every season ends with some of those sure things—sure to make it, or sure not to—swapping places. Better teams now aren't that much better than worse teams. A 60-minute game, more often than not, separates a slightly superior team from a slightly inferior one, but a 4-on-4 (now a 3-on-3) overtime, or a shootout, is a crapshoot. Teams play the regular season only a few points apart. Injuries or slumps at the wrong time can turn everything upside down fast. No team is good enough to run away and hide.

When the Wings and Canadiens won the Stanley Cup nearly every year during the 1950s, they dominated nearly every regular season too. The Leafs in the early 1960s were different—their players were too old to dominate every night but were able to rise to a Cup-winning level over the short two rounds and four short weeks of the playoffs. Then, during the next 25 years, the season-long dominant teams returned: the Canadiens, then the Islanders and Oilers. They didn't finish first every year—there were a lot more teams in the league by this time—but they came close. And the coaches pushed the idea, and their players bought it, that every game in November and February was both two points in the standings for then, and a message delivered for later: beat the other guy now and he won't believe he can beat you when it counts. And he won't beat you. And he didn't. During the 1990s and early 2000s, every year that Detroit, Colorado, New Jersey, and Dallas won Cups, they were also at or near the top of the league from October to April.

As competitive and financial advantages and disadvantages have receded, it has become harder to dominate. To dominate one year meant you had to dominate for eight months, no let-up, then begin the next season four months later and dominate for the next eight months after that, no let-up. And now with all the extra hours of training during the season and the extra weeks and months of training during the off-season, no letting up is harder. So why play that way? Why does a message in November matter in June? Why not just deliver it in June? And does finishing higher in the standings and getting home-ice advantage really make a difference? Is there truly such a thing as home-ice advantage now, what with every team flying on luxury charters, staying in luxury hotels, and playing in arenas all of which are 200 by 85 feet? Even if home ice does matter a little, is it worth all the grinding and never letting up to get it?

So if super-teams aren't possible any longer, why try to create one? If super-players *are* possible, why not get a few, manage their contracts, and put together a Cup-contending team around them?

That's what Chicago did. And if you have that right core of players, the best in every other player has a chance to emerge, and the worst can be hidden away. For the Blackhawks, that meant a mid-level pick like Dave Bolland can turn into a useful player; an end-of-draft selection like Dustin Byfuglien, 245th overall, can become an important piece; a sideways trade like that for Patrick Sharp can turn into something special; and a free agent signing like Marián Hossa can put you over the top. And when the best in these support players begins to emerge, and they can feel themselves getting better, they are infused with such excitement that they get even better, and then better still, until they can't work hard enough, try hard enough, or do enough for their teammates, their coaches, and their team, and feel like they are just going to explode. The right core is the rising tide that raises all ships. And as these mid-level players get better, the players who always had a bigger upside begin to show that too, and become stars. A Cup-contending team needs surprises to become a Cup winner.

Duncan Keith was a second-round pick, 54th overall, in the 2003 draft. He had bounced between Tier II junior and Michigan State, then major junior and the AHL, before finally arriving in Chicago for the 2005–06 season. He was 22. Brent Seabrook also joined the team that season, two years younger and a first-round selection, 14th overall. Seabrook finished 13th in the Calder voting that year; Keith received no votes at all. The two of them became regulars on Blackhawk teams that missed the playoffs in their first few years, but then they and the team got better. As a defence pair, they would play more than 1,000 games together (a league record) and average close to 25 minutes a game (Keith, slightly more)—the tough minutes, against the other teams' best players, on penalty kills, at a game's most decisive moments—and even more in the playoffs. By doing so, this allowed the other four defencemen to be matched up against only those they could play against and succeed against—mostly third and fourth liners, in routine, non-decisive moments—and, in doing so, feel the satisfaction of their own success and of the team's, and succeed even more.

In 2009–10, the Blackhawks became one year better at what they were already becoming. They scored a few more goals, allowed a few less, and earned a few more points. The year before, they had made the playoffs for the first time in six seasons and had gone to the conference finals. This season, the players were becoming more certain of themselves and of each other. Hossa, a smart, two-way veteran, was signed as a free agent. Keith broke through, going from 44 points to 69 during the regular season and winning the Norris Trophy as the league's best defenceman. In the playoffs, the Blackhawks didn't blow anybody away—that's not how they played—not even San Jose, whom they swept in the third round. They beat Nashville and Vancouver each in six hard-fought games, before defeating the Sharks, then faced the Flyers in the final. It didn't hurt that by this time the Capitals, who had won the regular season, had crashed out in the opening round against the Canadiens. It also didn't hurt that, for the Blackhawks, unexpected players emerged. That's what happens with good, solid, winning teams.

Sharp, who had scored 25 goals during the regular season, scored 11 in the playoffs, co-leading the team alongside the immense, unmissable, sometime-defenceman, sometime-forward Dustin Byfuglien, who also led *all* players during the entire playoffs with five game-winning goals. Antti Niemi gave the team good-enough—and better-than-expected— goaltending. Kane did the expected and found space, but did so on the more tightly congested, highly contested playoff ice, to score at important moments. And Keith found even more in himself. Stretched by the circumstances of the playoffs and by his own talent, he averaged more than 28 minutes of ice time a game.

Then there was Toews. Captain Serious. Playoffs are made for players like him, and he is made for the playoffs. You can't win the Cup with one great game or series or week or month. You win by creating little edges and being unrelentingly slightly better than your opponent. Toews is about every shift, about every faceoff; his opponent is about almost every shift and almost every faceoff. Toews doesn't blow you away, he wears you down. He's not a game changer, he's a game shifter. He goes onto the ice, and when he leaves it 45 seconds later, the chaos he inherited is a little less chaotic; the offensive threat his team was generating is a little more threatening; its secure lead a little more secure; the game a little more winnable. Every night, every week, every month, every round. He makes the punishing test of the playoffs a little less discouraging at discouraging moments, a little easier, a little more likely to survive—and win.

He was awarded the Conn Smythe Trophy as the playoffs' most valuable player. The Blackhawks were Stanley Cup champions, for the first time in 49 years—for only the second time in 72 years. It was Stan's first Cup.

Four months later, the Blackhawks were back at it again. They got off to a mediocre start, but that was all right, they were the Stanley Cup champions; then they drifted some more, and some more, and almost missed the playoffs, finishing eighth in the Western Conference. But that was all right too; they were a team made for the playoffs. Then they lost to the Canucks in the first round. That was not all right. But now they had six months off, they would be rested and ready, they had learned their lesson. And then they lost in the first round again, this time to the Coyotes. Now they had *really* learned their lesson, and they were still young, and with the NHL lockout not ending until mid-January that next season, they had nine months, from April 23, 2012, to January 19, 2013, to get themselves really, really ready—and they did, winning 21 of their first 24 games, their only three losses coming in shootouts. In the first round, they beat Minnesota; in the next series they fell behind Detroit three games to one, then won three in a row, the seventh game in overtime, to face the Stanley Cup winners from each of the previous two seasons—L.A. and Boston—in the final two rounds. This year, goalie Corey Crawford was the breakthrough player the Blackhawks needed.

Crawford had been a solid second-round pick, 52nd overall, in the 2003 draft. He had followed his four solid years in junior with five solid years in the AHL on Chicago's top farm team, yet had never been considered good enough to displace the big team's goalies: the veteran, often-injured Nikolai Khabibulin, then Patrick Lalime, Antti Niemi, and Cristobal Huet. Finally, in 2010–11, at age 26, he became a regular, yet still the Blackhawks hedged their bets—pairing him first with Marty Turco, then Ray Emery. Crawford wasn't as good as the league's best goalies, and everyone knew it. He wasn't as good as the Bruins' Tim Thomas or the Kings' Jonathan Quick, who had led their teams to Cup wins the previous two years. Even in this shortened 2012–13 season, Crawford played only two-thirds of the games.

Having beaten Minnesota and Detroit in the opening rounds, he had to go head-to-head with Quick. Chicago won. Then it was the turn of the Bruins and Tuukka Rask—who the following year would win the Vezina Trophy as the league's top goalie. Crawford played at least as well as Rask and Quick, and in doing so—instead of representing the disadvantage he was expected to be—he gave the Blackhawks an immense boost. More excitement. And Chicago won again. The NHL had had seven straight one-and-done Cup winners after the lockout year of 2004–05. The Blackhawks were the first team to win twice.

The next season, Chicago drifted back into the competitive mix, one of five or six teams that might win—or might lose. They had learned their lesson a few years earlier and made it comfortably into the playoffs, then went to the conference finals—where they lost to L.A., who became the post-lockout league's second double Cup winner. It was a disappointing end of season for the Blackhawks, but it was no reason for recriminations. The core of Chicago's players was still strong and young. There was no talk of "blowing up" the team to take a fresh run at a next stretch of Cup wins. Toews and Kane were still only 26 and 25, Keith and Seabrook were 30 and 29—not likely to get better but not yet ready to get worse—and Crawford, at 29, was a late bloomer. The Blackhawks fans were still packing the United Center. The Cubs and White Sox would both finish the year with 73–89 records, the Bears would go 5–11, the Bulls had lost in the first round of the NBA playoffs. The Blackhawks were still Chicago's exciting success story, and they were still good enough to win. And which other NHL team was definitively better? For Chicago, in this post-salary-cap era, it would be less about blowing up the team entirely than blowing up its middle. The mid-level players that had ridden the success of the team to salaries too high to fit under the cap had to be culled. Stan Bowman had managed this challenge to a second Cup win. He would just have to do it again.

As always, behind the bench was Quenneville. He was a steady, unspectacular coach for a steady, unspectacular team. Someone who as a player had been good enough to spend 12 years in the league but had never been good enough to take anything for granted; who had learned that if you got yourself ready, worked hard, didn't let up, and didn't think you were more or less than you were—if you just hung in—you had a chance. And with that chance, then it was up to you to pull it off.

He coached the same way, and in more than 16 NHL seasons he missed the playoffs only once. He never expected anything easy; he had been trained for struggle and was good at it. In Chicago, he had helped the Blackhawks to find a way to win after losing for five decades, and then to get through the two losing seasons that followed, and to win again.

It was this resilience that saw the Blackhawks through to their third Cup win, in 2014–15.

Scotty had watched this team for seven years—sometimes live, most often on TV. He went every year to training camp, and when the team hit the road for its pre-season games he watched their Rockford farm team before heading back to Buffalo. He and Suella would sometimes go to Chicago for Christmas to see Stan and his family, and Bob, and he would watch some games. Twice he had gone on the team's "parent-child" trips with his kids; twice with two of his grandkids.

For the playoffs, he and a Chicago scout, Don Lever, would watch first- and second-round games involving teams the Blackhawks might play in later series. Lever watched one team, Scotty the other. Then, if Chicago advanced, Lever would send Quenneville and the players a report of what he and Scotty had seen. During the regular season, Scotty also talked to the team's head of pro scouting, Ryan Stewart, maybe once a week, about players he had seen, or ones he knew the team had interest in. And always there were the analytics. After every period of every Blackhawks game, they were there on his iPad—the action of the previous 20 minutes laid out in numbers and comparatives. It was "sometimes irrelevant stuff," Scotty says, but every so often it was something that made him think, that found its way into his neurons, caused unknowable havoc, and came out as *something*. Then, every two weeks or so, Stan would call and they would talk. Maybe the team was thinking of making a move. Maybe Scotty had a thought to add.

He almost never spoke to Quenneville or the other coaches. That was Stan's job, and the coaches knew where to find him if they wanted to talk. He knew Quenneville a little—first and mostly as a player. "He was a defensive defenceman," Scotty recalls. "He didn't have a lot of offensive ability so he stayed back. He used to play on the edge, he wasn't easy to play against, he thought defence all the time. As a coach, he had some pretty good teams in St. Louis. He had [Al] MacInnis and [Chris] Pronger. Pronger was more of a two-way defenceman, MacInnis was an offensive threat."

As Scotty did, as all winning coaches do, "[Quenneville] coached the way he did because of what he had." In Chicago, he knew they could score, but they couldn't overwhelm. He knew they could defend, but they couldn't smother. "He wants them to play as tight as they can," Scotty explains. "The longer a game goes being real tight is to their advantage. If they can survive, they know they can score."

Other teams seemed more likely winners in that 2014–15 season: St. Louis, finally; Washington, always; Nashville, for the first time; Anaheim or Pittsburgh, again. The Blackhawks finished an irrelevant 7th during the regular season. In the voting for the league's all-stars, Kane finished 4th and Hossa 11th among right wingers; Toews was 7th among centres; Keith was 7th and Niklas Hjalmarsson 27th among defencemen; and Crawford, despite the team allowing the second-fewest goals in the league, was 10th among goalies. But it turned out that this very imperfect season made the Blackhawks even more ready for what was ahead.

The Western Conference was stronger than the Eastern Conference that year, and its Central Division was the strongest division in the league. As its top three teams, St. Louis, Nashville, and Chicago, made the playoffs, and Minnesota and Winnipeg, also in the division, qualified as the conference's two wild-card teams. Even Dallas and Colorado, the division's other two teams, recorded 90 points or more, but they missed the playoffs. Each team played their divisional rivals a combined 29 times during the regular season, and in the Central Division, with no easy nights off, the Blackhawks had only a 15–14 record.

In the opening round of the playoffs, Chicago had to face the Predators. The first game was in Nashville, and Scotty was there. "[The Blackhawks] really got outplayed and Crawford let in three goals in the first period," he recalls. "So they brought in [Scott] Darling and he played a hell of a game, and Chicago won in double overtime. Then they got beaten badly, 6–2, in the second game."

Returning to Chicago, the Blackhawks won both games, the second on Seabrook's goal in triple overtime. But Nashville came back and won at home, riding the blowing-the-roof-off energy of its fans. Game 6 was in Chicago. Nashville scored two quick goals, and before the 12-minute mark of the first period led the Blackhawks, 3–1. Quenneville removed Darling and put in Crawford, who shut out the Predators the rest of the game. Toews and Kane scored, then Keith late in the third period, and the Blackhawks won the series.

Chicago then swept Minnesota in the second round, but, as Scotty recalls, it wasn't easy. "Minnesota played a really good series. Goaltending was a big difference. Crawford was outstanding." Anaheim was next. The Ducks had won the Western Conference regular season, yet in the two previous years, they had gone out of the playoffs in a seven-game series, first to Detroit and then to L.A. This series with Chicago also went seven games, the teams splitting the first four games—each winning and losing at home, the first Blackhawks victory in triple overtime, the second in double overtime. Back home in Anaheim, the Ducks went ahead, 4–2, and were closing out Game 5 when Toews scored twice late in the third period, at 18:10 and 19:22, to force overtime. The Ducks won the game, but two nights later Chicago won again to tie the series. Game 7 was in Anaheim. By midway through the first period the Blackhawks were ahead, 2–0, both goals scored by Toews; by midway through the second it was 4–0, and the game was over. The Blackhawks were headed back to the Stanley Cup final, this time against Tampa Bay.

"All the games in the [Chicago–Tampa Bay] series were decided by one goal, except the last one," Scotty says. "In that game, there was no score with three minutes to go in the second period, then Keith scored. It was 1–0 all the way through the third, and Tampa was all over [Chicago], then Kane scored with five minutes to go. Crawford was outstanding. In the six games of the series, Chicago only scored 13 goals, Tampa 10. Not very many."

The Blackhawks had won the Cup because they did what they do best: they survived the worst moments, and scored when they needed to. And other things that you can't strategize or plan for had also fallen their way. The Blackhawks began their run of success in 2007–08 as a young team. By 2014–15 they were old—especially their defence. Keith was 31 and Seabrook 29; in their next pairing, Hjalmarsson was 27 and Johnny Oduya 33; and of their other regulars, Kimmo Timonen was 39 and Michal Rozsíval 36. Crawford was 30.

In four rounds of playoffs, veteran players can wear out. They get injured more often; they get tired. Winning a long, desperately contested series moves a team ahead, but also sets it back, especially an aging team. "The Blackhawks got a good break in round two by sweeping Minnesota," Scotty explains. "That gave them a good rest, and it was well timed because they then had to go against Anaheim, the conference champion, and start on the road. They needed everything they had in those seven games, and the final against Tampa could easily have gone seven too."

Fortunate for the Blackhawks was that "they basically got by using four and a half defencemen. The team had to play only 23 games [in the playoffs], but five of them were in overtime—[including] two in double overtime and two in triple. But their four defencemen never missed a game, *ohmygawd* not one, and their top seven or eight forwards played every game. I don't know how they got through the playoffs with the defence they had. It's just amazing they could play 23 games, and play a lot of hockey, and use only four guys, and a fifth a little bit."

Seabrook averaged 26:17 a game, Hjalmarsson 26:02, Oduya 24:45, and Keith, who, like Seabrook, also played on power plays and penalty kills, 31:07 a game! He won the Conn Smythe Trophy as the playoffs' most valuable player. As for the forwards, "Toews, Kane, and Hossa, and then Sharp, [Brandon] Saad and [Brad] Richards, they all played pretty regular, but after them, not many minutes. Not at very important times." For both the forwards and defence, "It was a very short bench."

Chicago's goaltending "was also very good after Crawford got back in the net," Scotty recalls. "He seemed to play better as the series went on, and in the key games he was outstanding." Scotty travelled with the team and saw every one of their playoff games. "They were just an experienced team," he explains, "and they were experienced in the playoffs. They had won twice before, in '10 and '13. The core guys knew they were core guys, and the other guys just sort of fit in. They knew how to win."

The 2014–15 Chicago Blackhawks were a team defined by Toews and Kane, by Keith, by Quenneville, and by the salary cap. They couldn't dominate, they couldn't be discouraged, they were never out of any game, they were never home free. Their greatness was in their resilience. They won three times in seven years—about as often as any post-salary-cap team is likely to win. The gap between the top teams now is so small that talent can't always be the difference maker. Sometimes that difference is inspiration, sometimes it's the capacity to survive the grind of what isn't perfect.

Toews and Kane have been a remarkable match. Individually, they are not in the league of Crosby or Ovechkin or McDavid. When they had very good years but not great ones and the team didn't win, they didn't face the same scrutiny or carry the same expectations as the biggest stars. They could come back the following season with a better year a lot more easily. The complications of the salary cap may have kept them in Chicago, but they would have likely remained together in any event. They are not like Gretzky and Messier, Crosby and Malkin—better together but almost as good alone. Toews and Kane need each other. The Blackhawks' fortunes rose with them, and—for Chicago fans—with some sadness but not much regret, those fortunes now fall with them. The Blackhawks are the first dynasty of the modern, post-cap NHL era.

CHAPTER EIGHTEEN

The best eight teams in NHL history.

They cover a period of 63 years, from 1951–52 to 2014–15—four Canadian teams, four American, four from the "Original Six" franchises, two from the expansion era, two represented twice, at least one team in each decade from the 1950s to the present, except one, only one U.S. team from before 1982, only one Canadian team from after 1984. They span a league that went from six teams—two Canadian and four American—to 30 teams—7 Canadian and 23 American. From rosters of 15 skaters and one goalie, helmetless and maskless, to rosters of 18 skaters and two goalies, helmeted and masked. From players who trained on the ice but not off it, played two-minute not 40-second shifts, used straight sticks not curved, shot at Gumby-sized not Michelin Man–sized goalies—and were all Canadian, not half American or European. From organizations with one coach, one manager, and one trainer, to ones with multitudes of each. From offices that used pen, paper, and instincts, to iPads and analytics. From fans who watched by newspaper and radio (once a week), to all-sports channels and the Internet (and games all the time). From kids signed as 14-year-olds to a universal draft, from players bound to their teams forever to free agency, from $5,000 contracts that were ceiling-less to $12 million ones limited by a salary cap. From Maurice Richard at age 30, Gordie Howe 23, Bobby Orr 3, Guy Lafleur at less than a month old—and Wayne Gretzky (at age –9), Mario Lemieux (–14), Alexander Ovechkin (–33), Sidney Crosby (–35), and Connor McDavid (–45)—to the birth year of the first overall pick of the 2033 draft. From Scotty at age 18 to when he was 81.

Now, the best eight teams in NHL history against each other. I didn't know which ones Scotty would pick, nor which matchups he would set for the four quarter-final series, nor those winners, nor the winners of the two semifinal series, nor the ultimate winner. I told him I didn't want to know. I didn't want to know because I didn't want anything to get in the way of the questions I would be asking him about each team. That said, I couldn't stop myself from imagining what his selections might be. From the way he talked about certain players, and from what he seemed to value most in a team or in a way of playing, some teams did seem to emerge. I knew the Canadiens of the 1950s and 1970s would. I knew the Oilers would. I thought the Wings of the early 2000s might, but I was surprised at the feeling he had for the Wings of the early 1950s. But even if I was right about what I heard, this still added up to five teams, and only four could advance to the semifinals. I was pretty sure these teams, minus one, would move on.

I was wrong.

Here are Scotty's matchups:

Toronto 1962–63 vs. Chicago 2014–15. I found this choice intriguing because, from what he had said, the two teams are similar in many ways. One of them would now be eliminated, but the other would go on to the semifinals, and I hadn't thought either of them would.

New York Islanders 1981–82 vs. Edmonton 1983–84. I was surprised only because the core of these two teams played against each other for six or seven straight seasons during the 1980s—the Islanders winning the early years, the Oilers the later ones.

Montreal 1976–77 vs. Detroit 2001–02. This was a big surprise to me. Of the eight teams, these are the two that Scotty coached. He knows them intimately, and has a deep affection for them. I thought they would both make it to the semifinals, and maybe go further. Now one would be losing in the first round.

Detroit 1951–52 vs. Montreal 1955–56. This was my biggest shock. Again, these two teams are from the same decade, and in a six-team league they not only played each other 14 times every regular season, but often in the playoffs too. More than that, I knew this Canadiens team was great—they won an NHL-record five straight Stanley Cups—and I knew that Scotty thinks they are great, and from what he said I know he thinks the Wings of the early 1950s are also great. I thought both of these teams would make the semifinals and at least one would go to the final. Now one would lose right away.

With the four matchups set, this was now about bringing each series to life. To take all of what Scotty has said about the teams and their players, and all he has learned in his more than seven decades in hockey, and apply it to make the series real. Great players are not great in every-thing, and some great players are greater than others. Who is who then, and what is what? A coach sees strength *and* weakness. A coach enhances one, and exploits the other. How was this going to play out?

Because these are set as actual series, each is a best-of-seven, and the team with the higher number of points during the regular season gets home-ice advantage. We decided to play the four series more or less in chronological order, so first up would be the 1951–52 Wings against the 1955–56 Canadiens, with the opening game at the Forum in Montreal.

I looked at scoring summaries from games that the teams had played against each other in adjacent playoff years—which team started games fast and got an early lead and which didn't; and tried to figure out how each would respond, and which players would rise to the moment and which wouldn't. And what about penalties and power plays, what about the crowd, how much did home-ice matter—to the teams, to each player? I wanted to create a real-life, real-game atmosphere for Scotty.

I asked him what the Forum might sound like, what Toe Blake would say to his team and Tommy Ivan to his, how each saw the other team and its players, what their game plans would be. If Béliveau, not the Rocket, was now the key player for the Canadiens, how would the Wings play against him? Ted Lindsay wasn't afraid of anyone or any situation, so would he go right after Béliveau, as Dickie Moore had done in junior, high-sticking him, slashing him—to bring him down, to bring his whole team down? Would he do it in the first shift, and if so, what would Béliveau do? Would Lindsay get a penalty? Would the Canadiens score on the power play? If they did, would the Wings come right back? And what if they did, and what if they didn't? What would Howe do, and what about the Rocket, and what about Metro Prystai and Floyd Curry, two mostly unseen players during the regular season who were big producers in the playoffs? Would they produce now, or somehow—against these players, and this team, at this moment, at their age and in their circumstances—not at all?

I asked Scotty these questions. He tried to put himself into each situation, inside the skins of the players and coaches. He imagined. He had answers. But the further we went in that first game, the more uncomfortable he sounded. He is a practical person. He has ideas and theories, but he doesn't deal in fantasies. He is a coach—he deals in real life, in real games, not in what has often been or what might predictably be. In what *is*. In what is right there in front of him, in front of his players, on that ice. *Now.*

Yes, he knows his own team and knows the other team, and yes, he has a game plan, but it's also up to him to surprise his opponent and it's up to his opponent to surprise him, to come up with something that the other doesn't have an answer for, or not enough of one. If the game is at home, if it's away, if one team gets a lead, if it falls behind, if it gets a penalty, if one of its big scorers scores, if one of its opponent's shutdown guys scores—you just deal with it. That's what a coach does, what players and teams do. Games aren't played in scenarios. Any script can be written. Any script can also be ripped up, flipped on its ear, and written again. To approach a game otherwise is to pretend a game is precisely what it isn't. As if *this* will happen, then *that*, then something else you don't expect but know will happen because something always does, then something else again that you don't expect, or perhaps that you do expect.

Any imagined game with imagined scenarios is fake—phony. The Rocket gets hot, Howe gets shut down, Moore gets hurt, all of these are possible. But so are a thousand other things. Tony Leswick scores a Cup-winning goal; Doug Harvey bats the puck into his own net to lose a Cup; Terry Sawchuk posts four shutouts in eight games. Impossible. Except they happened.

What was bothering Scotty—what I was hearing in his voice—was that he had no idea how to make these scenarios work. He couldn't do it. He had learned through his hockey life that theories are wonderful, and that anybody can make a brilliant, plausible case for an underdog winning, because sometimes an underdog does win—the U.S. Olympic hockey team in 1980, for example—but what almost always happens in reality is that the best team wins. Because whether they are ahead or fall behind, in a game or a series, whether they have injuries or not, or are in a slump or not, or lose disastrously at home or win triumphantly on the road—the best finds a way to win. That's why they're the best.

So Scotty and I started again. Let's forget scenarios, I told him. Let's talk about the teams in each series, thoroughly, completely, and then he would give his answer—between this great coach and that great coach, this great scorer, defender, and goalie and that one, who is a little bit better than the other? That is the team that will win.

Genius isn't theory. Genius is performance.

CHAPTER NINETEEN
The Elite Eight

SERIES 1
Detroit Red Wings 1951–52 vs. Montreal Canadiens 1955–56

"I was 17 playing junior," Scotty relates. "I was lucky, I saw this Detroit team from 1950 on. I also saw the 1955–56 Canadiens. I saw them both in the playoffs, in their two seven-game series in '54 and '55. I saw them play overtime games. And I mean, they were head and shoulders above the other teams.

"Detroit finished in first place in '49, '50, and '51 and they finished first that year, in '52, too. It was the fourth straight time. Yet they had only won the Cup once." That was in 1950. Two years later, the Wings were still young but now they were better, and now they were driven by their unconscionable loss to the Canadiens the year before, who during the regular season had finished 36 points behind them. The Wings had lost the first two games of that 1951 series, both in Detroit—the opener in four overtimes, the second in three—but then had come back, showing everyone just who they were by beating the Canadiens twice, decisively, at the Forum. The ship had been righted. But then the Wings lost again at home, 5–2, and then in Montreal, and their season was done. Scotty had watched those games too.

The image of the 1951–52 Detroit team still sticks in his mind. "They had such a big lineup. They were tough. The Production Line [Howe, Lindsay, and Abel] was so good. They had so much depth. I remember their checking line [Skov, Leswick, and Pavelich] was so good too. The other teams couldn't match up. And their defence. That was a really good team." Scotty doesn't use the words *so* or *such* or *really*

1951-52 DETROIT RED WINGS

GP	W	L	T	Pts	GF	GA
70	44	14	12	100	215	133

Tommy Ivan, Coach
Jack Adams, General Manager

FORWARDS	Pos	Age	GP	G	A	Pts	PIM
Sid Abel (C)	C	33	62	17	36	53	32
Ted Lindsay	L	26	70	30	39	69	123
Gordie Howe	R	23	70	47	39	86	78
Glen Skov	C	21	70	12	14	26	46
Marty Pavelich	L	24	68	17	19	36	54
Tony Leswick	R	28	70	9	10	19	93
Alex Delvecchio	C	19	65	15	22	37	22
Vic Stasiuk	L	22	58	5	9	14	19
Metro Prystai	R	24	69	21	22	43	16
Johnny Wilson	L	22	28	4	5	9	18

DEFENCE	Pos	Age	GP	G	A	Pts	PIM
Red Kelly	D	24	67	16	31	47	16
Bob Goldham	D	29	69	0	14	14	24
Marcel Pronovost	D	21	69	7	11	18	50
Leo Reise	D	29	54	0	11	11	34
Benny Woit	D	24	58	3	8	11	20

GOALTENDER	GP	GA	GAA	W	L	T	SO
Terry Sawchuk	70	133	1.90	44	14	12	12

1955-56 MONTREAL CANADIENS

GP	W	L	T	Pts	GF	GA
70	45	15	10	100	222	131

Toe Blake, Coach
Frank Selke, Sr., General Manager

FORWARDS	Pos	Age	GP	G	A	Pts	PIM
Jean Béliveau	C	24	70	47	41	88	143
Bert Olmstead	L	29	70	14	56	70	99
Bernie Geoffrion	R	24	59	29	33	62	66
Henri Richard	C	19	64	19	21	40	46
Dickie Moore	L	25	70	11	38	49	55
Maurice Richard	R	34	70	38	33	71	89
Ken Mosdell	C	33	67	13	17	30	48
Claude Provost	L	22	60	13	16	29	30
Floyd Curry	R	30	70	14	18	32	12
Don Marshall	C	23	66	4	1	5	8

DEFENCE	Pos	Age	GP	G	A	Pts	PIM
Doug Harvey	D	31	62	5	39	44	60
Dollard St. Laurent	D	26	46	4	9	13	58
Tom Johnson	D	27	64	3	10	13	75
Jean-Guy Talbot	D	23	66	1	13	14	78
Bob Turner	D	22	33	1	4	5	35
Butch Bouchard (C)	D	36	36	0	0	0	22

GOALTENDER	GP	GA	GAA	W	L	T	SO
Jacques Plante	64	119	1.86	42	12	10	7

Until 1982, teams that finished regulation time with an equal number of goals scored recorded a "Tie" (T) and one point.

very often—nouns and verbs, and the occasional adjective, are enough—but he uses them a lot when he talks about the Wings. "Abel was a great player, an experienced guy, sort of on the back end of his career. Howe and Lindsay were so good at attacking, and Abel was so good at defending. It was a perfect system. He was being pushed quite a bit that year by Delvecchio. He had come out of junior and they were priming him to play with Howe and Lindsay." Abel scored 17 goals that season; Delvecchio 15. When Delvecchio didn't play with Howe and Lindsay, he centred a line with Vic Stasiuk and Metro Prystai, or sometimes with Johnny Wilson.

"I remember Prystai, the Wings getting him from Chicago—he'd scored 29 goals his last year there. He scored 21 that 1951–52 season with the Wings as a *third*-line guy, and he had a hang of a playoffs." He, Howe, and Lindsay led the team in points. "And their defence was so good. Bob Goldham, it was amazing how he blocked shots. He played with Kelly, and there was no defenceman in the league who was close to playing like Kelly. He was up the ice all the time. He was a forward-playing defence." And he could play that way because of Goldham. "He got 16 goals as a defenceman that year," Scotty recalls. "That was unheard of in those days."

That season, no other defenceman on a team that made the playoffs scored more than five goals, aside from his teammate Marcel Pronovost, with seven, and Harvey, with six. The Wings' two other regular defence-men, Goldham and Leo Reise, didn't score a goal. One pairing, an unmatchable offensive and unmatchable defensive defenceman together; the other, a top-level offensive and top-level defensive defenceman together. And behind them, Terry Sawchuk.

"I remember watching [Sawchuk] play," Scotty says. "He was big, about 190 or 200 pounds. He started his pro career at 18 in the USHL, then was in the AHL. He hardly played junior. Even by this time [1951–52] he was only 22. He had five straight seasons with [a goals against] average below two. When they talk about the goalies of that era, they talk about Sawchuk, Plante, and Hall, and I had two of them in St. Louis [Plante and Hall]. If you look at longevity, Plante played the longest. Hall played the most games, and I'm a big Glenn Hall supporter."

In 1973, Scotty and Suella would name their second-born son Stanley Glen Bowman, after the Cup and the goalie. (*Glen* is spelled with one *n* because, while Hall's name was spelled with two, Scotty had written it wrongly on Stan's birth registration.) But as big a fan as Scotty is of Hall's, as he relates: "Sawchuk is still rated by people as the best of those three. I think the fact that Sawchuk had a checkered career after winning those Cups in '52, '54, and '55 took a lot away from his reputation. He got some kind of malaise, or disease—I don't think they ever found out what it was. He lost a lot of weight. He was in Boston then, and when he came back to Detroit they were on the decline, then he was in Toronto. But after he left Detroit the first time I don't think he was ever the same goalie." Yet in the early 1950s—in 1952: "Nobody was close to him."

This is the Detroit Red Wings, 1951–52. Three lines: Howe, Lindsay, and Abel/Delvecchio, the scorers; Skov, Pavelich, and Leswick, the defenders; Prystai, Stasiuk/Wilson, and Delvecchio, the two-wayers. Two sets of defence: Kelly and Goldham; Pronovost and Reise. The spares: Wilson and Benny Woit. Sawchuk in goal; Ivan behind the bench; Jack Adams the GM.

"I know this Montreal team," Scotty says of the 1955–56 Canadiens. He had watched different variations of it since he got his standing-room pass in 1947. He had watched Toe Blake, Elmer Lach, and Bill Durnan, and he had seen them retire. He saw Béliveau, Geoffrion, Moore, and Plante arrive. He saw the Rocket, Harvey, and Butch Bouchard in mid-career, and in 1955 they were all still there. (Harvey, it turned out, was still in mid-career.) He had seen them all practise. He had watched Dick Irvin as coach, then saw him go, and saw Blake return, this time behind the bench. He saw the arrival that season of Henri Richard and Claude Provost. He had watched the Canadiens the year before when they had put it all together, and he had been at the game when it all fell apart, after the Rocket had been suspended, when first place and the scoring title that was in Richard's grasp went up in the tear-gas smoke bomb that had targeted Clarence Campbell, and all had been lost. He had felt the build-up for this next season, 1955–56, the Canadiens having lost for two straight years in the final, both times in seven games, once in overtime. The Rocket now back, his brother in the lineup, Blake behind the bench. The young players getting better; the slightly older ones—Béliveau, Geoffrion, Moore, Plante—coming to the fore; the older ones—the Rocket and Harvey—and except for Bouchard, barely past their prime.

"They had a great regular season. It was the best record they had in their run of five [Cups] in a row." Just as the Wings had done in 1951–52, the Canadiens scored more goals than anyone else *by far*, and they allowed fewer *by far*. Béliveau, still only 24, outscored Howe 47 goals to 38 and 88 points to 79; he even out-penalized him 143 minutes to 100.

"They had two lines that could score. Béliveau, Geoffrion, who could really shoot—those two could put it in—and Olmstead, who was very good in the corners and on the puck, and a good defensive player. Then the Rocket, and Henri—Henri wasn't a great player then, but he was one of those guys who came up and made it right away. And Moore. He wasn't Dickie Moore yet, but he was a really good player."

Then their checking line: Ken Mosdell, a smart, solid veteran; Floyd Curry, defensively reliable and hard-working, with offensive skills that could surprise, especially in the playoffs; and Provost, who at 22 was on his way to becoming an important two-way player for the team.

Then their defence. "Kelly was better offensively but Harvey was better all-round." He was tough in every way, and his teammates looked to him. The Rocket, they honoured; Béliveau amazed them. In Harvey, they trusted. "[Tom] Johnson was a workmanlike defenceman and a very good skater. And a competitor. After that, their defence [Dollard St. Laurent and Jean-Guy Talbot] wasn't as good." But the Canadiens had a weapon no other team had. Their power play. "Oh, it was so strong," Scotty recalls. Harvey moved from right defence over to left, Geoffrion from right wing back to right defence, Olmstead played out of the left corner, Béliveau was at centre, and the Rocket on right wing. A power play that was so good that after the season, the league changed the rule.

Then there was Plante. Until the 1955–56 season, Plante, it seemed, couldn't be that good—because no one who played that way could be good. But that year, he began to be seen as what he was.

This is the Montreal Canadiens, 1955–56. Three lines: Béliveau, Geoffrion, and Olmstead, the scorers; the Rocket, Henri Richard, and Moore, the also-scorers; Mosdell, Curry, and Provost, the defenders. Two sets of defence: Harvey and St. Laurent; Johnson and Talbot. The spares: Donnie Marshall and Bob Turner. Plante in goal; Blake behind the bench; Selke the GM.

The two teams: the Wings 100 points; the Canadiens 100 points. The Wings, first by 22 points over the second-place Canadiens; the Canadiens, first by 24 points over the second-place Wings. The Wings, four first-team all-stars; the Canadiens, four first-team all-stars and two second-team all-stars. Both teams having lost the year before, busting with embarrassment, desperation, anger, pride, and a need to win. The two best teams of the decade, *by far*, year after year after year. The two greatest stars, Richard and Howe; the two best defencemen, Harvey and Kelly; the two best goalies, Sawchuk and Plante; the two best coaches, Ivan and Blake. The Canadiens, 45 wins; the Wings 44. So Games 1 and 2, and 5 and 7, if necessary, are at the Forum.

"It's a tough call," Scotty says. "I was looking over their records again. Montreal lost 15 games, and Detroit 14, but Montreal had more wins. There's no question it's really tough to figure [out] which is the best of the two.

"The teams would match lines," he continues. "The coaches didn't have much choice except to do that"—because the shifts were long, the teams didn't change on the fly much, and stoppages were few—"and they didn't juggle lines much either. Maybe if you're down in a game you might try to double-shift some guys. But again the shifts were so long, it was really hard. And the big lines didn't play against each other. The Rocket and Gordie Howe hardly ever did. The spare guys weren't good enough to slot in, and there wasn't anybody in the farm system to bring up. Only if there was an injury."

The Wings and the Canadiens would have to go head-to-head with what they had and what they were.

"There wasn't much difference in the big scorers. Howe, Béliveau, Lindsay, Geoffrion. The second-line guys, there wasn't much difference either. Sure, the Rocket—but Henri only scored 19 goals that year, and Dickie Moore 11. They were important guys, they could skate and were so competitive, but they were young. They didn't become scorers until later. And [for Detroit] Prystai, it's easy to forget him. He was such a good player. I don't know why Chicago traded him."

But Scotty does see a difference in the teams' checking lines—Glen Skov, Tony Leswick, and Marty Pavelich for Detroit; Ken Mosdell, Floyd Curry, and Claude Provost for Montreal. Curry, a right winger, was always effective playing against Lindsay, a left winger. They had grown up together in Kirkland Lake, one street apart; they were the same age (Lindsay was two weeks older); they both went south to play junior—Lindsay with St. Mike's in Toronto (and then Oshawa), Curry with the Oshawa Generals. They won the Memorial Cup together in 1944. They were lifelong friends, which only heightened the ferocity with which they competed against each other. But Curry didn't play against Lindsay as a pest or a shadow but as a player. He could skate, and the year before, in the playoffs, he had tied for the most goals with eight (in only twelve games)—so Lindsay didn't stick him, and he didn't try to intimidate and defeat him.

But for Scotty, Curry wouldn't be enough to level an imbalance. "Skov, Leswick, and Pavelich, I don't know how many years they played together, but the Montreal checking line didn't stand out to me. It was

more just put together than a real line, guys coming in and out. That
Detroit line was as good a checking line as I've ever seen." To Scotty,
that means the Béliveau line would have a harder time against the Wings'
defensive line than Howe's line would have against the Canadiens'
checkers.

Another difference for Scotty: Harvey was great, Johnson was good,
but together the four Wings defencemen were more solid. And then
Sawchuk. No matter how good Plante was, in the 1952 playoffs Sawchuk
had four shutouts in eight games. His goals against average was 0.62.

"I think Detroit would win in six games," Scotty says. "They would
win at home."

The Wings' checking line, their depth on defence, and Sawchuk.
Detroit's best players were also at their absolute peak—Howe,
Lindsay, Kelly, Sawchuk. For the Canadiens, Béliveau, Geoffrion, and
maybe Harvey were at their peak, but not yet Plante, Henri Richard,
or Moore—and the Rocket was slightly past his. Not much of a difference, but enough.

In fact, the whole Detroit organization was at its pinnacle. General
manager Jack Adams was at his best, coach Tommy Ivan was at his best,
Howe and Lindsay together were at their best. Everything for Howe and
Lindsay was still about winning and being great players, and *only* about
winning and being great players. For Adams and Ivan it was still all
about winning too. Later, there were distractions—or to Adams there
seemed to be. Lindsay got into some outside businesses and became a
driving force in the creation of the NHL Players' Association; so, in 1957,
as punishment, he was traded to the league's rock pile, Chicago. Sawchuk
had his own troubles and was traded to Boston. Ivan left for Chicago to
salvage the Norris family's other team, the Black Hawks. The Wings
won two more Cups, in 1954 and 1955, but they might have won more had
their team on the ice not been undone by their team off it.

The Canadiens of the 1950s were never *not* about winning and being
great players. Their team on the ice was never undone by their team off

344

it, and while the Canadiens' five straight Cups between 1956 and 1960 might have made those teams collectively better than Detroit's, this challenge, set before Scotty, is about one team, one year—who was the best?

The Detroit Red Wings 1951–52 move on. The Montreal Canadiens 1955–56 are out.

SERIES 2
Toronto Maple Leafs 1962–63 vs Chicago Blackhawks 2014–15

These two teams Scotty got to know in different ways. He knew the 1962–63 Leafs from watching many of their players as juniors: Pulford, Harris, Baun, Brewer, and Nevin with the Marlies; Duff, Mahovlich, and Keon with St. Mike's; Shack with Guelph. He had coached against these players. He had watched them get stronger and better, take on bigger roles, and finally—on those Leafs teams of the early 1960s—become what he had seen in them. And now they were Stanley Cup champions.

Scotty had also seen the Leafs mature as a team. He was there in Peterborough, coaching the Petes, when Imlach arrived for his first training camp. He watched the team practise. He talked to Imlach. Imlach talked to him. Training camps lasted six weeks in those years, and you get to know a coach, and a player, when you watch them practise. When he became head scout for the Canadiens in Eastern Canada, he was in Toronto the entire month of November, every year. He'd hang out in the canteen at Maple Leaf Gardens with the other scouts. He would read the Toronto papers, listen to Toronto radio, watch Toronto TV, hear Toronto gossip. He also watched the Leafs practise and went to a few of their games.

He knew the 2014–15 Blackhawks from being the father of the team's GM. From seeing the team at training camp every year, from watching them play against the Lightning in Tampa, from travelling on Chicago's annual "parent-son" road trip with his kids and grandkids and with the team, from watching them in real time on TV or online and sometimes watching them again on tape the following day. He also knew them from the analytics he received, from live-streaming the games of the Rockford

IceHogs, from being part of the team's extended "brain trust" during the playoffs, and from his frequent phone conversations with the team's pro scout and with Stan. He had watched the Blackhawk players too, year

1962-63 TORONTO MAPLE LEAFS

GP	W	L	T	Pts	GF	GA
70	35	23	12	82	221	180

Punch Imlach, Coach and General Manager

FORWARDS	Pos	Age	GP	G	A	Pts	PIM
Red Kelly	C	35	66	20	40	60	8
Frank Mahovlich	C	25	67	36	37	73	56
Bob Nevin	R	24	58	12	21	33	4
Dave Keon	C	22	68	28	28	56	2
George Armstrong (C)	C	32	70	19	24	43	27
Dick Duff	L	26	69	16	19	35	56
Bob Pulford	C	26	70	19	25	44	49
Eddie Shack	L	25	63	16	9	25	97
Ron Stewart	C	30	63	16	16	32	26
Billy Harris	C	27	65	8	24	32	20
Ed Litzenberger	R	30	59	5	13	18	8

DEFENCE	Pos	Age	GP	G	A	Pts	PIM
Tim Horton	D	33	70	6	19	25	69
Allan Stanley	D	36	61	4	15	19	22
Carl Brewer	D	24	70	2	23	25	168
Bob Baun	D	26	48	4	8	12	63
Kent Douglas	D	26	70	7	15	22	105

GOALTENDERS	GP	GA	GAA	W	L	T	SO
Johnny Bower	42	109	2.60	20	15	7	1
Don Simmons	28	69	2.47	15	8	5	1

2014-15 CHICAGO BLACKHAWKS

GP	W	L	OL	Pts	GF	GA
82	48	28	6	102	229	189

Joel Quenneville, Coach
Stan Bowman, General Manager

FORWARDS	Pos	Age	GP	G	A	Pts	PIM
Jonathan Toews (C)	C	26	81	28	38	66	36
Patrick Sharp	L	33	68	16	27	43	33
Marián Hossa	R	36	82	22	39	61	32
Patrick Kane	R	26	61	27	37	64	10
Brandon Saad	L	22	82	23	29	52	12
Brad Richards	C	34	76	12	25	37	12
Antoine Vermette	C	32	82	13	25	38	40
Kris Versteeg	L	28	61	14	20	34	35
Teuvo Teräväinen	L	20	34	4	5	9	2
Marcus Krüger	C	24	81	7	10	17	32
Andrew Desjardins	C	28	69	5	5	10	57
Andrew Shaw	C	23	79	15	11	26	67
Bryan Bickell	LW	28	80	14	14	28	38

DEFENCE	Pos	Age	GP	G	A	Pts	PIM
Duncan Keith	D	31	80	10	35	45	20
Niklas Hjalmarsson	D	27	82	3	16	19	44
Brent Seabrook	D	29	82	8	23	31	27
Johnny Oduya	D	33	76	2	8	10	26
Kimmo Timonen	D	39	16	0	0	0	2
Trevor van Riemsdyk	D	23	18	0	1	1	2
Michal Rozsíval	D	36	65	1	12	13	22

GOALTENDER	GP	GA	GAA	W	L	T	SO
Corey Crawford	57	126	2.27	32	20	5	2

In 2005, the shootout was introduced, eliminating all "Tie" (T) games. The winning team recorded a "Win" (W) and two points, the loser an "Overtime Loss" (OL) and one point.

after year. He had watched them mature—Kane, Keith, Seabrook, Crawford. He had watched Toews never be anything but mature. Now these two teams, the Leafs and the Blackhawks, would go head-to-head.

"Keon, Armstrong, and Duff were as good a line as you could get at that time," Scotty recalls. "They could play offence, they could play defence. They had good speed—Keon and Duff—and Armstrong was really a good corner guy. He wasn't a great skater, but he was strong. And he was a big guy. When I watched in those days, Béliveau and Armstrong stood out. They seemed much bigger than the other guys. But that was a hell of a line."

Then there was Kelly, Mahovlich, and Nevin. "Kelly and Mahovlich were so good together, a great passer and a great shooter, one more on the defensive side, one more offensive, and again they were big. And Nevin was a strong young guy. All of their forwards, maybe not Shack, could play both ways."

It is a theme that Scotty returns to often, especially when he talks about the Leafs. Like Sam, he likes the guys who can "light the light," but he also likes guys who can keep the other team from lighting the light. "And Pulford was smart and physical, he could play any game. Stewart was steady. And the defence, they had four very good defencemen. When you think of it, they had good veterans, and they had good young guys who had won before. They had won [the Memorial Cup] with the Marlies in junior." And they had won the Stanley Cup in '62." The team was virtually unchanged from that season before—only Olmstead was gone, retiring after his fifth Cup; only Douglas had been added.

To play against the Leafs, first you had to run the gauntlet of their forwards—Armstrong, Pulford, Kelly, Nevin, Stewart, Mahovlich, Shack—big guys. Then you had to run the gauntlet of their defence— Horton, Stanley, Baun, Brewer, Douglas—big guys. Then there was Bower. Scotty describes the Leafs with two phrases he uses with admiration: they were "hard to play against," and they "played on the edge." The Leafs made nothing easy. And nothing was easy for them either. They didn't win big; they didn't even lose big. They couldn't coast through minutes of a game they were certain to win or lose—they didn't have that luxury; their games were too close. They always had to compete. Not that Imlach would let them coast anyway. The players who he thought coasted on their skills at times—Mahovlich and Brewer—he was the toughest on. The veterans who he was afraid might use age as a crutch, he drove the hardest, so they couldn't and wouldn't need to.

The Leafs that season won only 35 of the 70 games they played (losing 23 and tying 12), but they made everyone they played against know that if they wanted to beat them, they would have to pay a price. Not every opponent is willing to do that every moment of a game.

This is the Toronto Maple Leafs, 1962–63. Three lines: Kelly, Mahovlich, and Nevin, the scorers; Keon, Armstrong, and Duff, the two-wayers 1; Pulford, Shack, and Stewart, the two-wayers 2. Two sets of defence: Horton and Stanley; Brewer and Baun. The spares: Billy Harris, Ed Litzenberger, and Kent Douglas. Bower in goal (with Don Simmons); Imlach behind the bench; Imlach the GM.

When Scotty talks about the Blackhawks, he talks differently. With the Wings, it's always "Howe and Lindsay," or sometimes "Howe, Lindsay, and Abel (or Delvecchio)." And generally he talks in lines, or at least tandems. It's "Gretzky and Kurri," "Messier and Anderson," "Trottier and Bossy." With the Canadiens, it is usually full lines: "Lemaire, Lafleur, and Shutt," "the two Richards and Moore," or just by the name of the centre, "the Béliveau line" or "the Jarvis (or Gainey) line." Even with the Leafs, who played such a team game, it is "Kelly and Mahovlich," "Keon and Armstrong."

With the Blackhawks, he doesn't talk in lines, or even tandems. He does say "Toews and Kane" just as he says "Gretzky and Messier"—not as linemates but as two powerhouse players their teams could run on back-to-back lines. But Scotty doesn't talk much about "Toews, Sharp, and Hossa," or "Kane, Saad, and Richards," or even "Toews and Hossa" or "Kane and Saad (or Richards)." Teams are put together differently now. Understood differently.

"The salary cap has had such an effect," Scotty says. "You win, and the players expect more [money], and they've earned more, but now you can't keep everybody." With every other team he has seen or coached, and in the seven other teams he has selected, you *could* keep everybody. You wanted to keep everybody, unless you thought that, while good enough that season, some player or other would get in the way of some better emerging player the next year and so you traded him. Or if you were Detroit in the 1950s and were willing to cut off your nose (Ted Lindsay) to spite your face (the team) because Lindsay got too cozy with the Players' Association.

The lockout in 2004–05, the cancelled season, the rout of the NHLPA, and the resulting salary cap changed all that. "You've got to know who your core guys are now," Scotty says. "You've got to keep them, then fill in the rest." And on the Blackhawks, the core guys were Toews and Kane, then Keith, and maybe Seabrook and Crawford. Hossa, Sharp, Saad, and Richards were good players who were made better by those around them, and who made the other good players around them better too. They weren't "fillers," but they had to be allowed to go, and come, from year to year. Teams can't fall in love with players like them now, and can't overpay them. And they weren't talked about much, even by Scotty. The Blackhawks were going to go as far as Toews and Kane, and Keith, were able to take the others along with them.

"Toews is like Béliveau—tall, strong, good on offence and defence, good on faceoffs. He isn't the scorer Béliveau was; he doesn't have quite the same force to his game." But the 1962–63 Leafs, Scotty says, had no one who could match him. Not Kelly, not Pulford. "Kane is like Lafleur," Scotty continues. "Not only can he make plays, but he can score. He's one of those guys who can do both. He's a great playmaker. He's got a good knack around the net, and his shooting is underrated." The Leafs had no one to match him either, not even Keon. Keon was also a dartingly quick skater—he could do everything—but he couldn't finish the way Kane can.

"Keith can play all over the ice, sometimes too much," Scotty says. "He's a big part of their offence too." On the Leafs, Horton wasn't a big part of their offence. (Horton, as a defenceman, was like Tim Hortons is as a brand of coffee—solid, reliable, hard to compete against, never lets you down, good, maybe better than good.) Neither was Brewer an offensive force. Brewer had the skills, but he would go on solo rushes; he didn't bring the team forward with him. The Blackhawks of 2014–15 weren't talented enough to overwhelm, they weren't physical enough to grind down, but nor could they be overwhelmed or ground down themselves. They kept games close. That's what Crawford and Seabrook, what Hossa, Sharp, and all the other good players did, and then in those tight moments the Blackhawks had three game-breakers: Kane, Toews, and Keith.

This is the Chicago Blackhawks, 2014–15. Four lines: Toews, Sharp, and Hossa, the two-wayers; Kane, Saad, and Richards, the two-wayers with flair; Vermette, Versteeg, and Teräväinen, and Krüger, Desjardins, and Shaw, the guys who kept the ship steady until the big guys returned. Three sets of defence: Keith and Hjalmarsson; Seabrook and Oduya; Timonen and van Riemsdyk. Crawford in goal; Quenneville behind the bench; Stan Bowman the GM.

The Leafs and Blackhawks both played a tight, disciplined game—the Leafs more so, because hockey in 1963 was tighter and more disciplined. The Leafs were tough and grindingly physical; theirs was a tougher, more physical time. The Blackhawks were quicker and more skilled, because the NHL of 2015 was quicker and more skilled. In a league of fewer than 120 players, the 1962–63 Leafs had two on the league's first all-star team, Mahovlich and Brewer, and one on the second, Horton. They had one player, Mahovlich, in the top 10 in scoring. In a league of more than 600 players, the 2014–15 Blackhawks had no all-stars, and no scorers in the top 10. Both teams had outstanding players, but neither had any who today would be considered among the greatest of all time.

Not Mahovlich, not Keon, not Bower, not Kelly as a centre; not Toews or Kane or Keith. Both had stars of a time, but not of all time. They won their Stanley Cups with grit and grind, not ease.

Yet the Leafs had a much bigger presence in hockey in their time than the Blackhawks did in theirs. There were only six teams then, not 30, and the league was overwhelmingly, undeniably Canadian. Not just all of its players, or that the league's head office was in Montreal, but that almost every year a Canadian team—and there were only two—won the Stanley Cup. Beginning 21 years before this Leafs team and extending through to the end of the 1970s, out of 38 years, Montreal (18) or Toronto (10) won the Cup 28 times. Narrow the focus further, count back a few years from this 1962–63 team and forward a few more, from 1956 to 1969, and Canadian teams, two of them, won the Cup 13 times out of 14. The Canadiens of these years were legendary because of all the Cups they won, and because of all the great players they had. The Leafs were legendary because of all their Cups—and, without the same great stars, because of how else they won. They, like the 2014–15 Blackhawks, weren't good enough to win except as a team.

In February 1999, the Leafs played their final game at Maple Leaf Gardens. I was the team's president. Three years earlier, the Canadiens had closed the Forum with a highly emotional ceremony that focused on the 19 former Montreal players, still living, in the Hockey Hall of Fame. Each was introduced individually and walked on a red carpet set out in a giant rectangle around the Forum ice, while a video tribute played on the board and the crowd roared and wept. The Rocket was introduced last. It was a powerful, perfect moment.

Now it was the Leafs' turn to move to a new arena, and what the Canadiens had done three years before would serve as the model. Except, when I looked at the names of the Leafs' Hall of Famers, I realized it wouldn't work. In fact, it would be embarrassing, entirely misleading, and unfair. The Leafs' greatest names—Keon, Kennedy, Apps, Mahovlich, Bower, Sittler—came nowhere near the dimension of the Canadiens' greatest names—Richard, Béliveau, Harvey, Plante, Lafleur. The Canadiens had won with great stars; the Leafs with great teams. We decided instead to honour what had made the Leafs great, and invited back *all* those who had played on the team. In the end, more than 120 former players, wearing their Leafs' jerseys, walked onto the Maple Leaf Gardens ice. The Toronto team of 1962–63 embodied the best of them.

In these two years, 1962–63 and 2014–15, Toronto and Chicago had similar seasons. The Leafs finished first, "but the top four teams were separated by five points: Toronto had 82, Chicago 81, Montreal 79, and Detroit 77. It was amazing," Scotty recalls. The Blackhawks finished third in the league's seven-team Central Division, "but it was a tough division. St. Louis was first, then Nashville, and both of the wild-card teams [from the Western Conference] came from that division."

For both the Leafs and the Blackhawks, it was the players and coaches they had and what they had experienced—it was their capacity to survive seasons like this—that had seen them through.

The 2014–15 Blackhawks, in many ways, were the 1962–63 Leafs, 52 years later.

The Leafs played a 70-game schedule, the Blackhawks 82. Chicago had a higher win percentage, so the first two games of the series, and Games 5 and 7, if necessary, would be in the United Center.

"When I look at the way the Leafs would play," Scotty says. "The size of Toronto. They had some small players, but they had pretty good size. Chicago was average-sized, they were fast, but I don't know if they could handle some of these guys. The Leafs were very tough to play against. They had a big, strong, hard-checking defence." After Keith and Seabrook, Chicago's defence, Scotty says, was "pretty thin."

"Toronto was tough to beat at home too. Chicago not as much. I think the series would go six games, but it's pretty hard not to think the Leafs would win."

Two teams on to the semifinals—the 1962–63 Leafs and 1951–52 Wings. Two teams out—the 1955–56 Canadiens and 2014–15 Blackhawks.

SERIES 3
New York Islanders 1981–82 vs. Edmonton Oilers 1983–84

"Boy, I never realized those two teams finished within a point of each other in those two years," Scotty says of the 1981–82 Islanders and the 1983–84 Oilers. He had been looking at his notes. The Islanders in 1982 had 118 points; two years later the Oilers had 119. "And I never realized the Islanders scored 385 goals that year, and compared to the [1983–84] Oilers, gave up 64 less. The Oilers allowed 314. Holy mackerel."

Until Gretzky was sold to L.A. in 1988, the Islanders and Oilers were by far the two most dominant teams of the 1980s. "When I was in Buffalo, Boston was pretty good," Scotty recalls, "Quebec was really coming on, and Montreal was still pretty decent, and so were Philadelphia and Washington—and in the [Western] Conference, Calgary and Minnesota." But both the Islanders and Oilers knew that to win the Cup they would have to find a way to beat the other. And in 1982 and 1984 respectively, they were at their best. The Islanders had won two straight Cups, but in 1981–82 they also had the motivation of being almost the underdogs with the fast-rising Oilers coming at them. In 1983–84, the Oilers, the anointed ones, had everything but they still hadn't won anything. During the first two-thirds of each of those seasons, both teams were good, but in the last third, with the playoffs looming, both went crazy. The Islanders lost only three times in their final 36 games. From January 21 to February 20, they won 15 in a row. The Oilers, in their final 22 games, lost four times, scoring 12 goals in one game, and 6 or more goals in 11 of the others.

"Trottier and Bossy played together continuously," Scotty says, "and then the Islanders would switch up, sometimes Gillies, sometimes

Bourne. They had two good centremen, Trottier and Goring, and then Wayne Merrick, a pretty fast skater—on the shy side, but that wasn't a problem on the Islanders because they had enough sandpaper. And then Billy Carroll and Brent Sutter. Then their left wingers, Gillies, Bourne, and Tonelli, that's a pretty strong left side. And on the right, Anders

1981-82 NEW YORK ISLANDERS

GP	W	L	T	Pts	GF	GA
80	54	16	10	118	385	250

Al Arbour, Coach
Bill Torrey, General Manager

FORWARDS	Pos	Age	GP	G	A	Pts	PIM
Bryan Trottier	C	25	80	50	79	129	88
Mike Bossy	R	25	80	64	83	147	22
Clark Gillies	L	27	79	38	39	77	75
Butch Goring	C	32	67	15	17	32	10
John Tonelli	L	24	80	35	58	93	57
Bob Bourne	L	27	76	27	26	53	77
Wayne Merrick	C	29	68	12	27	39	20
Bob Nystrom	R	29	74	22	25	47	103
Anders Kallur	R	29	58	18	22	40	18
Duane Sutter	R	21	77	18	35	53	100
Brent Sutter	C	19	43	21	22	43	114
Billy Carroll	C	23	72	9	20	29	32

DEFENCE	Pos	Age	GP	G	A	Pts	PIM
Denis Potvin (C)	D	28	60	24	37	61	83
Stefan Persson	D	27	70	6	37	43	99
Tomas Jonsson	D	21	70	9	25	34	51
Ken Morrow	D	25	75	1	18	19	56
Dave Langevin	D	27	73	1	20	21	82
Gord Lane	D	28	51	0	13	13	98
Mike McEwen	D	25	73	10	39	49	50

GOALTENDERS	GP	GA	GAA	W	L	T	SO
Billy Smith	46	133	2.97	32	9	4	0
Roland Melanson	36	114	3.24	22	7	6	0

1983-84 EDMONTON OILERS

GP	W	L	T	Pts	GF	GA
80	57	18	5	119	446	314

Glen Sather, Coach and General Manager

FORWARDS	Pos	Age	GP	G	A	Pts	PIM
Wayne Gretzky (C)	C	23	74	87	118	205	39
Jari Kurri	R	23	64	52	61	113	14
Dave Semenko	L	26	52	6	11	17	118
Mark Messier	L	23	73	37	64	101	165
Glenn Anderson	R	23	80	54	45	99	65
Dave Hunter	L	26	80	22	26	48	90
Ken Linseman	C	25	72	18	49	67	119
Pat Hughes	R	28	77	27	28	55	61
Willy Lindström	R	32	73	22	16	38	38
Kevin McClelland	C	21	52	8	20	28	127
Jaroslav Pouzar	L	32	67	13	19	32	44
Dave Lumley	R	29	56	6	15	21	68

DEFENCE	Pos	Age	GP	G	A	Pts	PIM
Paul Coffey	D	22	80	40	86	126	104
Charlie Huddy	D	24	75	8	34	42	43
Randy Gregg	D	27	80	13	27	40	56
Don Jackson	D	27	64	8	12	20	120
Kevin Lowe	D	24	80	4	42	46	59
Lee Fogolin	D	28	80	5	16	21	125

GOALTENDERS	GP	GA	GAA	W	L	T	SO
Grant Fuhr	45	171	3.91	30	10	4	1
Andy Moog	38	139	3.78	27	8	1	1

In 1983, overtime was introduced. A game's winner recorded a "Win" (W) and two points, its loser an "Overtime Loss" (OL) and one point. If no goal was scored, both teams recorded a "Tie" (T) and one point.

Kallur, a left-hand shot but he played right wing, and Bossy, of course, and Nystrom, and then Duane Sutter as the fourth. They had a pretty well-balanced team."

And then, on defence, "There was Potvin, and then Persson and Jonsson, two Swedes—the three of them were the offensive guys; and the other guys, Morrow, Lane, and Langevin, were on the defensive side—they were big guys, they weren't offensive at all. Lane and Langevin, they used judiciously. Potvin played with Persson—I wonder how much Potvin played; they didn't keep track of ice time then—and then Morrow and Jonsson. There weren't a lot of teams that used three defence pairs at the time. Then they had McEwen on the power play. And Billy Smith was a good playoff goalie."

This is the New York Islanders, 1981–82. Four lines: Trottier, Bossy, and Gillies, the scorers; Goring, Tonelli, and Bourne, the two-wayers; Merrick, Nystrom, and Kallur, the checkers; Duane Sutter, Brent Sutter, and Billy Carroll, the checkers 2. Three sets of defence: Potvin and Persson; Jonsson and Morrow; Langevin and Lane. The spare: McEwen. Smith (with Rollie Melanson) in goal; Arbour behind the bench; Torrey the GM.

On any other team but the Oilers, the tandem everyone would talk about would be "Gretzky and Kurri." The two of them together were not just good, they were historically good, like "Howe and Lindsay" and "Béliveau and Geoffrion." Or everyone would talk about "Messier and Anderson," who were almost as good. But on the Oilers, there was only one tandem: "Gretzky and Messier." Back-to-back. If one doesn't get you, the other will.

That season, the Oilers also had Ken Linseman at centre, and in the playoffs Kurri scored 14 goals, Gretzky 13, and Linseman 10. When the big guys score, to an opponent it's disappointing. When the others do, it's crushing. "And McClelland [the team's fourth centre], he got four goals," Scotty adds. "And Hunter, Lindström, and Semenko each got five. These third- and fourth-line guys had 19 goals in 19 games that year—a goal a game. And *then* [the Oilers] had the big scorers."

As for their defence, Coffey was great, most of the time. The rest—Kevin Lowe, Randy Gregg, Charlie Huddy, Lee Fogolin, and Don Jackson—were solid and reliable, which was what the Oilers needed with the offence they had. And Grant Fuhr made the big saves. "They learned to play a much better defensive game in the playoffs too. I think they realized they had to tighten up a little bit, and they did."

This is the Edmonton Oilers, 1983–84. Four lines: Gretzky, Kurri, and Semenko, the mega-scorers; Messier, Anderson, and Hunter, the mega-scorers 2; Linseman, Hughes, and Lindström, the two-wayers; McClelland, Pouzar, and Lumley, the rest. Three sets of defence: Coffey and Huddy; Gregg and Jackson; Lowe and Fogolin. Fuhr (with Andy Moog) in goal; Sather behind the bench; Sather the GM.

This series would offer no surprises. In different conferences, the two teams rarely saw each other during the regular season but they had faced each other in the playoffs, and they *knew* about each other. Each was the standard for the other: if the Islanders were going to continue as champions, they would need to beat the future, and that was the Oilers. If the Oilers were going to become champions, they were going to have to defeat the past, and that was the Islanders. They knew that each represented the most fundamental test for their team. The Islanders were talented—Bossy, Potvin, and Trottier were all-time stars. The team was smart, experienced, and rock-solid—unrelentingly so. They could slow down faster opponents and beat them at their own Islanders speed. But what about a super-fast, super-talented opponent? Speed makes the almost-fast seem clumsy and slow. Skill makes the lesser-skilled seem inept. What would it be? Who would win out?

The Oilers had seemed big enough and competitively tough enough the year before, but then Gretzky and his teammates had walked by that Islanders dressing room as losers and peeked inside to see—all bruised and beaten up—what winners looked like. What happens when the super-fast and super-talented who are tough enough take on the super-tough and super-competitive who are talented enough?

This wouldn't be the 1982 Islanders that were too good for the 1982 Oilers, who hadn't yet learned their lesson. This wouldn't be the 1984 Oilers who blew away the 1984 Islanders, who, after winning 19 straight series, had run out of gas. The Islanders' tank was full, the Oilers' jaw was set. The first two games would be in Edmonton. Who would win out?

Very simple.

"I think that year the Oilers really came into their own," Scotty says. "They had missed the year before and missed pretty handily. They probably thought it could never happen to them, but it did. But they grew up pretty fast after that. There was a lot of experience there now. And the Islanders, except for Potvin, didn't have a lot of guys on defence. It would be their big, strong guys chasing those Oilers guys around. It would be awfully tough for the Islanders to beat them."

Three teams moving on; three teams going home.

SERIES 4
Montreal Canadiens 1976–77 vs. Detroit Red Wings 2001–02

These are the two teams that Scotty coached—the 1976–77 Canadiens when he was 43 years old and had won two Stanley Cups, and the 2001–02 Red Wings when he was 68 and had won eight. He had already coached the Canadiens for five years and the Wings for eight. He had seen the teams develop; he had seen how the players reacted when they won and when they lost. He knew what they had and what they didn't have. He knew these teams and these players inside out.

"Nobody had four lines like we had," Scotty says of his Detroit team. "We had five centres—Yzerman, Fedorov, Larionov, Draper, and Datsyuk. We had enough that in the playoffs we could move Yzerman to the wing. He played with Fedorov and Shanahan. Brett Hull was with two young guys, Datsyuk and Boyd Devereaux—Datsyuk was a rookie. Larionov played with Holmström and Robitaille, they were like a fourth line. Then we had Draper, Maltby, and McCarty, that was our go-to checking line.

"On power plays, we had Lidström and Yzerman on the points, then up front we had Fedorov and Hull, and Holmström in front of the net, or [on the second unit] Shanahan and Larionov, and Robitaille instead of Holmström. God, we scored a lot of power plays. We had 19 in the playoffs, only 7 against. We could take guys from each line because when the power play was over we always had the Draper line ready to go. Killing penalties, they were our go-to guys, and Fedorov and Yzerman were really, really good there too. We had specialty players, a lot of guys who could fit different roles."

The Wings had a lot of players who in their younger years and on less competitive teams had bigger responsibilities. Scotty knew that—at their age and on a team with the Wings' ambitions—that wouldn't work. He had a lot of great players—nine who became Hall of Famers and one future one—but he knew they were past their prime, and if not used right they could get sour and grumpy. *Right* meant putting them in situations where they could still be great; it meant playing the forwards 16 minutes a game, not 22, so they didn't

1976-77 MONTREAL CANADIENS

GP	W	L	T	Pts	GF	GA
80	60	8	12	132	387	171

Scotty Bowman, Coach
Sam Pollock, General Manager

FORWARDS	Pos	Age	GP	G	A	Pts	PIM
Jacques Lemaire	C	31	75	34	41	75	22
Guy Lafleur	R	25	80	56	80	136	20
Steve Shutt	L	24	80	60	45	105	28
Doug Jarvis	C	21	80	16	22	38	14
Bob Gainey	L	23	80	14	19	33	41
Réjean Houle	R	27	65	22	30	52	24
Doug Risebrough	C	23	78	22	38	60	132
Mario Tremblay	R	20	74	18	28	46	61
Yvon Lambert	L	26	79	24	28	52	50
Pete Mahovlich	C	30	76	15	47	62	45
Yvan Cournoyer (C)	R	33	60	25	28	53	8
Murray Wilson	L	25	60	13	14	27	26
Jimmy Roberts	R	36	45	5	14	19	18

DEFENCE	Pos	Age	GP	G	A	Pts	PIM
Larry Robinson	D	25	77	19	66	85	45
Serge Savard	D	31	78	9	33	42	35
Guy Lapointe	D	28	77	25	51	76	53
Bill Nyrop	D	24	74	3	19	22	21
Pierre Bouchard	D	28	73	4	11	15	52
Rick Chartraw	D	22	43	3	4	7	59

GOALTENDERS	GP	GA	GAA	W	L	T	SO
Ken Dryden	56	117	2.14	41	6	8	10
Bunny Larocque	26	53	2.09	19	2	4	4

2001-02 DETROIT RED WINGS

GP	W	L	T	OL	Pts	GF	GA
82	51	17	10	4	116	251	187

Scotty Bowman, Coach
Ken Holland, General Manager

FORWARDS	Pos	Age	GP	G	A	Pts	PIM
Steve Yzerman (C)	C	36	52	13	35	48	18
Sergei Fedorov	C	32	81	31	37	68	36
Brendan Shanahan	L	33	80	37	38	75	118
Kris Draper	R	30	82	15	15	30	56
Kirk Maltby	L	29	82	9	15	24	40
Darren McCarty	R	29	62	5	7	12	98
Brett Hull	R	37	82	30	33	63	35
Pavel Datsyuk	C	23	70	11	24	35	4
Boyd Devereaux	L	23	79	9	16	25	24
Igor Larionov	C	41	70	11	32	43	50
Luc Robitaille	L	35	81	30	20	50	38
Tomas Holmström	R	29	69	8	18	26	58

DEFENCE	Pos	Age	GP	G	A	Pts	PIM
Nicklas Lidström	D	31	78	9	50	59	20
Fredrik Olausson	D	35	47	2	13	15	22
Chris Chelios	D	40	79	6	33	39	126
Jiří Fischer	D	21	80	2	8	10	67
Mathieu Dandenault	D	25	81	8	12	20	44
Steve Duchesne	D	36	64	3	15	18	28

GOALTENDERS	GP	GA	GAA	W	L	T	SO
Dominik Hašek	65	140	2.17	41	15	8	5
Manny Legace	20	45	2.42	10	6	2	1

get tired, didn't get injured, and didn't feel old; so they succeeded and felt, miraculously, that they—different from everyone else on earth—had reversed time, which only added a new measure to their greatness, which only made them feel even greater. So that they had less bad stress, more possibilities, more good stress, and more fun. And they did.

Because these Wings forwards were so skilled, they had the puck more, chased it less, and had to defend less often. Which was a good thing because the team's defence was not great. "Basically we were strong up front," Scotty recalls, "and I would say just so-so on the back end." Lidström was outstanding all over the ice; he played about 30 minutes a game. Chelios, at age 40, was a force (and freak) of nature. He worked out before practice, he practised, he worked out after, he dragged his exercise bike into the sauna, he played about 26 minutes a game, and it was never enough for him.

"We didn't have to play him in the wrong situations," Scotty says. "Lidström, we had to play him against the best line. Chelios played against the next level of player." Lidström was teamed with Fredrik Olausson, a 35-year-old veteran and "project" who was grateful for a final and unexpected shot at glory. Chelios played with Jiří Fischer, a 21-year-old rookie "who had a really good year for a young defenceman," remembers Scotty.

"Our third set of guys was Dandenault and Duchesne. One was an ex-forward; the other had bounced around a bit. Both were puck-moving guys, not as much defenders. Our defence was a bit of a question mark." The team needed the right goalie to stabilize the defence and to stand up to Roy, Belfour, and Brodeur. "When Kenny [Holland] made the trade for Hašek, that gave our team a real shot in the arm. A goalie like that gives you an awful lot of confidence. When we got Hašek, and you're never sure it will work, that put us over the top."

And crucial to the maximizing and slotting in and mixing and matching of these older players: "We didn't have to overuse anybody." Only Lidström, but he was a kid at 31 and he could handle it.

This is the Detroit Red Wings, 2001–02. Four lines: Yzerman, Fedorov, and Shanahan, the super-all-rounders; Draper, Maltby, and McCarty, the super-checkers; Hull, Datsyuk, and Devereaux, the sniper and the kids; Larionov, Robitaille, and Holmström, the all-rounders. Three sets of defence: Lidström and Olausson; Chelios and Fischer; Dandenault and Duchesne. Hašek in goal (with Manny Legace); Scotty behind the bench; Holland the GM.

"I saw some games recently," Scotty says about the Canadiens of the late 1970s. "All the games where we won Cups, and also the last year in '79 against the Rangers, the fifth game. And every time you saw the puck, if the other team was chasing it or coming out of their own end with it, there's one of our guys right there. And then once they beat our guy and move the puck to another guy, there's our guy there. We had speed on the forecheck, and our defence, as soon as the other team made a pass, a guy was right on him. They had no time and space. I mean, when you can skate fast enough and can always have somebody pursuing the puck, the other team can't get going. It's because we had that speed."

He coached those Canadiens teams in hundreds of games. He coached them to that style of play. Yet nearly 40 years later, it was as if he was seeing this for the first time.

Scotty is a numbers guy. He was when he was in school; math was his best subject. He was in the stockroom at Sherwin-Williams, learning the code numbers of the paints that he would someday sell. He was as a scout and coach, poring over all the stats sheets he could find, in search of anything he could find. He is today, with his iPad and stylus. Numbers on a page or screen say something, he knows. When he was watching those Cup-winning games again, he saw those numbers in motion.

"One line scored 150 goals—Lafleur, Shutt, and Lemaire, 56, 60, and 34. Then Risebrough, Lambert, and Tremblay, 22, 24, and 18. That's 64, and that would be in a bit of a defensive role. Then Jarvis, Gainey, and Réjean Houle, that's 52. Then Pete [Mahovlich], Cournoyer, and Murray Wilson. Every player except Shutt had more assists than goals. And only four other teams in the league that year scored over 300 goals—and two of them had 301—and the next-most had 64 less. Nearly a goal a game. The difference between our goals for and against was *216*. I've never seen any other spread like that—nobody has come close to that. But it's the defence scoring, that's what really gets to me. Robinson had 19, Lapointe 25, Serge [Savard] 9, Nyrop 3, Bouchard 4. That's 60 goals—five defence-man and one [Bouchard] who didn't play much. On the '02 team in Detroit, our defence scored 31."

A few more numbers: "We lost only one game at home. The whole season. It was around October 30, just before Halloween. That's it. We had only eight losses in all, and after January 17 [just] one. That was in Buffalo, 4–1. We had played the night before against the Rangers at home. That's just short of three months."

This is the Montreal Canadiens, 1976–77. Four lines: Lemaire, Lafleur, and Shutt, the scorers; Jarvis, Gainey, and Houle, the super-checkers; Risebrough, Tremblay, and Lambert, the kids; Pete Mahovlich, Cournoyer, and Wilson, the scorers 2. Two sets of defence, plus one: Robinson and Savard; Lapointe and Nyrop; Bouchard. Dryden (with Bunny Larocque) in goal; Scotty behind the bench; Pollock the GM.

For the 2001–02 Wings, it was their third Stanley Cup in six years. For the 1977 Canadiens, it was their second of what would be four in a row. Both teams had a need. For the Wings, it came from an unprecedented collection of great stars who knew this was their last chance. For Montreal, it came from being a team that had won the year before while focusing almost solely on the Flyers, almost unaware of itself. Now it was its own focus. The Canadiens were just beginning to realize how good they were, the responsibility they had, the possibilities before them—and their own hunger to achieve them.

For Scotty, it is the Canadiens' defence that has always stood out—Robinson, Savard, and Lapointe. But, watching those Stanley Cup–winning games again, there's something else in the words he kept repeating: "*There's a guy right there. There's a guy right there.*" Always there was a guy right there. Right there to score, right there to defend, again, and again, shift after shift, game after game. "That is more than depth," he says.

With a higher win percentage than the Wings during the regular season, the Canadiens would open at home.

"It would be pretty tough to ever think this Montreal team could lose," Scotty says. "The forward matchups wouldn't be the biggest problem for Detroit, because they both had four lines. The biggest problem would be on defence. The Detroit defence doesn't match up. Too much offence for that defence. That's what I think. That's my strong opinion."

Four teams are left. And Scotty has chosen his matchups. It will be the 1951–52 Wings against the 1962–63 Leafs, and the 1976–77 Canadiens against the 1983–84 Oilers.

CHAPTER TWENTY
The Final Four

Scotty and I were getting close to the end of more than a year of conversations. He had chosen his top eight teams; he had talked about each with the dissecting eye of a coach. There wasn't much more to say. No details to add, just reminders about the essence of each team: what made them good enough—or not quite good enough—to win.

Detroit Red Wings 1951–52 vs. Toronto Maple Leafs 1962–63

"[The Wings] finished first seven years in a row—'49, '50, '51, '52, '53, '54, '55, then not in '56 but again in '57—eight times in nine years, and won four Cups. They had Howe and Lindsay, and Kelly in his prime was like a fourth forward. There have been other great defensive lines, but theirs was so good I think they could nullify a really good scoring line. And they were so stingy, [with] Sawchuk, it would be so hard to score on them. They had everything going for them. The Leafs were big, they were solid, they had two very strong defence pairs and their players were used to winning. I think it would be a homer series. I pick Detroit in seven, because of home ice."

We have one finalist.

Montreal Canadiens 1976–77 vs. Edmonton Oilers 1983–84

"Nobody had a back-to-back like Gretzky and Messier. Then Gretzky with Kurri, and Messier with Anderson—nobody could match that," Scotty says. "They had a deficiency on defence, but they didn't have to play defence much. Coffey and Huddy were a good combination that could add to the offence a little bit. Lowe, Fogolin, Gregg, Jackson were more-sizable guys, not much offence, but they didn't need much because of their forwards. And Fuhr was a good match for a high-scoring team like that."

When Scotty thinks of the Canadiens, he thinks of the team's New Year's Eve game in 1975 against the Central Red Army team at the Forum. A big game, a showdown game, against a very good offensive opponent. He remembers the fast skating and quick passing; how the team rose to the moment; how they showed they could handle that. "When you think of that game, then about the four-game sweep of the Flyers to win the Cup a few months later, then the Canada Cup a few months after that with lots of Canadiens players on that team, and then another Cup on top of that some months later, this team had a lot of confidence."

He thinks about how he would try to deal with Gretzky and Messier. "Messier dominated players when teams tried to play him one-against-one. If a player challenged him, if he made it all about him and Messier, that's when Messier was at his best. You're better to give him a dose of someone good defensively, then one who was a little bit aggressive and would bother him. I think we'd have Pete Mahovlich, then Doug Risebrough—he could be a good thorn in your side—and then Lemaire, who was always good defensively. So you've got a good cross-section of guys. Guys who wouldn't make it personal. Then Jarvis against Gretzky, so Gainey lines up against Kurri. But you'd have to judge as the games were going on."

Then he adds, "But you'd have to put some offence against them. You can't just play defence. You can't go in thinking you're just going to stop them. You've got to think the opposite. They're a little bit vulnerable if you throw some offence against them. Both teams had superstar forwards if you talk about the top three or four, but the bottom end of the Canadiens' forwards, maybe from eight to twelve, was pretty strong. And I don't think the Oilers had the defence. Nobody had the defence we did, with the offence that came from the defence.

"I think Montreal would win. They would win the first two games at home, split in Edmonton, and then come home and win in five."

And then there were two.

CHAPTER TWENTY-ONE
The Final Two

Detroit Red Wings 1951–52 vs. Montreal Canadiens 1976–77

One American, one Canadian. Both Original Six teams—one from the Original Six era and one from post-expansion times. Every player but two (Bill Nyrop and Rick Chartraw) a Canadian. Almost all of the greatest of them from small towns: Howe from Floral, Saskatchewan; Lafleur from Thurso, Quebec; Lindsay from Kirkland Lake, Ontario; Robinson from Marvelville, Ontario; Kelly from Simcoe, Ontario; Savard from Amos, Quebec. Only Sawchuk (Winnipeg) was from a big city.

One a team that Scotty watched up close as a fan at 18; the other, at 43, he coached.

Whenever we're done talking about teams and I ask him which one will win a series, I expect Scotty will say a name—like *Detroit* or *Edmonton* or *Montreal*. Definitively. Emphatically. Instead he says something like, "I think it would be hard not to say . . ."

At first I thought this was just his long way around of saying the same thing, but it isn't. He doesn't declare a winner; he says "I think" because he knows anything can happen. He knows a better team can lose and a lesser team can win. Because he's a coach. And he says what he says not just because he remembers everything—and what he once saw is still there in his head, so that whatever was, still is, and forever will be. He says what he says because he scours his old notebooks and the electronic pages of his iPad; he talks to others, he thinks, he scours his own mind. And it's only after this that he answers. Because he knows that what he sees in those numbers matters. This—choosing the best eight teams of all time—is not really about what he, Scotty Bowman, thinks. This is about what happened. This is about results. This is what's real.

In this series, Lindsay, as always, would be a key player. "He is a tough, tough loser," Scotty says. "He would try to be disturbing, but Howe is the guy I would try to concentrate on. You'd want your best left winger on him, which would be Gainey for sure, and go from there." As with Messier, with Howe you get on him but you don't challenge him. You don't make it mano-a-mano, because then you lose for sure. "The player who did the best against Howe, and he played junior with us, was Gilles Tremblay. He didn't challenge him in any real physical way. He just poked at him. He could skate, he knew how to play, he had a good defensive mind about him, and he didn't showboat. He didn't try to get Howe off his game, he just diligently did his job."

He did enough to get Howe's respect, and not enough to get up his anger. He didn't try to defeat him. He didn't make it personal. And that's how Gainey played too. Trying to get Howe or Messier—or the Rocket—off their game was only forcing them to be *on* their best game. A fierce, passionate game that was scary and beyond control, and you didn't want to do that. You didn't want Howe or Messier or the Rocket to hate you. Instead—diffuse, distract; temper hatred with respect.

"Against Howe, I'd also like size. Savard and Robinson. When I was in St. Louis I played Doug Harvey against him. He could stymie Howe—not physically, or by riling him up, but just by getting his stick on him and knowing where he was.

"You can't just go on statistics," Scotty says. But you don't ignore them either. They are smarter than you think you are. "You look at the

Canadiens' road record, losing only 7 games out of 40. That record is going to stand for as long as any record does. And the domination of that team the whole season—including the playoffs. I think the series would go seven games; it would be a homer series, but a little more depth offensively, and more defensively. The Canadiens would come at Detroit with just a little too much for Detroit to handle.

"I'm feeling that Montreal would win the series."

The Montreal Canadiens, 1976–77: Scotty Cup champions.

Being There, Doing That

July 2, 2018.

"Your son's gotten better. His skating, he's really improved, and he's gotten bigger," Scotty says to a man in the high-ceilinged front lobby, warming area, and gathering place between the four ice pads of the Northtown Center in Amherst, New York. It is where Scotty is—same arena, same time—every year.

"Yeah, he was five-eight last year. Now he's about five-eleven," the man replies. He is Pat Brisson, who once played in the Quebec junior league and now lives in L.A.—the agent for Sidney Crosby, Jonathan Toews, Patrick Kane, John Tavares, Nathan MacKinnon, and many others. His son is Brendan Brisson, an "'o1," as the scouts say—he was born in 2001, which would normally make him draft-eligible in 2019, but he has a "late birthday," October 22, after the September 15 cut-off date, so he has to wait another year. Brisson attends Shattuck-St. Mary's School in Faribault, Minnesota, an hour south of Minneapolis. It is the best hockey high school in the U.S., where even Canadian kids go— including, not so many years ago, Crosby, Toews, and MacKinnon themselves. He is here as one of 180 players invited to USA Hockey's Boys Select 17 Player Development Camp. Today is the seventh and last day of the sessions. After a week of practices, off-ice presentations

("Team Success at Short Events," "Nutrition," "USA Hockey Pride"), and intra-squad games, 40 players have been chosen to play in an all-star game. Brisson is one of them.

Pat Brisson, who has played in many big games and been involved in many big negotiations, had flown in the night before to get here, and looks nervous. He is about to watch his son—and so are lots of college, junior, and NHL scouts. He is happy and proud that Scotty remembers Brendan. He goes up the stairs into the rink, and a short time later, Scotty follows.

About a hundred or so people are inside, dressed in their winter wear. A few are parents like Brisson; most are scouts of some form; others are agent-recruiters, or "family advisors" as they are called, because the word *agent* connotes money, and high schools and colleges are amateur. They are mostly entry-level guys in their agencies, paying their dues and making first contact with prospects for the heavy-hitter agents like Brisson, Don Meehan, or Bobby Orr to come in later and make the sale. Most of the scouts stand at one end of the rink, along the top row, like birds on a telephone wire; their programs and stats sheets in their hands. They have watched all these kids before on their high school or prep school or club teams, but it has been a year since—in this same rink—they saw *all* of them together. This is the chance for the scouts to see what these kids can do when they have others on their same line who can skate and pass and shoot and make plays as well as they can; when they have others as good, or better, *against* them. The scouts need to know: Against the best, who is the best? Who do they draft? Who gets the scholarship?

That's why *they* are here. But Scotty is here too. Every year.

They are watching the future. These kids are from everywhere because rinks can be built anywhere, and because cold winters no longer give Canada home (outdoor) ice advantage. Nobody makes the NHL from Willibrord Park anymore. And now NHL players play in 24 U.S. cities, and retire in 24 U.S. cities—especially where the sun shines—and they retire with kids, with money, with time, and with the hope of doing something they are good at and love to do. They have grown up with hockey schools and off-ice training; they have lived the life of the road; and now they can keep on living the life of the road and the spirit of the team on weekend trips with their kids to tournaments that might be anywhere.

Once, the only U.S. players that mattered came from Minnesota and Massachusetts. Here, of the 180 players, only 29 are from Minnesota and only 15 from Massachusetts—26 are from Michigan, 17 from New York, and (impossible to imagine even a decade ago) 8 are from California, 7 from Texas, 3 from Missouri, 2 each from Georgia, Arizona, and Alaska, and 1 each from Utah, Idaho, North Carolina, Tennessee, Nevada, and lots of others. They are from 31 states in all, the best of the best. Scouts always have their biases—Canadian kids are tougher, U.S. kids more skilled; junior kids more competitive, college kids better-trained. But now, scouts say, park that ancient wisdom at the door. Canadian kid, U.S. kid, it makes no difference. It's not where they're from, it's what they do.

Scotty walks towards the far end of the rink to take his seat, saying hello to familiar faces before they can get up the nerve to say anything to him. He is on the lookout for his nephew, Steve, who is the head amateur scout for the Washington Capitals and the son of Jack, Scotty's younger brother, a long-time scout with Buffalo, who died suddenly 20 years ago.

Steve is with Ross Mahoney, the Caps' assistant general manager, and both of them are still over the moon. Less than four weeks earlier, Washington won the Stanley Cup, and both Steve and Mahoney were in Las Vegas for the final game. Afterwards, they both went onto the ice and they both carried the Cup, surrounded by the players they had watched, argued about, and drafted; lived with and died with; and lived with, to their indescribable victory. Almost no one else at that moment thought this, but they and their families did, and every scout in this rink knows it—this is *their* Cup too. As they talk with Scotty, other NHL scouts walk by and congratulate them—and mean it. Two weeks later, Steve would have his day with the Cup in the backyard of his home in London, Ontario. His family, friends, neighbours, and all those important to his achievement would be there, except for his father. The Cup will now have the name *Bowman* on it 18 times—14 his uncle's, 3 his cousin Stan's, and once his own. Both Scotty and Stan had *raised* the Cup, but Steve decided to do it his way. He raised *himself* up, in a handstand, his head above the Cup, and drank from it upside down.

Scotty has already made some notes in his program. This is the third day of the U17 camp he has attended. Two weeks earlier he was here for the U15 camp, and last week for the U16s. Scotty has his own system: for every player who has totalled five or more points in the five games they've played, he has written their stats beside their program bios. Beside Brisson's name he has written: *5 GMS 4 Goals—5 Assists*. On a separate handout, he has put a star beside the names of players born after September 15, 2001 (those who aren't eligible for the draft until next year)—Brisson and seven others in today's game included.

The game begins. It flies. It isn't until 6:01 of the first period that there is a whistle. All the players can skate, they can pass, they don't risk loss of possession with an offside or an icing; no shot is taken that hasn't been rushed or screened, or that isn't from in close so a goalie can catch, smother, or control it—there is nothing to cause a whistle. "It's so fast now," Scotty exclaims. He sees it every day in these camps; he sees it when he watches his own grandkids play during the winter. He is never not amazed. These are *17-year-olds*.

He watches them as he does every time he scouts, focusing on one team one period, the other team the next. He doesn't sit at the middle of the ice because the middle of the ice doesn't matter much. It may be where a game picks up steam, where its patterns develop, but the game must make its way into the offensive/defensive zones, and it's what happens there—between the blue line and the end boards—that decides the game. As in golf, you "drive for show, and putt for dough." It is in this final third of the ice where the defenders defend and the scorers score. It's where, for both the defenders and scorers, you see their skills and their "compete." That's why Scotty sits where he does.

When he sits here, he sees what he can't not see, and thinks what he can't stop himself from thinking. If this final third of the ice matters so much to a game's outcome, if scoring is so hard, why can't we do more about it? He sees a blue line that is now 64 feet from the net and not 60, and he sees the game as a coach. He sees four more feet of extra space and time in front of the net, in "the house," where almost every goal is scored, so he wants to get the puck to his guys there, and now with players who can pass better both here and in the NHL, they can do that. But he's also the coach of the other team, so he wants to keep the puck from getting there, to take away that four extra feet of space and time, and so if the league insists on expanding this space, as a coach he'll shrink it himself. He won't move his forwards four feet further from the net to cover the points; he'll move them four feet back to cover the house. But, he's also still the other team's coach, so he won't pass the puck into the house now, he won't have his forwards trying to find open ice that doesn't exist; he'll get them to go to the net to jam things up, so the goalie can't see, so his own point men can blast away, so there will be screens, deflections, and rebounds. And goals. But then he's also the other team's coach too, so he'll get his forwards to rush out and dive in front of the point men's shots *before* they can be screened, deflected, or rebounded. So goals *aren't* scored. But also, unfortunately, so his forwards aren't in any position to break back up the ice. And score. So the result, what he sees right there in front of him: there's a lot of action, and no goals at either end. And as the coach of both sides, he wonders why.

"If you've got the blue lines way out, if you've got the [defensive] forwards all down low," he says, "do you want Crosby and Ovechkin and these guys blocking shots? I always wonder, where would Gretzky and Lemieux play in today's game? They played up high, they were always looking to break out. Do you want them blocking shots? I've talked to some of the [NHL] coaches I still know. I say, 'Why can't you play different styles with different players? It's only the top two lines who score anyway, and they're up against the checkers, and the checkers can't score on them. So if the scorers play out further, they'd take away the point shot *and* be able to jump into the offence, and if the puck gets by them into the middle near the net, those checkers can't score anyway.' But [the coaches] just say, 'The game's too fast. The shifts are too short. It's too complicated.' But why? And why don't they try?"

It's not about these other coaches being wrong; it's about there being another way. And what might that be?

Once the puck is dropped, Scotty doesn't look at his papers. He watches. He has heard from others the players that are special, but he doesn't watch for them. He watches what's in front of him. If somebody does something special, he'll see it. Good *and* bad. It's the players who decide what he sees and what he doesn't. When the whistle blows, it's then that he looks at his notes, and maybe makes one or two more.

The players he sees in front of him are not only from everywhere, but they come in every dimension. Size doesn't matter so much anymore. That's what a short-shift, full-sprint, puck-possession game does. For the first 70 years of Scotty's hockey life, size was its own "skill," like skating and shooting. When he was a scout he looked for size. If a kid was big, his size was already there—he might even get bigger—and he could always get better. But if he was small, he might *never* get big. Now, out on this ice, he and the scouts can't not see size because they always did and size is impressive, but more striking is the quickness, or lack of it. Instead of wondering whether a small kid will get big enough, they wonder if a big kid will get quick enough.

Eventually, a few goals go in. Brisson scores one of them. "He wasn't a good skater last year," Scotty says. "His stride was too short." Scotty also sees a big, smooth-skating forward—it's his quickness he notices, and how even in the frenzy of the action he still looks "commanding." A presence. Then he scores on a hard shot to the top corner. "He's good," Scotty says. His name is Sam Colangelo, he's from Stoneham, Massachusetts, and he goes to Lawrence Academy, a prep school in Groton, Massachusetts. He, too, is a late birthday, and isn't eligible for the draft until 2010.

Scotty saw Bobby Orr at 13 in Parry Sound, and he saw Mario Lemieux at 12 and Wayne Gretzky at 17, both at the Forum. He has watched the best all his life. He saw the Rocket almost all of his career. He saw Howe and Béliveau, Sawchuk, Harvey, and Plante; he saw Esposito, Lafleur, Messier, Crosby, Ovechkin, and McDavid. Of the 40 players now on the ice at Northtown Center, only about five will play major junior in Canada—the rest will go to U.S. colleges, some Division I, some Division II—and only four or five will someday make the NHL. None of them, as good as they are, will be anything like the players he has seen. Yet he circles their numbers and puts stars beside their names. He nods and murmurs when Colangelo hits the top corner. He has seen it all, but he also hasn't. He has been there and done that, but he has also never stopped being there and doing that. Unlike Vince Lombardi and his growl, Red Auerbach and his cigar, Phil Jackson and his "guru" persona, Scotty blends in. When you're bigger than life, you distort it.

Why is he here—he's Scotty Bowman?

He's Scotty Bowman. That's why he's here.

ACKNOWLEDGEMENTS

I have a lot of people I want to thank, and a few people I would like to thank a lot.

I didn't know what I was getting into when I began this book. I should have. I had known Scotty since September 1971, his first training camp, and my second, with the Canadiens. I got to know him as he got to know me through our emerging years, through Stanley Cups lost and won. After I retired from hockey, I watched him go from being special, to being amazing, to becoming legendary, all by never really changing. By the time we first talked about this book in 2015, I knew he was incomparable, and that as long as anyone trusts stories of the past, he would remain so.

I had to focus on what set him apart, and that was his coaching, his records, and Stanley Cups, but also that what he achieved he did so over such a long time. His first Stanley Cup and his last were 29 years apart—from when he was 39 to when he was 68. He had to be healthy enough and physically strong enough to succeed all of this time. He had to be smart, but more than that he had to be willing *and* able to change, to deal with players who remained young as he got older, who were no longer all Canadians, who had gone from being privileged and well-off to mega-privileged and mega-rich. And perhaps most of all, he had to have in him something beyond ambition and hunger because ambition and hunger almost always become complacent or satisfied.

I had to get at this in *Scotty*, but I didn't really know how. And, because I didn't know, I needed to work with people who trusted me. I want to thank Bruce Westwood for believing in this project from the beginning. Jared Bland and Scott Sellers for their unfailing enthusiasm and for seeing the book's possibilities. Evelyn Armstrong for transcribing endless hours of interviews into more than 1,500 pages, and for her little asides when she sent the transcriptions back to me, most often, "Scotty, he's so funny." Dan Diamond, who for 25 years put together the *NHL Official Guide and Record Book*, who loves the game and its cultural connection to Canada, and who loves its numbers. When I was in my office in Toronto and Scotty was at his kitchen table in Siesta Key, we each had in front of us binders that Dan created, one for each team that told the statistical story of each of Scotty's selections. I want to thank too whomever it is that created and operates Hockey-Reference.com and Hockeydb.com. For Scotty's and my conversation to work, it had to flow. It had to go fast, because Scotty's mind moves fast, and it had to be able to go in whatever directions his mind took it. He has his amazing memory to draw on, but he needed more, to confirm what he remembered, to give confidence to it, but also to push it and feed it. We needed at our fingertips something that would allow us to grab the moment and turn it into something, into questions, ideas, other thoughts. Both websites were immensely helpful.

I also want to thank Professor Serge Durflinger of the University of Ottawa. I wanted to know more about Verdun, and online I found a reference to his master's thesis, which I read, and which he later turned into the book *Fighting from Home: The Second World War in Verdun, Quebec*. His writing, and the long conversations we had, helped me to understand what life on the Avenues was like. Also very helpful was Chrys Goyens, who allowed me to use transcripts of interviews he had done with Scotty during four memorable (for him) and transformational (for his young son who accompanied him) days in 2002. His son is now a minor hockey coach in Montréal.

I want to thank my editor, Jenny Bradshaw, Joe Lee who assisted her, and Gemma Wain, our copy editor. Joe is almost as much a hockey fan as he is a Leafs fan, and his commitment to the book was evident at every stage. Gemma had to check many hundreds of facts, shifts of time and tense, to ensure both accuracy and meaning, never losing sight of the forest while she focused on every tree. She did so undaunted. Jenny drew on her many different backgrounds, her skill, and on her knowledge that whichever way this book evolved, the right structure for it was the one that allowed Scotty's story to be told to the fullest. Always patient and encouraging, she has been a pleasure to work with.

Also my wife, Lynda. Lynda first met Scotty when I did, in September 1971, and came to know Suella better, though a coach's wife– player's wife divide is even wider than that between a coach and a player. Lynda is always my first reader and editor. She can't stop herself from noticing typos, wrong verb tenses, and any words that include the phrase "human beings." But most irreplaceably, page by page, she conveys her reactions to what she reads—whether something really works, or really doesn't, or doesn't but could—"Right here, right now, we are beginning to feel your and Scotty's relationship"; "OK, you have me"; and many, many times, "I wish I had known this in Montreal!" And my favourite, when I wrote about how Sam Pollock, as a 20-year old, gained the acceptance of the Canadiens players because of all the gofer work he did that they didn't want to do that made their softball team go, "This is the only part of any team I had any hope of making," Lynda wrote. After I had finished a final draft, she thought of an image to describe what she had been saying all along. She talked about how she likes Pittsburgh, especially where the rivers come together, where the Allegheny and Monongahela join, and become the Ohio. She said, "For me, that's what happened in this book. At some point there was this confluence," she said, "and the two of you became the Ohio."

And finally Scotty and Suella. Not long after Scotty and I decided to go ahead with the book, I got a handwritten letter from Suella. In it, she asks if I was recording our conversations, and if so, "would I be able to get any copies to share with the grandkids and family?" She goes on to say, "Scotty has never done a book of his career. I am amazed at all he remembers—people, places, dates, and hockey scores! I'm sure he might not want me to be asking but he remembers so much and I would like to document some of it to share with the family." Later, she told me this story. It was their first year in Montreal, a game at the Forum and she was sitting beside a man who was some years older. As the game went on, she noticed, then couldn't stop noticing that the woman beside him, who appeared to be with him, just kept looking down, at her lap, at the back of the person in front of her, anywhere but at the game. Finally between periods, Suella leaned over and whispered to the man, "Is she OK?" The man said yes, that she gets nervous at games, that her son, their son, is down on the ice. He's the Canadiens' goalie. Suella whispered back to him, "My husband is down there too, behind the bench. He's the Canadiens' coach."

Scotty's joy, I think, isn't in knowing what got him to where he is, but in what will take him to someplace else. His memory is such a treasure not because it allows him to live in the past, but because it enables him to figure out a different future. It's not easy to be written about, or to want to be. Both Scotty and Suella are in their eighties. They are what they've done and what they do each day with their children and grandchildren. They will be how those closest to them will remember them. Why allow someone else to mess around with their story? I want to thank them for their trust. The book began as something I knew I needed to write. It turned out to be a book I loved to write.

PHOTO CREDITS

First photo section:

Pages i, iii, iv, v, vi, vii (top © David Bier), viii courtesy of Scotty Bowman; page ii (top) courtesy of the Bibliothèque et Archives nationales du Québec, P48, S1, P2642; page ii (bottom) courtesy of Ken Dryden.

Second photo section:

Pages i, ii (bottom © Michael Burns Photography), iii, iv, v, vi (top and bottom right), viii courtesy of Scotty Bowman; page vi (bottom left) © Denis Brodeur/Getty Images/NHL; page vii © Elsa/Getty Images/NHLI.

KEN DRYDEN was a goalie for the Montreal Canadiens in the 1970s, during which time the team won six Stanley Cups. He also played for Team Canada in the 1972 Summit Series. He has been inducted into the Hockey Hall of Fame and the Canadian Sports Hall of Fame. He is a former federal member of parliament and cabinet minister, and is the author of seven books, including *The Game*, *Home Game* (with Roy MacGregor), and *Game Change*. He and his wife, Lynda, live in Toronto and have two children and four grandchildren.